A HOME FOR MR. EASTER

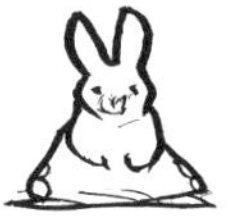

THE EVENTS, INSTITUTIONS, AND CHARACTERS PRESENTED IN THIS BOOK ARE FICTIONAL. ANY RESEMBLANCE TO ACTUAL PERSONS, LIVING, DEAD, OR UNDEAD, IS PURELY COINCIDENTAL.

ISBN 978-1-56163-580-1
LIBRARY OF CONGRESS CONTROL NUMBER: 2010922846

5 4 3 2 1

A HOME FOR MR. EASTER

BY BROOKE A ALLEN

FOR: VIVIAN 'MEMA' BRANTLEY & JEREMY MULLINS

BROOKE IS CURRENTLY A STUDENT AT SCAD AND LIVES IN THE SECRET GARDEN THAT IS SAVANNAH, GA WITH HER TWO DOGS AND BRAVE LITTLE HAMSTER (APTLY NAMED) BATMAN. WHEN SHE'S NOT DRAWING COMICS HER FAVORITE ACTIVITIES INCLUDE SLEEPING, EATING, AND FIGHTING CRIME WITH BATMAN. HER FAVORITE PREHISTORIC ANIMAL IS THE GIANT SLOTH FOR ITS CALM, NOBLE APPEARANCE. SHE LOOKS FORWARD TO MOVING NORTHWEST TO MAKE MORE COMICS AND RETURN HER DOG LINUS BACK INTO THE WILD.

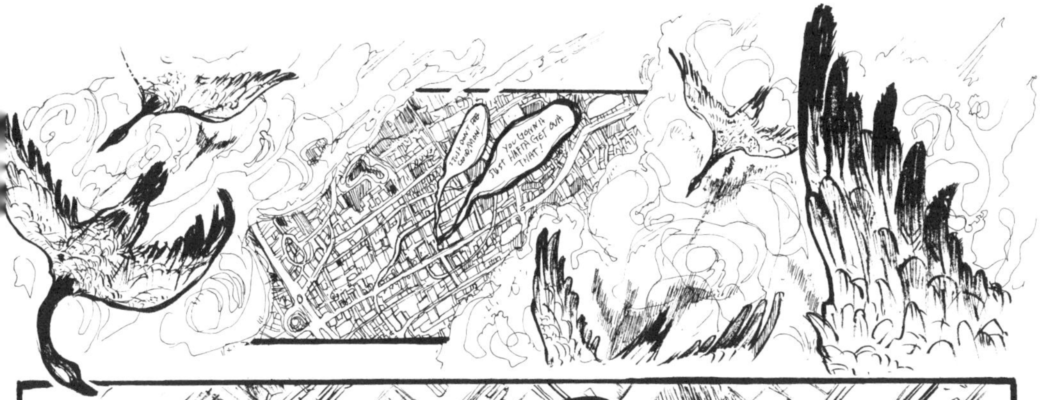
I JUST DON'T FEEL GOOD, MOM!
YOU GONNA JUST HAFTA GET OVA THAT!

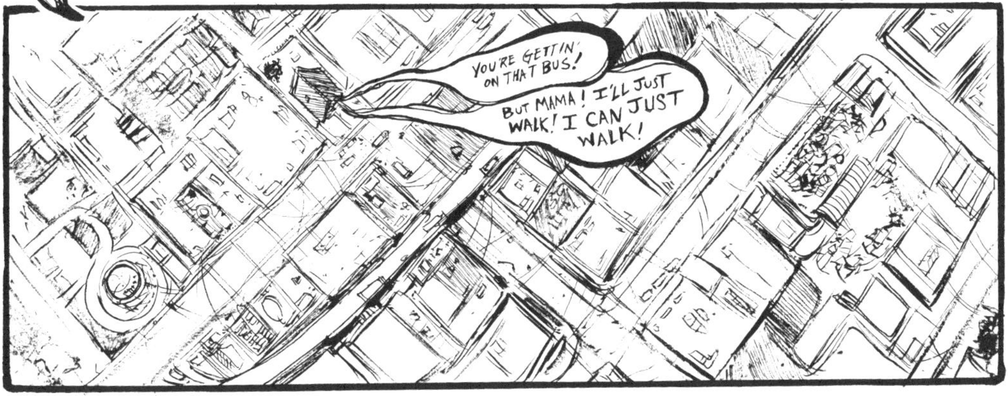
YOU'RE GETTIN' ON THAT BUS!
BUT MAMA! I'LL JUST WALK! I CAN JUST WALK!

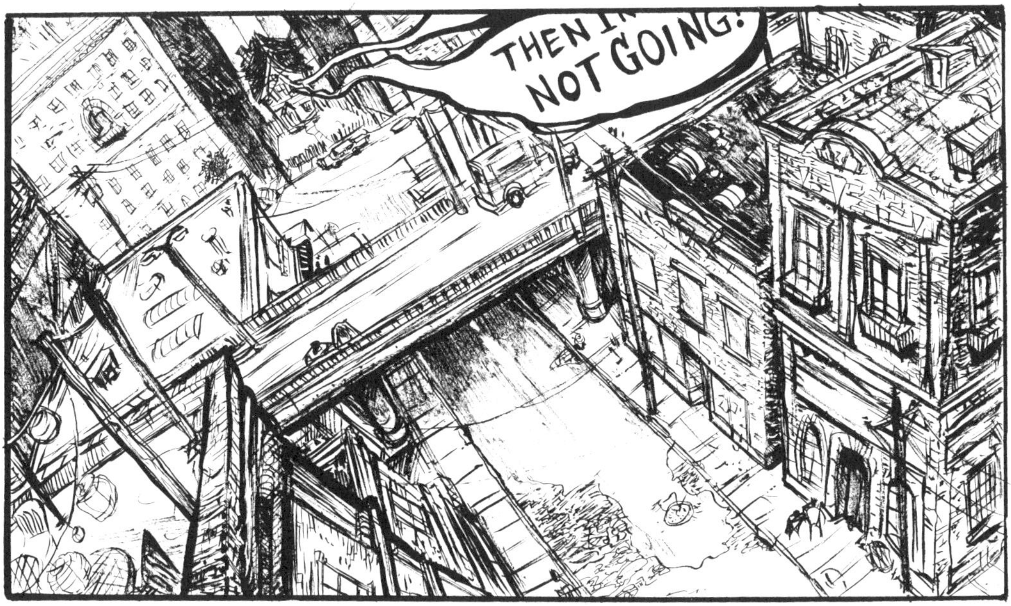
THEN I
NOT GOING!

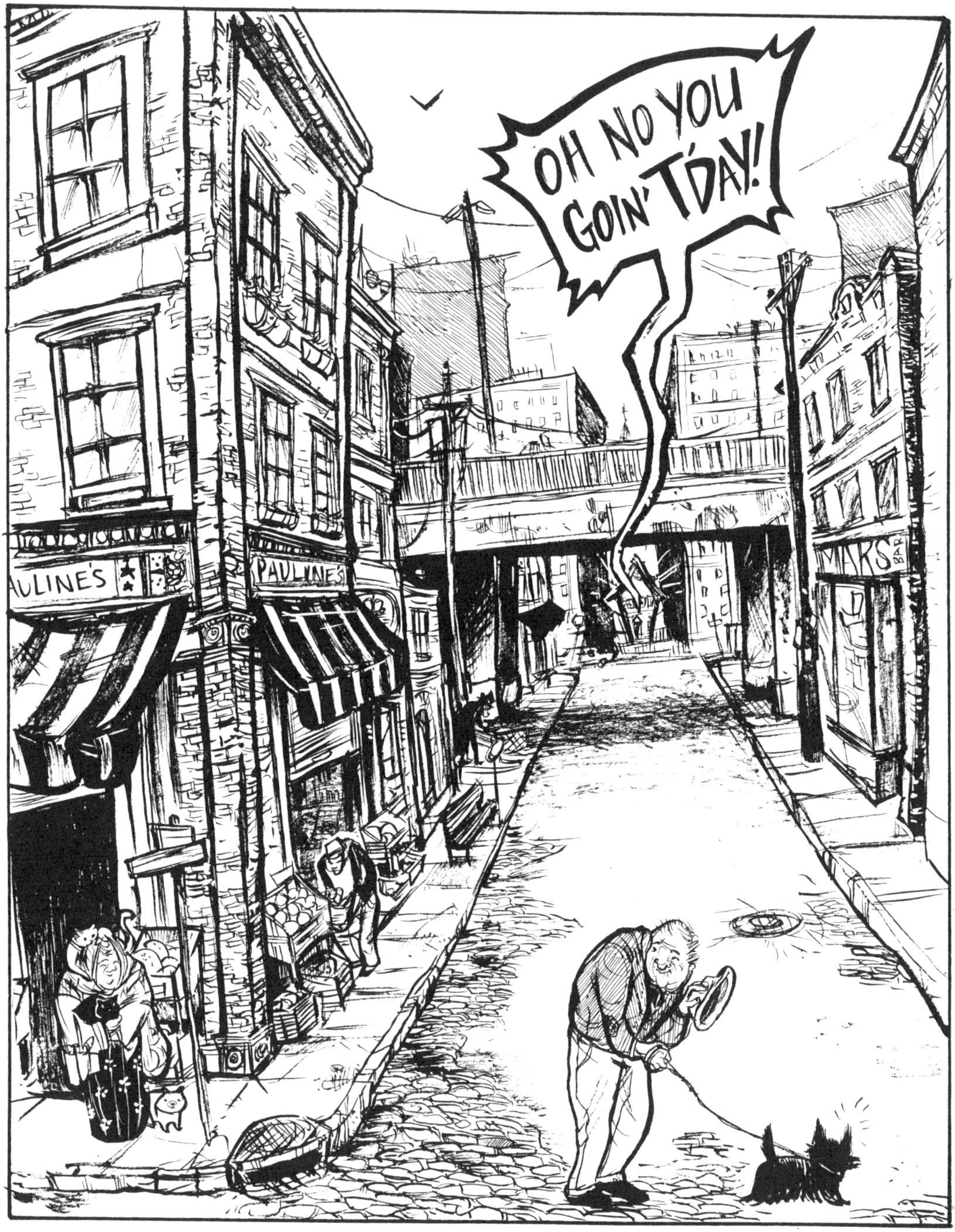

OH NO YOU GOIN' T'DAY!
AULINE'S
PAULINE'S
MARKS
BAR

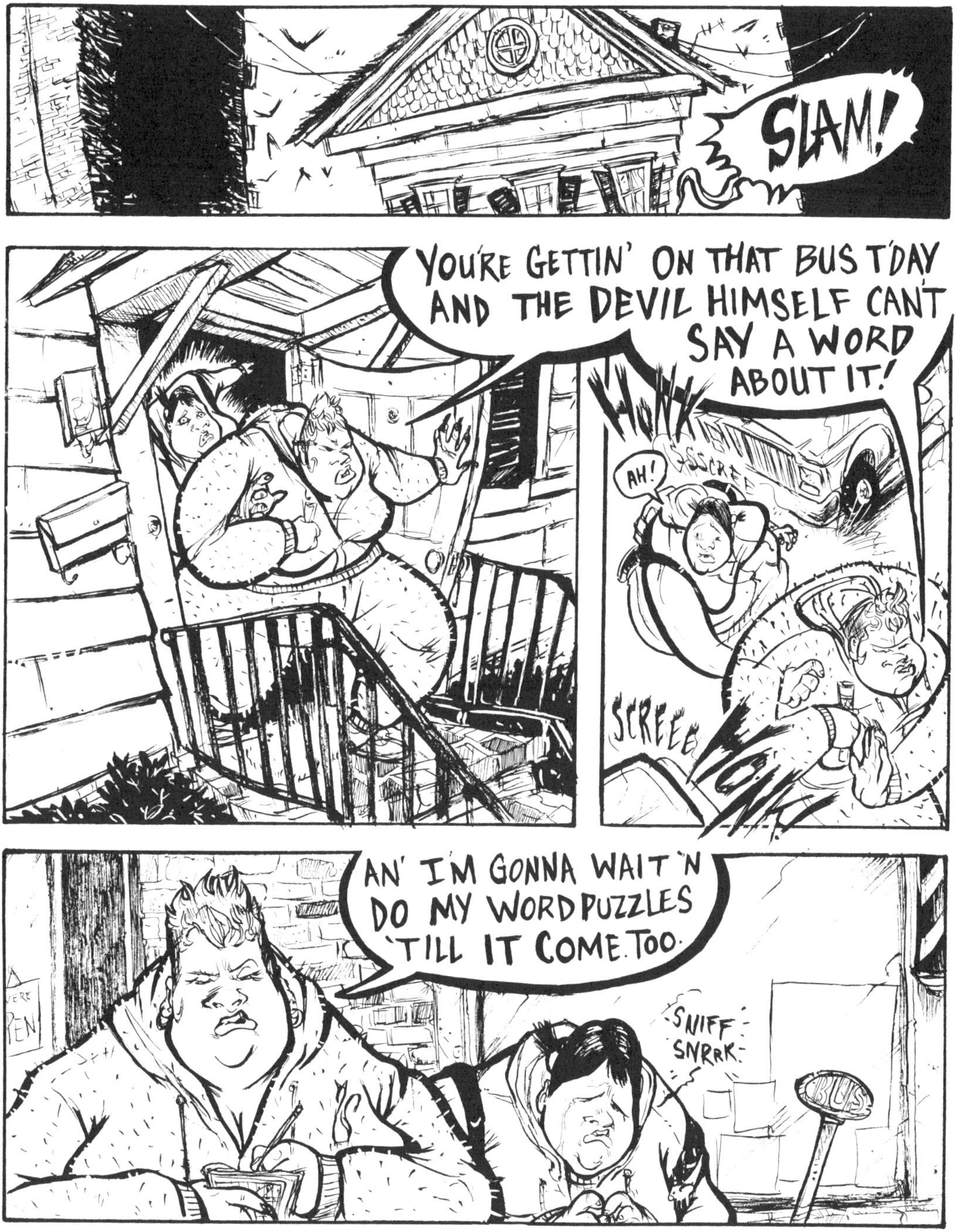
SLAM!
YOU'RE GETTIN' ON THAT BUS T'DAY AND THE DEVIL HIMSELF CAN'T SAY A WORD ABOUT IT!
HONK
SSSCREE
AH!
SCREEE
AN' I'M GONNA WAIT 'N DO MY WORDPUZZLES 'TILL IT COME. TOO.
SNIFF SNRRK
BUS

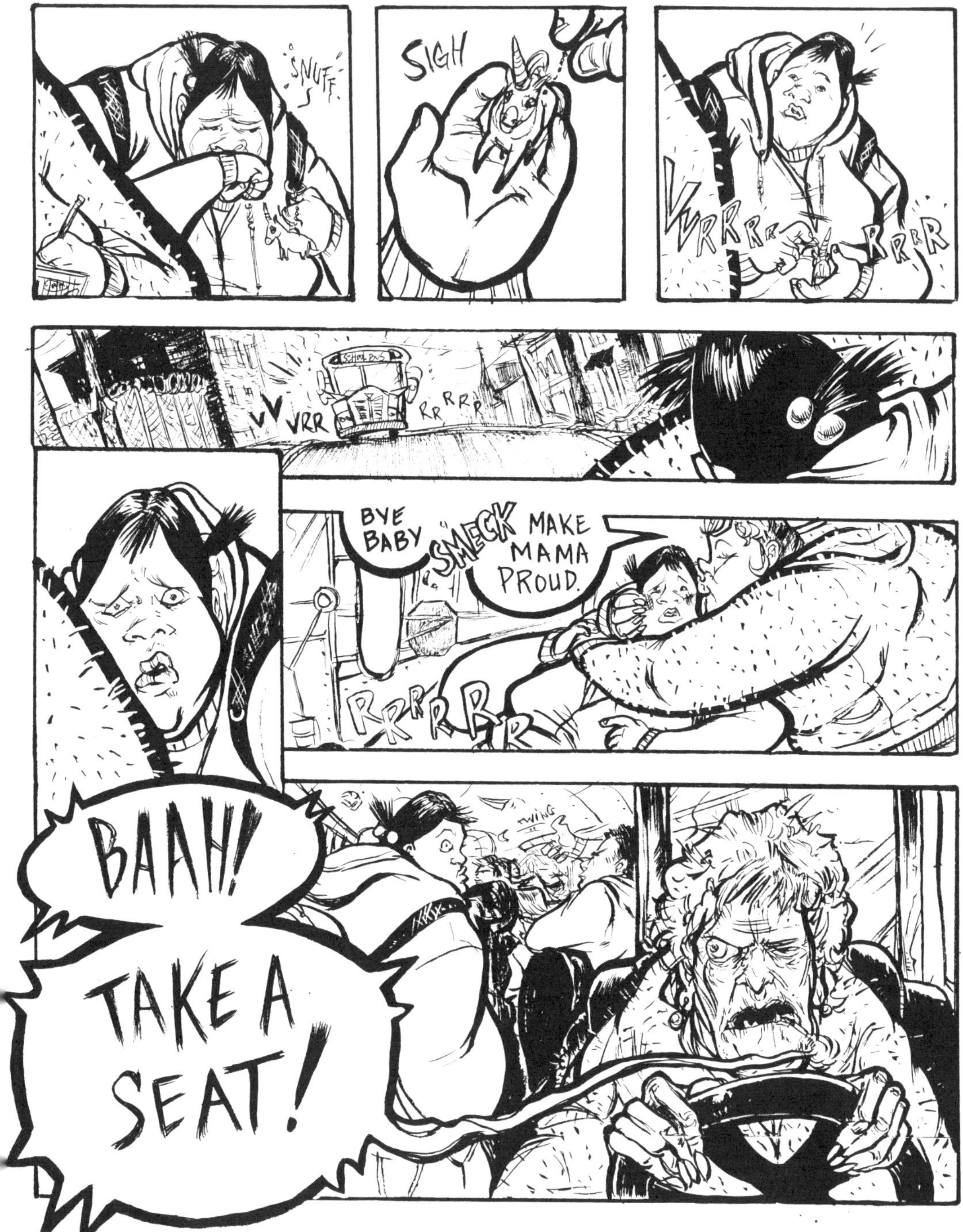
SNUFF
SIGH
VRRRRRRRRR
SCHOOL BUS
VVRR RRRRR
BYE BABY
SMECK
MAKE MAMA PROUD.
RRRRRR
TWING
BAAH!
TAKE A SEAT!

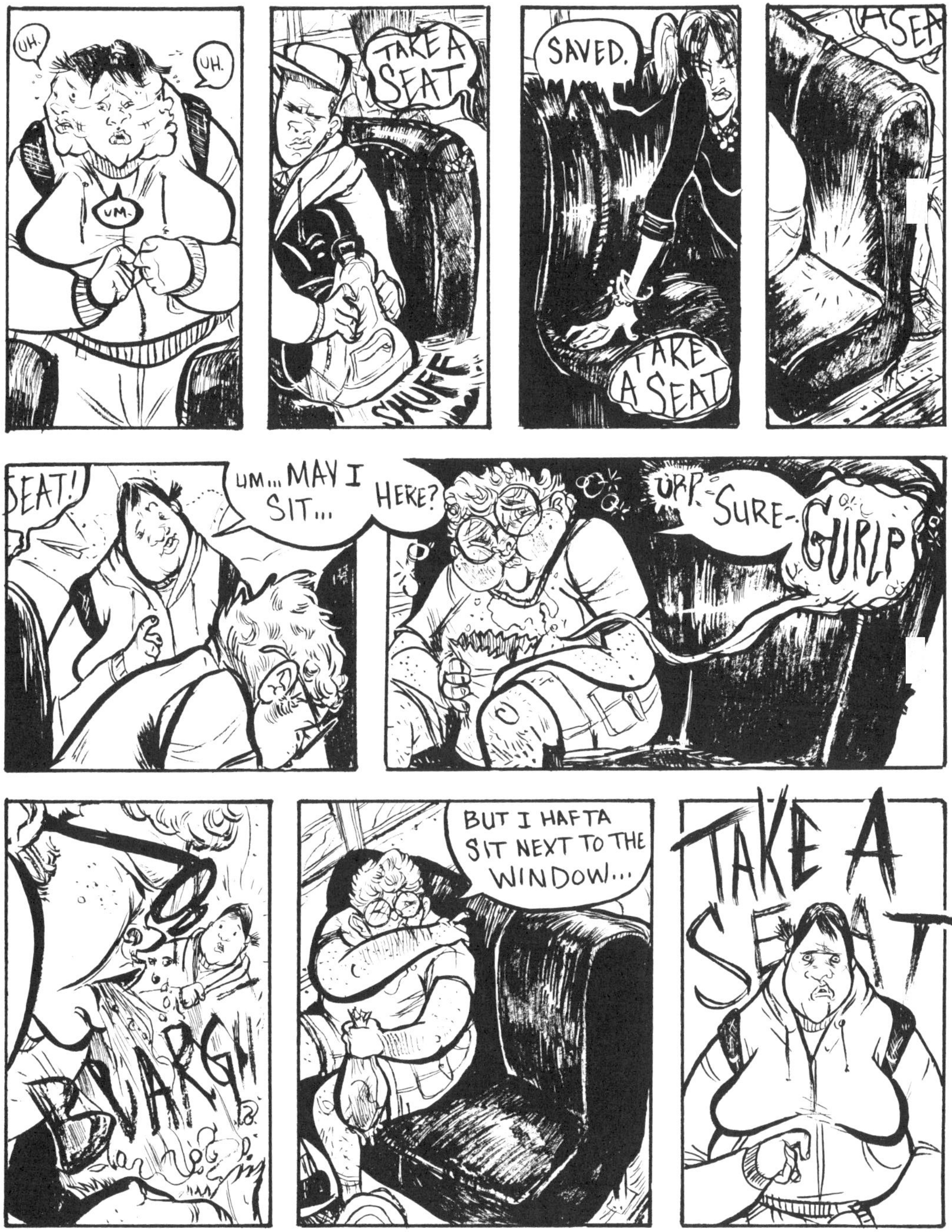
UH.
UH.
UM.
TAKE A SEAT
SHUFF
SAVED.
TAKE A SEAT
ASEA
SEAT!
UM... MAY I SIT...
HERE?
URP-SURE-GURLP
BLARG!!
BUT I HAFTA SIT NEXT TO THE WINDOW...
TAKE A SEAT

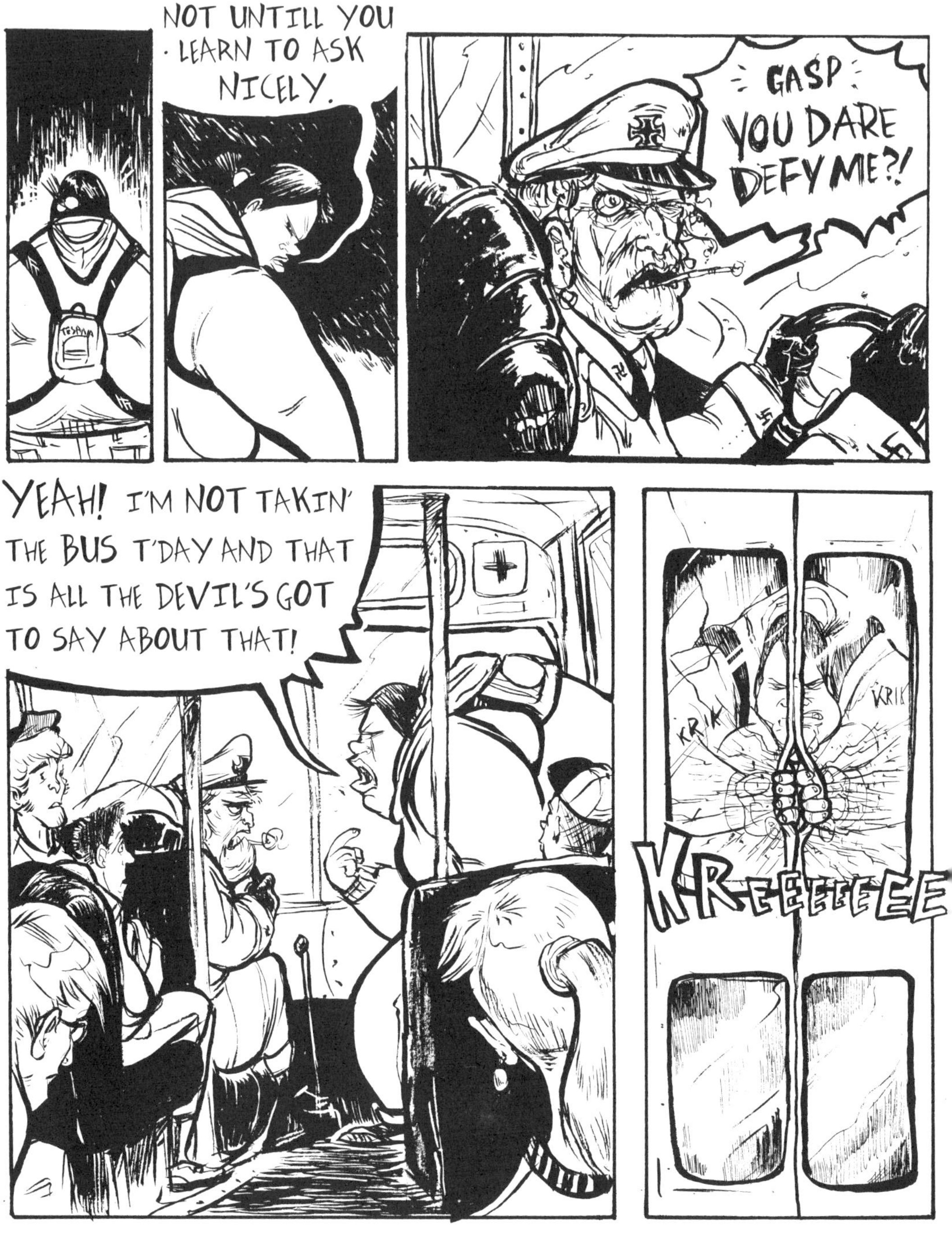
NOT UNTILL YOU LEARN TO ASK NICELY.
GASP YOU DARE DEFY ME?!
YEAH! I'M NOT TAKIN' THE BUS T'DAY AND THAT IS ALL THE DEVIL'S GOT TO SAY ABOUT THAT!
KRIK
KRIK
KREEEEEEE

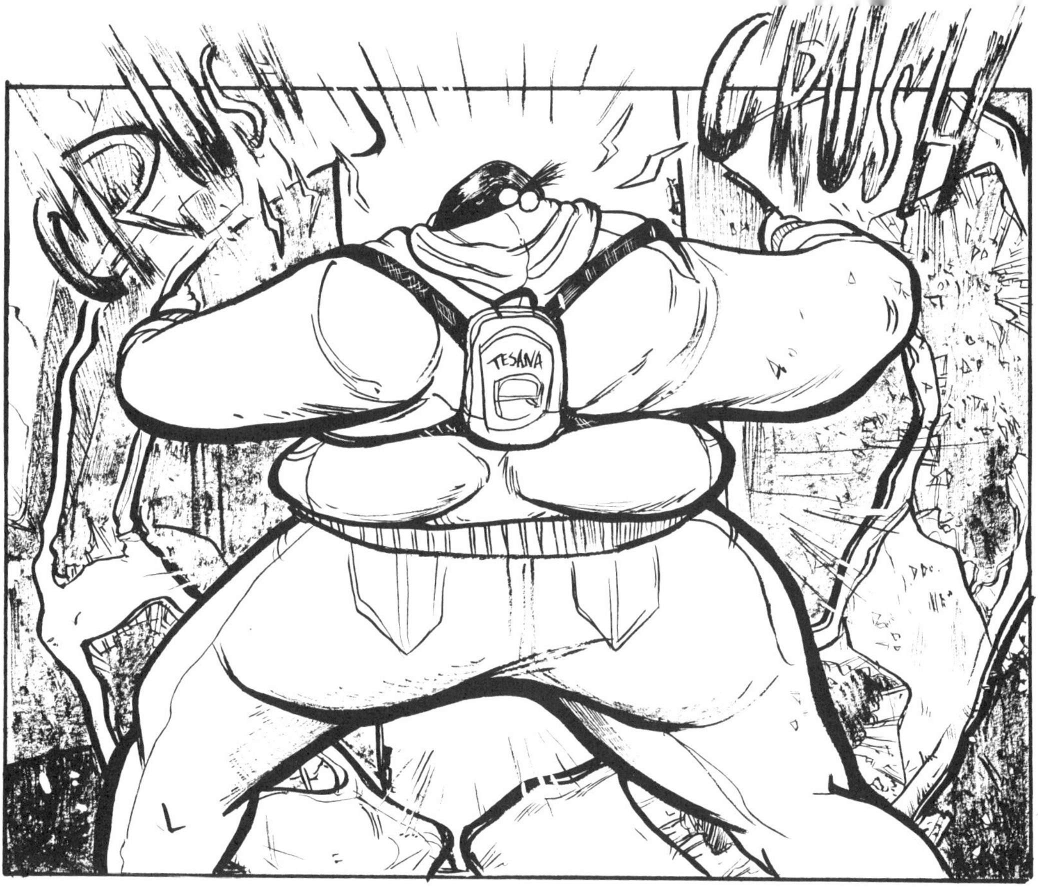
CRUSH
CRUSH
TESANA

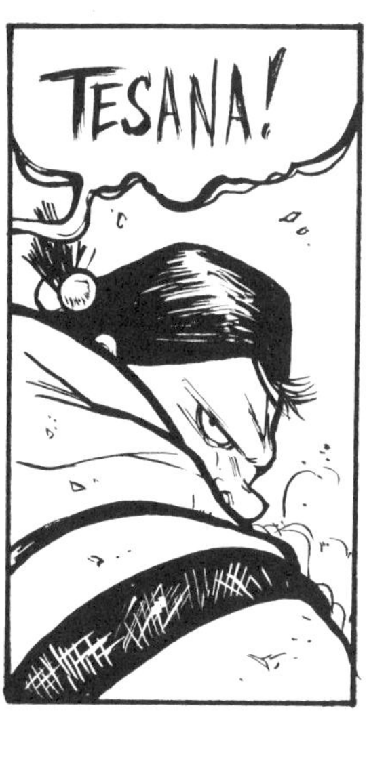
TESANA!

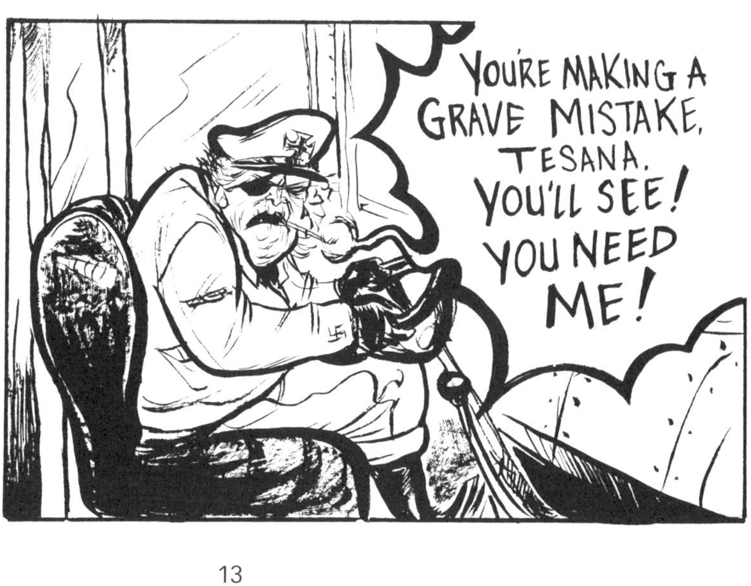
YOU'RE MAKING A GRAVE MISTAKE, TESANA. YOU'LL SEE! YOU NEED ME!

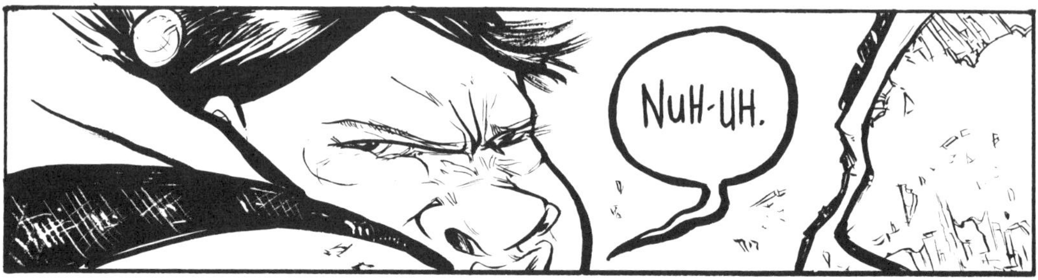
NUH-UH.

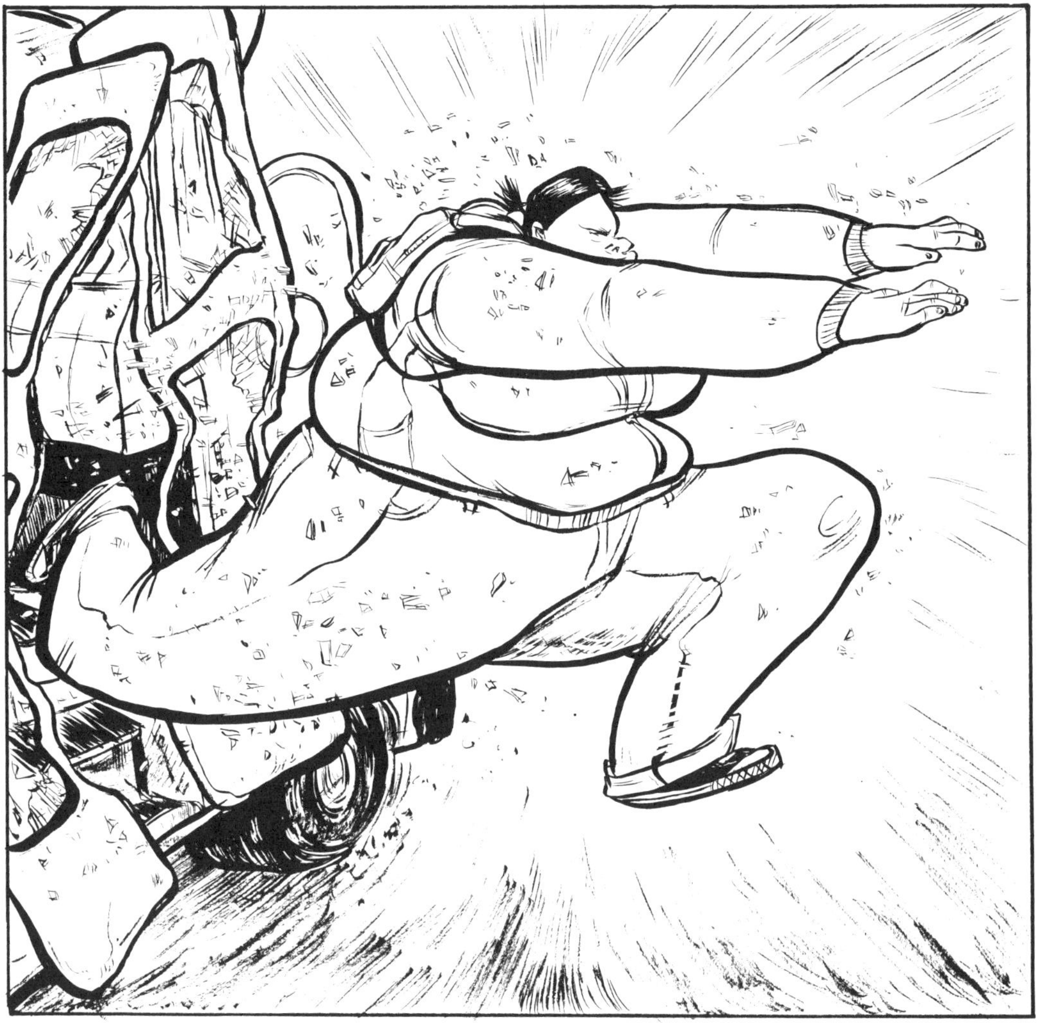

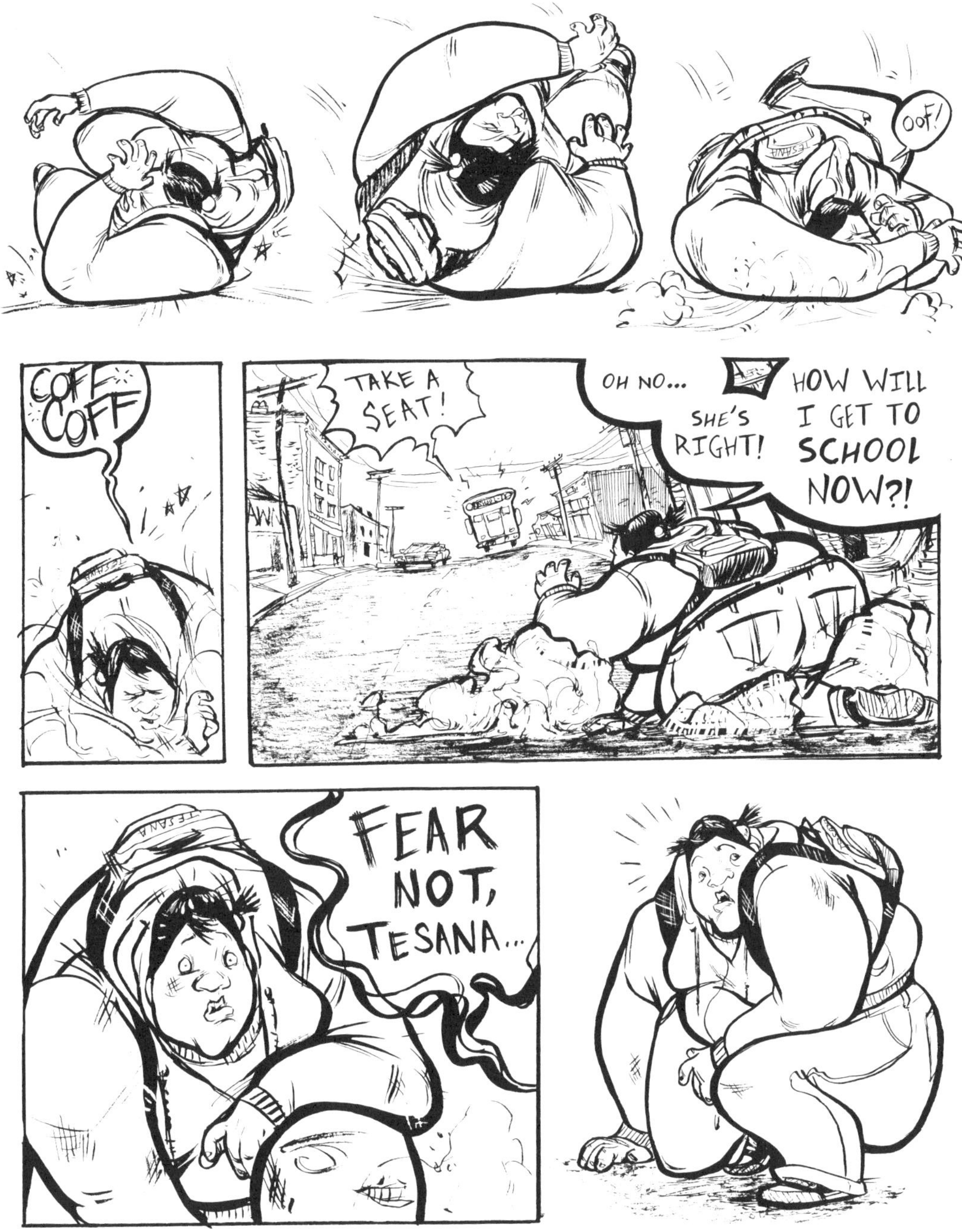
OOF!
TESANA
COFF COFF
TESANA
TAKE A SEAT!
OH NO...
SHE'S RIGHT!
HOW WILL I GET TO SCHOOL NOW?!
TESANA
FEAR NOT, TESANA...

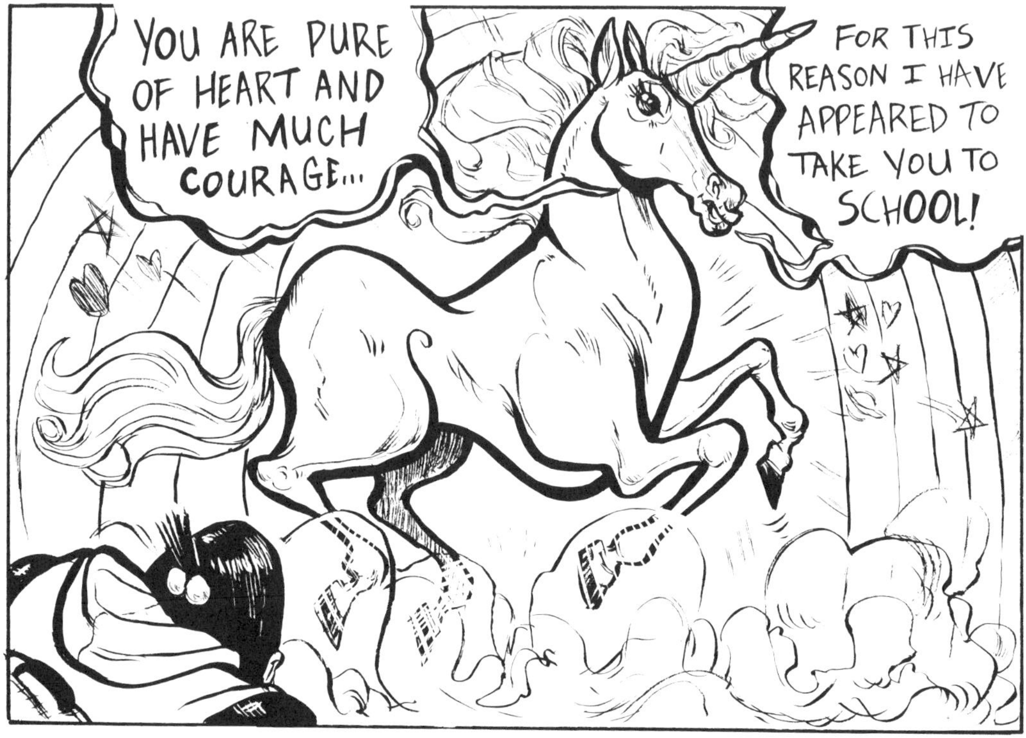
YOU ARE PURE OF HEART AND HAVE MUCH COURAGE...
FOR THIS REASON I HAVE APPEARED TO TAKE YOU TO SCHOOL!

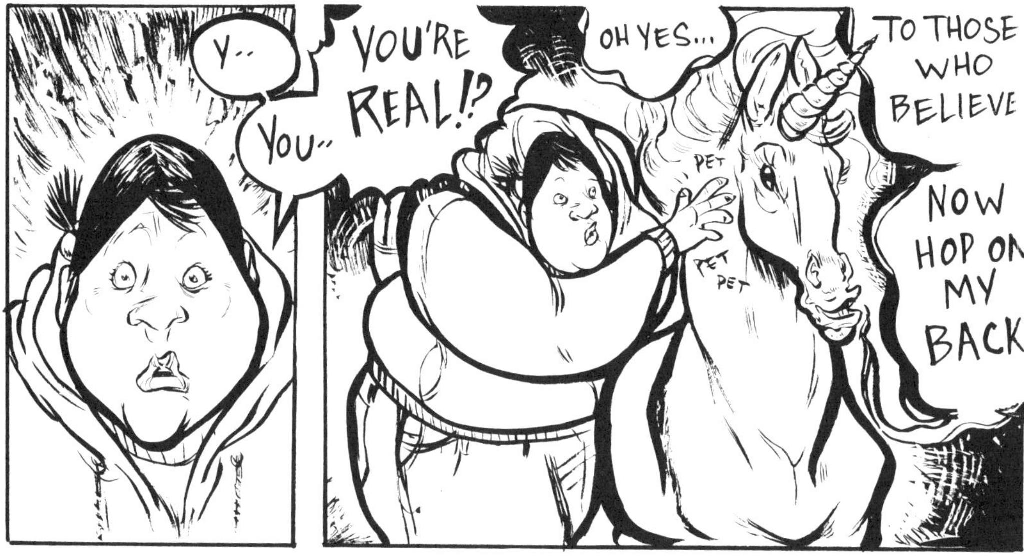
Y..
YOU..
YOU'RE REAL!?
OH YES...
TO THOSE WHO BELIEVE
PET
PET PET
NOW HOP ON MY BACK!

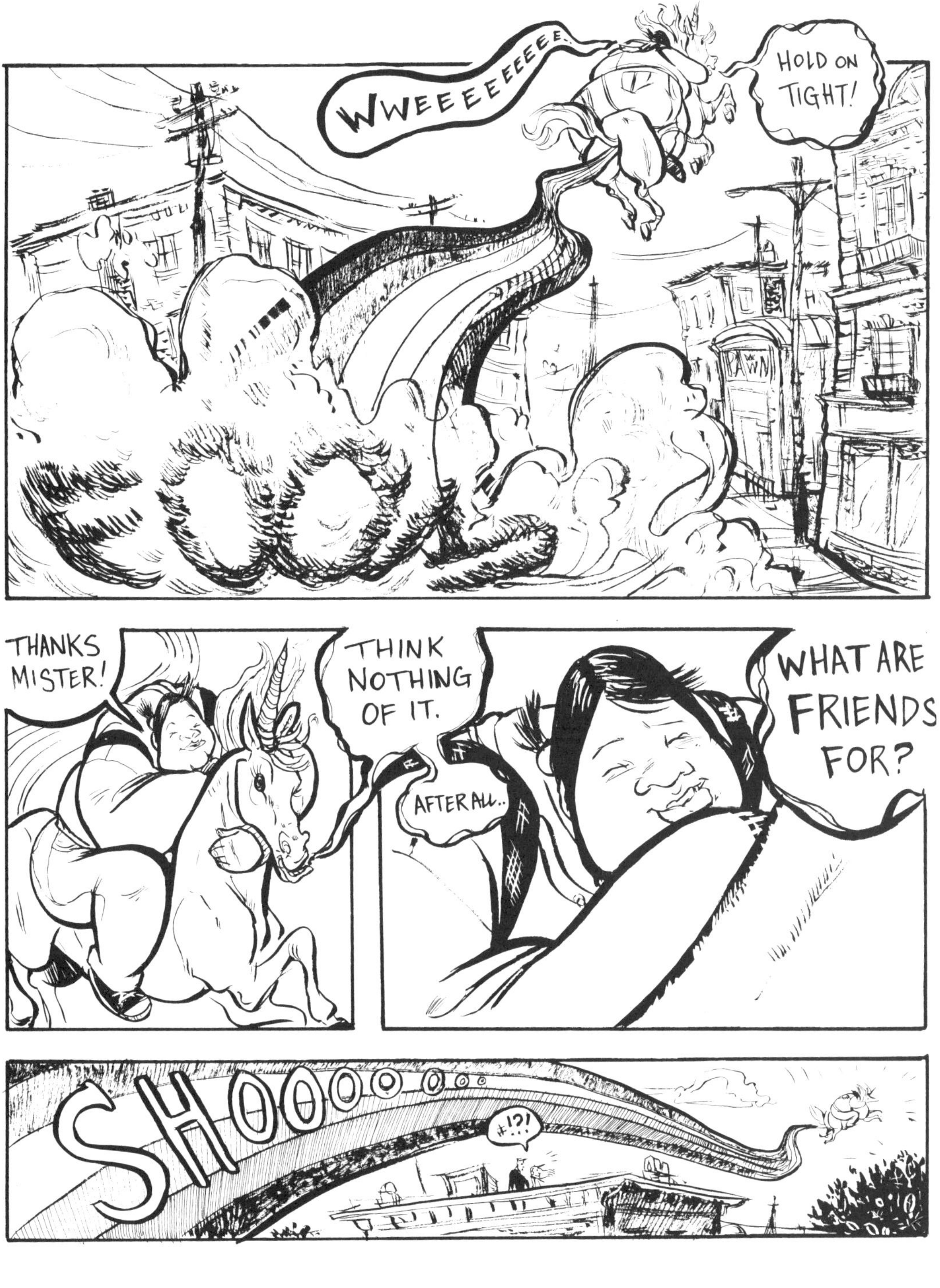
WWEEEEEEEEEE...
HOLD ON TIGHT!
PAWN
THANKS MISTER!
THINK NOTHING OF IT.
AFTER ALL..
WHAT ARE FRIENDS FOR?
SHOOOOooo
#!?!

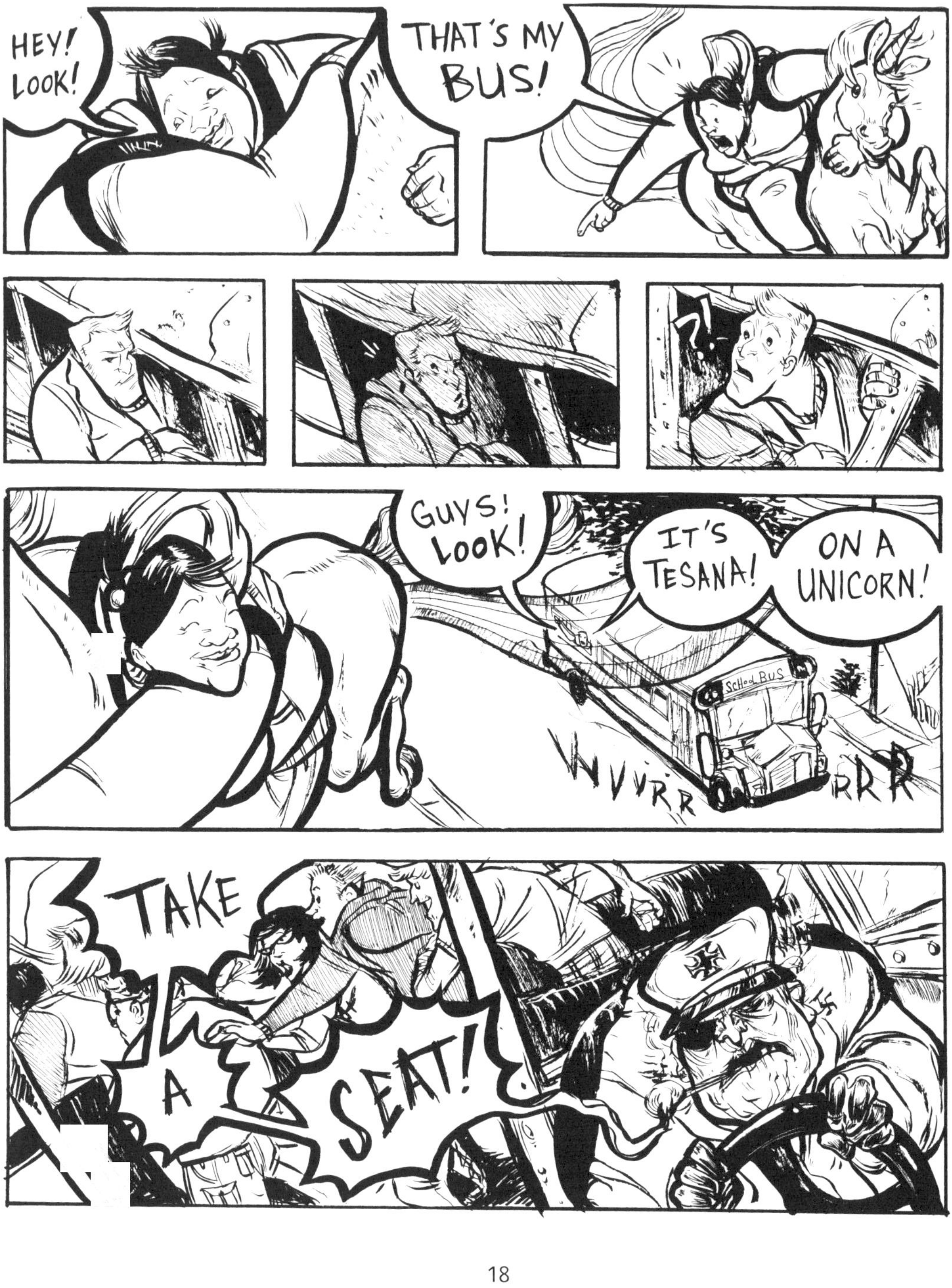

HEY! LOOK!
THAT'S MY BUS!
?!
GUYS! LOOK!
IT'S TESANA!
ON A UNICORN!
SCHOOL BUS
WVVRR
RRR
TAKE A SEAT!

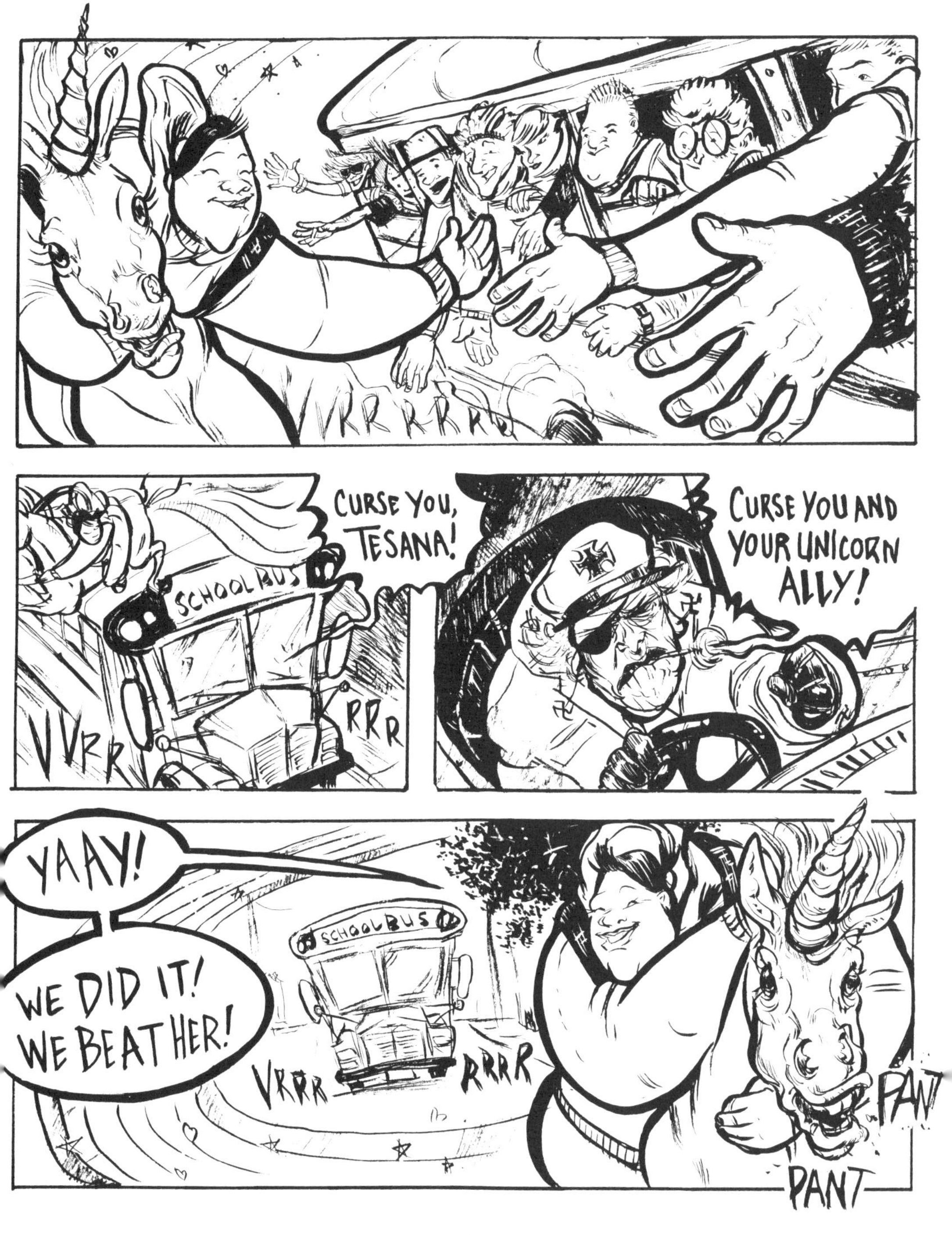
VRRRRRR
SCHOOL BUS
CURSE YOU, TESANA!
VVRRR
RRR
CURSE YOU AND YOUR UNICORN ALLY!
YAAY!
WE DID IT! WE BEAT HER!
SCHOOL BUS
VRRR
RRRR
PANT
PANT

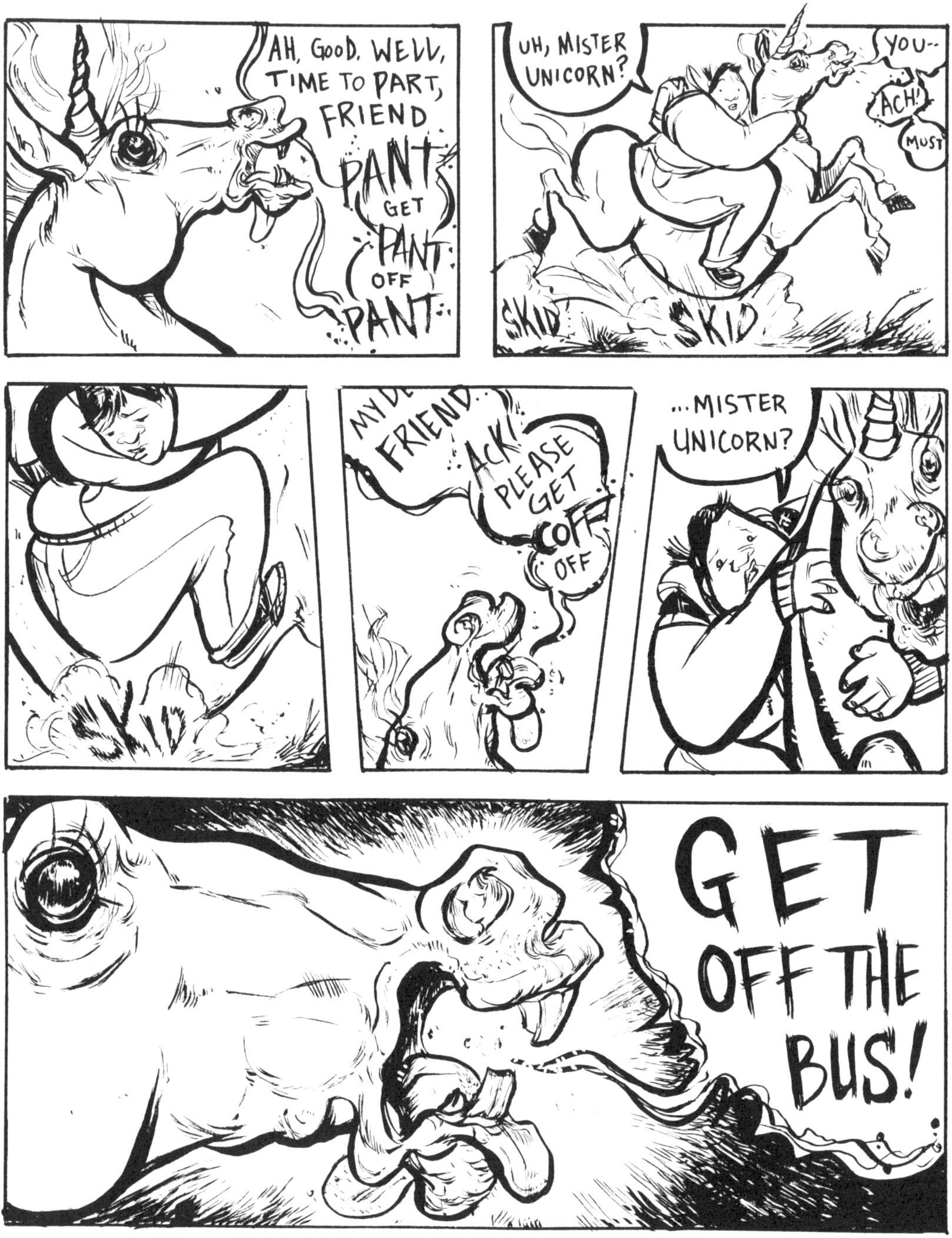
AH, GOOD. WELL, TIME TO PART, FRIEND
PANT
GET
PANT
OFF
PANT
UH, MISTER UNICORN?
YOU--
ACH!
MUST
SKID
SKID
SKID
FRIEND
ACK! PLEASE GET
COFF
OFF
...MISTER UNICORN?
GET OFF THE BUS!

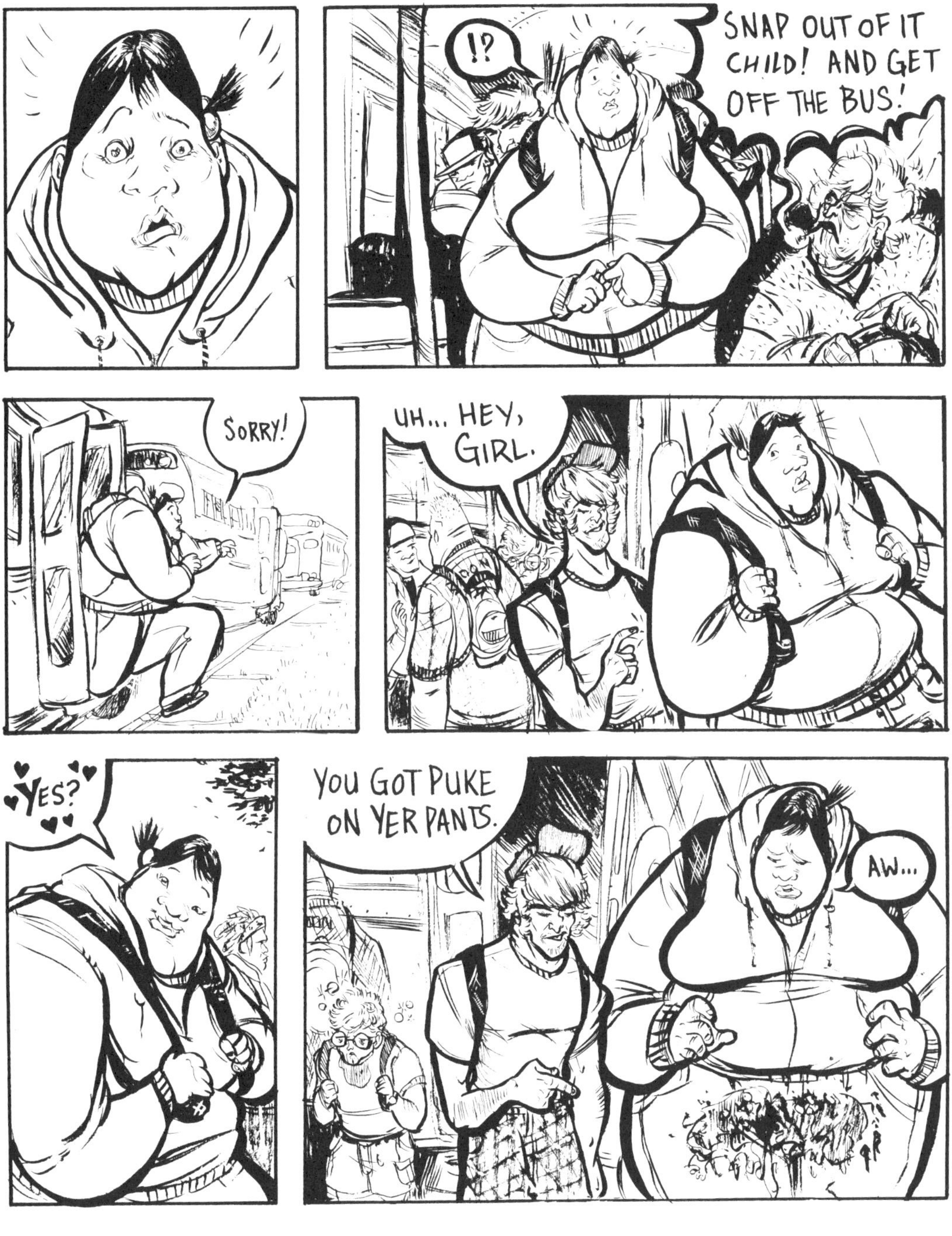
!?
SNAP OUT OF IT CHILD! AND GET OFF THE BUS!
SORRY!
UH... HEY, GIRL.
YES?
YOU GOT PUKE ON YER PANTS.
AW...

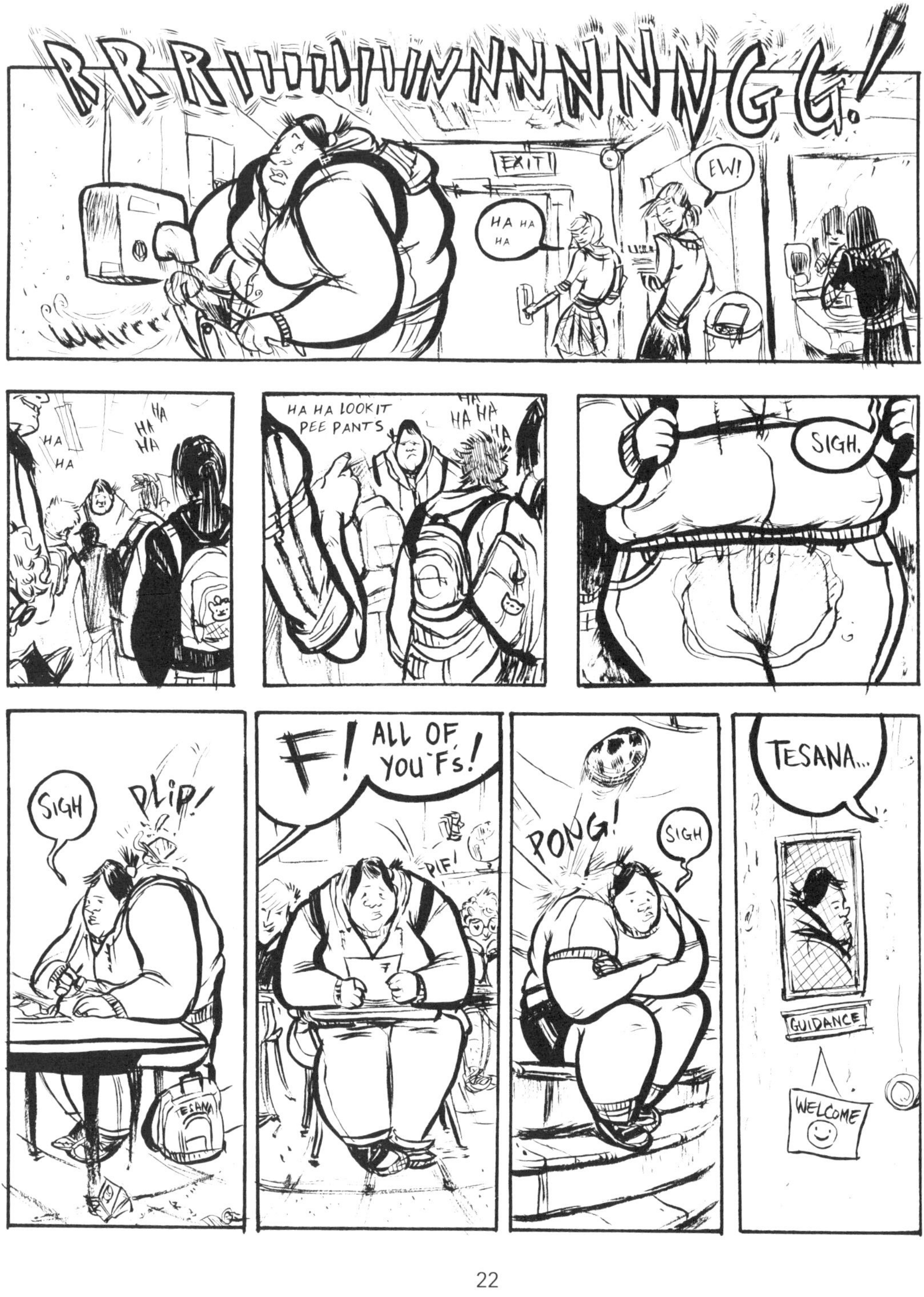
BRRIIIIIIIINNNNNNGG!
EXIT
HA HA HA
EW!
Whirrrr
HA HA
HA HA
HA HA
HA HA LOOKIT PEE PANTS
HA HA HA HA
SIGH.
SIGH
PLIP!
TESANA
F! ALL OF YOU F's!
PIF!
PONG!
SIGH
TESANA...
GUIDANCE
WELCOME

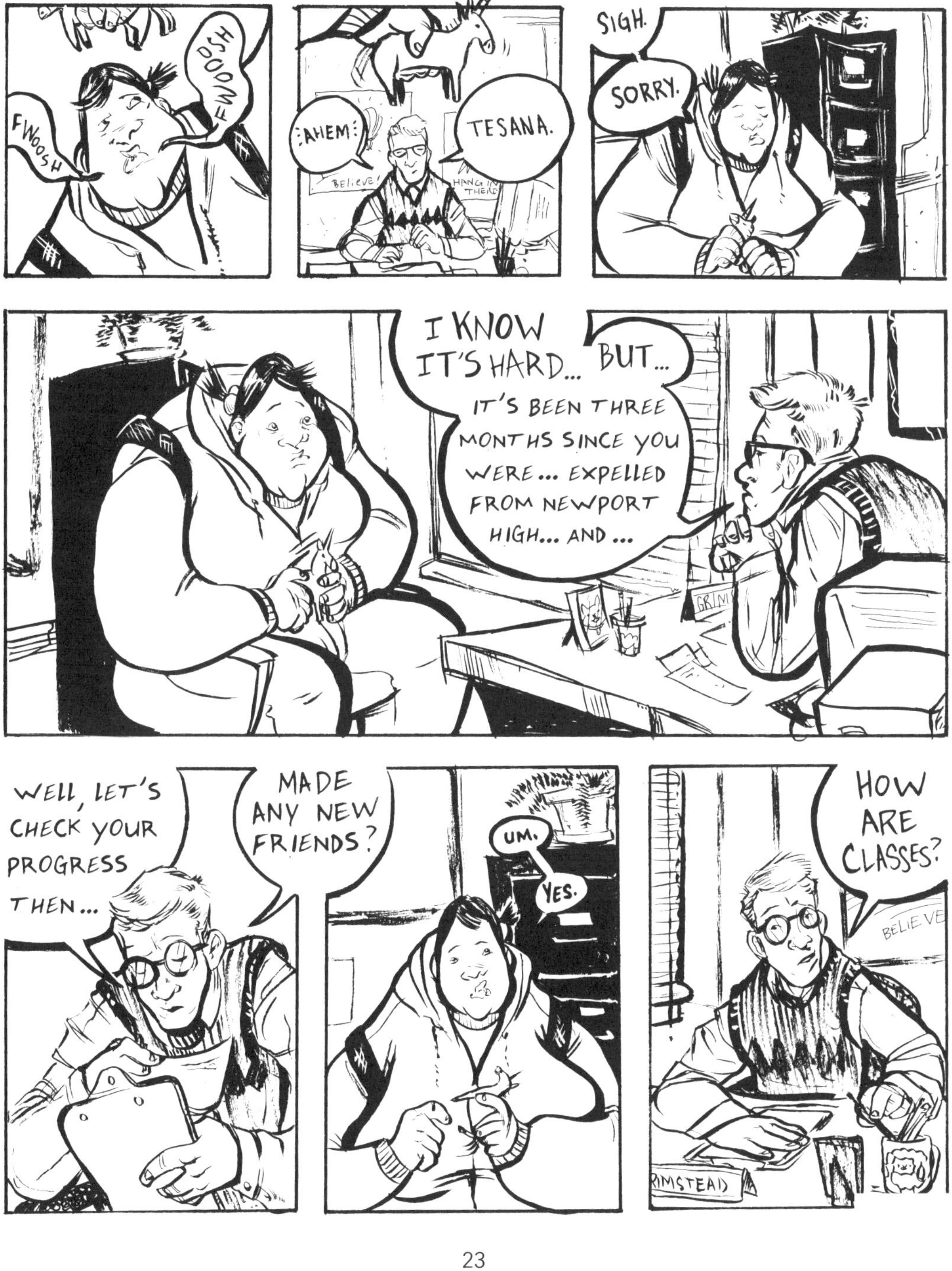
FWOOSH
FWOOOSH
AHEM
TESANA.
BELIEVE!
HANG IN THERE
SIGH.
SORRY.
I KNOW IT'S HARD... BUT...
IT'S BEEN THREE MONTHS SINCE YOU WERE... EXPELLED FROM NEWPORT HIGH... AND...
WELL, LET'S CHECK YOUR PROGRESS THEN...
MADE ANY NEW FRIENDS?
UM.
YES.
HOW ARE CLASSES?
BELIEVE
RIMSTEAD

GOOD.
AND YOUR HOMEWORK GRADES ARE...?
GOOD.
MHMM...AND HOW HAVE THINGS BEEN AT HOME?
GOOD.
TESANA, I NEED YOU TO ANSWER THESE QUEST-
GOOD.
TESANA, THIS ISN'T A GAME. I CAN'T HELP IF YOU WON'T LET ME...
GOOD.
UGH... OK I THINK WE NEED A LITTLE EXTRA TIME... LET ME SEE WHO'S SCHEDULED TO COME IN NEXT...
GASP
OH NO. WHAT'S THE TIME?
TICK
TICK
...JUDSON.

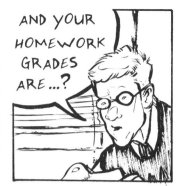

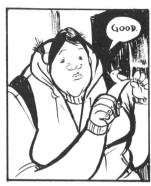

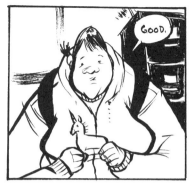

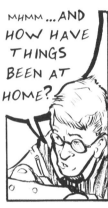

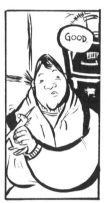

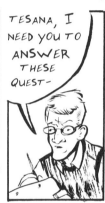

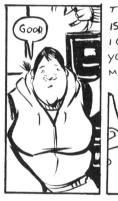

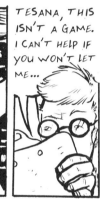

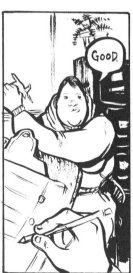

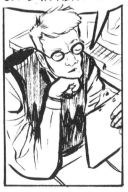

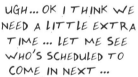

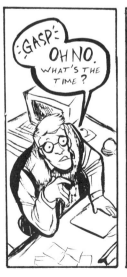

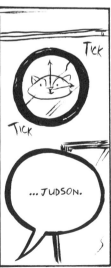

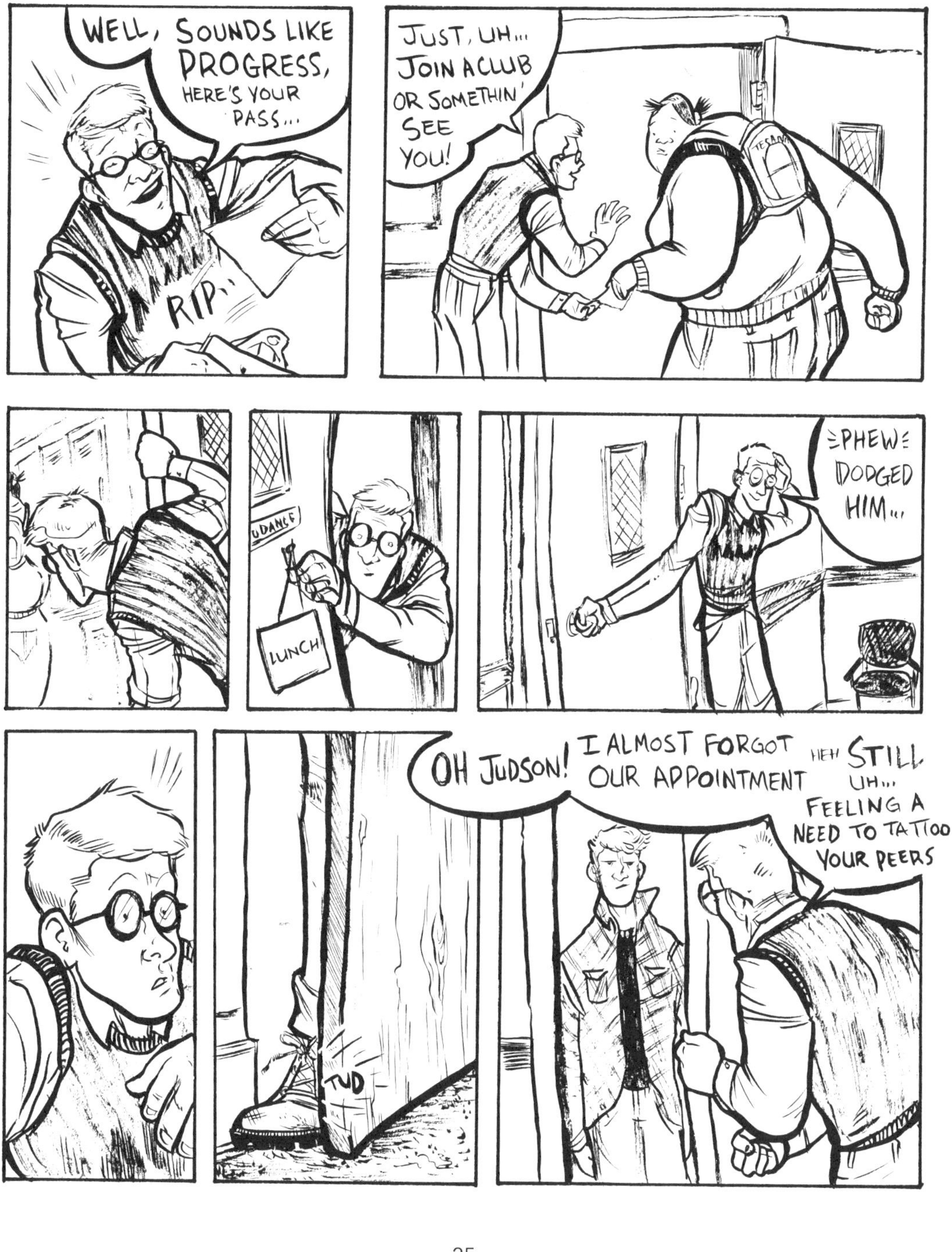
WELL, SOUNDS LIKE PROGRESS, HERE'S YOUR PASS...
RIP
JUST, UH... JOIN A CLUB OR SOMETHIN' SEE YOU!
DANCE
LUNCH
PHEW DODGED HIM...
OH JUDSON! I ALMOST FORGOT OUR APPOINTMENT HEH STILL UH... FEELING A NEED TO TATTOO YOUR PEERS
TUD

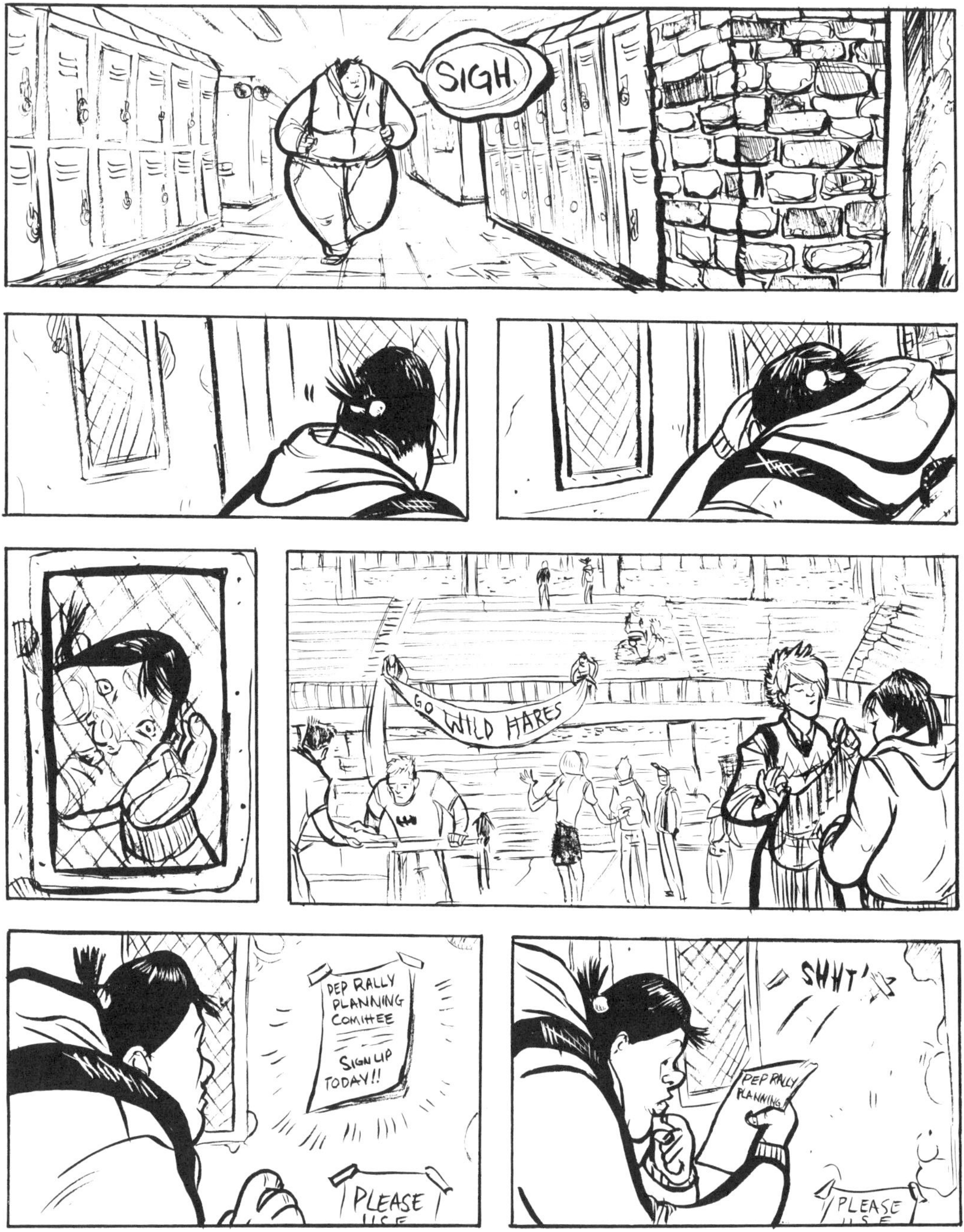
SIGH.
GO WILD HARES
PEP RALLY
PLANNING
COMITTEE
SIGN UP
TODAY!!
PLEASE
SHHT'
PEP RALLY
PLANNING
PLEASE

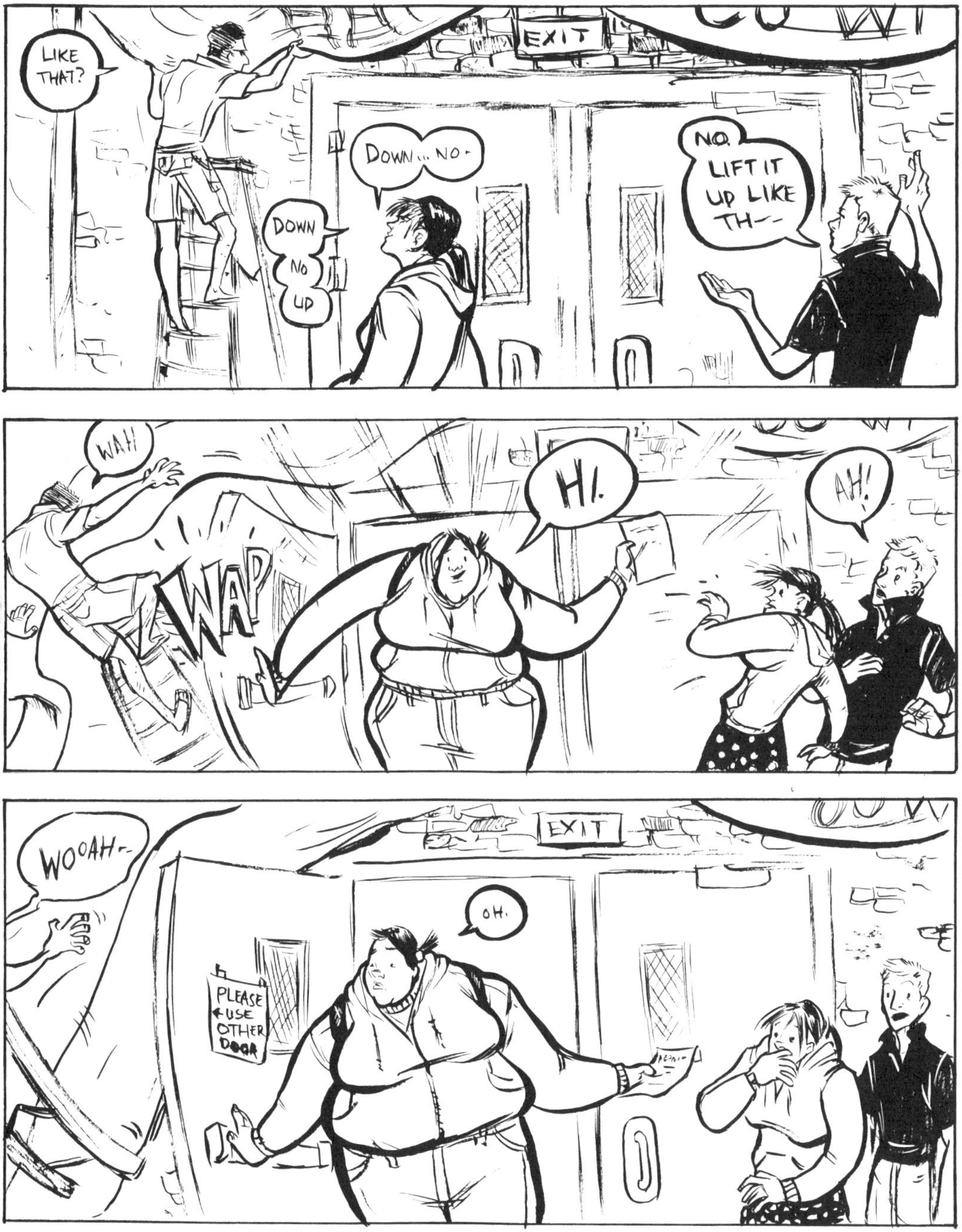
LIKE THAT?
DOWN... NO-
DOWN NO UP
NO. LIFT IT UP LIKE TH--
WAH!
WAP
HI!
AH!
WOOAH--
OH.
PLEASE ← USE OTHER DOOR

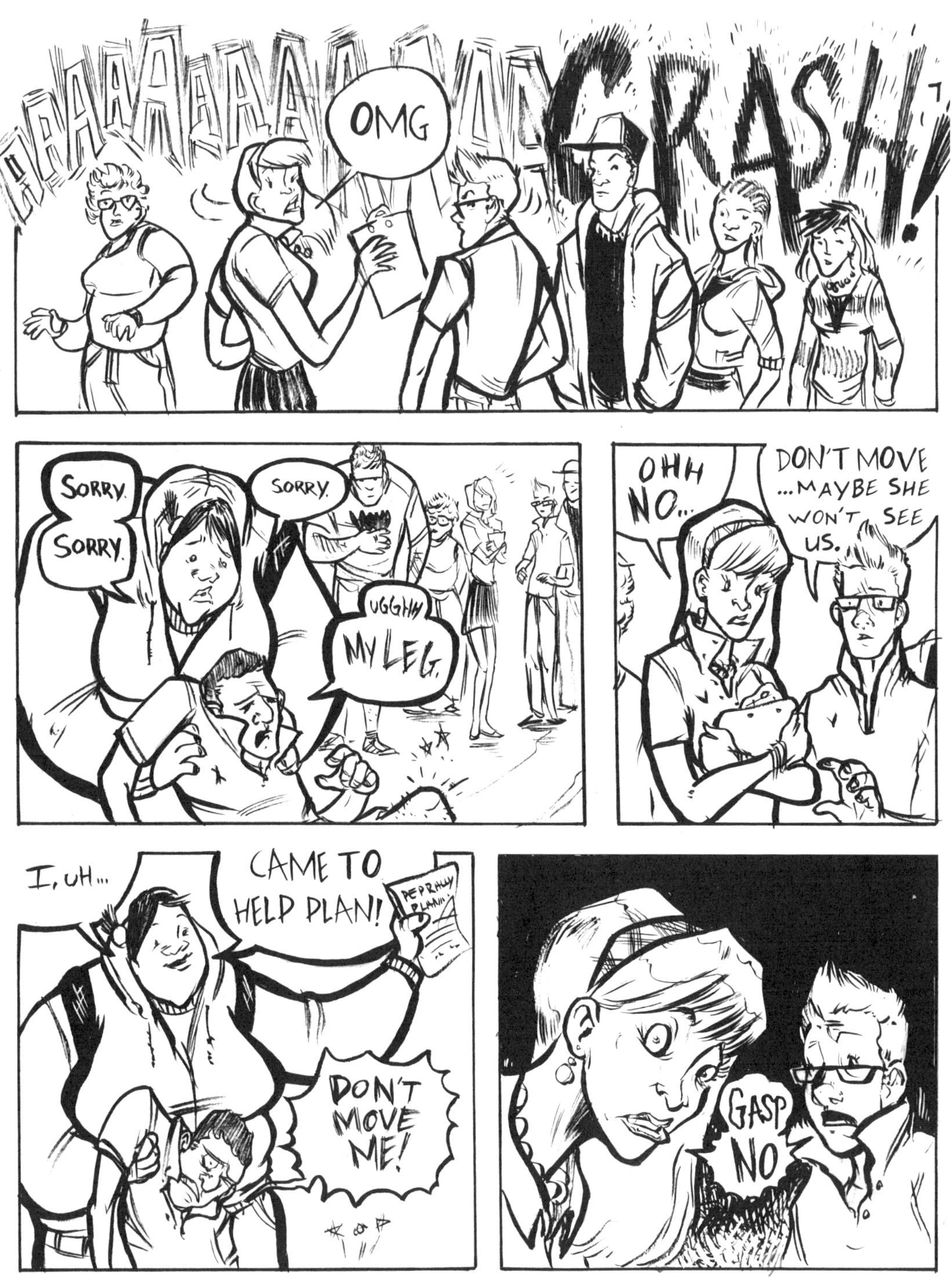
OMG
CRASH!
SORRY.
SORRY.
SORRY.
UGGHH
MY LEG.
OHH NO...
DON'T MOVE ...MAYBE SHE WON'T SEE US.
I, UH...
CAME TO HELP PLAN!
DON'T MOVE ME!
GASP
NO

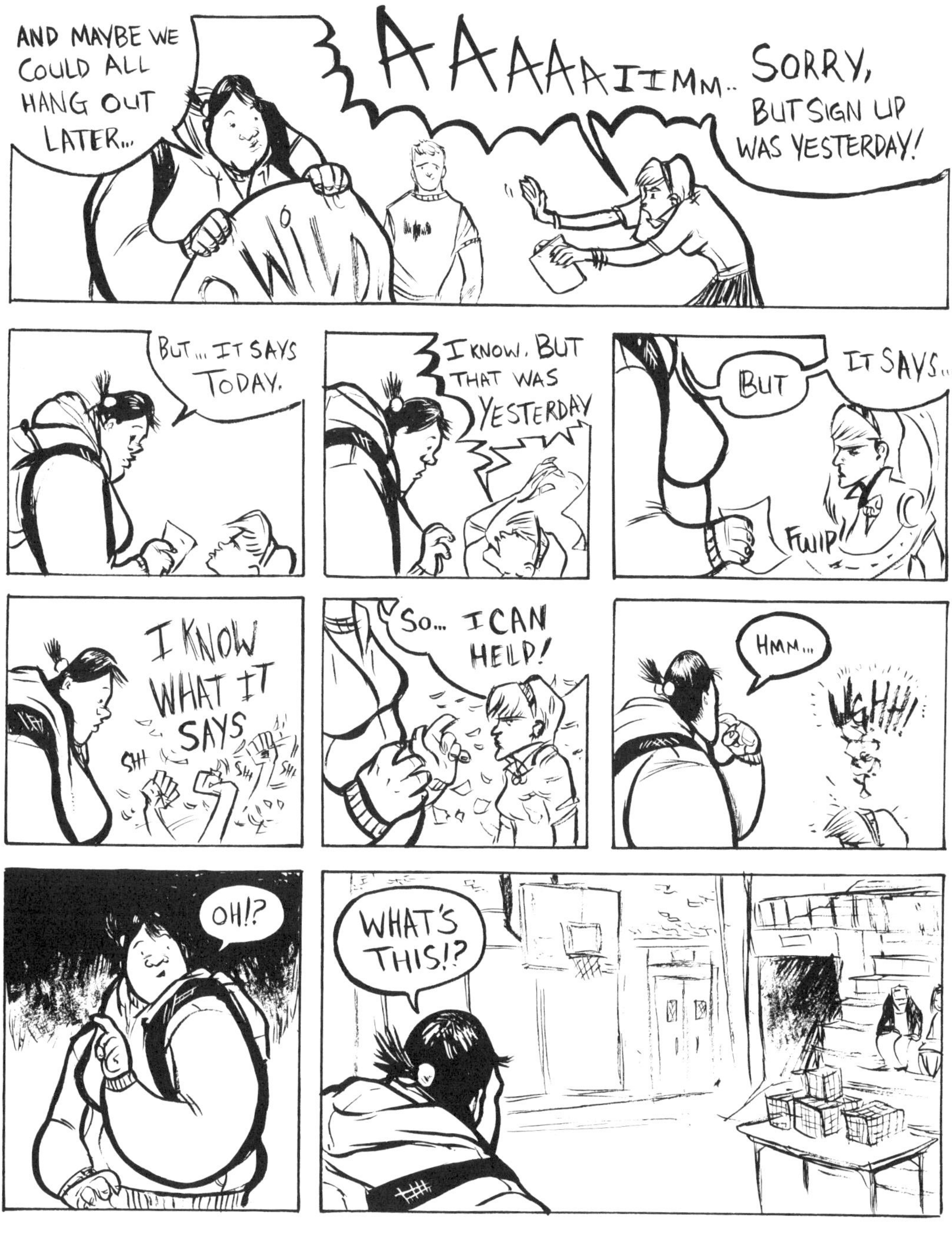
AND MAYBE WE COULD ALL HANG OUT LATER...
AAAAAIIMM.. SORRY, BUT SIGN UP WAS YESTERDAY!
BUT... IT SAYS TODAY.
I KNOW. BUT THAT WAS YESTERDAY
BUT
IT SAYS...
FWIP
I KNOW WHAT IT SAYS
SHH
SHH
SHH
SO... I CAN HELP!
HMM...
UGHH!
OH!?
WHAT'S THIS!?

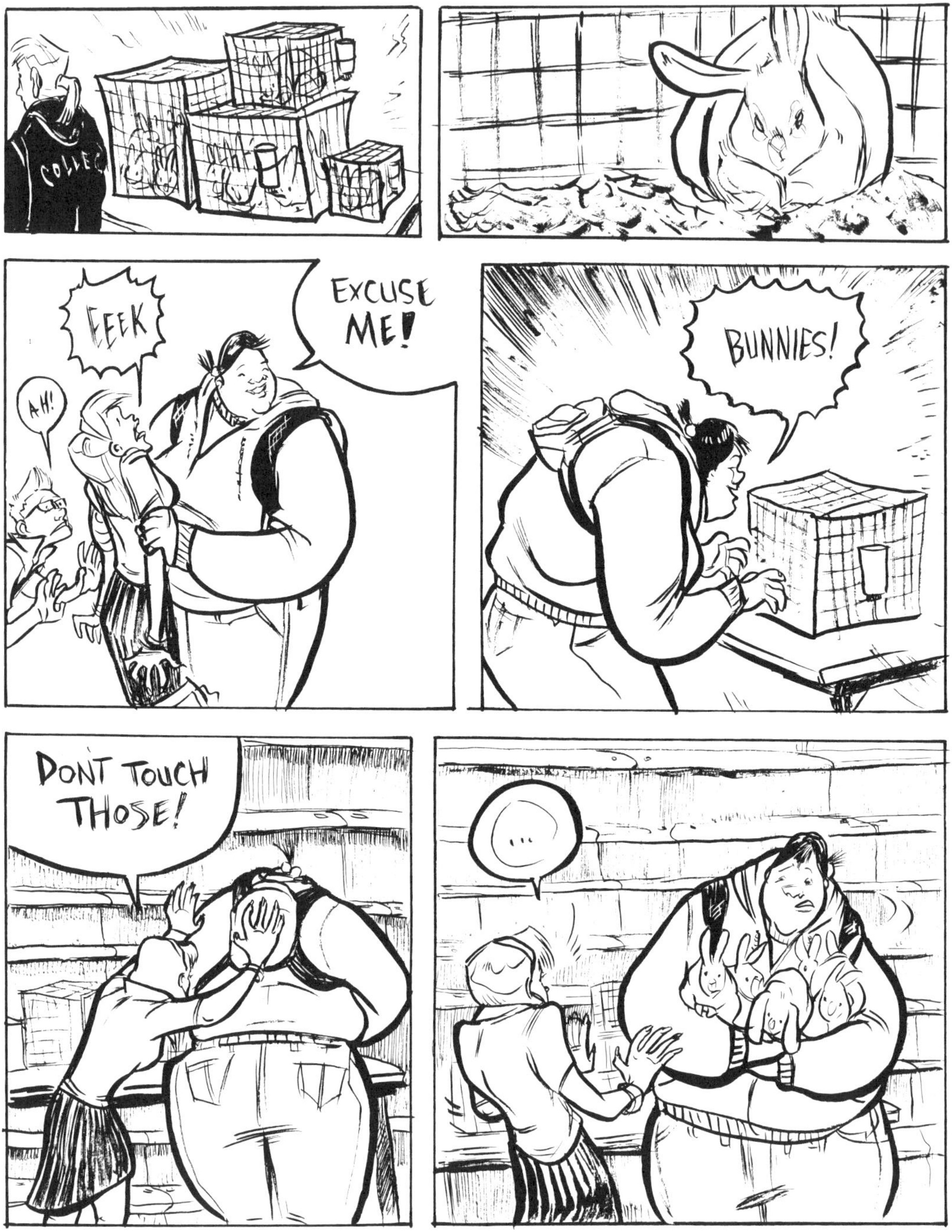
EEEK
AH!
EXCUSE ME!
BUNNIES!
DON'T TOUCH THOSE!
...

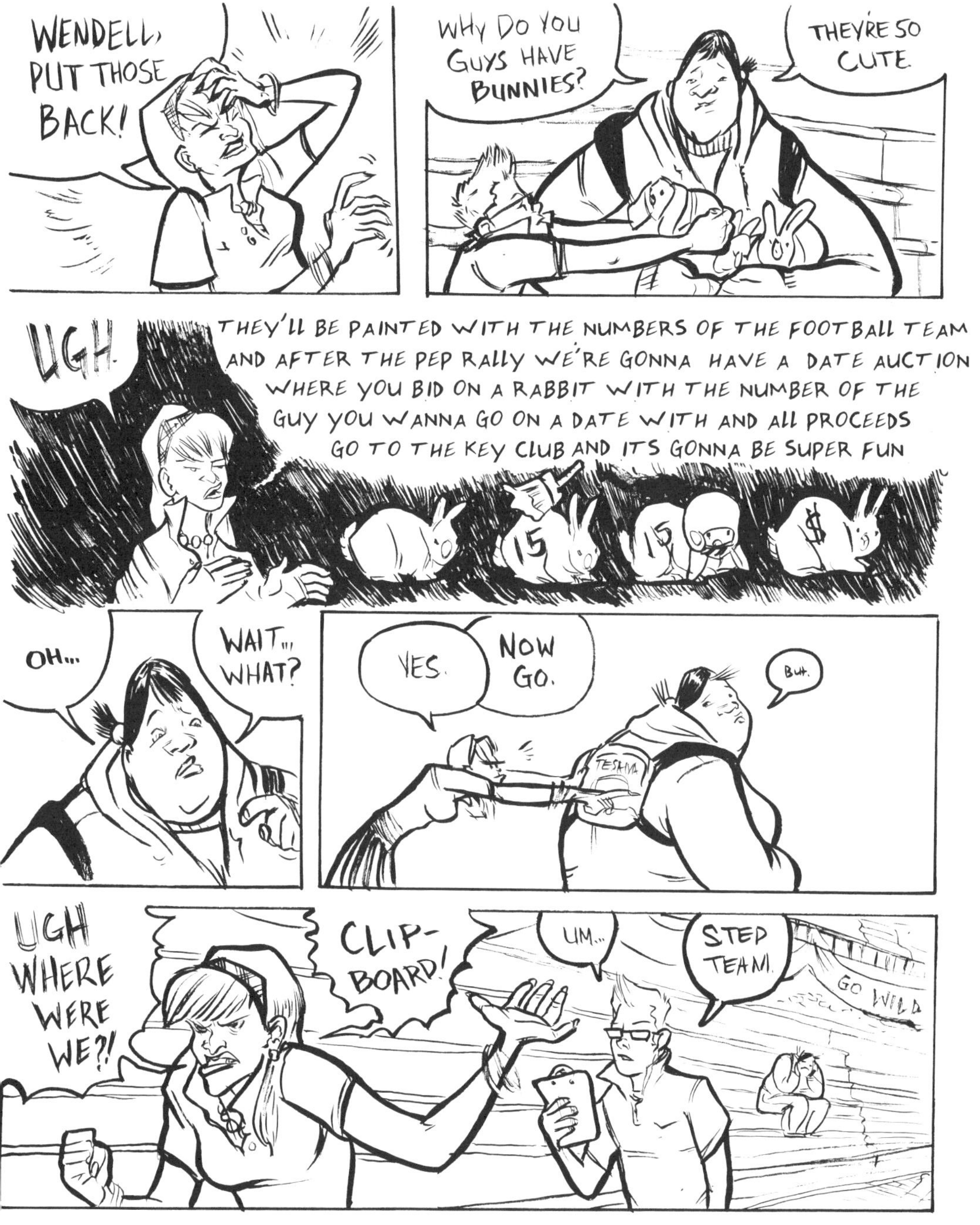

WENDELL, PUT THOSE BACK!
WHY DO YOU GUYS HAVE BUNNIES?
THEY'RE SO CUTE.
UGH.
THEY'LL BE PAINTED WITH THE NUMBERS OF THE FOOTBALL TEAM AND AFTER THE PEP RALLY WE'RE GONNA HAVE A DATE AUCTION WHERE YOU BID ON A RABBIT WITH THE NUMBER OF THE GUY YOU WANNA GO ON A DATE WITH AND ALL PROCEEDS GO TO THE KEY CLUB AND ITS GONNA BE SUPER FUN
15
15
$
OH...
WAIT... WHAT?
YES.
NOW GO.
But.
TESHIA
UGH WHERE WERE WE?!
CLIP-BOARD!
UM...
STEP TEAM.
GO WILD

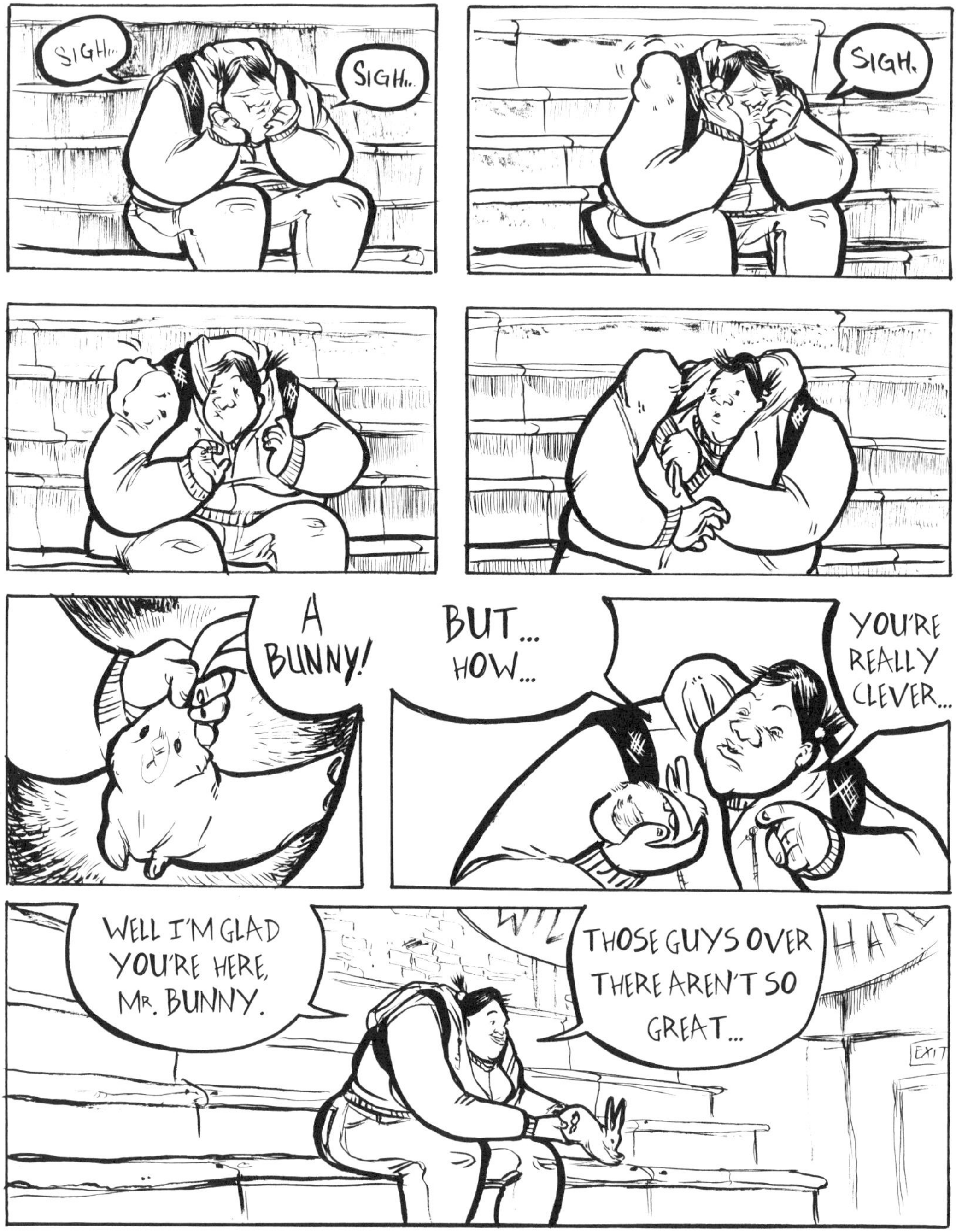
SIGH...
SIGH...
SIGH.
A BUNNY!
BUT... HOW...
YOU'RE REALLY CLEVER...
WELL I'M GLAD YOU'RE HERE, MR. BUNNY.
THOSE GUYS OVER THERE AREN'T SO GREAT...
EXIT

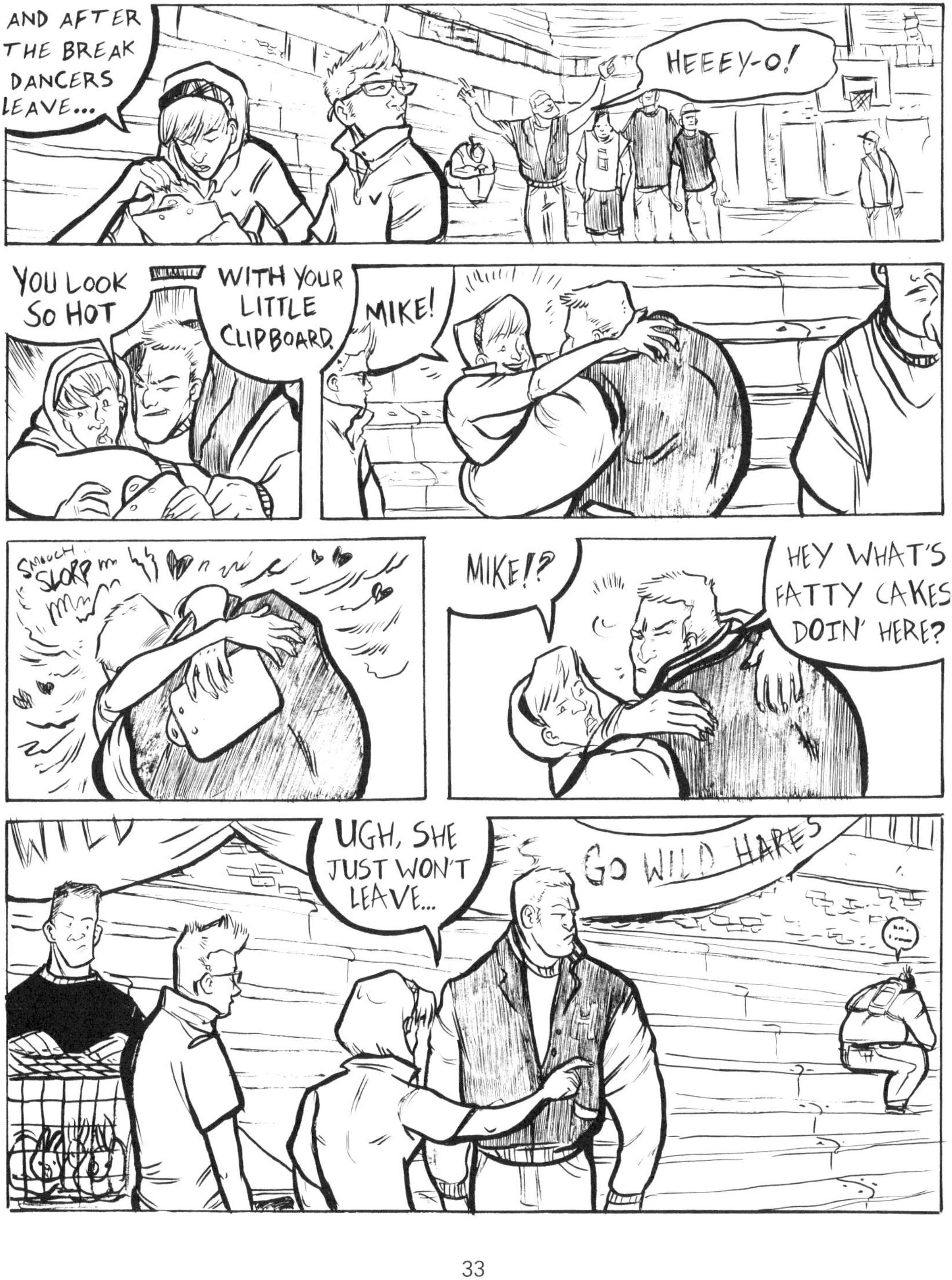
AND AFTER THE BREAK DANCERS LEAVE...
HEEEY-O!
YOU LOOK SO HOT
WITH YOUR LITTLE CLIPBOARD.
MIKE!
SMOOCH
SLORP
MIKE!?
HEY WHAT'S FATTY CAKES DOIN' HERE?
WILD
UGH, SHE JUST WON'T LEAVE...
GO WILD HARES

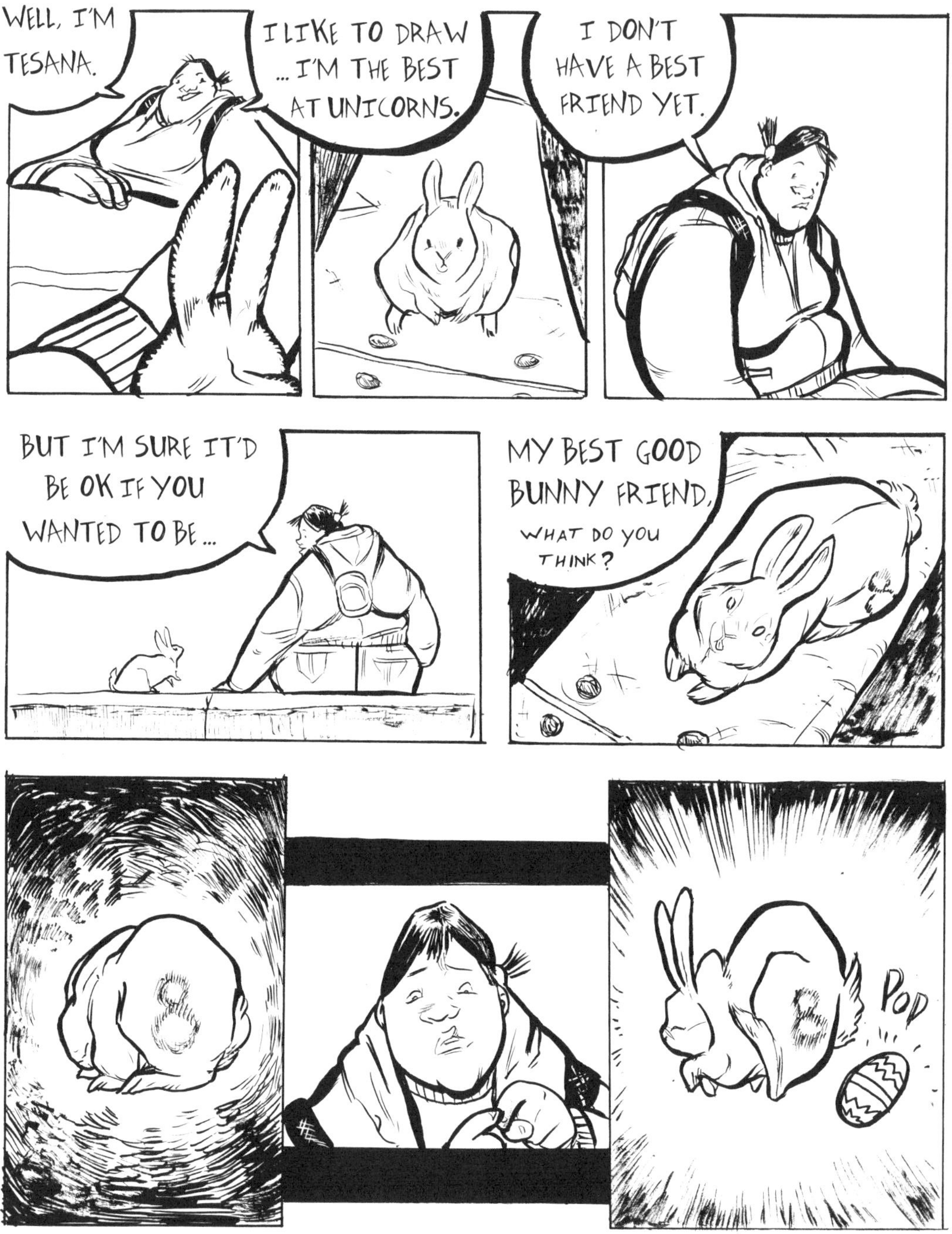
WELL, I'M TESANA.
I LIKE TO DRAW ... I'M THE BEST AT UNICORNS.
I DON'T HAVE A BEST FRIEND YET.
BUT I'M SURE IT'D BE OK IF YOU WANTED TO BE ...
MY BEST GOOD BUNNY FRIEND.
WHAT DO YOU THINK?
POP

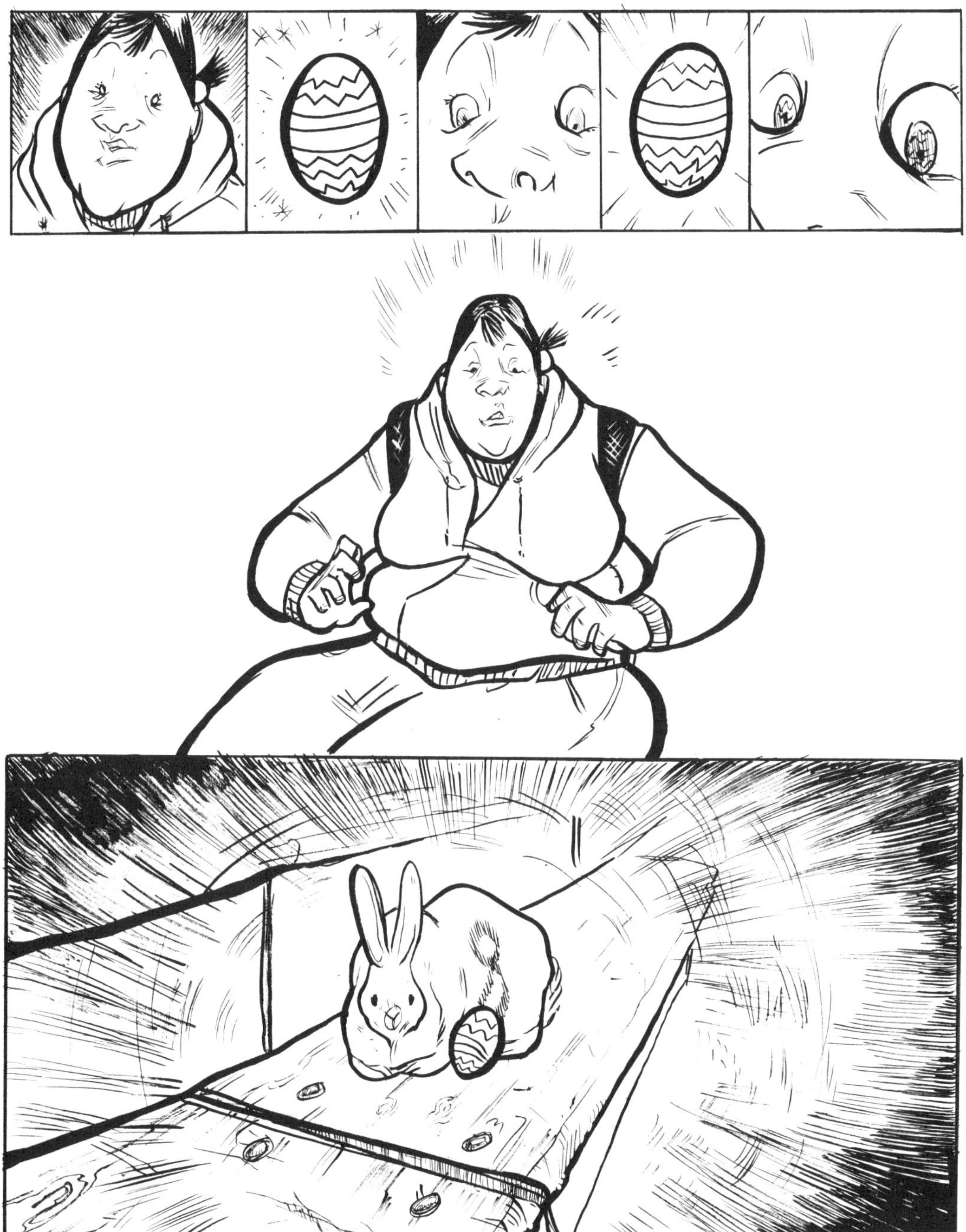

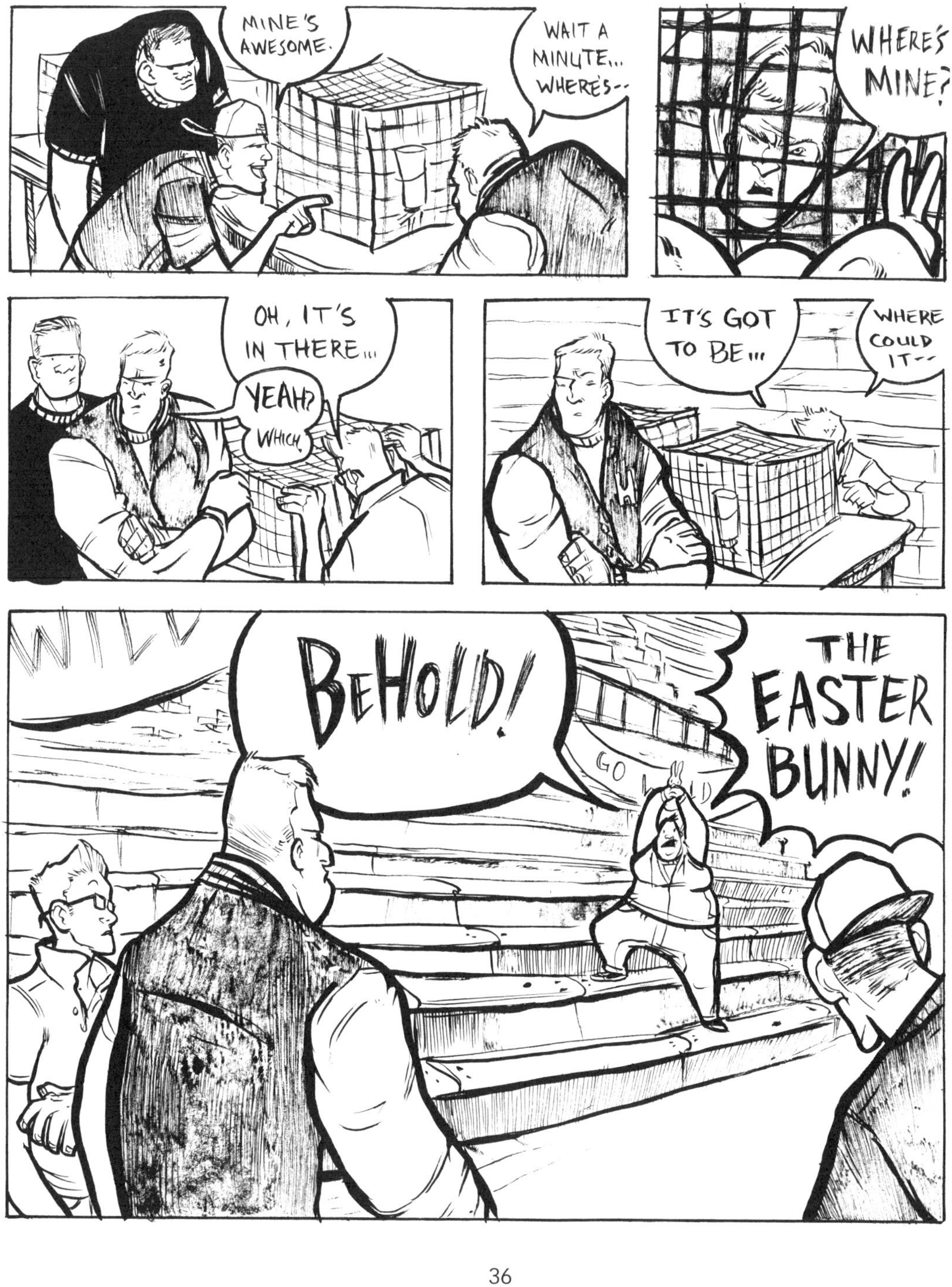
MINE'S AWESOME.
WAIT A MINUTE... WHERE'S--
WHERE'S MINE?
OH, IT'S IN THERE...
YEAH? WHICH.
IT'S GOT TO BE...
WHERE COULD IT--
BEHOLD!
THE EASTER BUNNY!

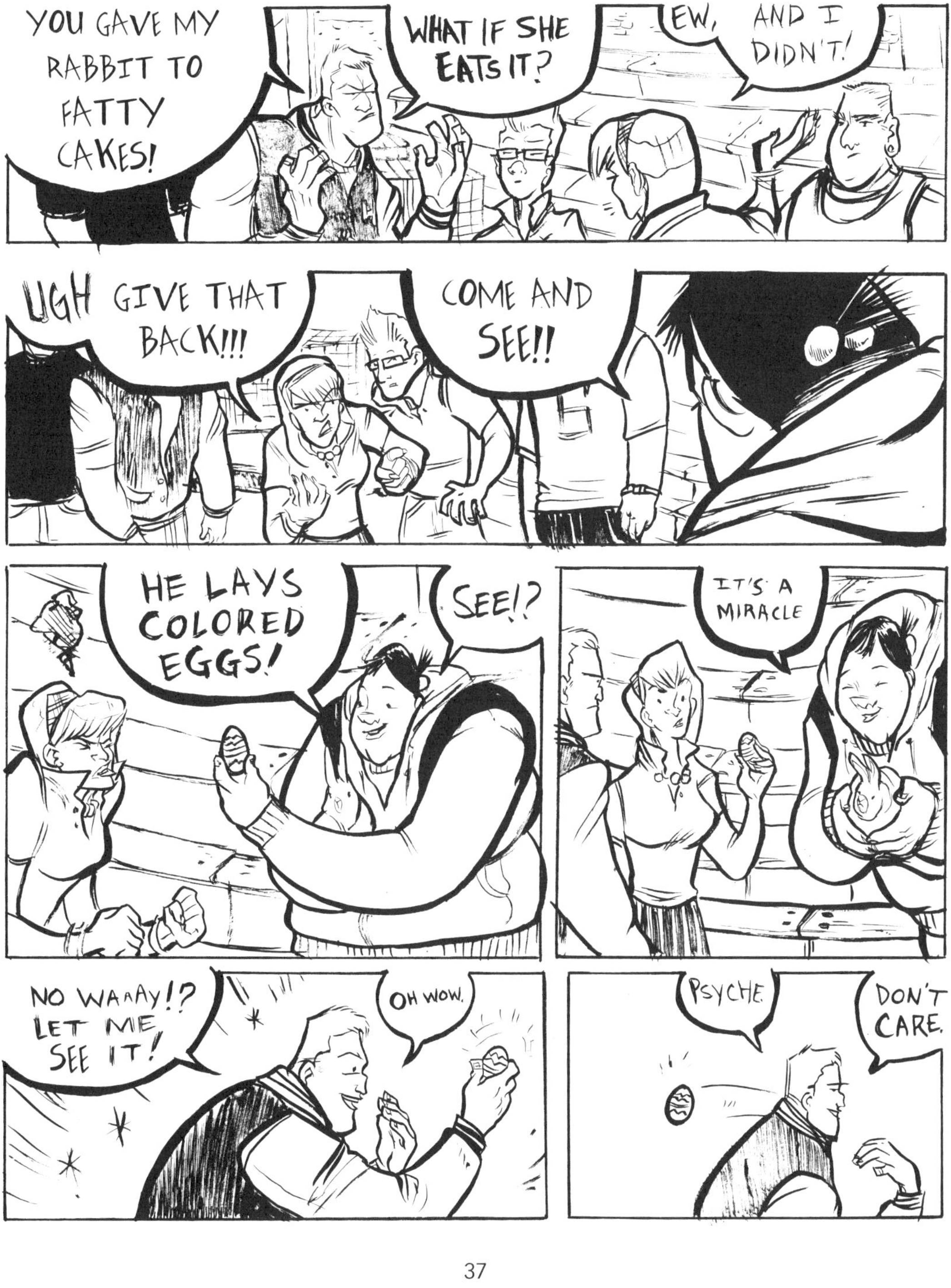

YOU GAVE MY RABBIT TO FATTY CAKES!
WHAT IF SHE EATS IT?
EW,
AND I DIDN'T!
UGH GIVE THAT BACK!!!
COME AND SEE!!
HE LAYS COLORED EGGS!
SEE!?
IT'S A MIRACLE
NO WAAAY!? LET ME SEE IT!
OH WOW.
PSYCHE.
DON'T CARE.

SPUT!

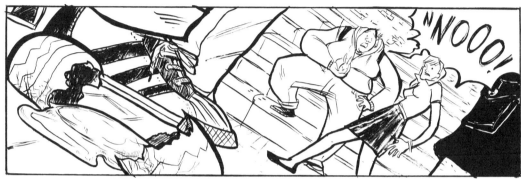

"NOOO!"

EASY TESANA!

COULD YOU HAND US BACK THAT BUNNY?!

NO! I'M TAKING HIM BACK WHERE HE BELONGS!

OH? AND WHERE'S THAT?

"DISCOUNT PET PROVIDER? BECAUSE THAT'S WHERE HE CAME FROM.

OR THE NORTH POLE WITH SANTA AND HIS DUMB DEER?

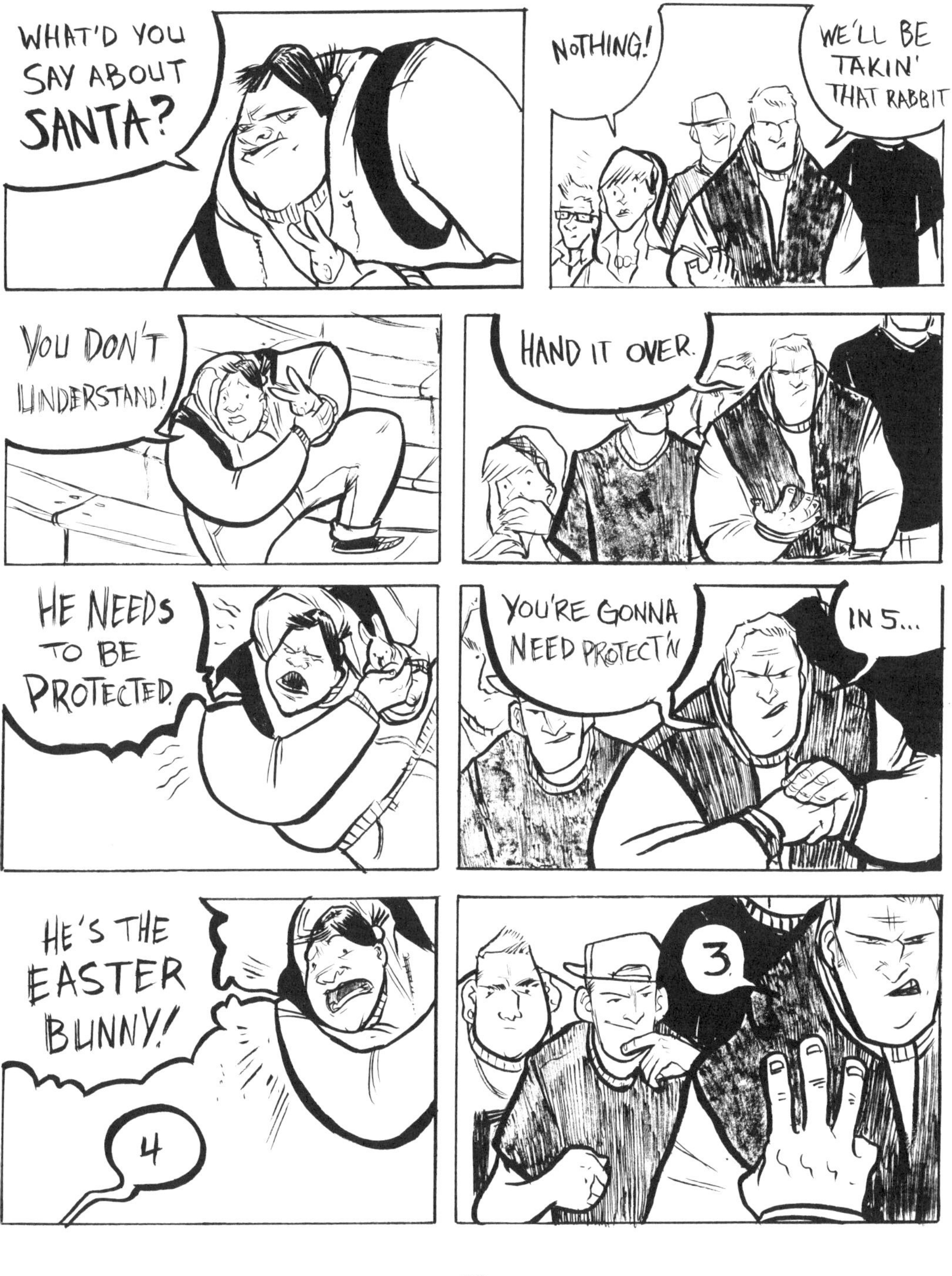
WHAT'D YOU SAY ABOUT SANTA?
NOTHING!
WE'LL BE TAKIN' THAT RABBIT
YOU DON'T UNDERSTAND!
HAND IT OVER.
HE NEEDS TO BE PROTECTED.
YOU'RE GONNA NEED PROTECT'N
IN 5...
HE'S THE EASTER BUNNY!
4
3

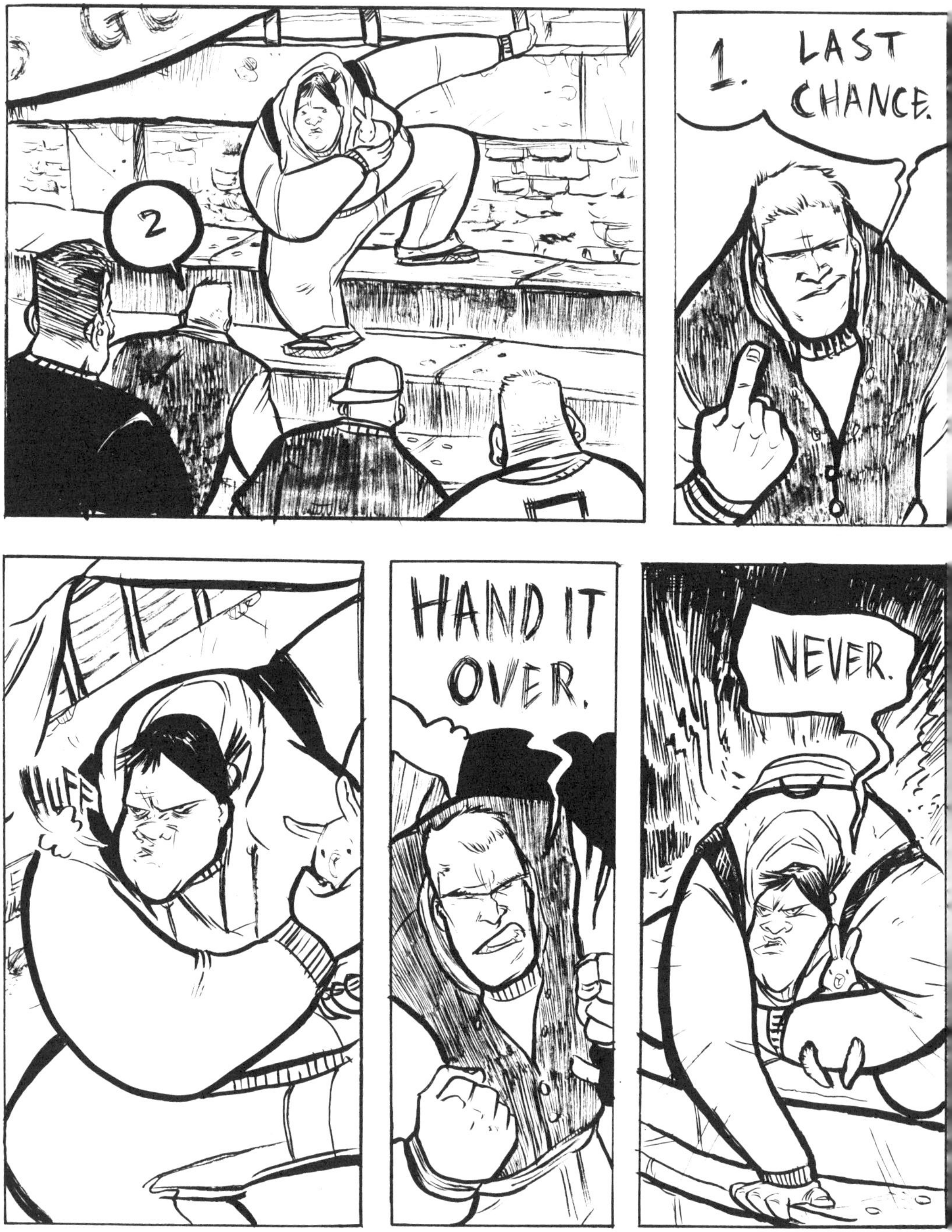
2
1. LAST CHANCE.
HUFF
HAND IT OVER.
NEVER.

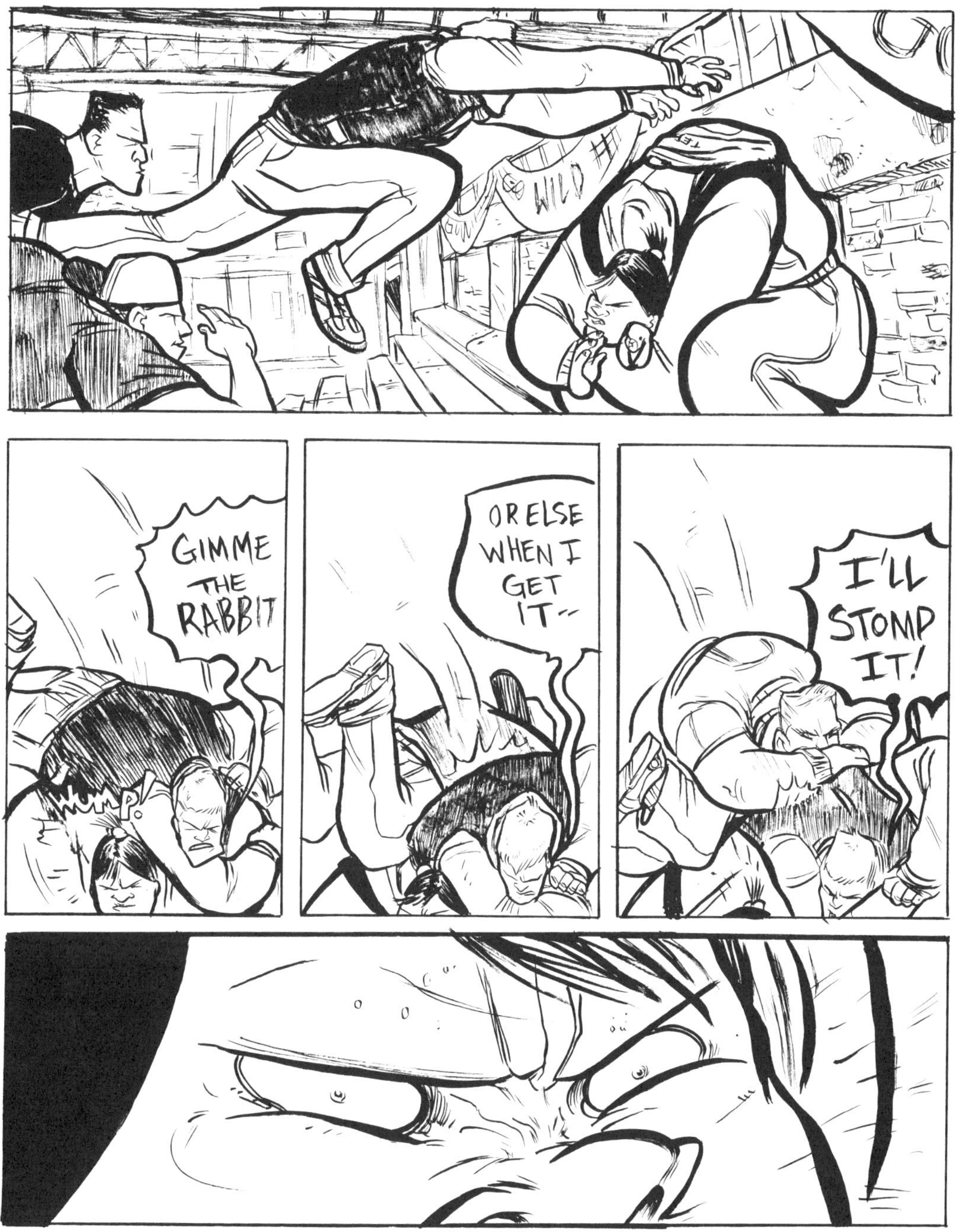
WILD
GIMME THE RABBIT
WOMP!
OR ELSE WHEN I GET IT--
I'LL STOMP IT!

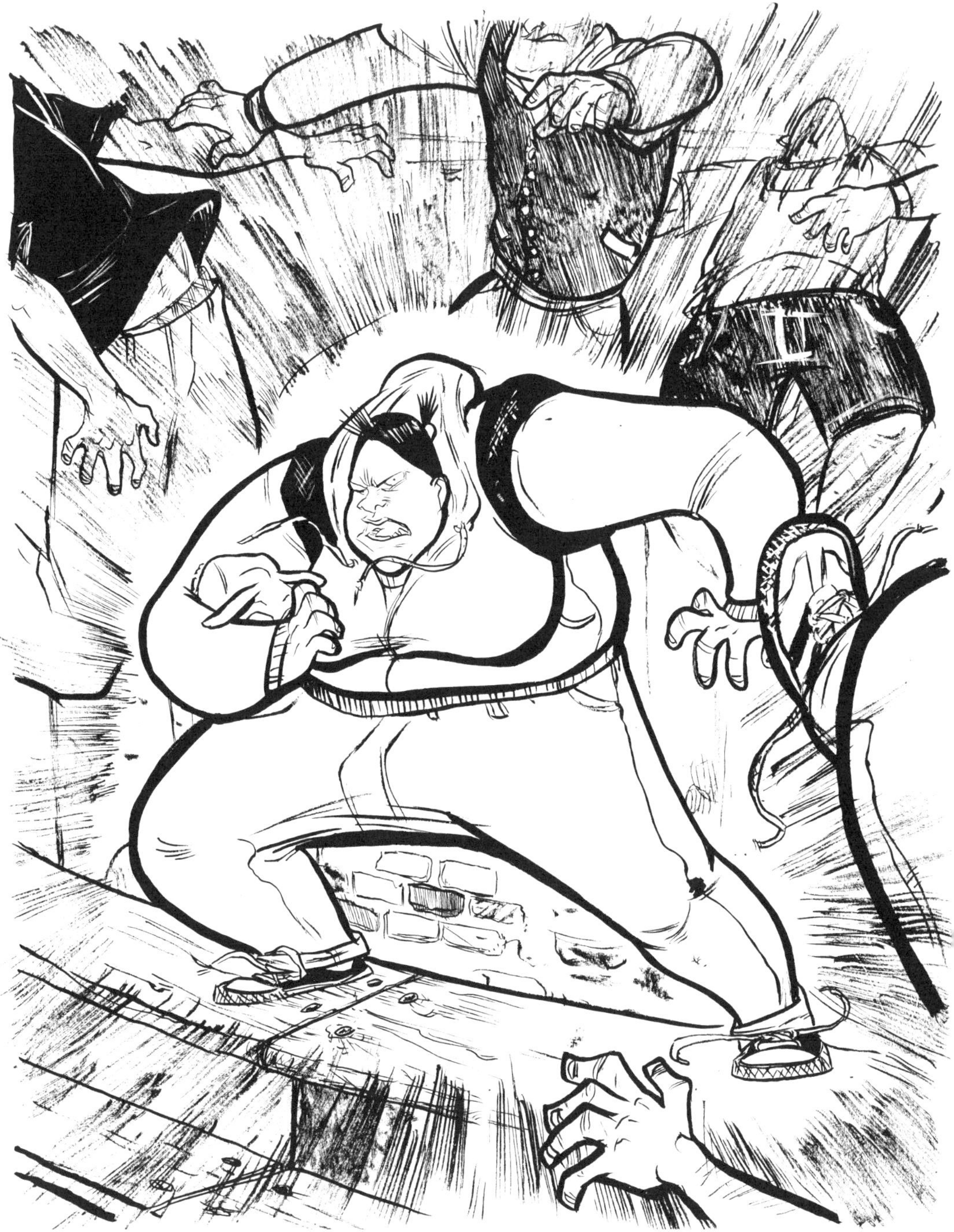

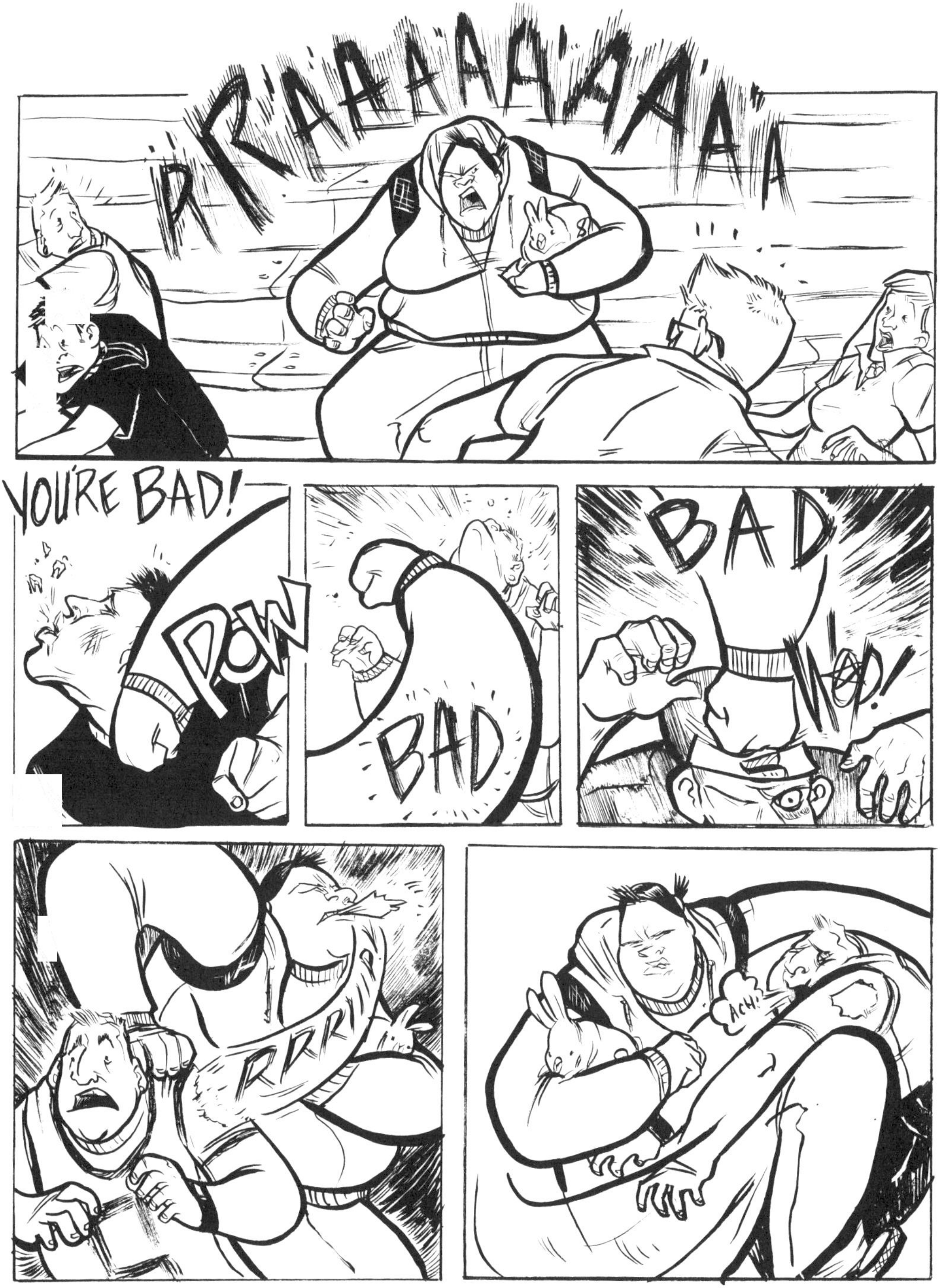
RAAAAAAAAA
YOU'RE BAD!
POW
BAD
BAD
RRRIIP
ACH!

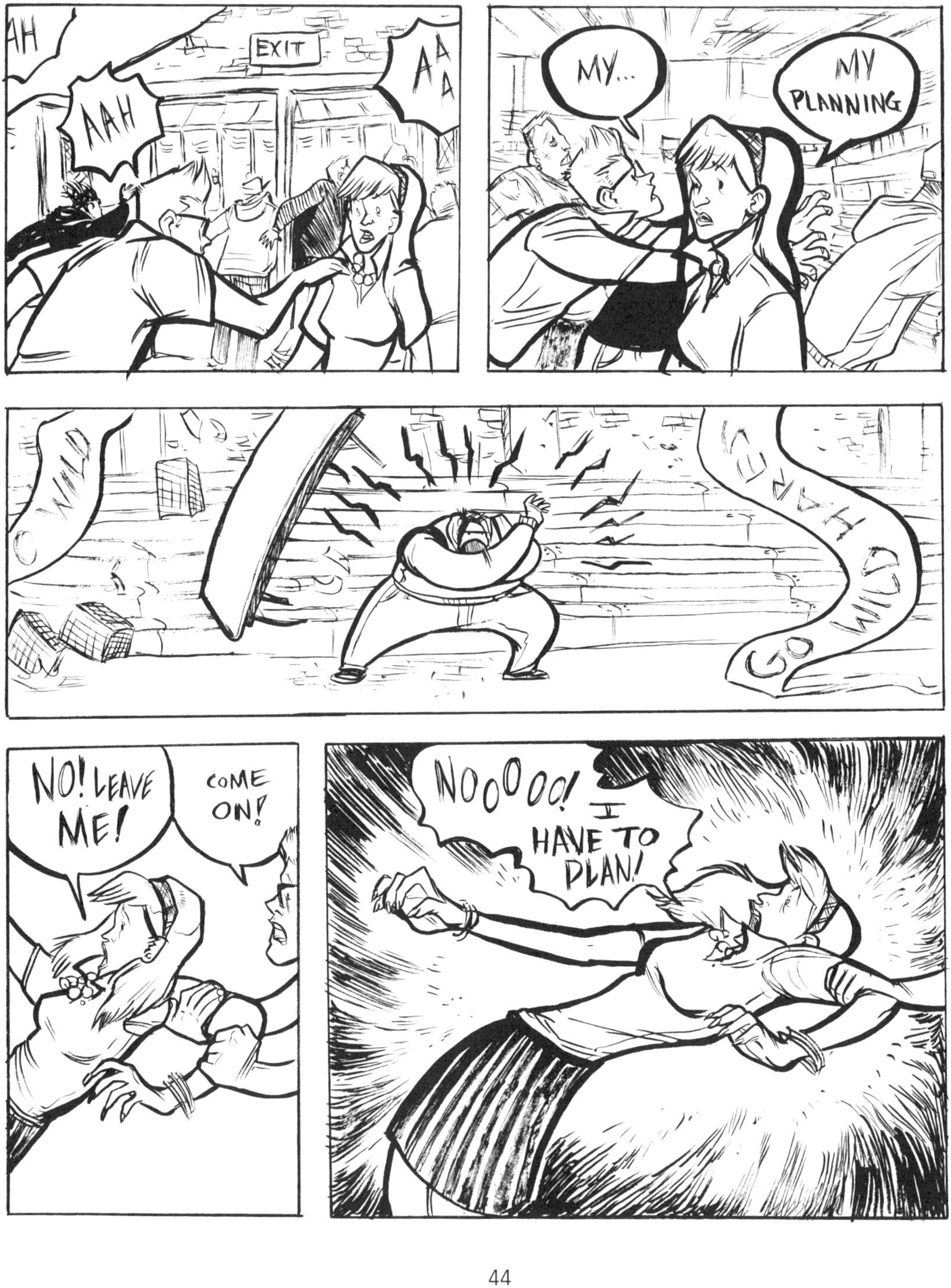
AH
EXIT
AAH
AAA
MY...
MY PLANNING.
GO WILD
GO WILD HARD
NO! LEAVE ME!
COME ON!
NOOOOO! I HAVE TO PLAN!

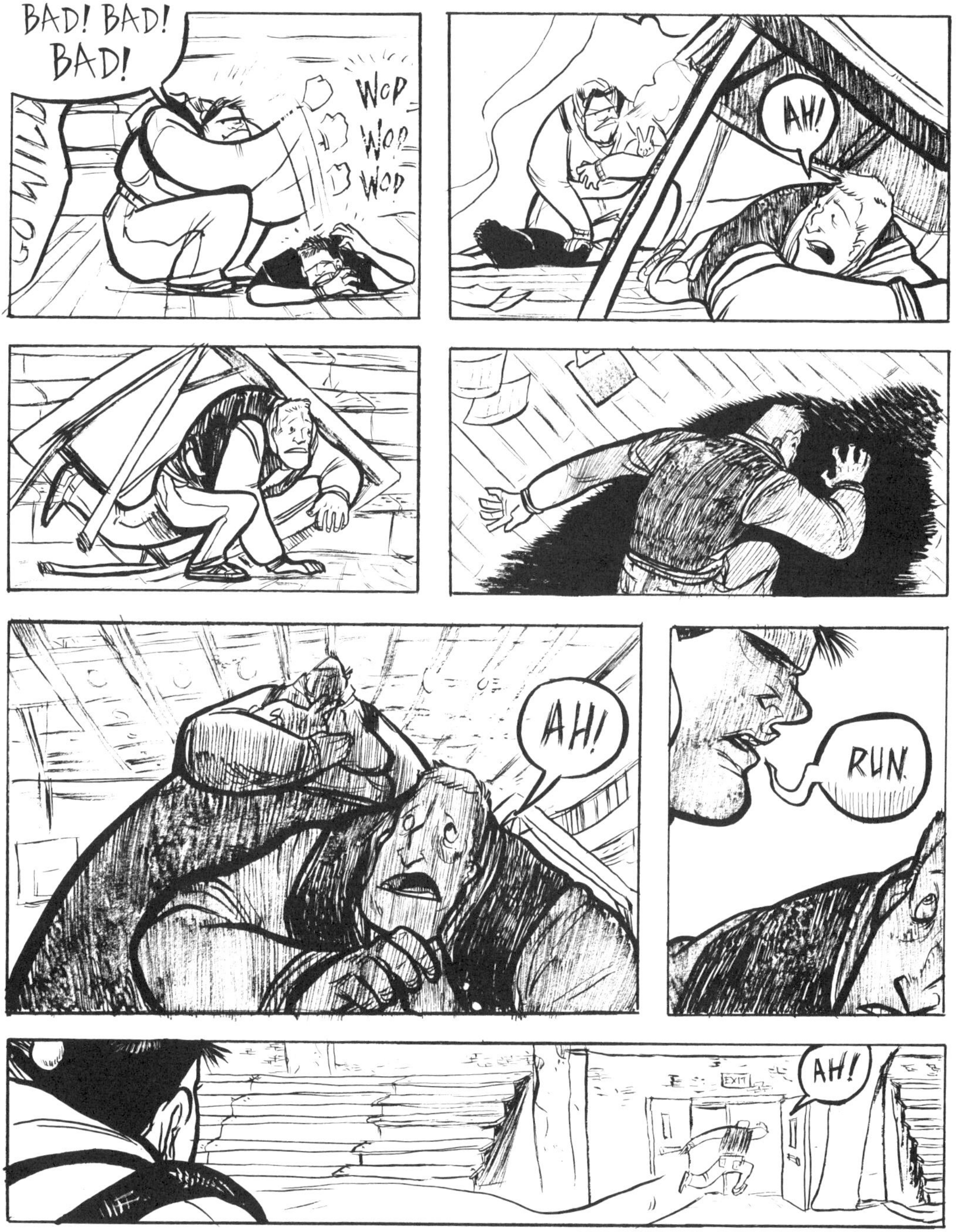
BAD! BAD! BAD!
GO WILD
WOP WOP WOP
AH!
AH!
RUN.
EXIT
AH!

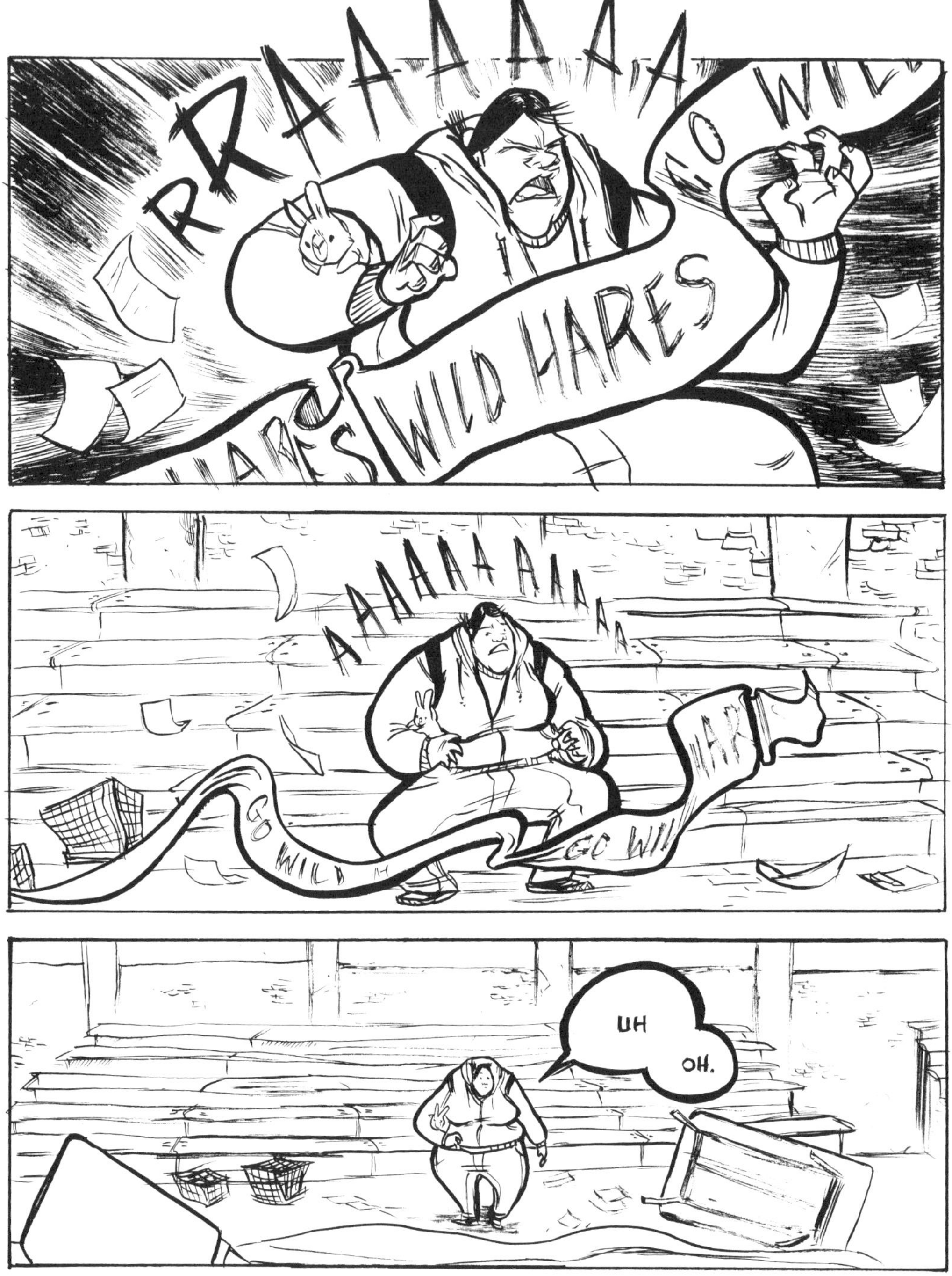
RRAAAAAAA
GO WIL
WILD HARES
HARES
AAAAAAAAAAA
GO WILD
GO WIL
UH OH.

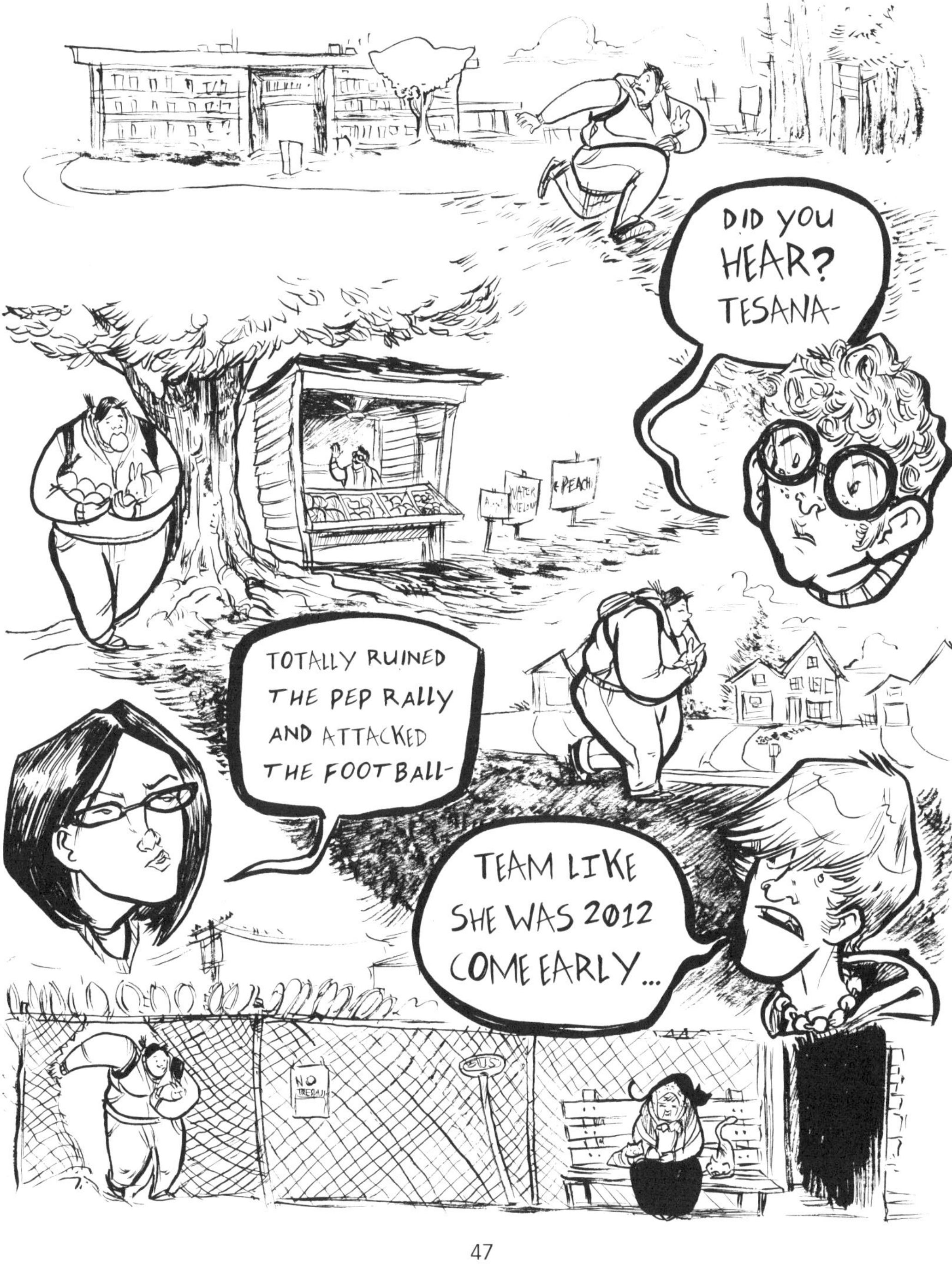
DID YOU HEAR? TESANA-
TOTALLY RUINED THE PEP RALLY AND ATTACKED THE FOOTBALL-
TEAM LIKE SHE WAS 2012 COME EARLY...

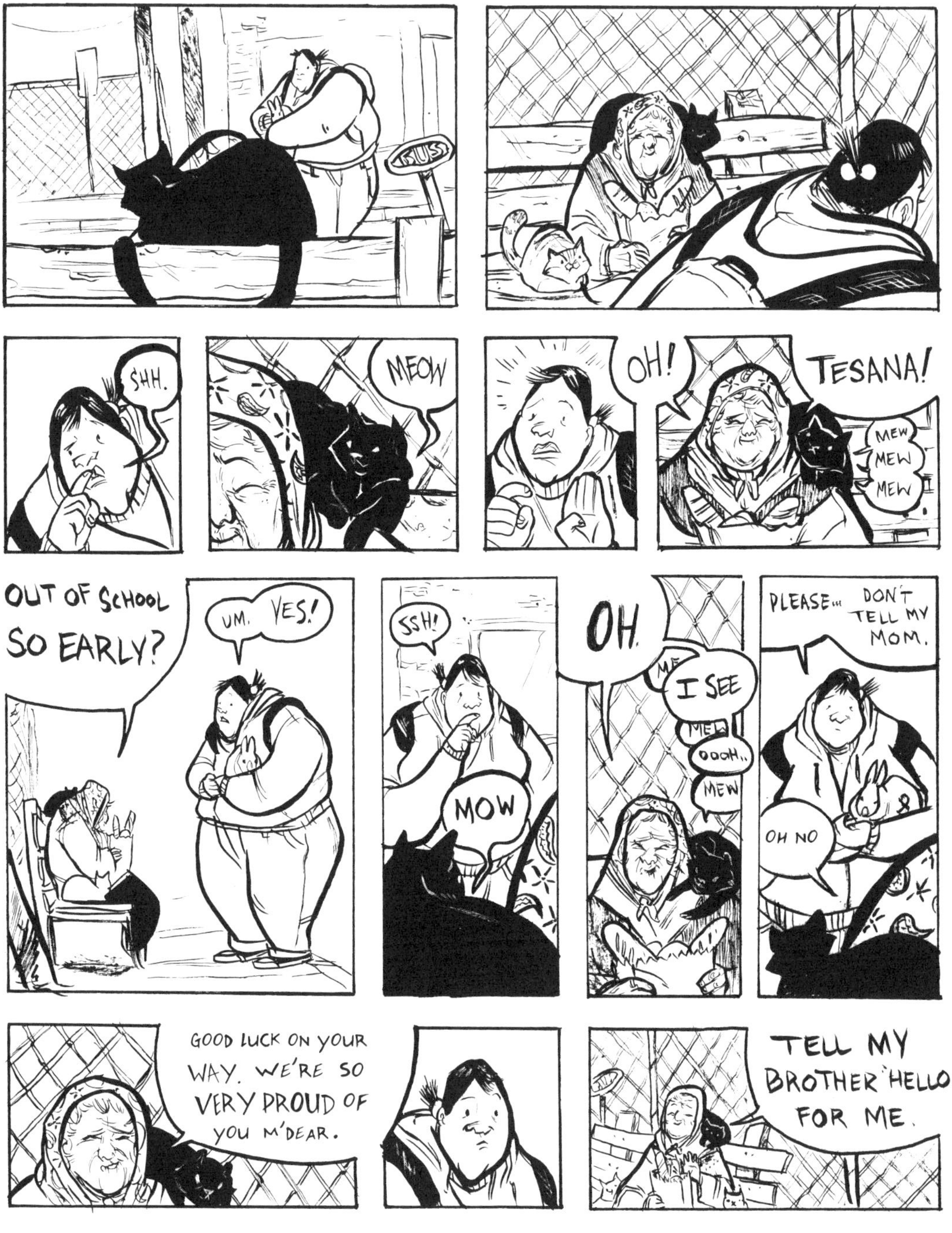
BUS
SHH.
MEOW
OH!
TESANA!
MEW
MEW
MEW
OUT OF SCHOOL SO EARLY?
UM.
YES!
SSH!
MOW
OH.
I SEE
OOOH...
MEW
PLEASE... DON'T TELL MY MOM.
OH NO
GOOD LUCK ON YOUR WAY. WE'RE SO VERY PROUD OF YOU M'DEAR.
TELL MY BROTHER HELLO FOR ME.

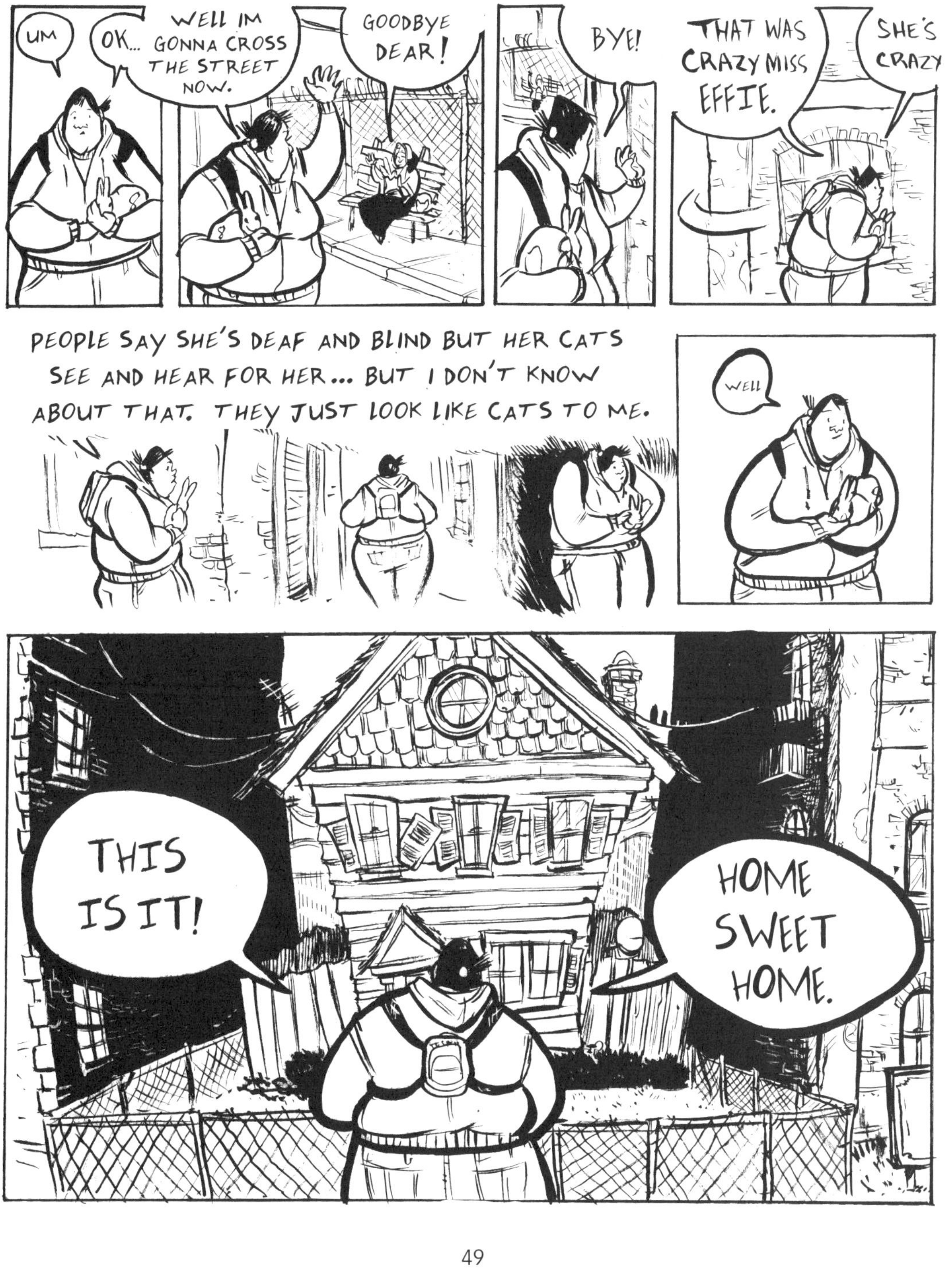
UM
OK...
WELL IM GONNA CROSS THE STREET NOW.
GOODBYE DEAR!
BYE!
THAT WAS CRAZY MISS EFFIE.
SHE'S CRAZY
PEOPLE SAY SHE'S DEAF AND BLIND BUT HER CATS SEE AND HEAR FOR HER... BUT I DON'T KNOW ABOUT THAT. THEY JUST LOOK LIKE CATS TO ME.
WELL
THIS IS IT!
HOME SWEET HOME.

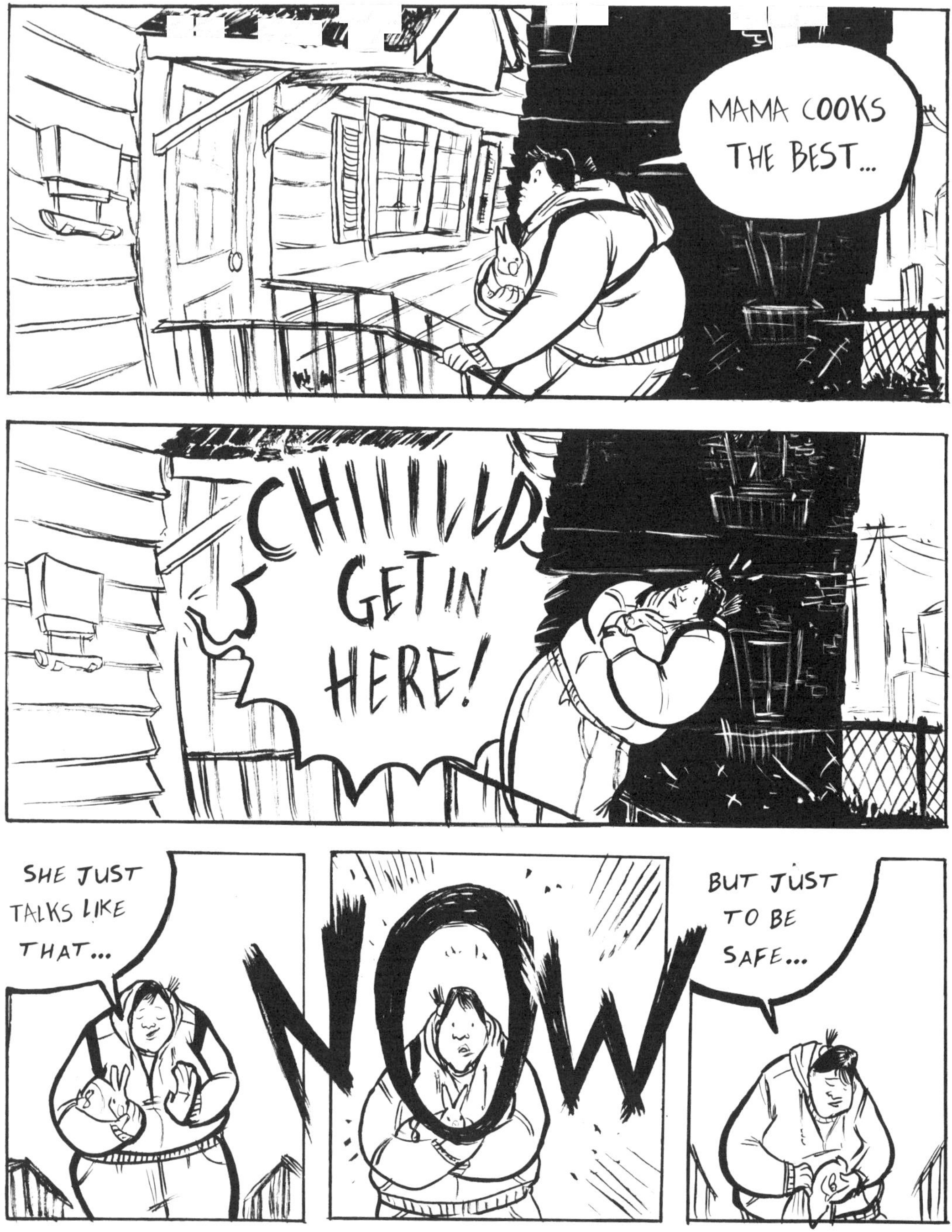
MAMA COOKS THE BEST...
CHIIILLD GET IN HERE!
SHE JUST TALKS LIKE THAT...
NOW
BUT JUST TO BE SAFE...

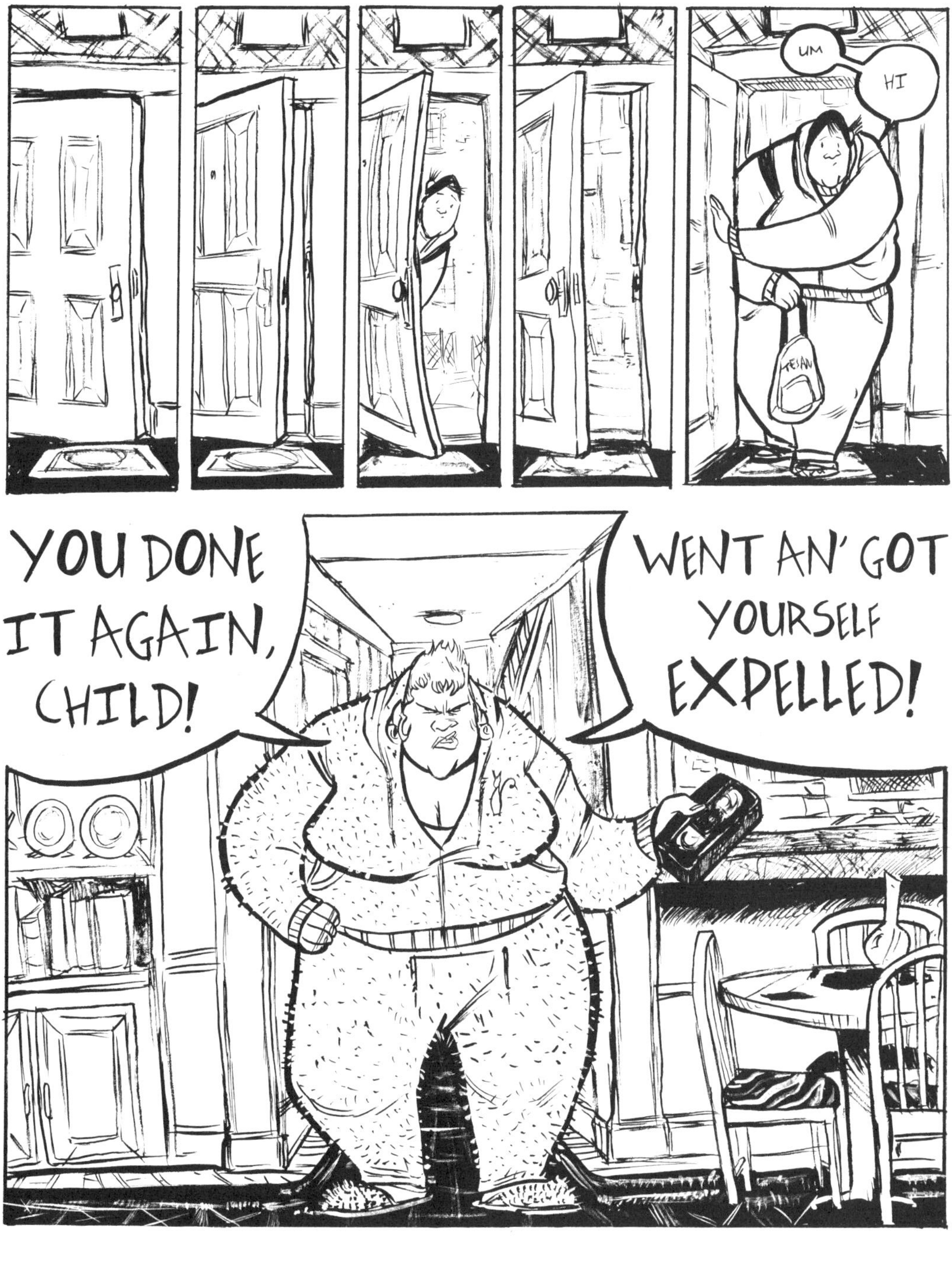
UM
HI
YOU DONE IT AGAIN, CHILD!
WENT AN' GOT YOURSELF EXPELLED!

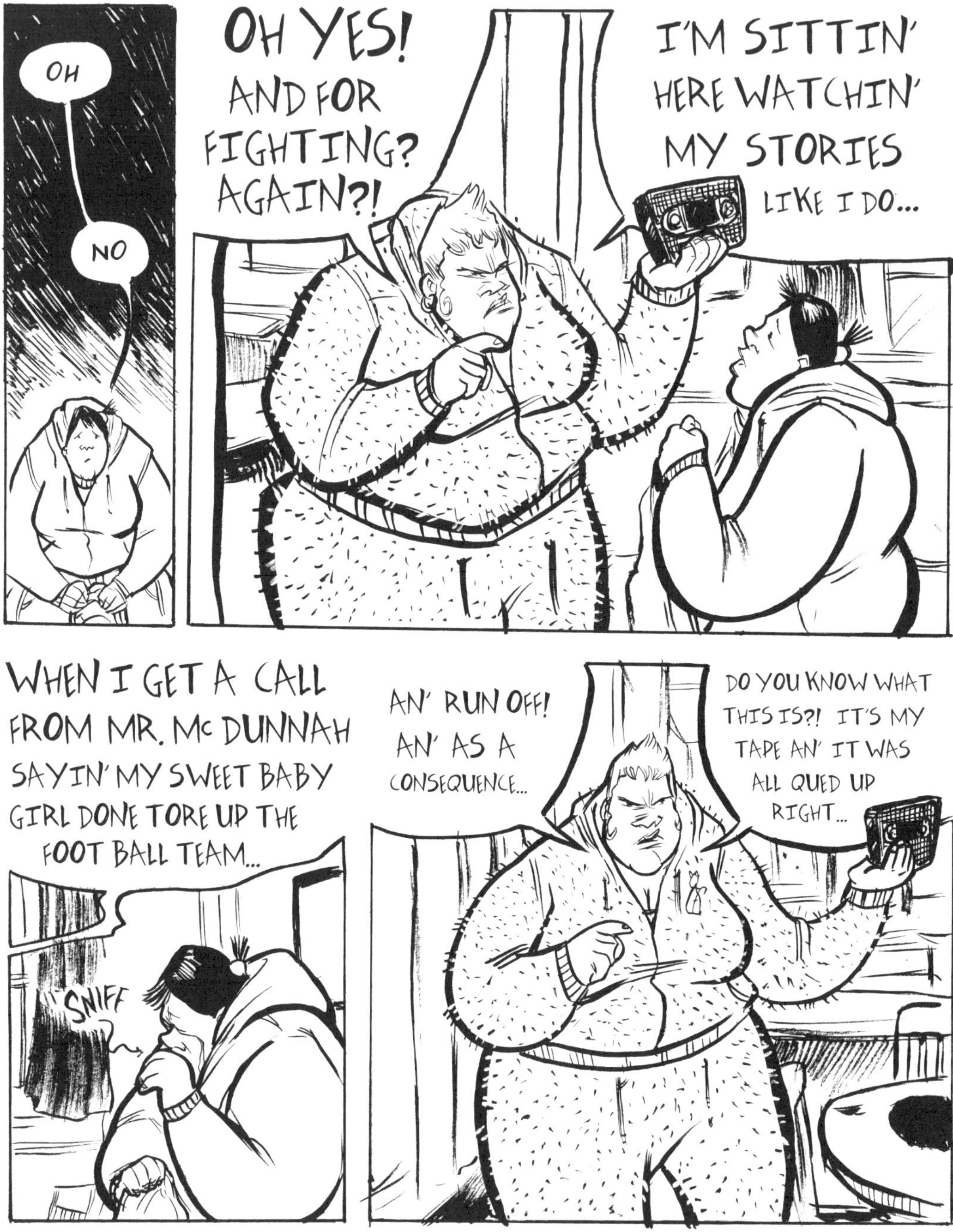
OH
NO
OH YES!
AND FOR FIGHTING? AGAIN?!
I'M SITTIN' HERE WATCHIN' MY STORIES
LIKE I DO...
WHEN I GET A CALL FROM MR. McDUNNAH SAYIN' MY SWEET BABY GIRL DONE TORE UP THE FOOT BALL TEAM...
SNIFF
AN' RUN OFF! AN' AS A CONSEQUENCE...
DO YOU KNOW WHAT THIS IS?! IT'S MY TAPE AN' IT WAS ALL QUED UP RIGHT...

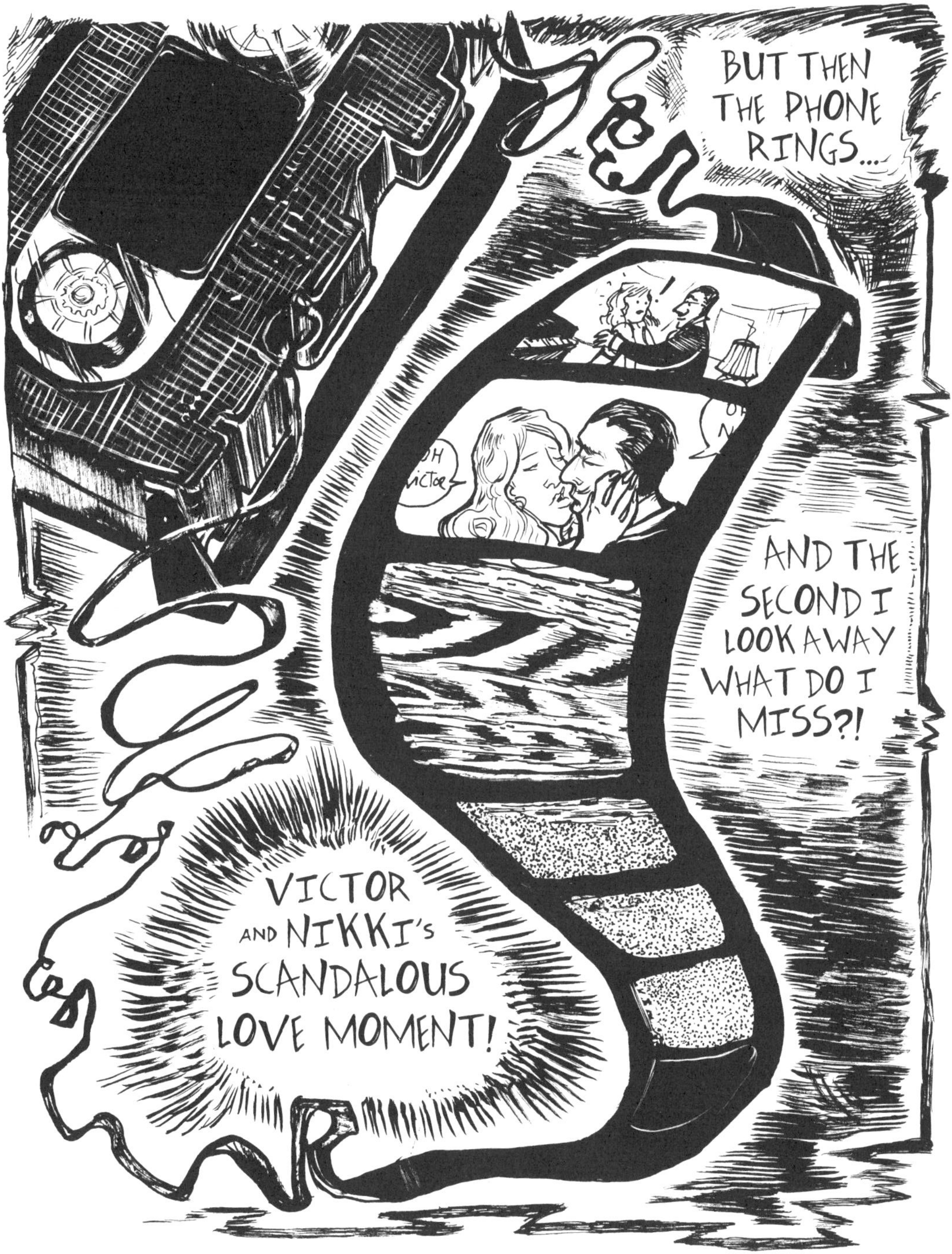
BUT THEN THE PHONE RINGS...
AND THE SECOND I LOOK AWAY WHAT DO I MISS?!
VICTOR AND NIKKI's SCANDALOUS LOVE MOMENT!

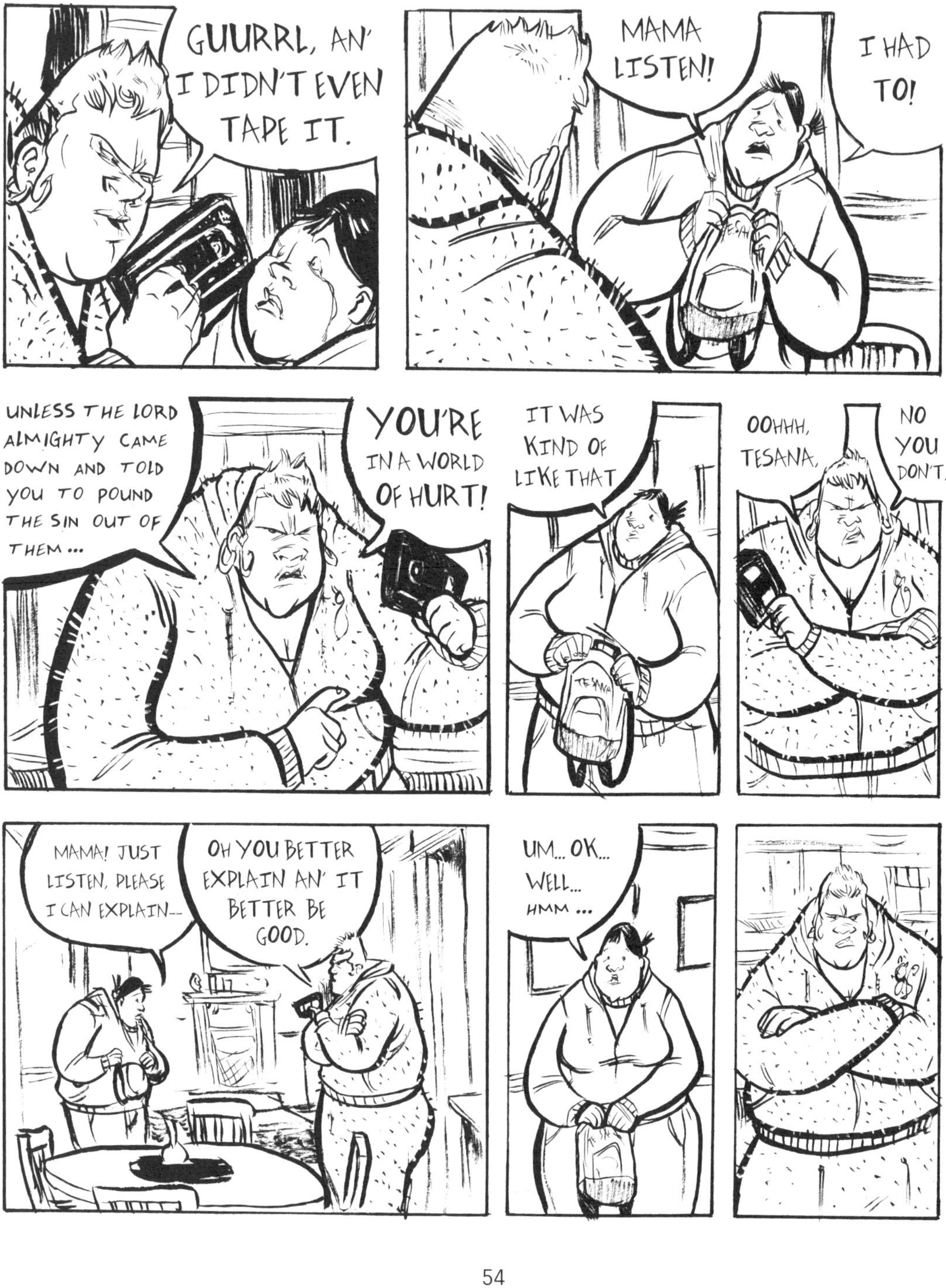
GUURRL, AN' I DIDN'T EVEN TAPE IT.
MAMA LISTEN!
I HAD TO!
UNLESS THE LORD ALMIGHTY CAME DOWN AND TOLD YOU TO POUND THE SIN OUT OF THEM...
YOU'RE IN A WORLD OF HURT!
IT WAS KIND OF LIKE THAT
OOHHH, TESANA,
NO YOU DON'T.
MAMA! JUST LISTEN, PLEASE I CAN EXPLAIN--
OH YOU BETTER EXPLAIN AN' IT BETTER BE GOOD.
UM... OK... WELL... HMM...

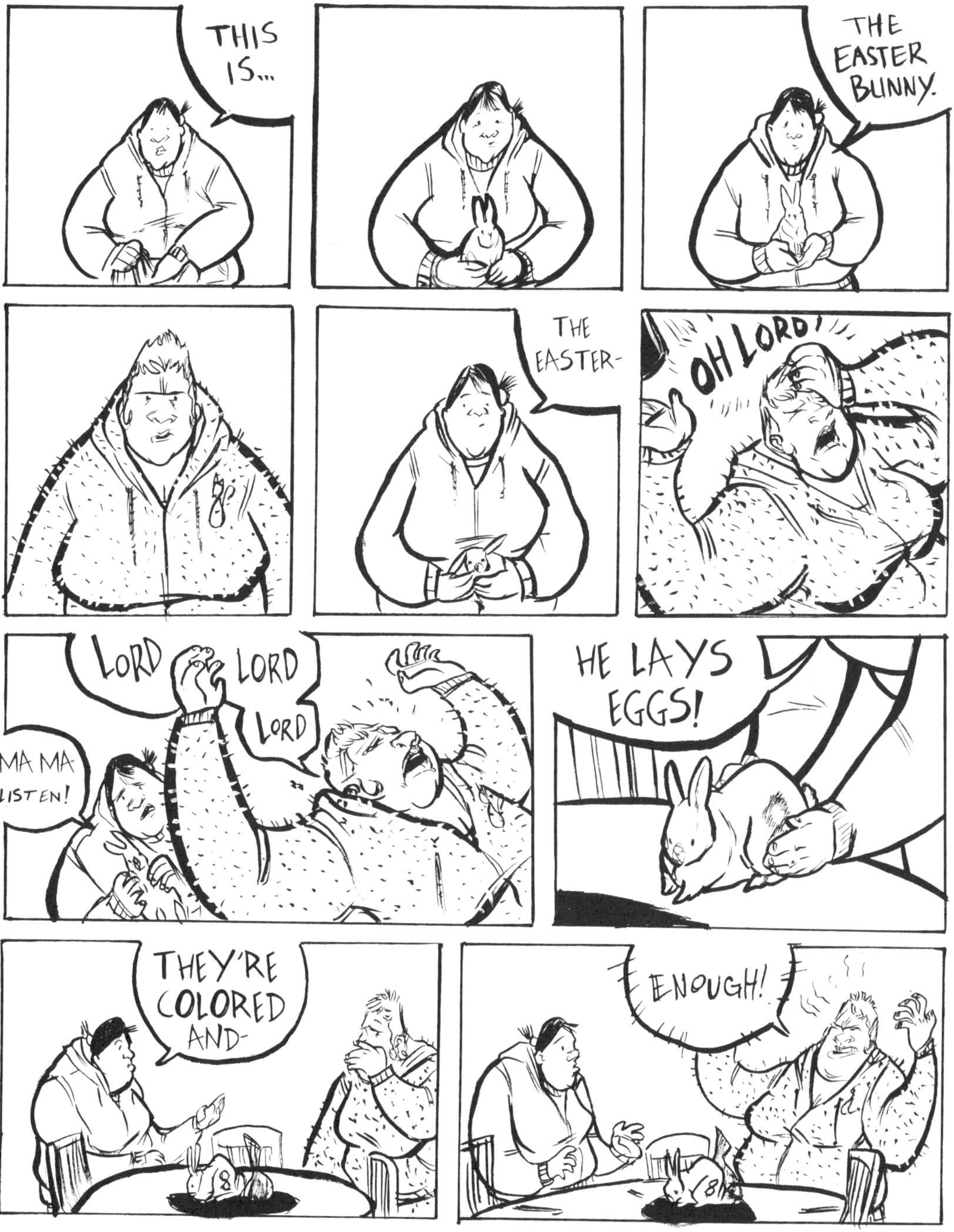
THIS IS...
THE EASTER BUNNY.
THE EASTER-
OH LORD!
LORD LORD LORD
MA MA LISTEN!
HE LAYS EGGS!
THEY'RE COLORED AND-
ENOUGH!

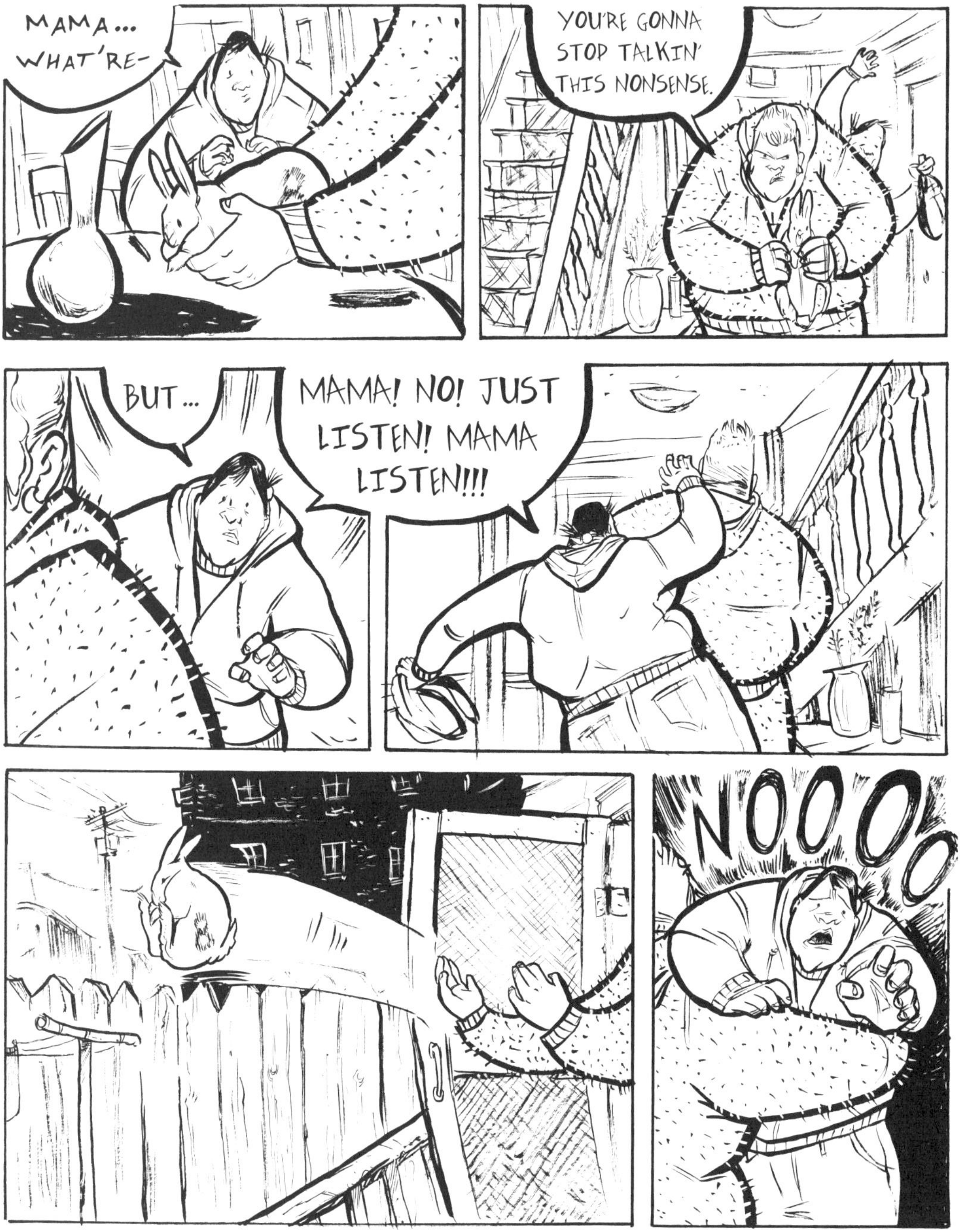
MAMA... WHAT'RE-
YOU'RE GONNA STOP TALKIN' THIS NONSENSE.
BUT...
MAMA! NO! JUST LISTEN! MAMA LISTEN!!!
NOOOOO

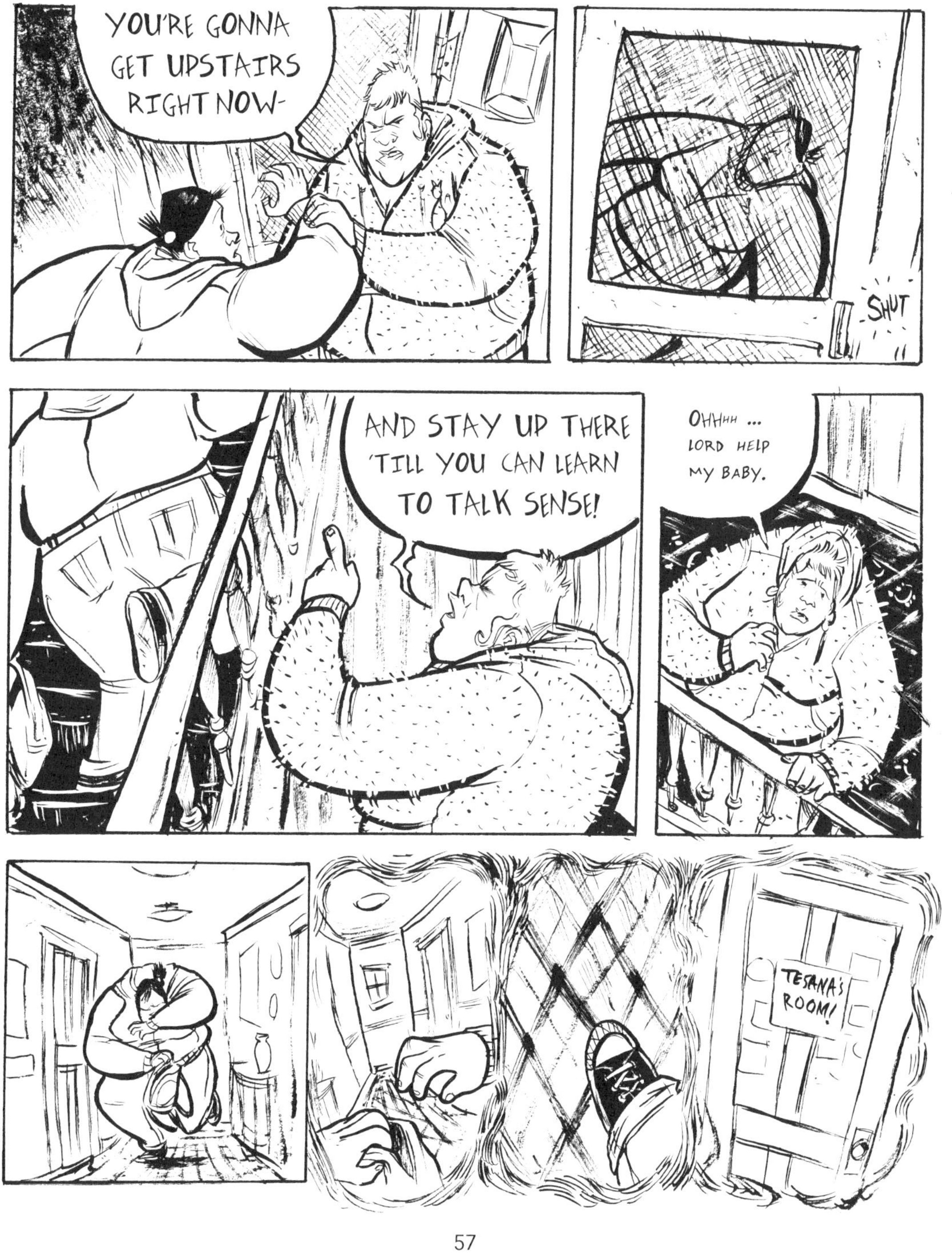
YOU'RE GONNA GET UPSTAIRS RIGHT NOW-
SHUT
AND STAY UP THERE 'TILL YOU CAN LEARN TO TALK SENSE!
OHHHH ... LORD HELP MY BABY.
TESANA'S ROOM!

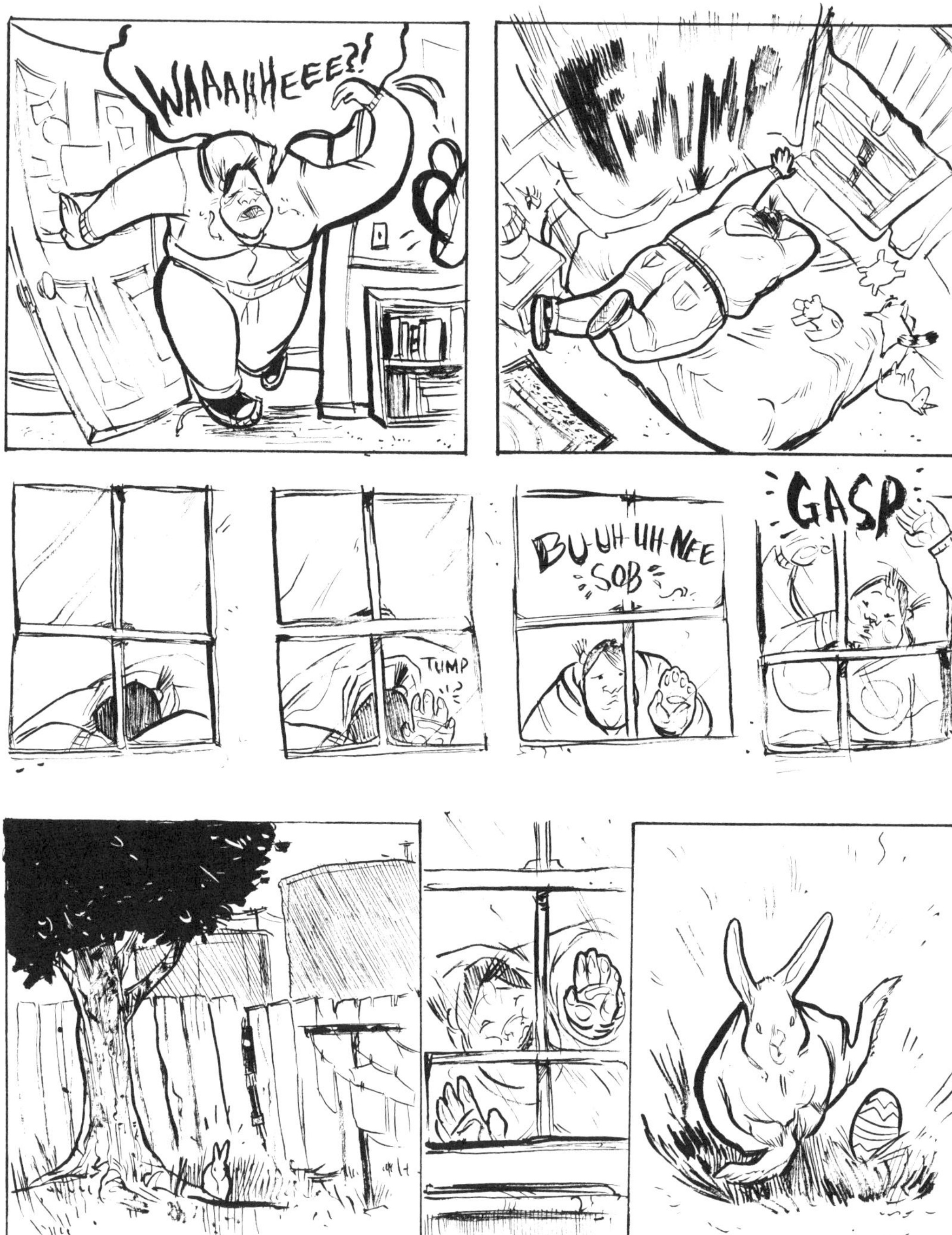
WAAAHHEEE?!
FWUMP
TUMP
BU-UH-UH-NEE
SOB
GASP

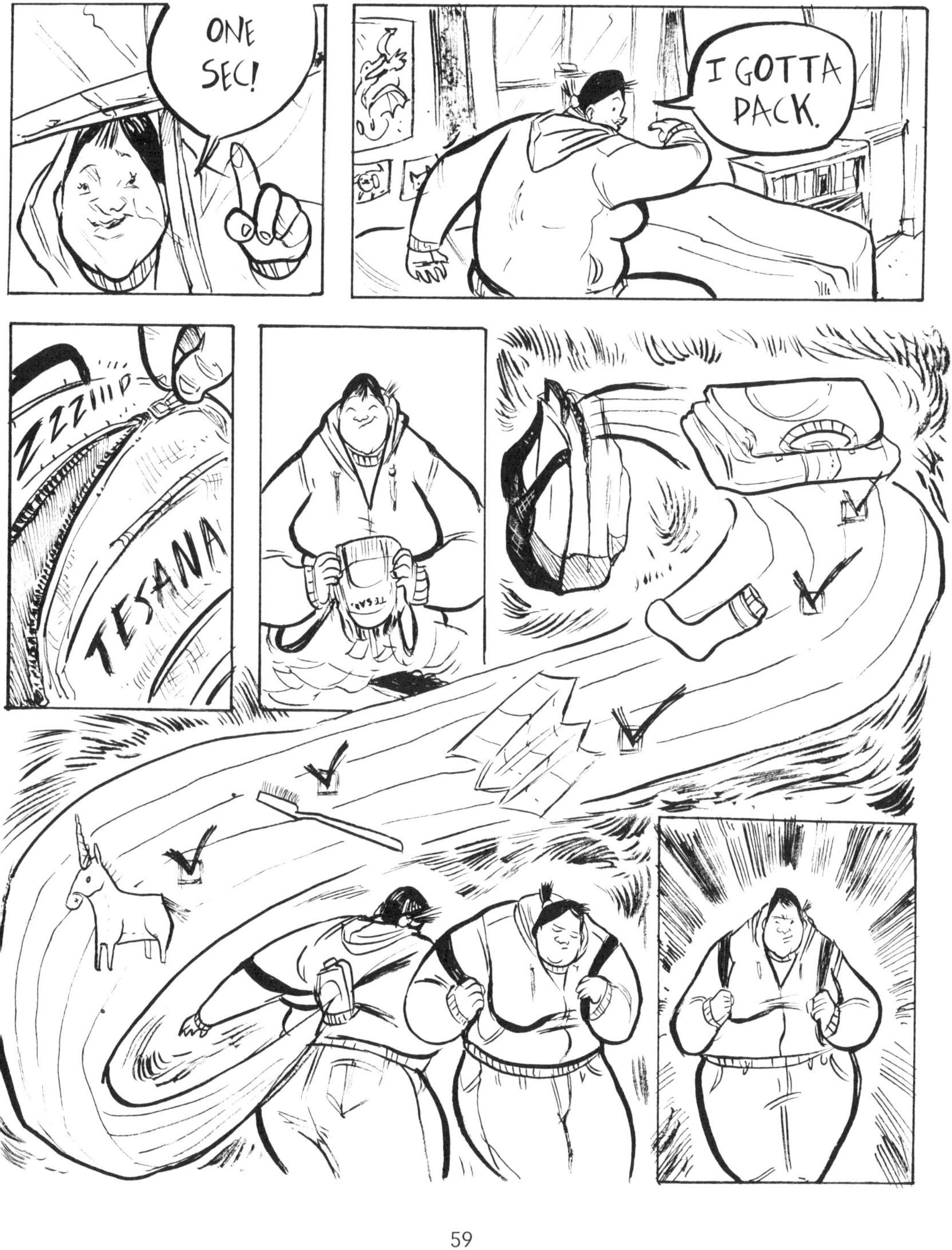
ONE SEC!
I GOTTA PACK.
ZZZIIIIP
TESANA

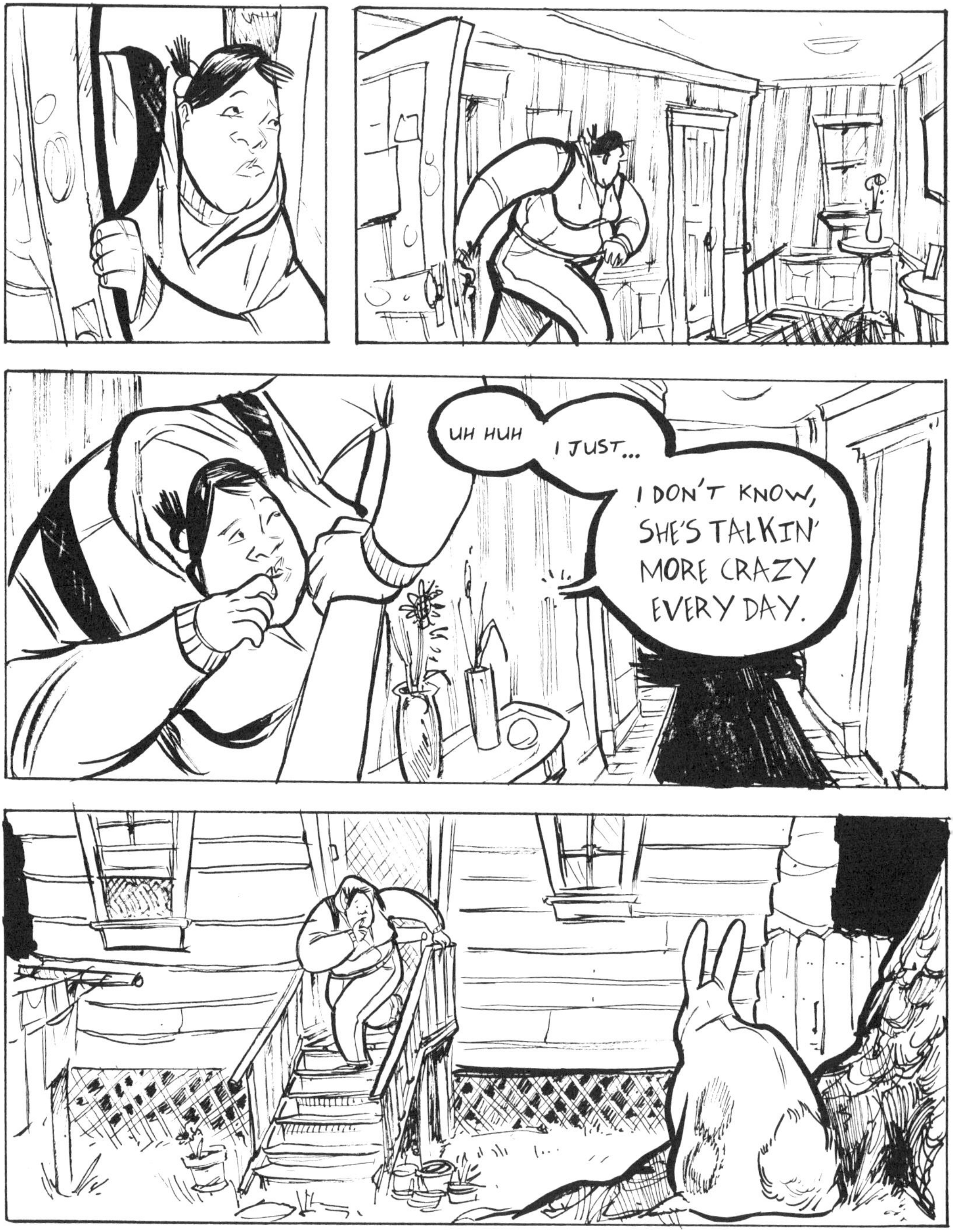
UH HUH
I JUST...
I DON'T KNOW, SHE'S TALKIN' MORE CRAZY EVERY DAY.

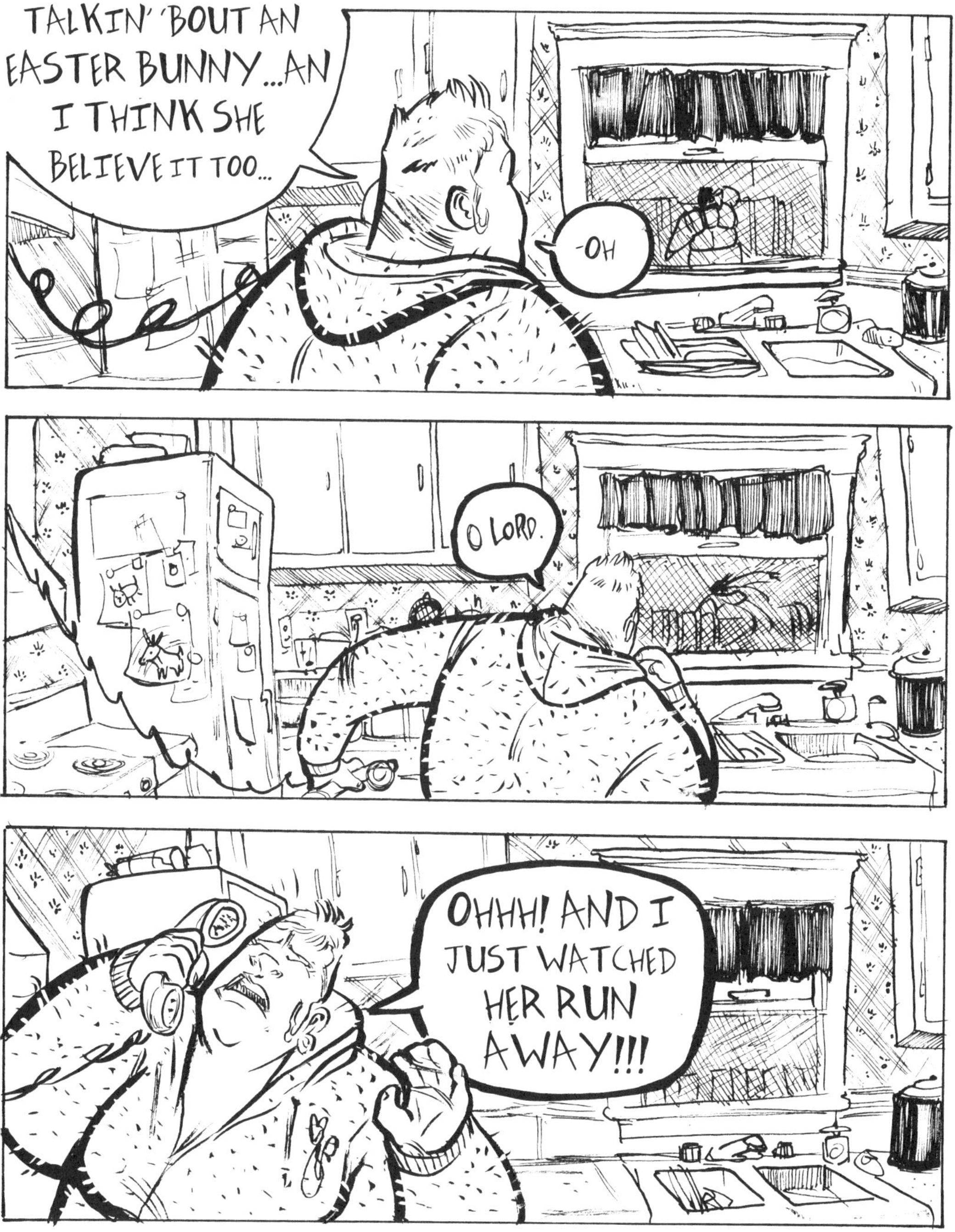
TALKIN' 'BOUT AN EASTER BUNNY...AN I THINK SHE BELIEVE IT TOO...
-OH
O LORD.
OHHH! AND I JUST WATCHED HER RUN AWAY!!!

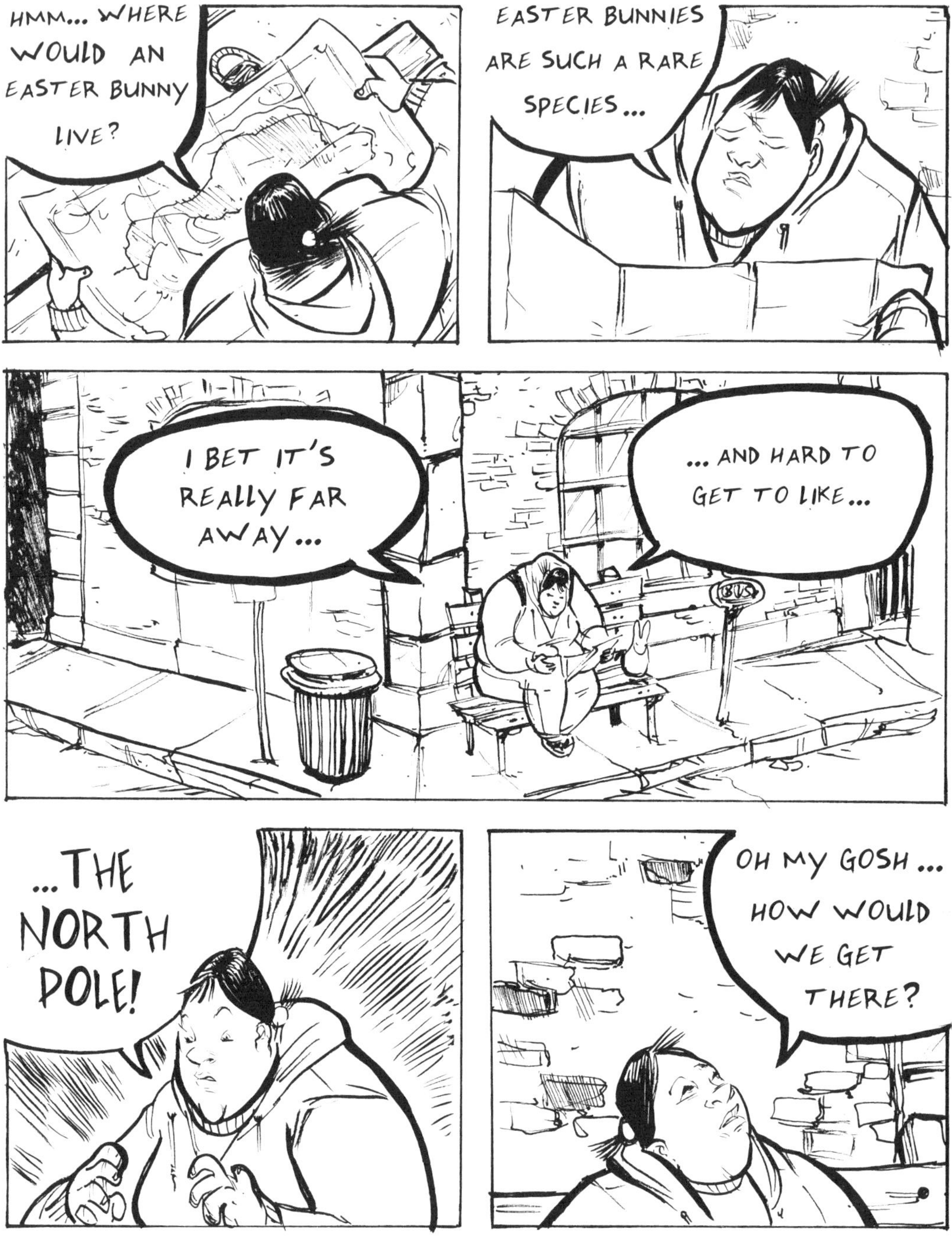
HMM... WHERE WOULD AN EASTER BUNNY LIVE?
EASTER BUNNIES ARE SUCH A RARE SPECIES...
I BET IT'S REALLY FAR AWAY...
... AND HARD TO GET TO LIKE...
BUS
...THE NORTH POLE!
OH MY GOSH... HOW WOULD WE GET THERE?

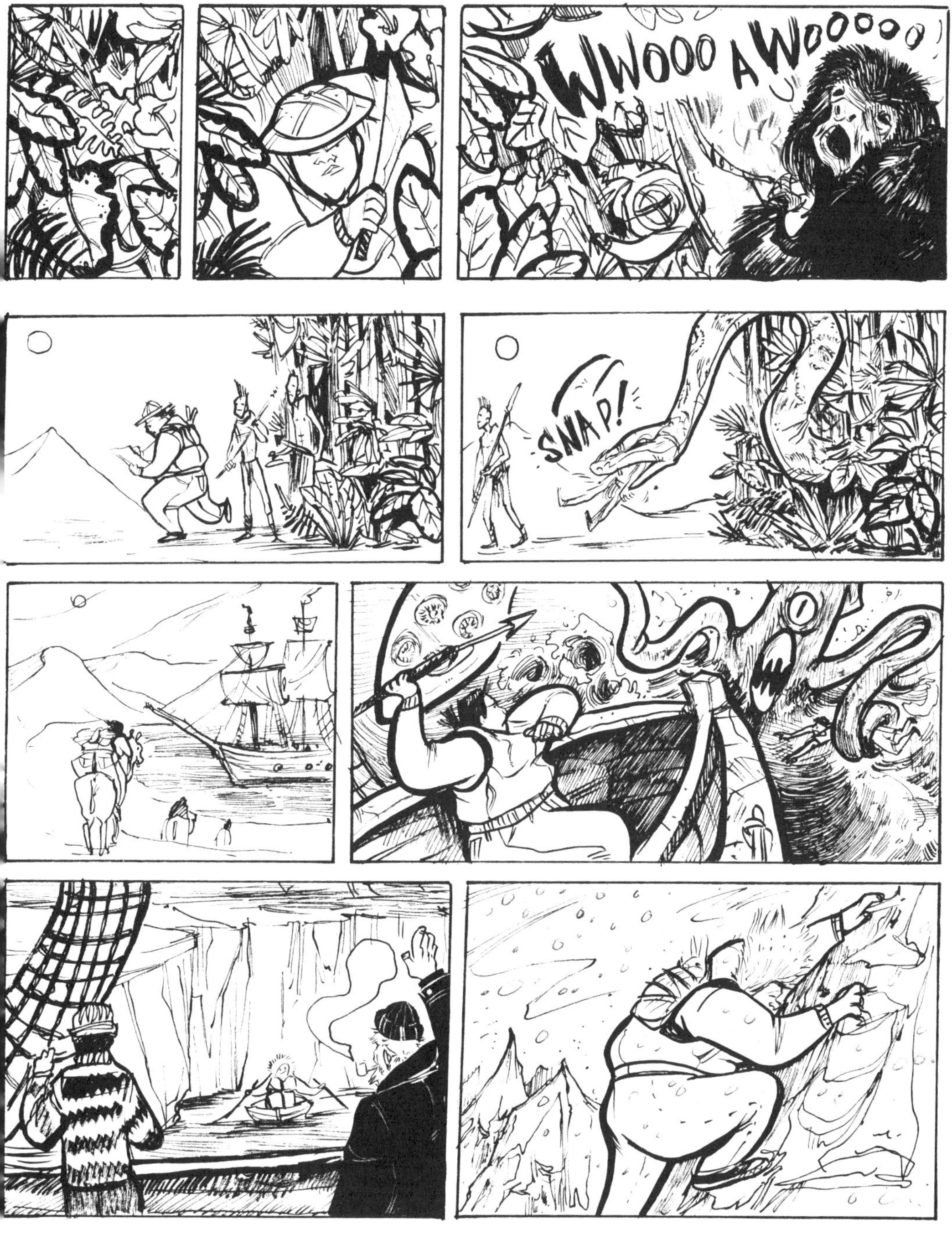
WWOOO AWOOOOOO
SNAP!

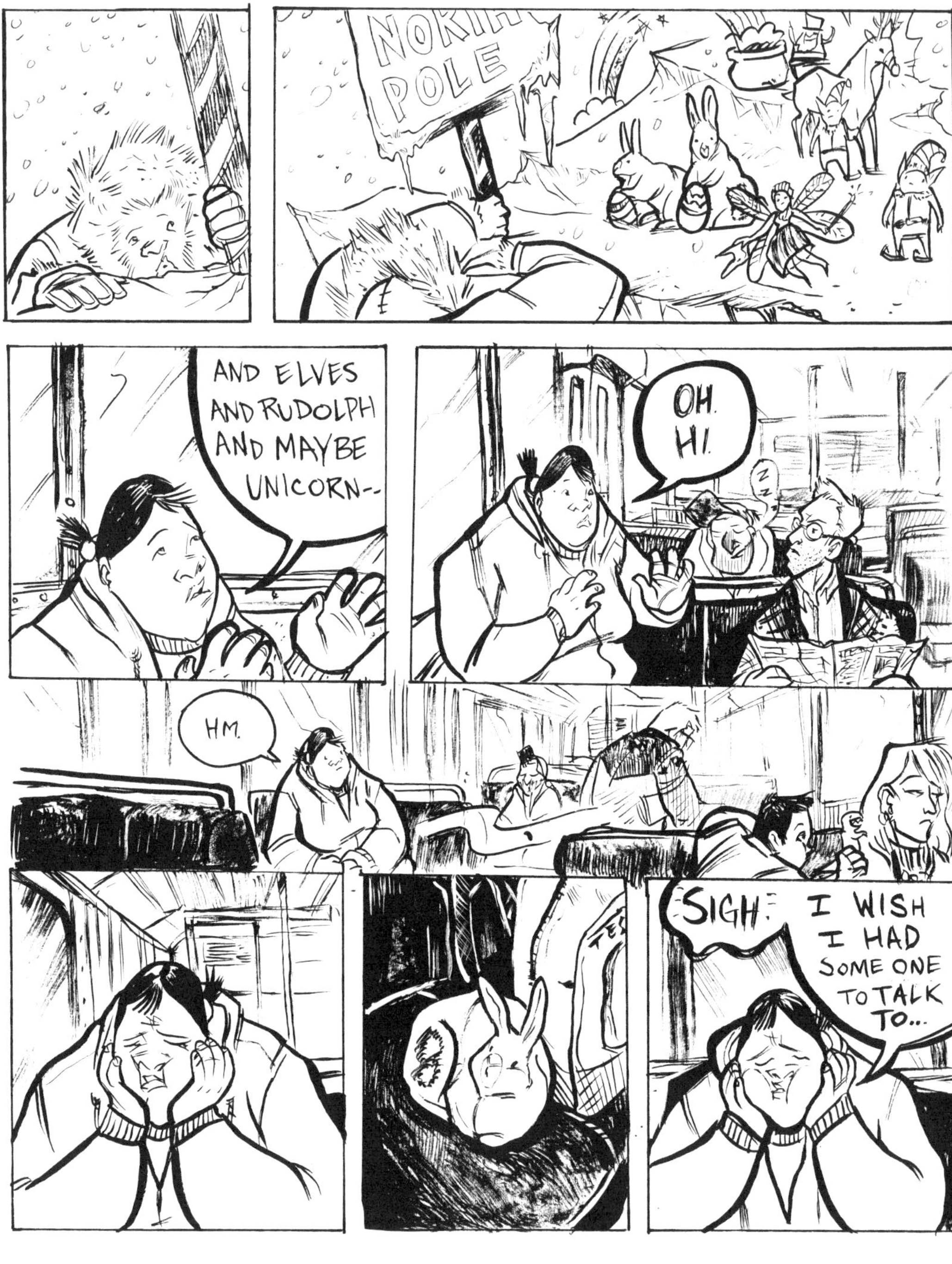
NORTH POLE
AND ELVES AND RUDOLPH AND MAYBE UNICORN--
OH. HI.
HM.
SIGH.
I WISH I HAD SOME ONE TO TALK TO...

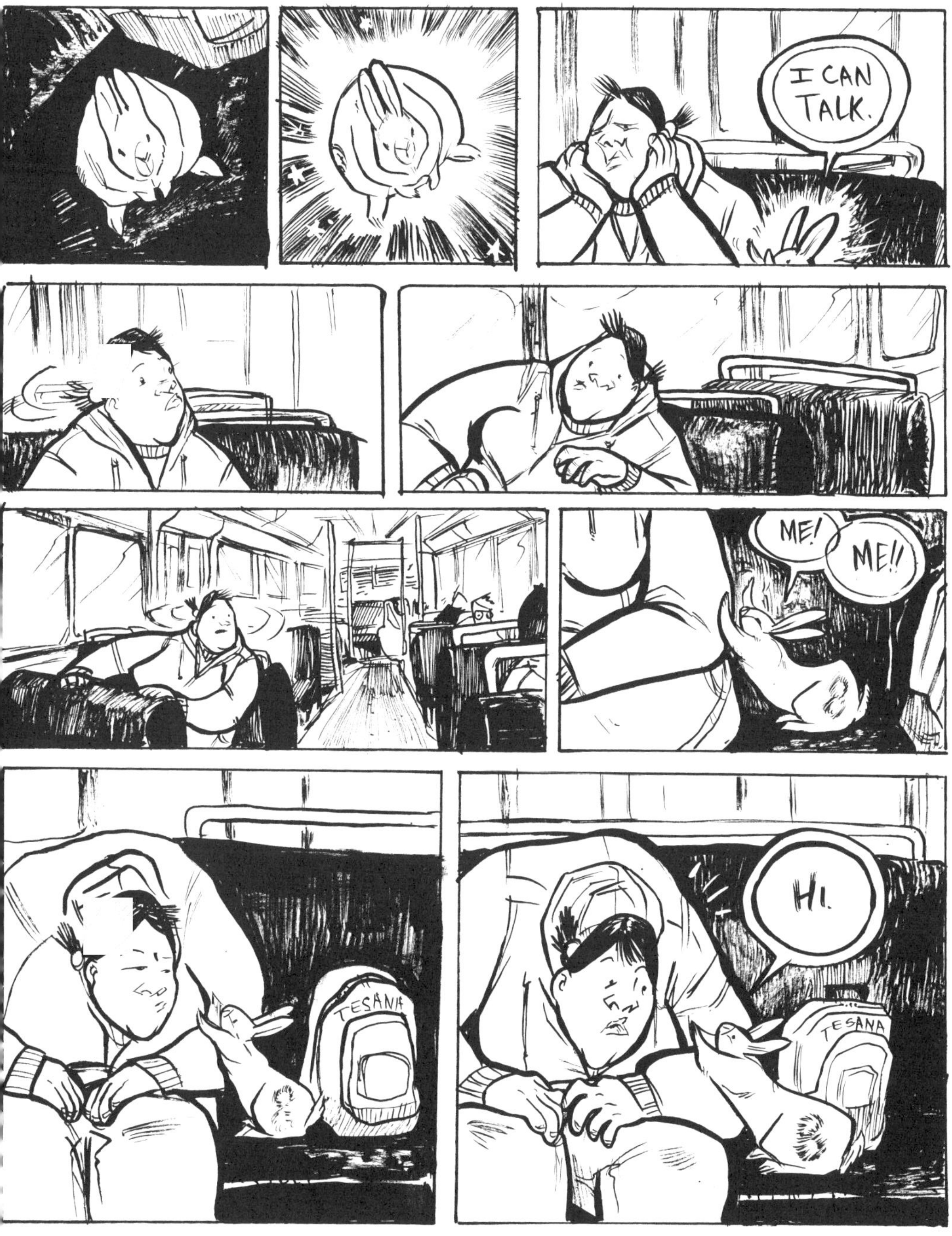
I CAN TALK.
ME!
ME!!
HI.

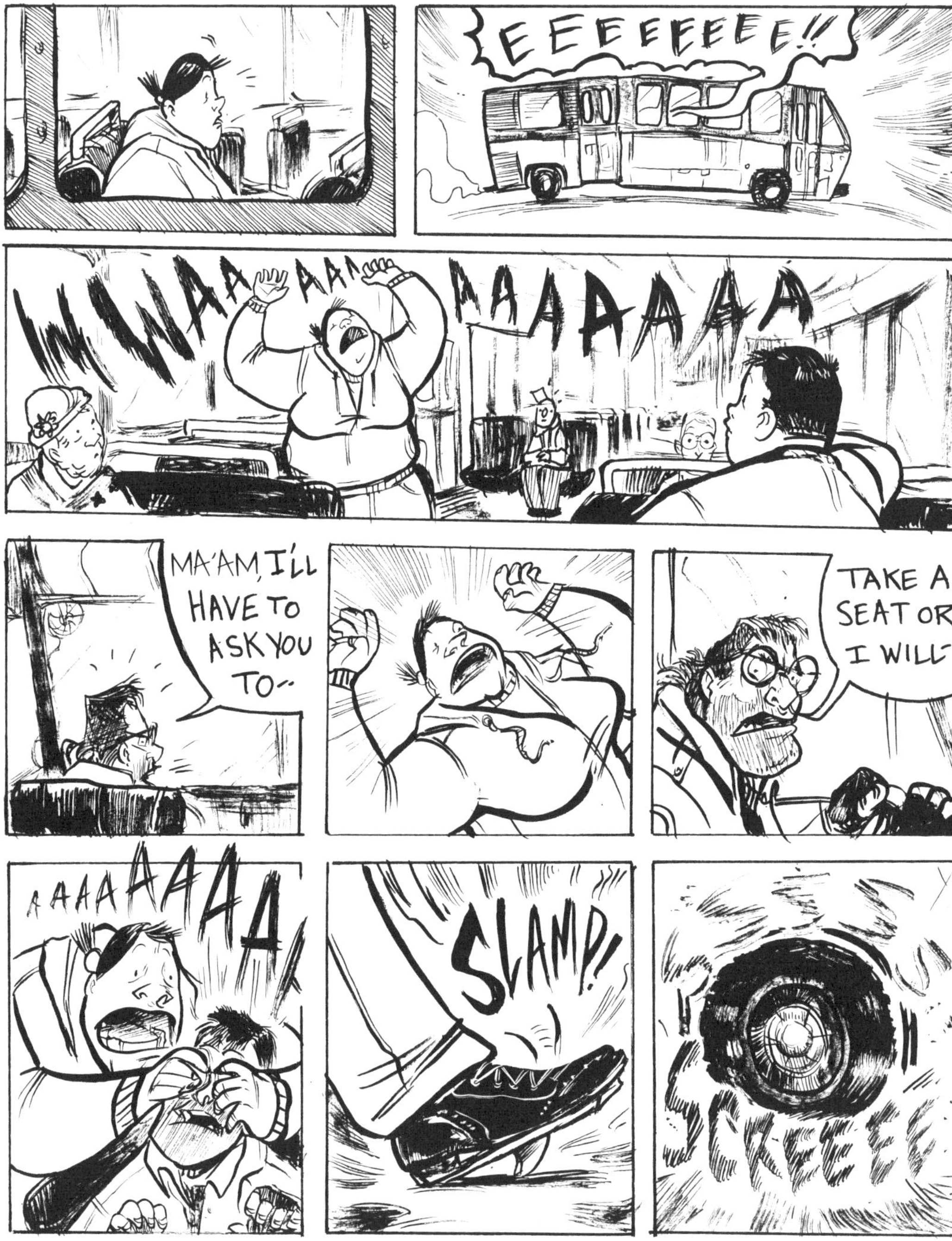
EEEEEEEE!!
MA'AM, I'LL HAVE TO ASK YOU TO--
TAKE A SEAT OR I WILL-
SLAMP!!

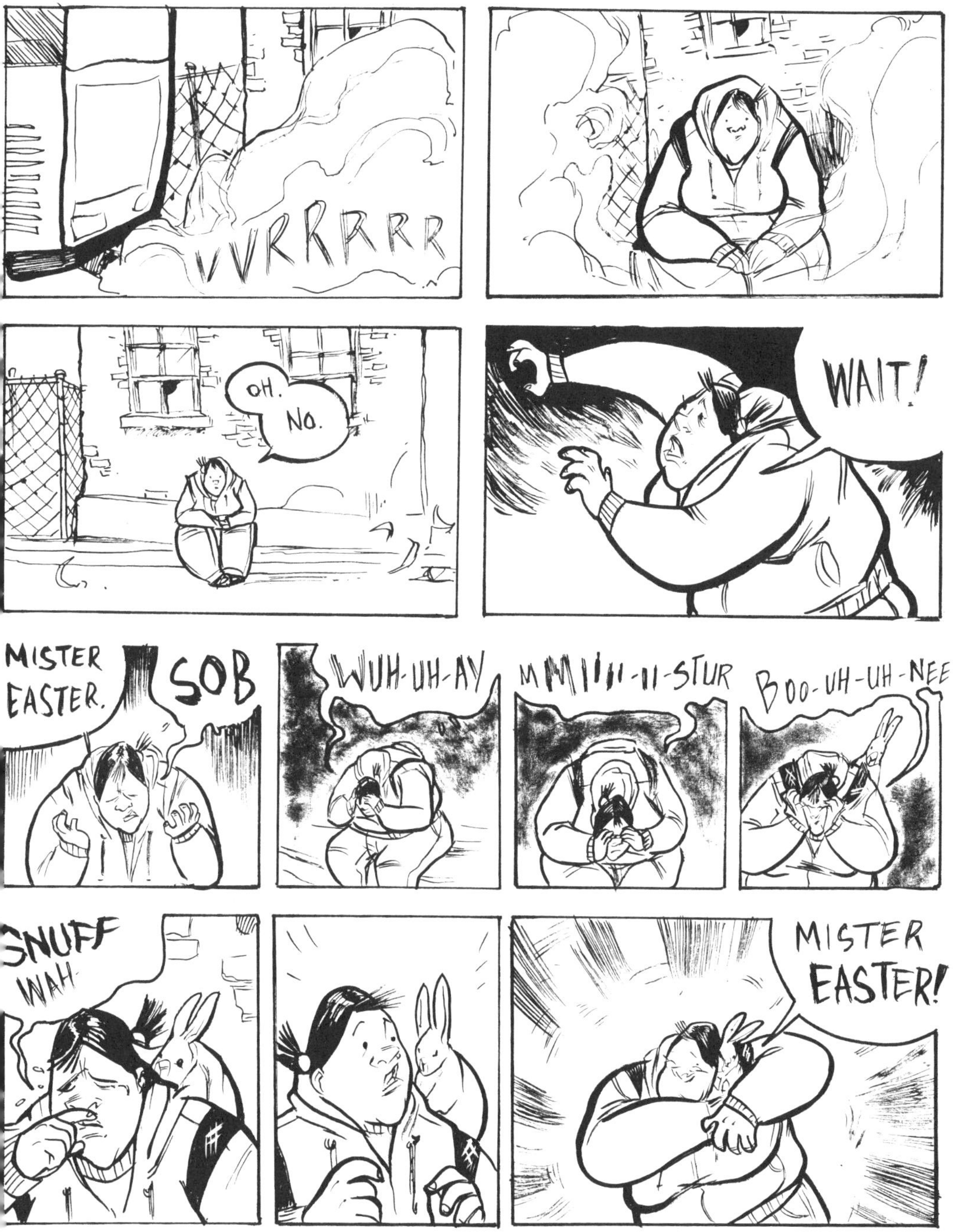
VVRRRRRR
OH. NO.
WAIT!
MISTER EASTER.
SOB
WUH-UH-AY
MMIIII-II-STUR
BOO-UH-UH-NEE
SNUFF
WAH
MISTER EASTER!

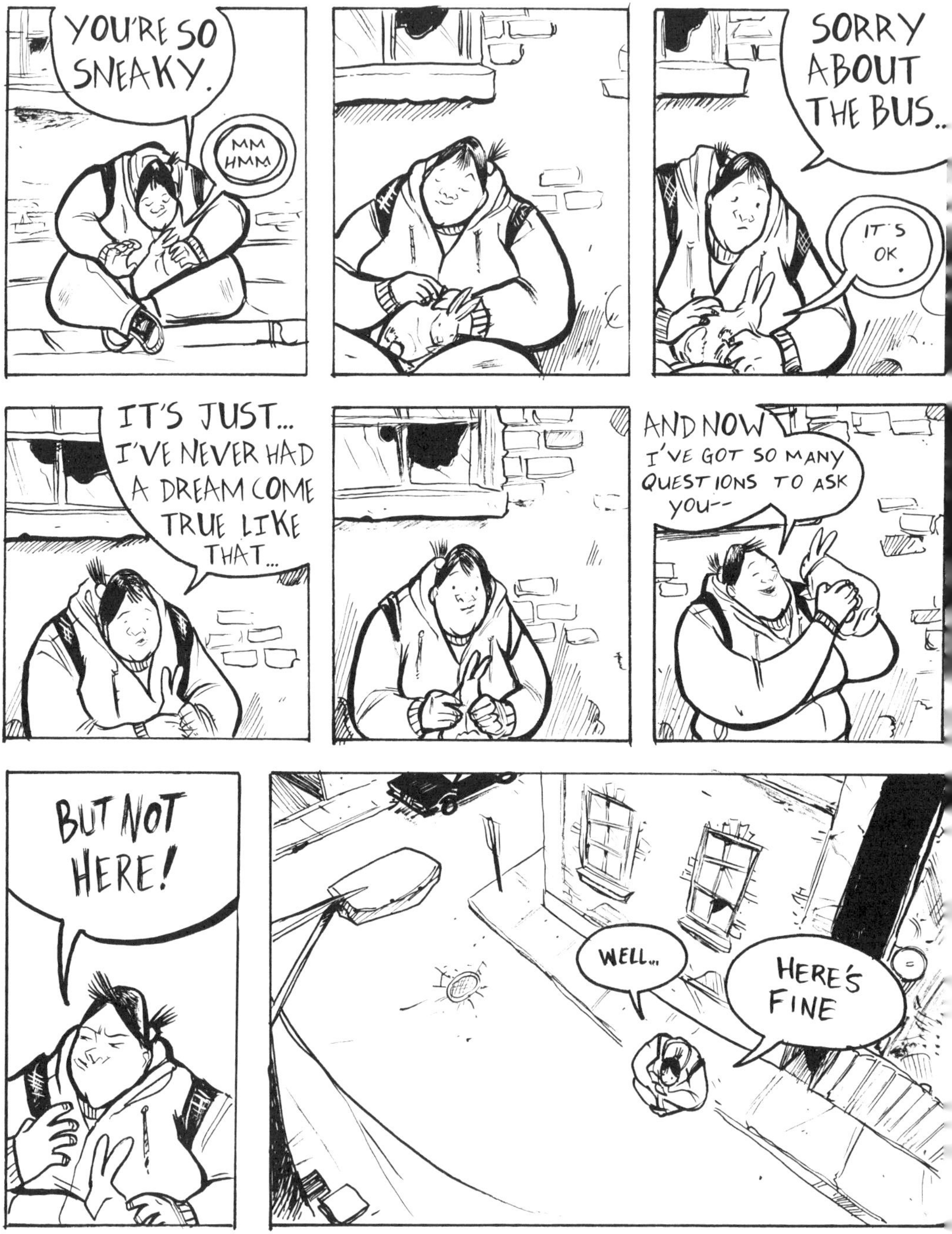
YOU'RE SO SNEAKY.
MM HMM
SORRY ABOUT THE BUS..
IT'S OK.
IT'S JUST... I'VE NEVER HAD A DREAM COME TRUE LIKE THAT...
AND NOW I'VE GOT SO MANY QUESTIONS TO ASK YOU--
BUT NOT HERE!
WELL...
HERE'S FINE

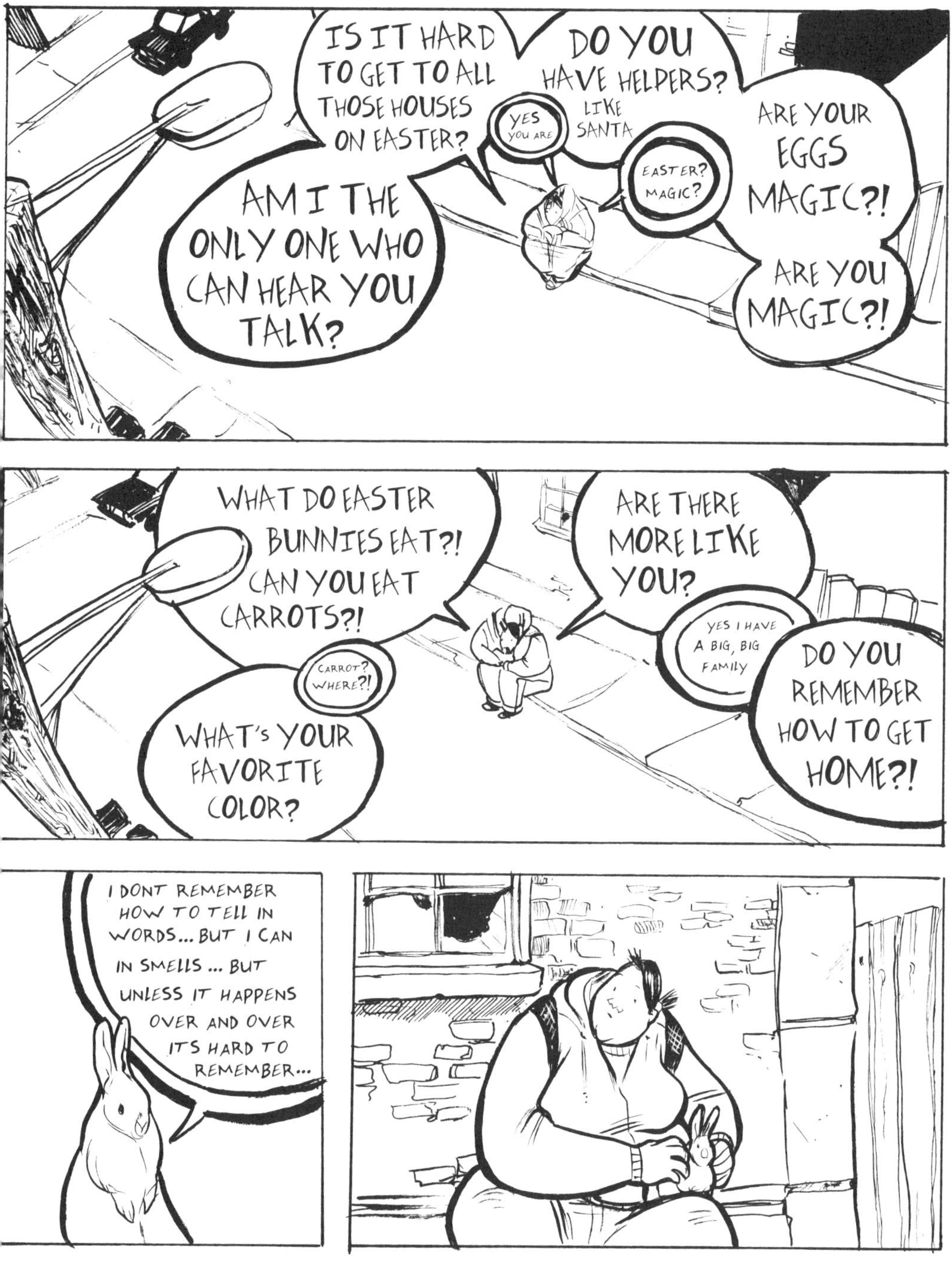
IS IT HARD TO GET TO ALL THOSE HOUSES ON EASTER?
DO YOU HAVE HELPERS?
LIKE SANTA
YES YOU ARE
EASTER? MAGIC?
ARE YOUR EGGS MAGIC?!
AM I THE ONLY ONE WHO CAN HEAR YOU TALK?
ARE YOU MAGIC?!
WHAT DO EASTER BUNNIES EAT?! CAN YOU EAT CARROTS?!
ARE THERE MORE LIKE YOU?
CARROT? WHERE?!
YES I HAVE A BIG, BIG FAMILY
WHAT'S YOUR FAVORITE COLOR?
DO YOU REMEMBER HOW TO GET HOME?!
I DONT REMEMBER HOW TO TELL IN WORDS... BUT I CAN IN SMELLS ... BUT UNLESS IT HAPPENS OVER AND OVER ITS HARD TO REMEMBER...

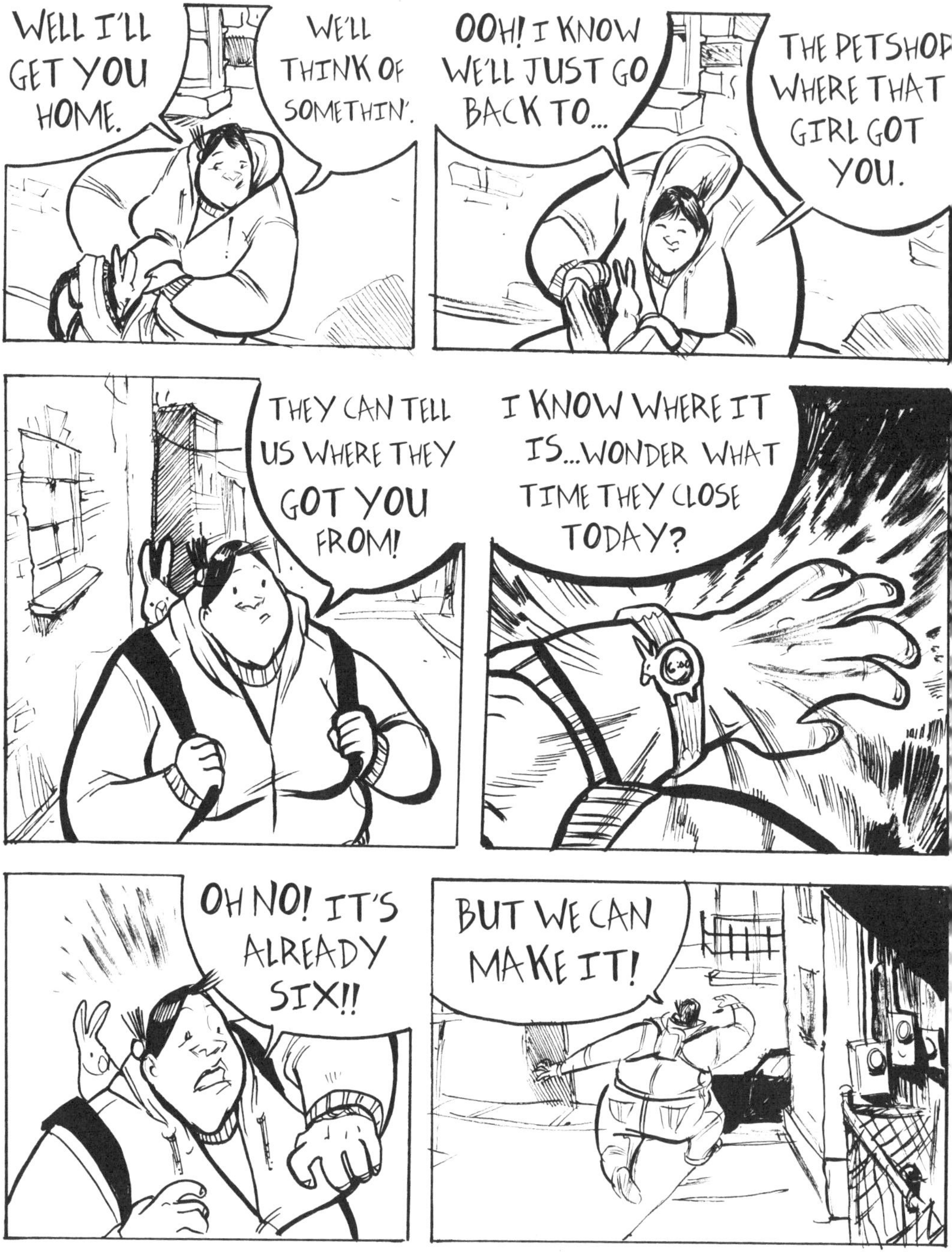
WELL I'LL GET YOU HOME.
WE'LL THINK OF SOMETHIN'.
OOH! I KNOW WE'LL JUST GO BACK TO...
THE PETSHOP WHERE THAT GIRL GOT YOU.
THEY CAN TELL US WHERE THEY GOT YOU FROM!
I KNOW WHERE IT IS...WONDER WHAT TIME THEY CLOSE TODAY?
OH NO! IT'S ALREADY SIX!!
BUT WE CAN MAKE IT!

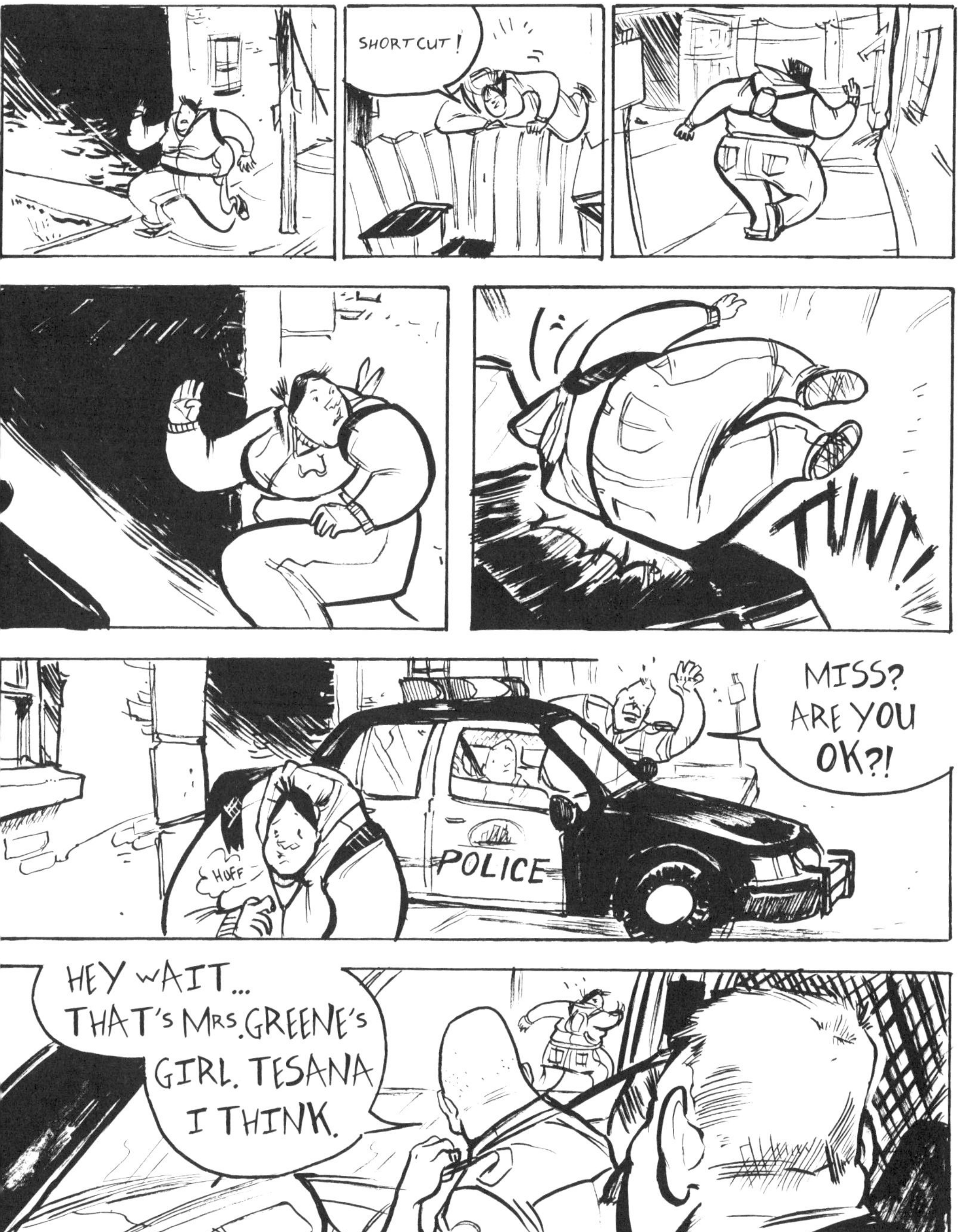
SHORTCUT!
TUNT!!
MISS? ARE YOU OK?!
HUFF
POLICE
HEY WAIT... THAT'S MRS. GREENE'S GIRL. TESANA I THINK.

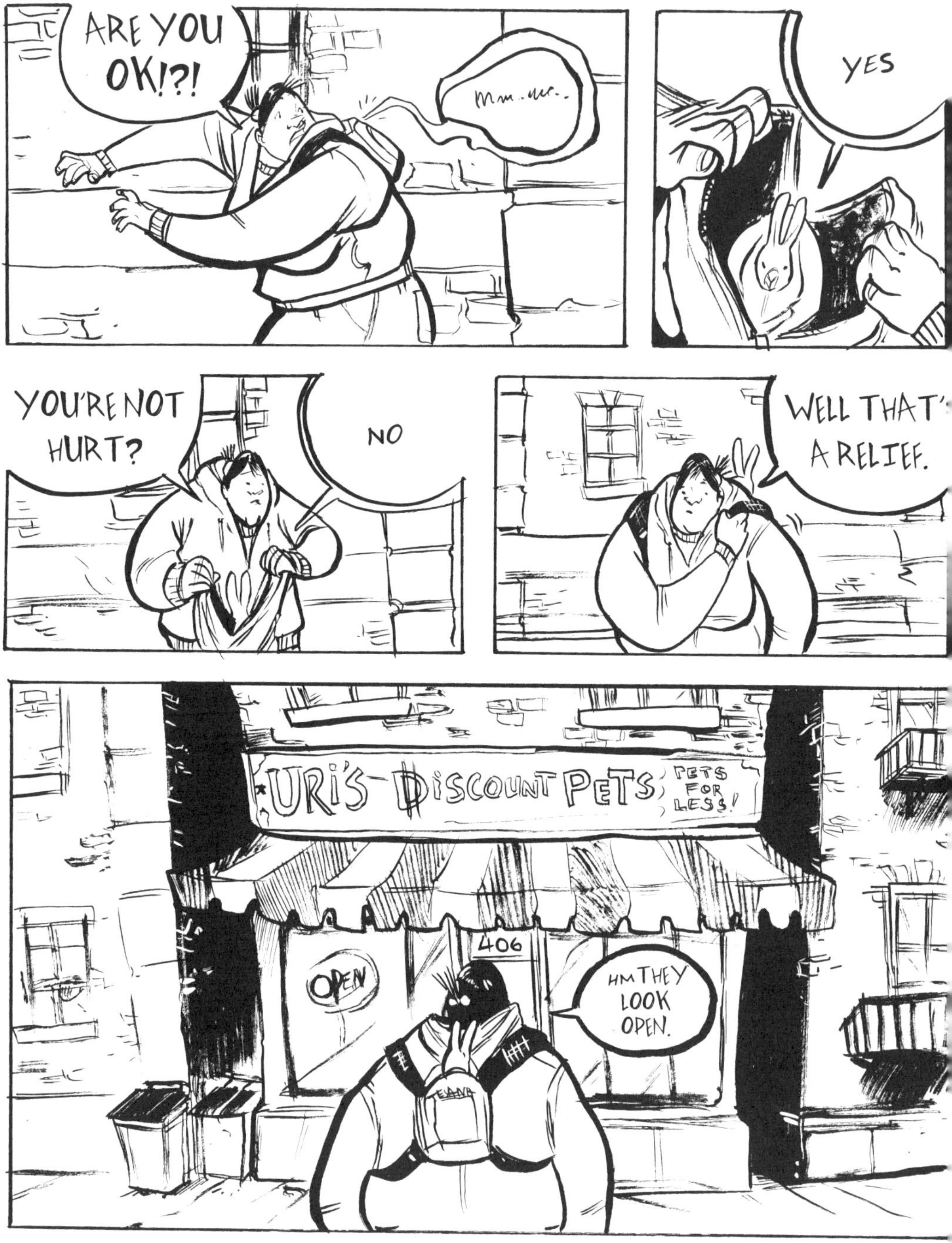
ARE YOU OK!?!
Mm...mr...
YES
YOU'RE NOT HURT?
NO
WELL THAT'S A RELIEF.
URI'S DISCOUNT PETS
PETS FOR LESS!
406
OPEN
HM THEY LOOK OPEN.

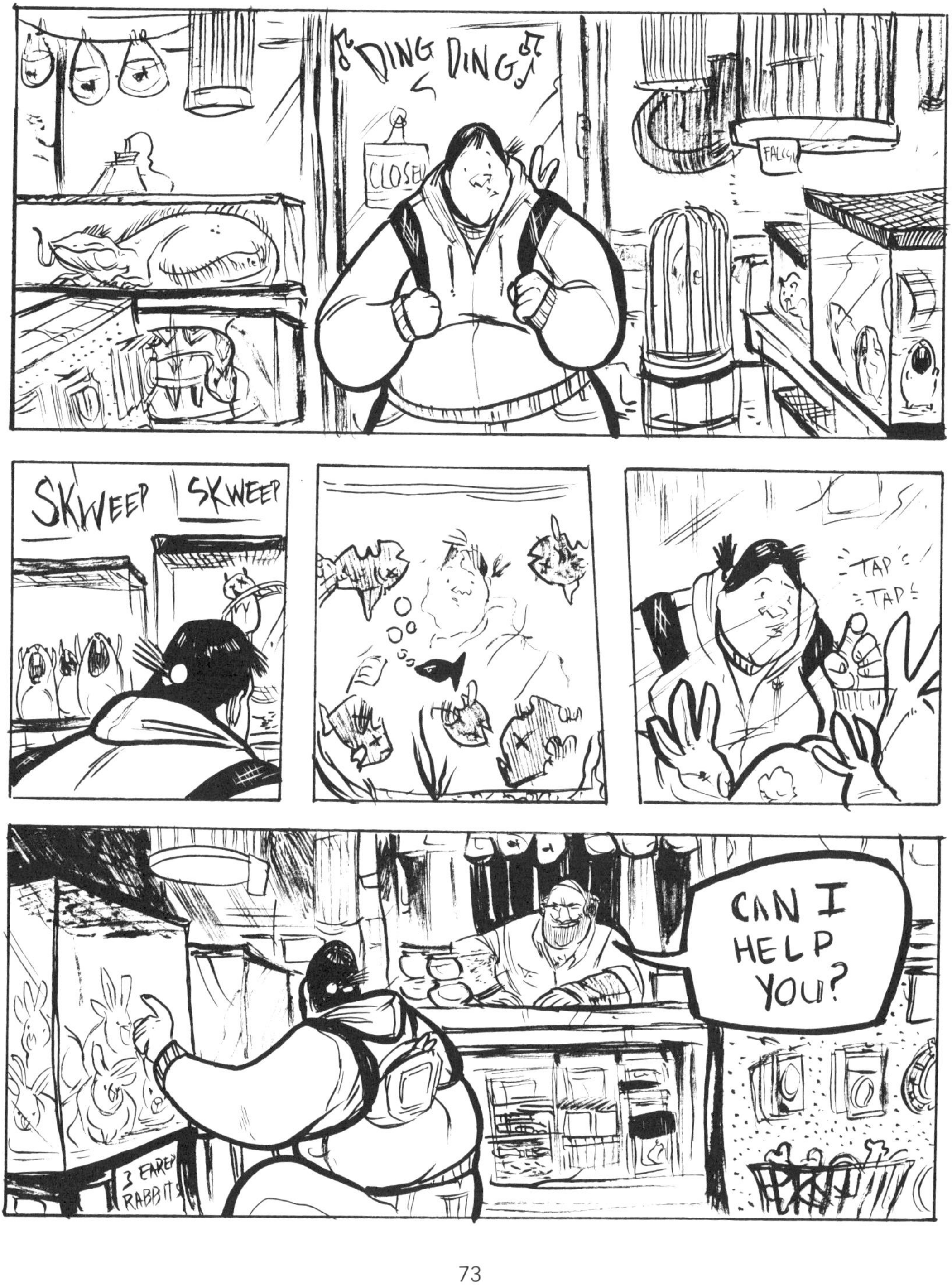

DING DING
CLOSED
FALCON
SKWEEP SKWEEP
TAP TAP
CAN I HELP YOU?
3 EARED RABBITS

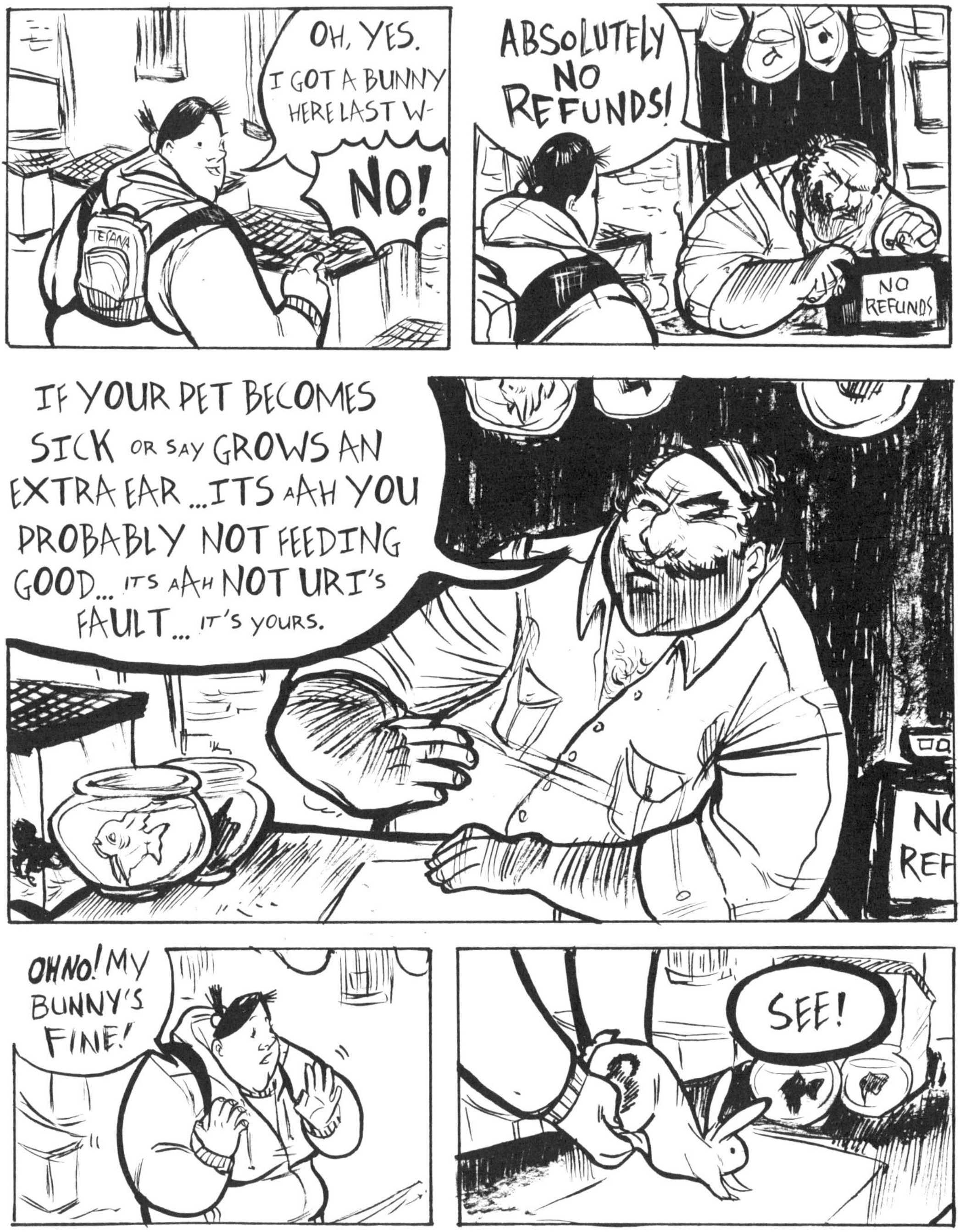
OH, YES. I GOT A BUNNY HERE LAST W-
NO!
TETIANA
ABSOLUTELY NO REFUNDS!
NO REFUNDS
IF YOUR PET BECOMES SICK OR SAY GROWS AN EXTRA EAR ...ITS AAH YOU PROBABLY NOT FEEDING GOOD... ITS AAH NOT URI'S FAULT... IT'S YOURS.
OH NO! MY BUNNY'S FINE!
SEE!

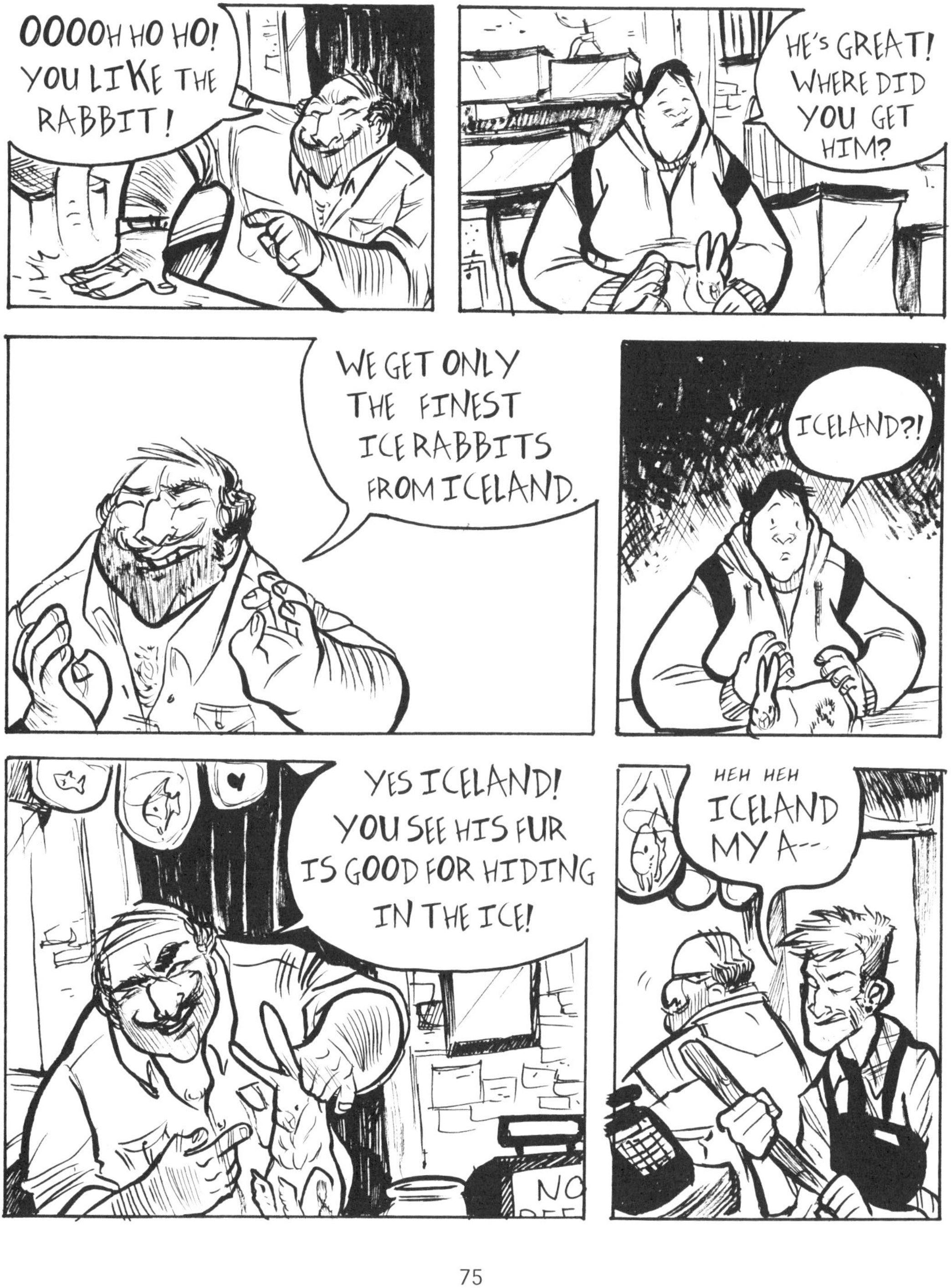
OOOOH HO HO! YOU LIKE THE RABBIT!
HE'S GREAT! WHERE DID YOU GET HIM?
WE GET ONLY THE FINEST ICE RABBITS FROM ICELAND.
ICELAND?!
YES ICELAND! YOU SEE HIS FUR IS GOOD FOR HIDING IN THE ICE!
NO
HEH HEH
ICELAND MY A--

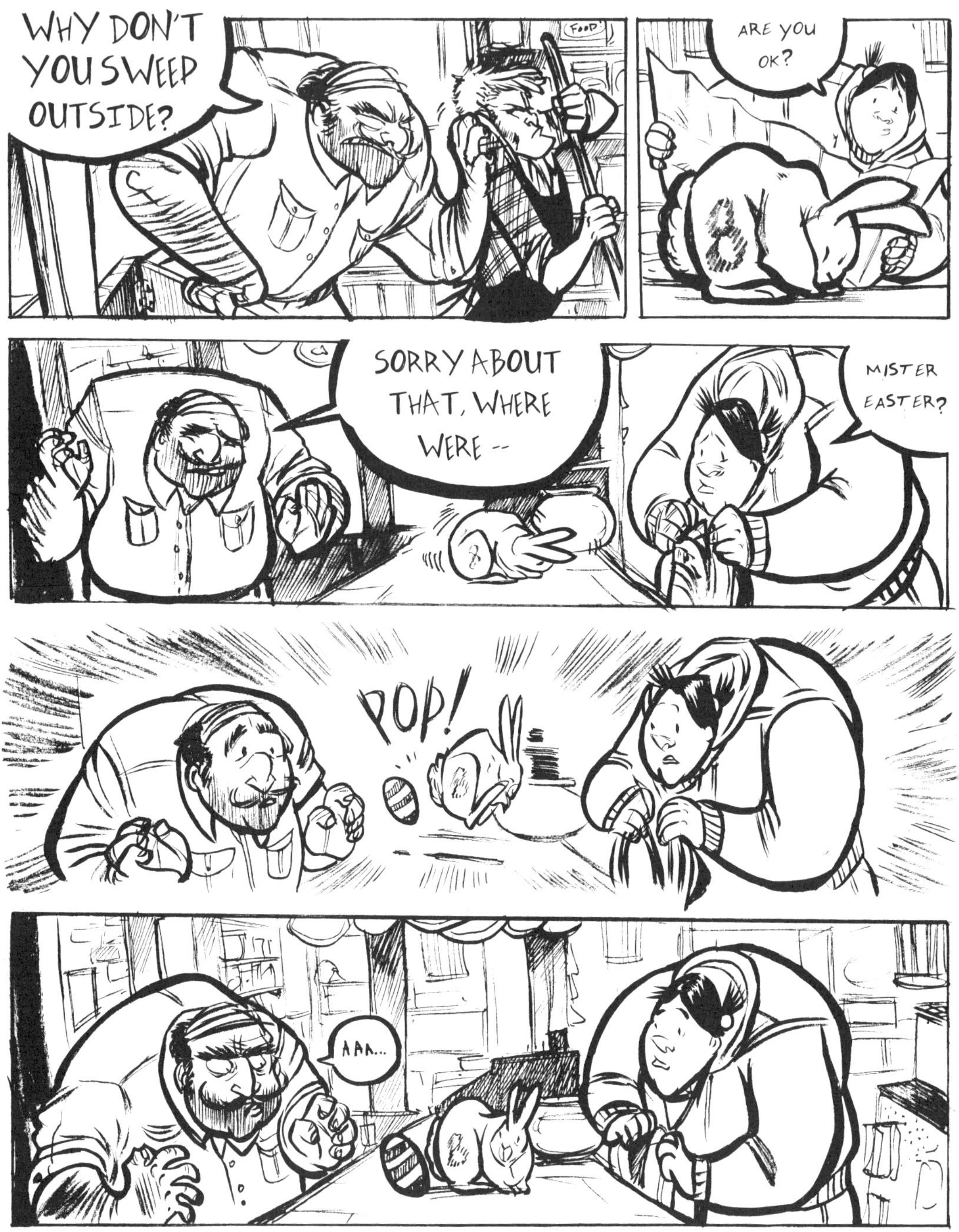
WHY DON'T YOU SWEEP OUTSIDE?
FOOD
ARE YOU OK?
SORRY ABOUT THAT, WHERE WERE --
MISTER EASTER?
POP!
AAA...

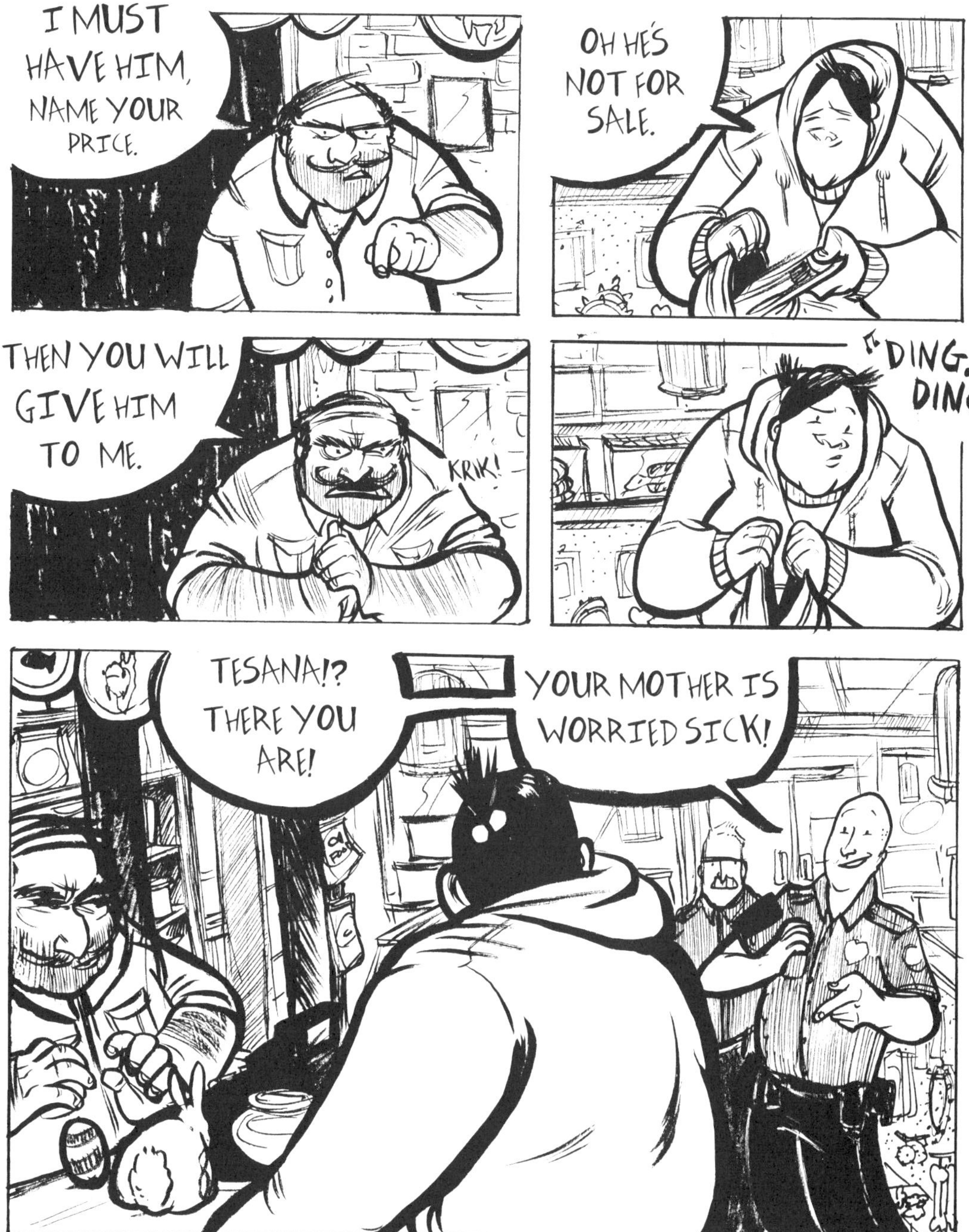
I MUST HAVE HIM, NAME YOUR PRICE.
OH HE'S NOT FOR SALE.
THEN YOU WILL GIVE HIM TO ME.
KRIK!
DING DING!
TESANA!? THERE YOU ARE!
YOUR MOTHER IS WORRIED SICK!

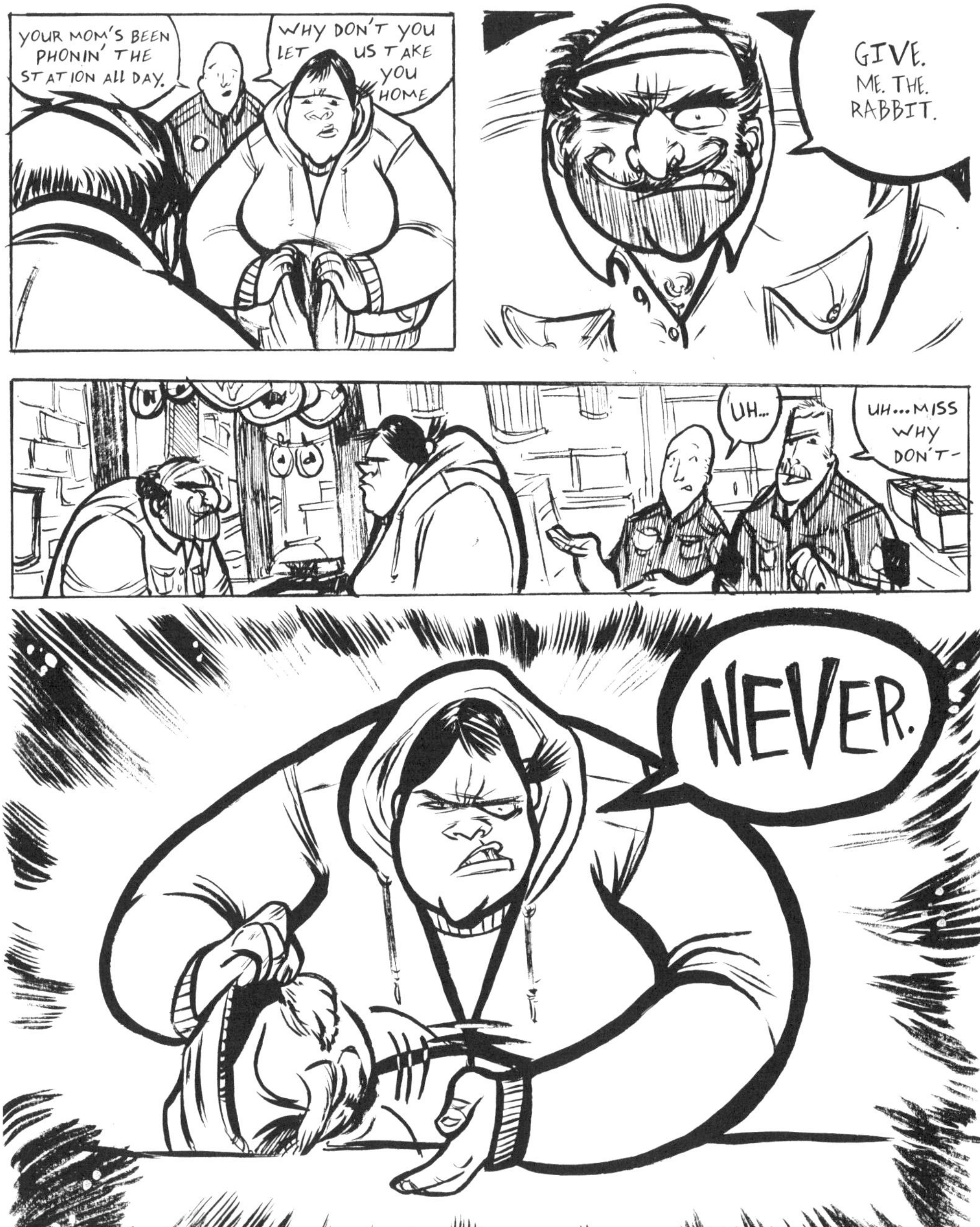
YOUR MOM'S BEEN PHONIN' THE STATION ALL DAY.
WHY DON'T YOU LET US TAKE YOU HOME
GIVE. ME. THE. RABBIT.
UH...
UH...MISS WHY DON'T-
NEVER.
72

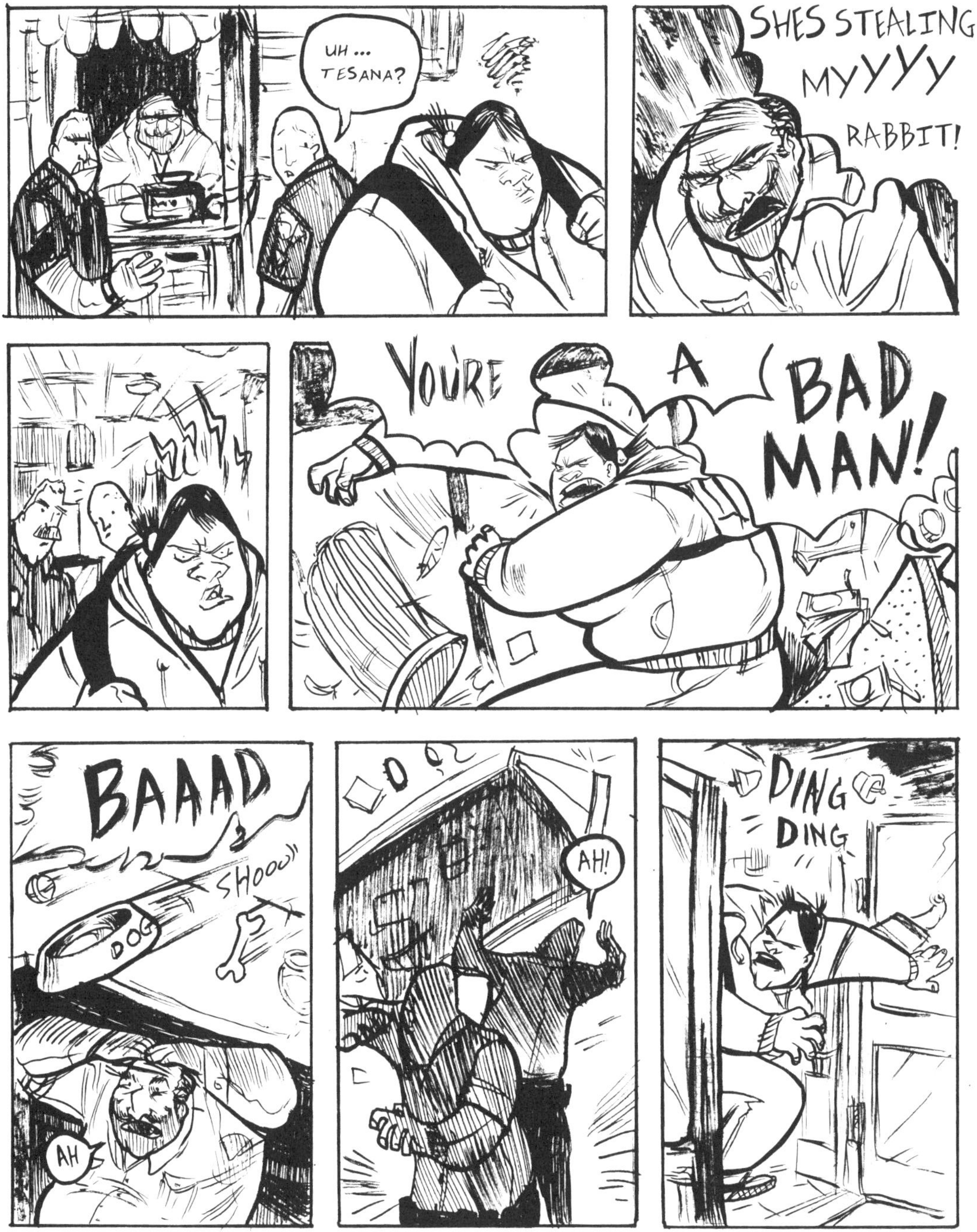
UH ... TESANA?
SHES STEALING MYYYY RABBIT!
YOU'RE A BAD MAN!
BAAAD
SHOOO
DOG
AH
AH!
DING DING

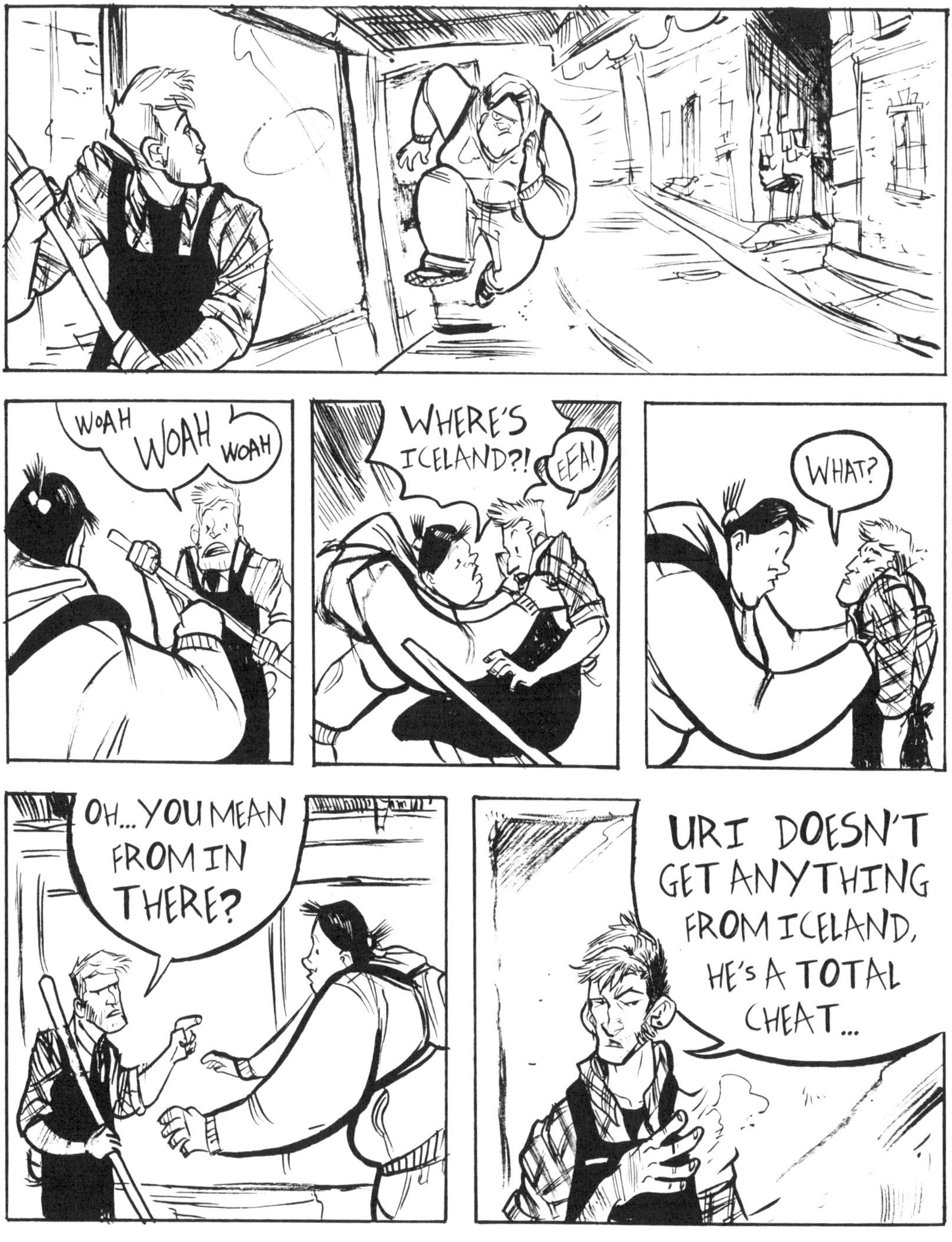

WOAH WOAH WOAH
WHERE'S ICELAND?!
EEA!
WHAT?
OH... YOU MEAN FROM IN THERE?
URI DOESN'T GET ANYTHING FROM ICELAND, HE'S A TOTAL CHEAT...

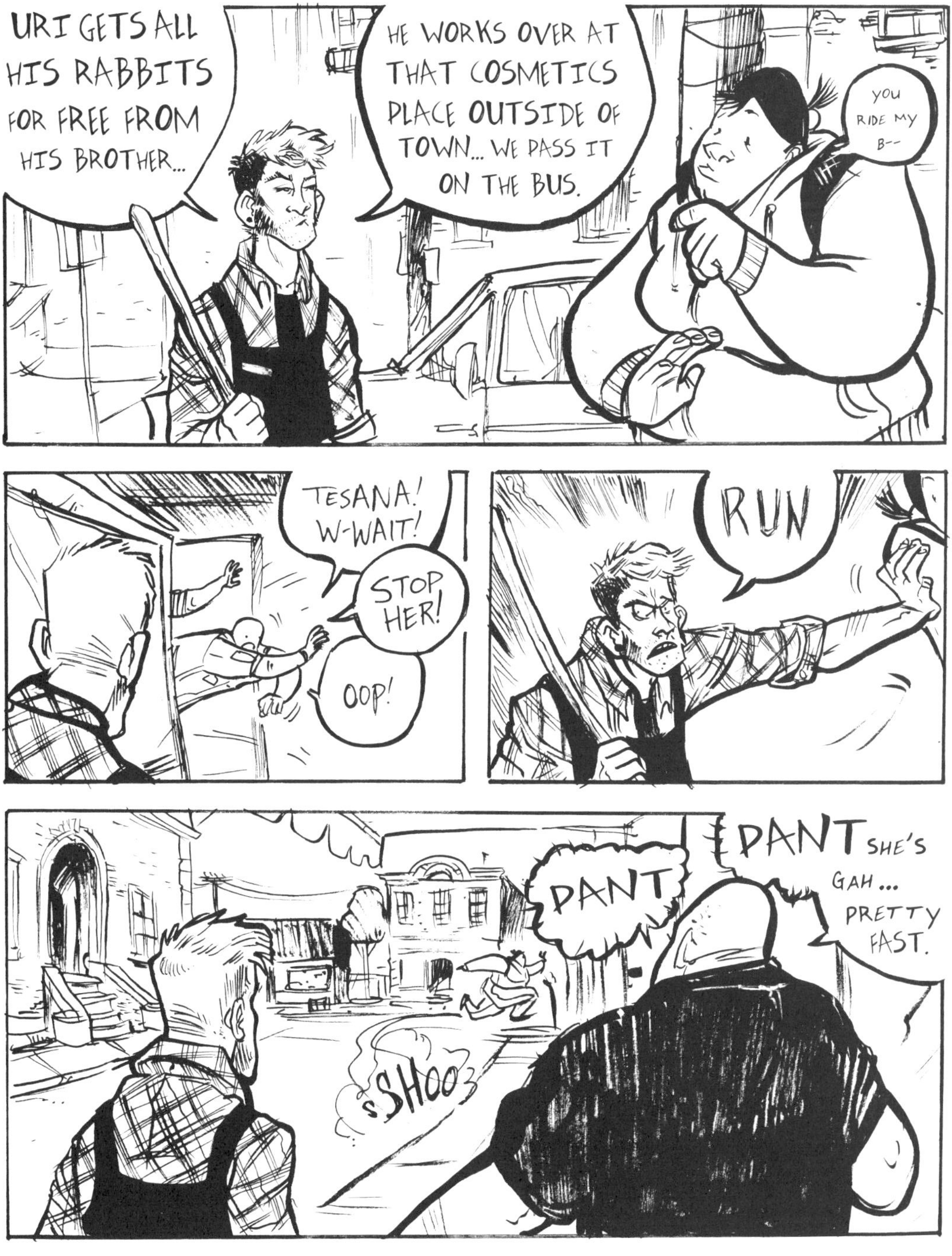
URI GETS ALL HIS RABBITS FOR FREE FROM HIS BROTHER...
HE WORKS OVER AT THAT COSMETICS PLACE OUTSIDE OF TOWN... WE PASS IT ON THE BUS.
YOU RIDE MY B--
TESANA! W-WAIT!
STOP HER!
OOP!
RUN
PANT
PANT SHE'S GAH... PRETTY FAST.
SHOO

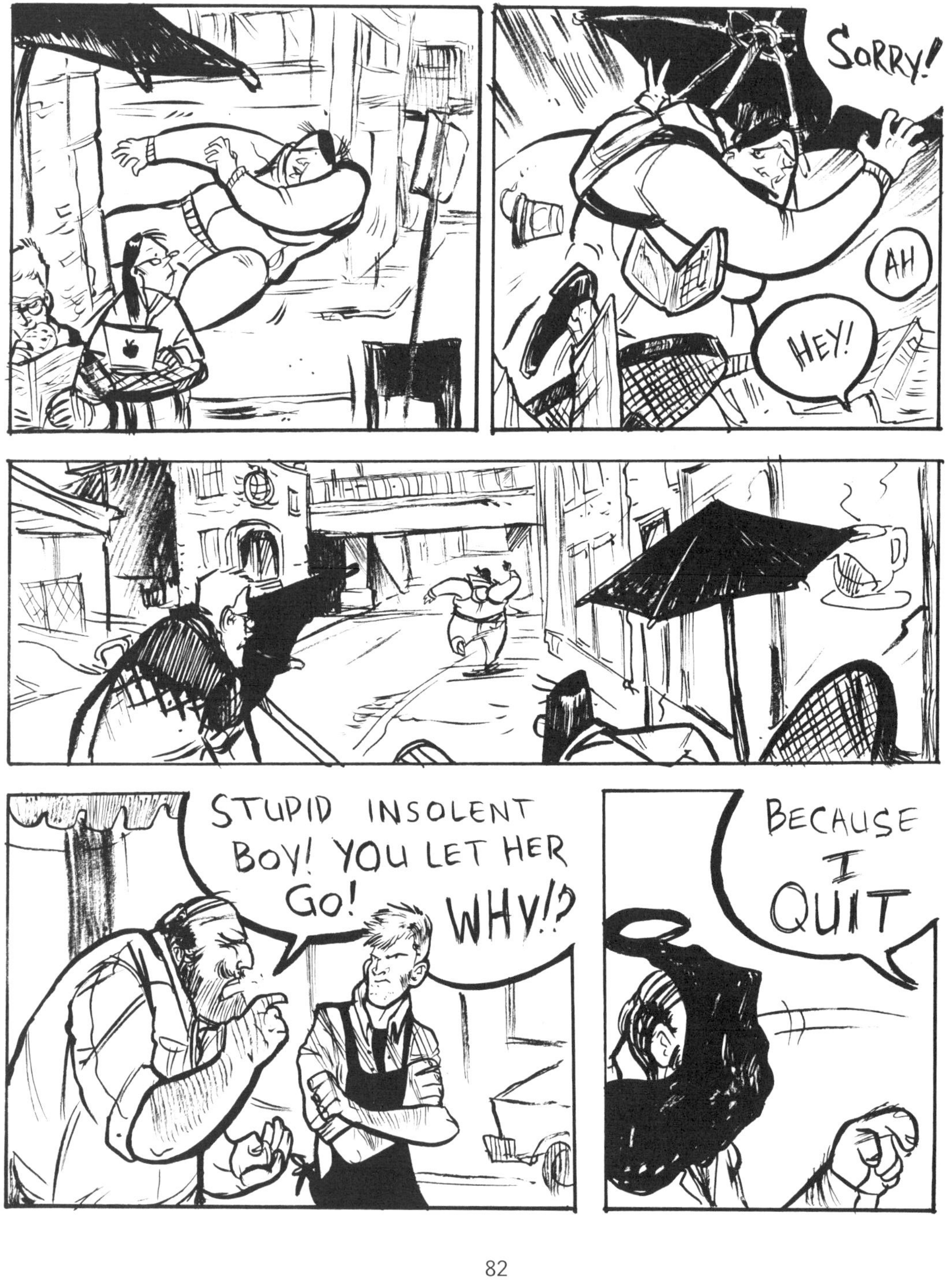
SORRY!
AH
HEY!
STUPID INSOLENT BOY! YOU LET HER GO!
WHY!?
BECAUSE I QUIT

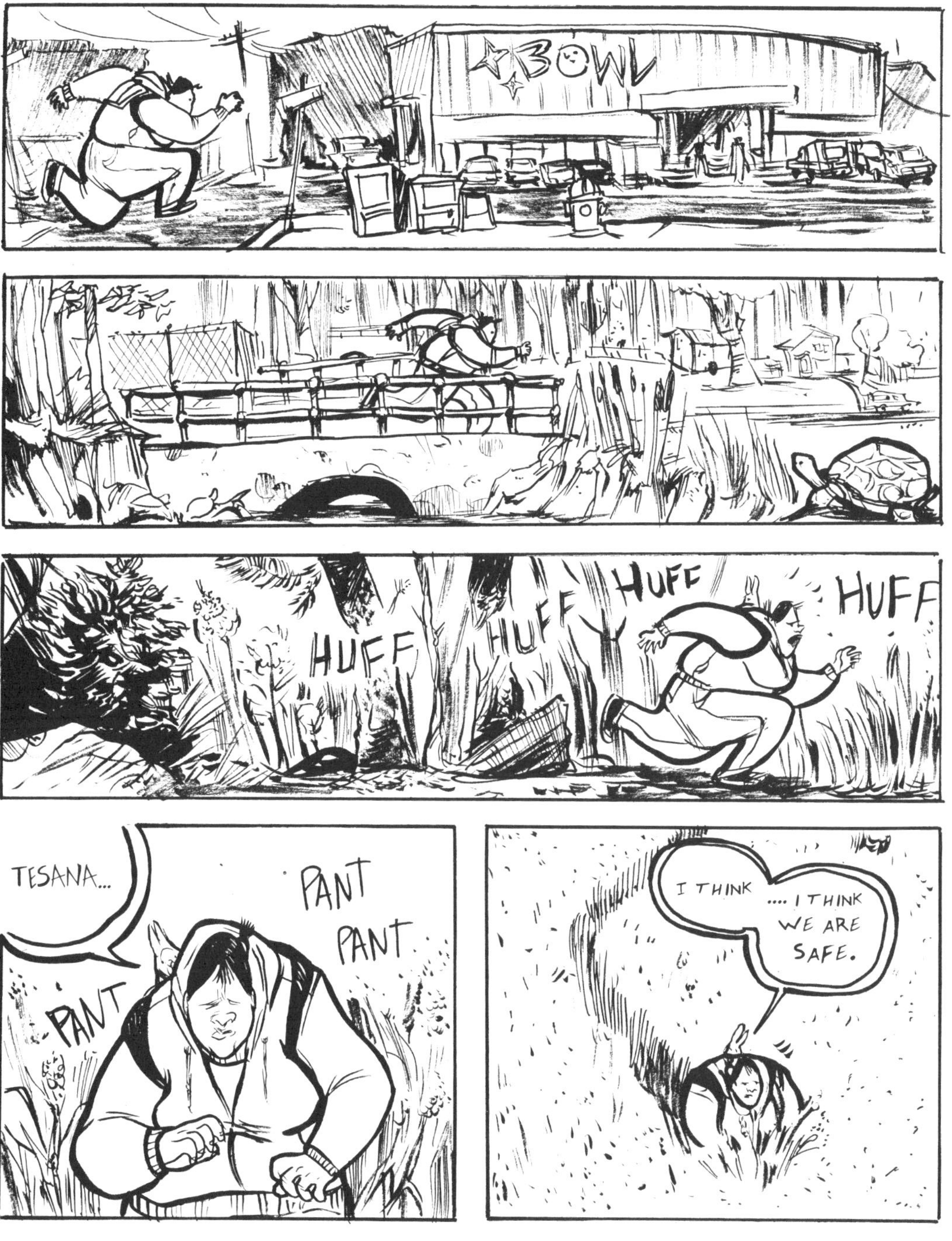

BOWL
HUFF
HUFF
HUFF
HUFF
TESANA...
PANT
PANT
PANT
I THINK ....I THINK WE ARE SAFE.

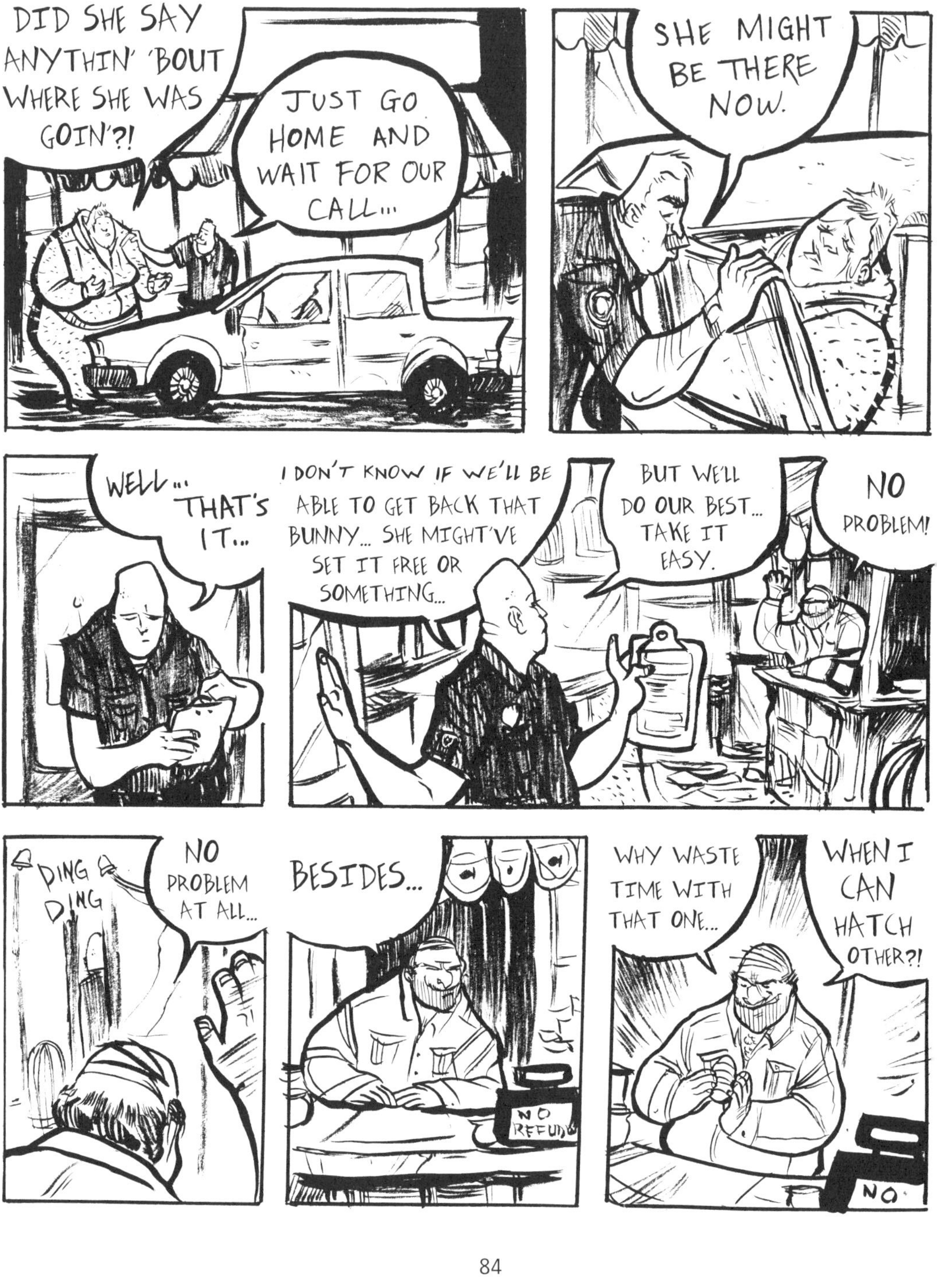
DID SHE SAY ANYTHIN' 'BOUT WHERE SHE WAS GOIN'?!
JUST GO HOME AND WAIT FOR OUR CALL...
SHE MIGHT BE THERE NOW.
WELL... THAT'S IT...
I DON'T KNOW IF WE'LL BE ABLE TO GET BACK THAT BUNNY... SHE MIGHT'VE SET IT FREE OR SOMETHING...
BUT WE'LL DO OUR BEST... TAKE IT EASY.
NO PROBLEM!
DING DING
NO PROBLEM AT ALL...
BESIDES...
NO REFUND
WHY WASTE TIME WITH THAT ONE...
WHEN I CAN HATCH OTHER?!
NO

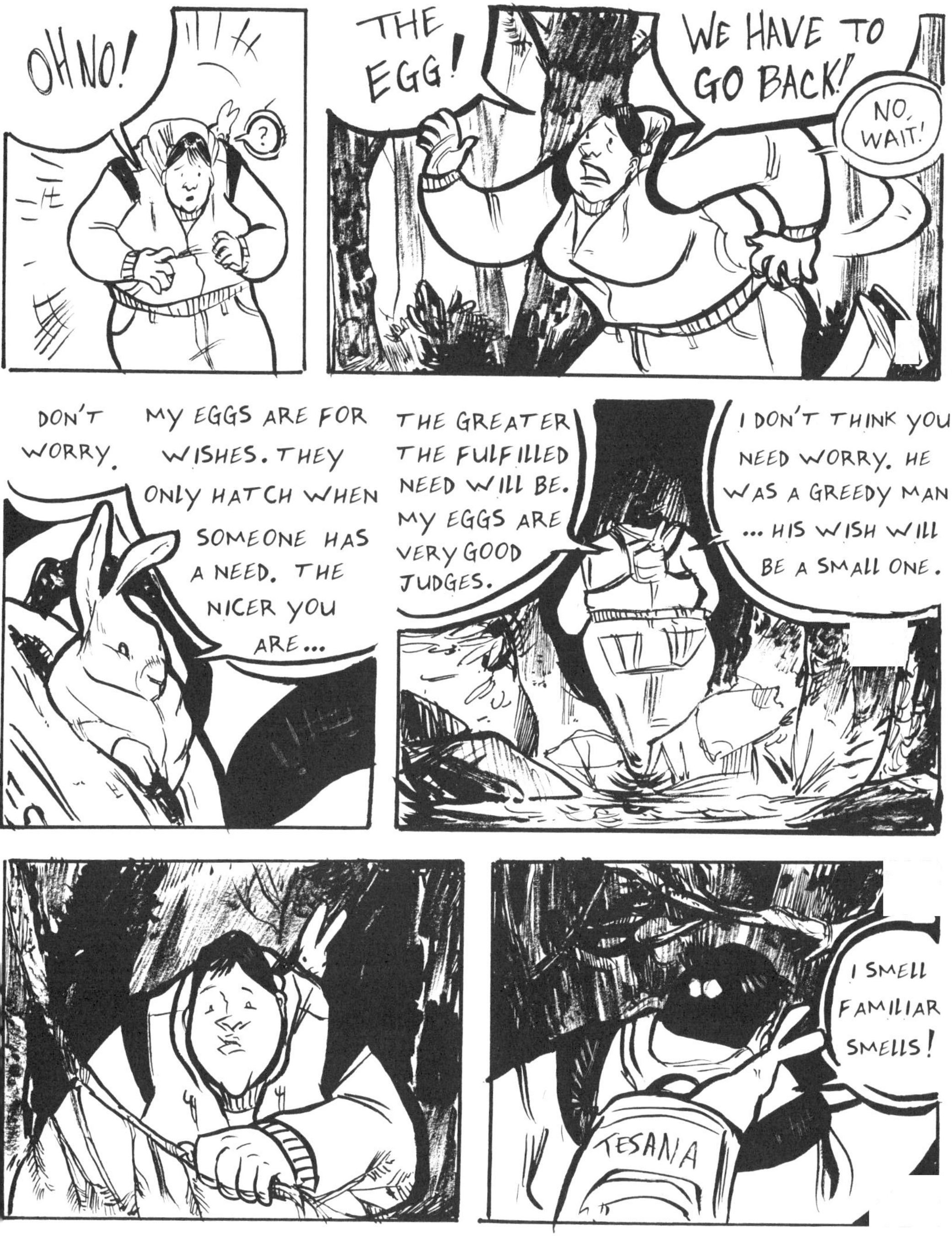

OH NO!
?
THE EGG!
WE HAVE TO GO BACK!
NO, WAIT!
DON'T WORRY.
MY EGGS ARE FOR WISHES. THEY ONLY HATCH WHEN SOMEONE HAS A NEED. THE NICER YOU ARE...
THE GREATER THE FULFILLED NEED WILL BE. MY EGGS ARE VERY GOOD JUDGES.
I DON'T THINK YOU NEED WORRY. HE WAS A GREEDY MAN ... HIS WISH WILL BE A SMALL ONE.
I SMELL FAMILIAR SMELLS!
TESANA

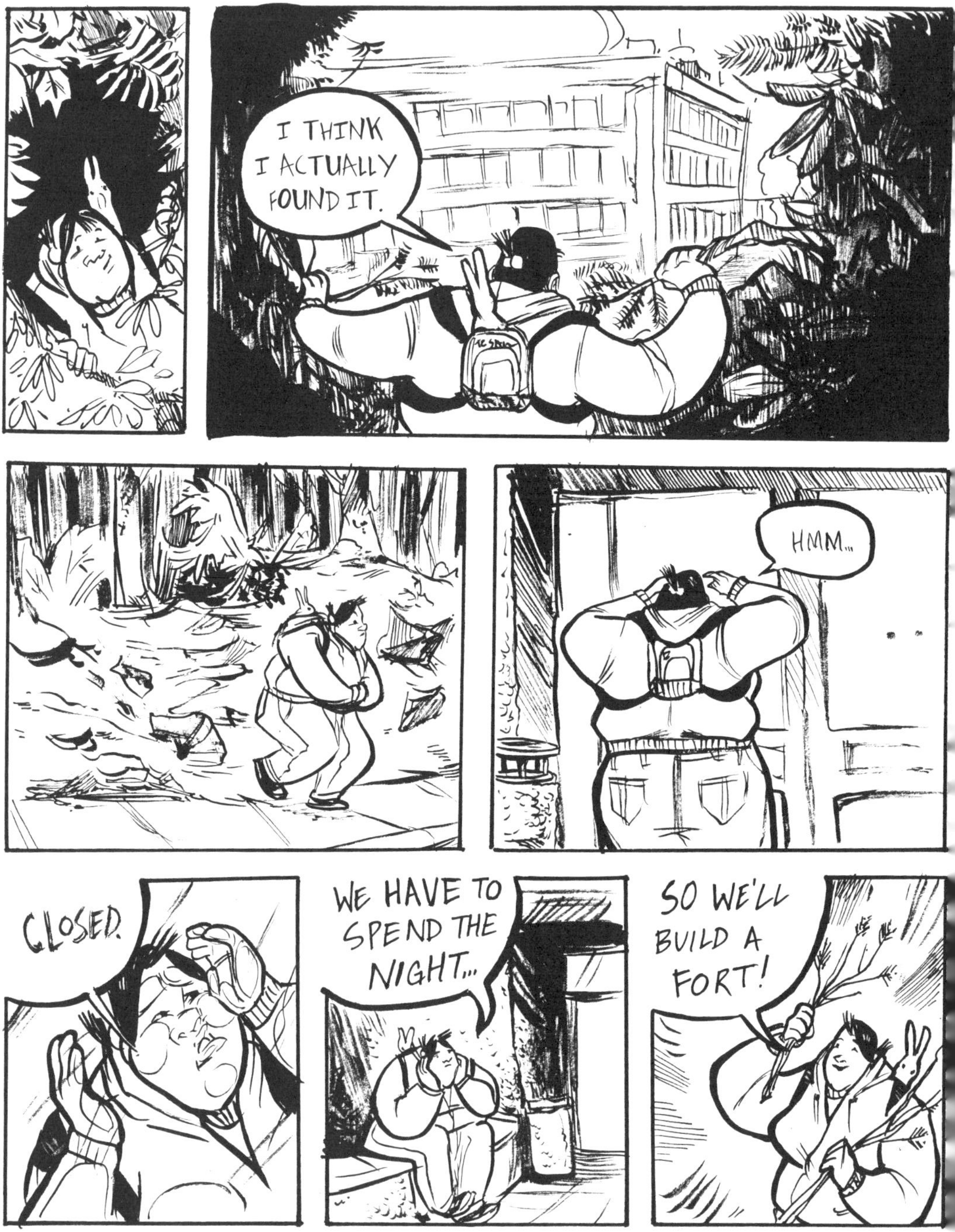
I THINK I ACTUALLY FOUND IT.
HMM...
CLOSED.
WE HAVE TO SPEND THE NIGHT...
SO WE'LL BUILD A FORT!

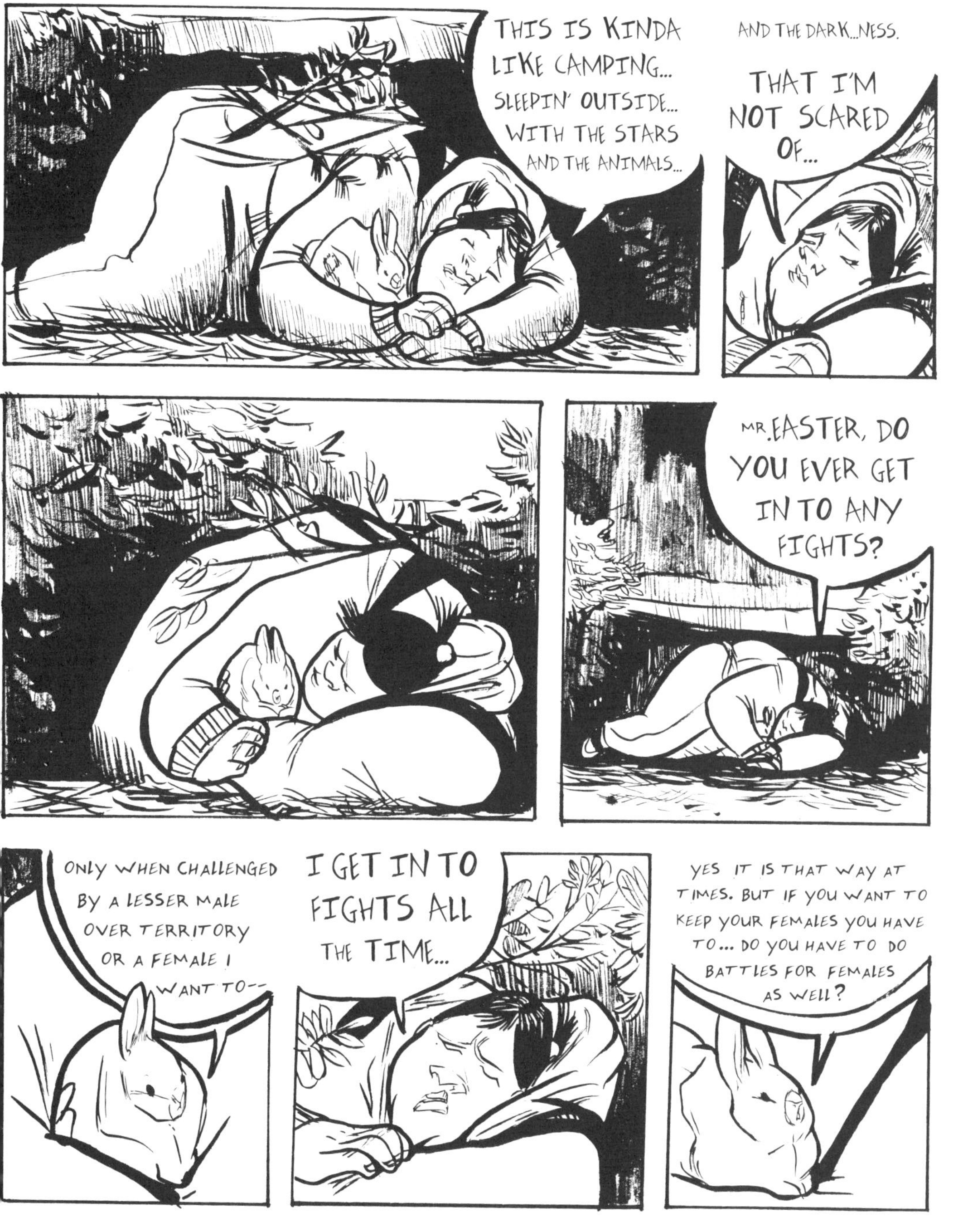
THIS IS KINDA LIKE CAMPING... SLEEPIN' OUTSIDE... WITH THE STARS AND THE ANIMALS...
AND THE DARK...NESS.
THAT I'M NOT SCARED OF...
MR. EASTER, DO YOU EVER GET IN TO ANY FIGHTS?
ONLY WHEN CHALLENGED BY A LESSER MALE OVER TERRITORY OR A FEMALE I WANT TO--
I GET IN TO FIGHTS ALL THE TIME...
YES IT IS THAT WAY AT TIMES. BUT IF YOU WANT TO KEEP YOUR FEMALES YOU HAVE TO... DO YOU HAVE TO DO BATTLES FOR FEMALES AS WELL?

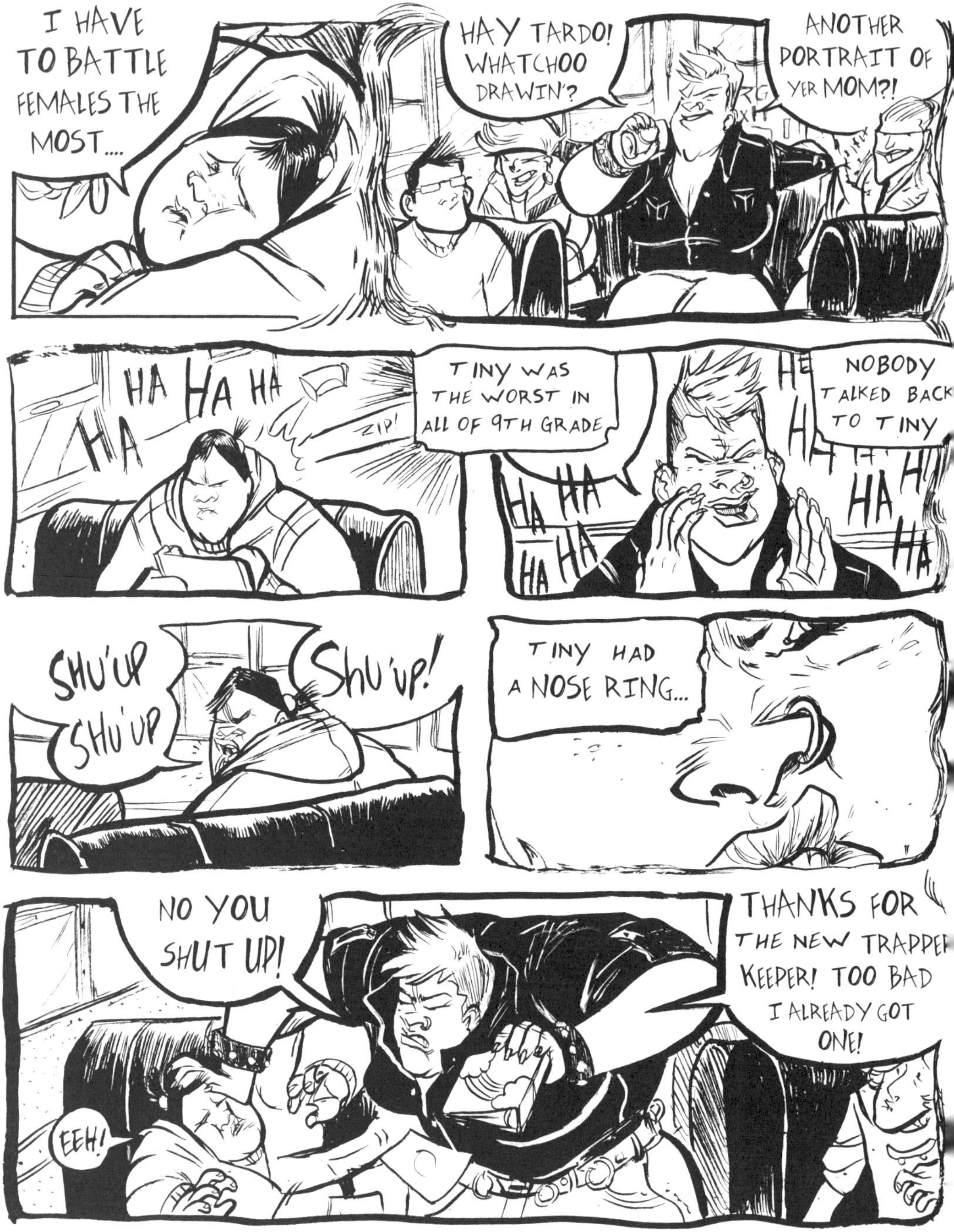

I HAVE TO BATTLE FEMALES THE MOST....
HAY TARDO! WHATCHOO DRAWIN'?
ANOTHER PORTRAIT OF YER MOM?!
HA HA HA HA
ZIP!
TINY WAS THE WORST IN ALL OF 9TH GRADE
NOBODY TALKED BACK TO TINY
HA HA HA HA HA HA HA
SHU'UP SHU'UP
SHU'UP!
TINY HAD A NOSE RING...
NO YOU SHUT UP!
THANKS FOR THE NEW TRAPPER KEEPER! TOO BAD I ALREADY GOT ONE!
EEH!

THAT.... WAS THE ... BEST... UNICORN

I'VE EVER DRAWN!!

ROOOOOAAA

SPARK

WAAAH

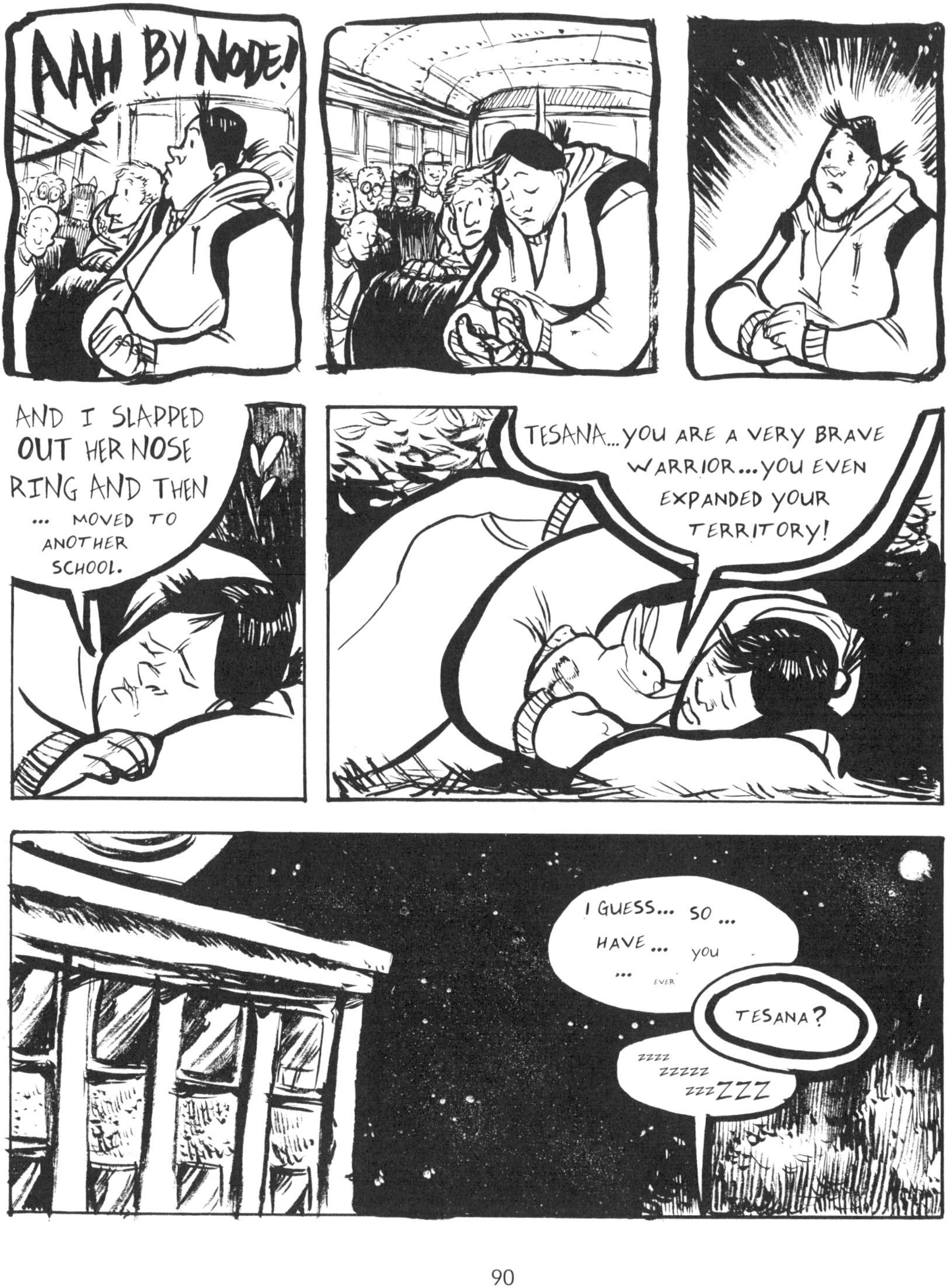
AAH BY NODE!
AND I SLAPPED OUT HER NOSE RING AND THEN ... MOVED TO ANOTHER SCHOOL.
TESANA...YOU ARE A VERY BRAVE WARRIOR...YOU EVEN EXPANDED YOUR TERRITORY!
I GUESS... SO ... HAVE ... YOU ... EVER
TESANA?
ZZZZ ZZZZZ ZZZZZZ

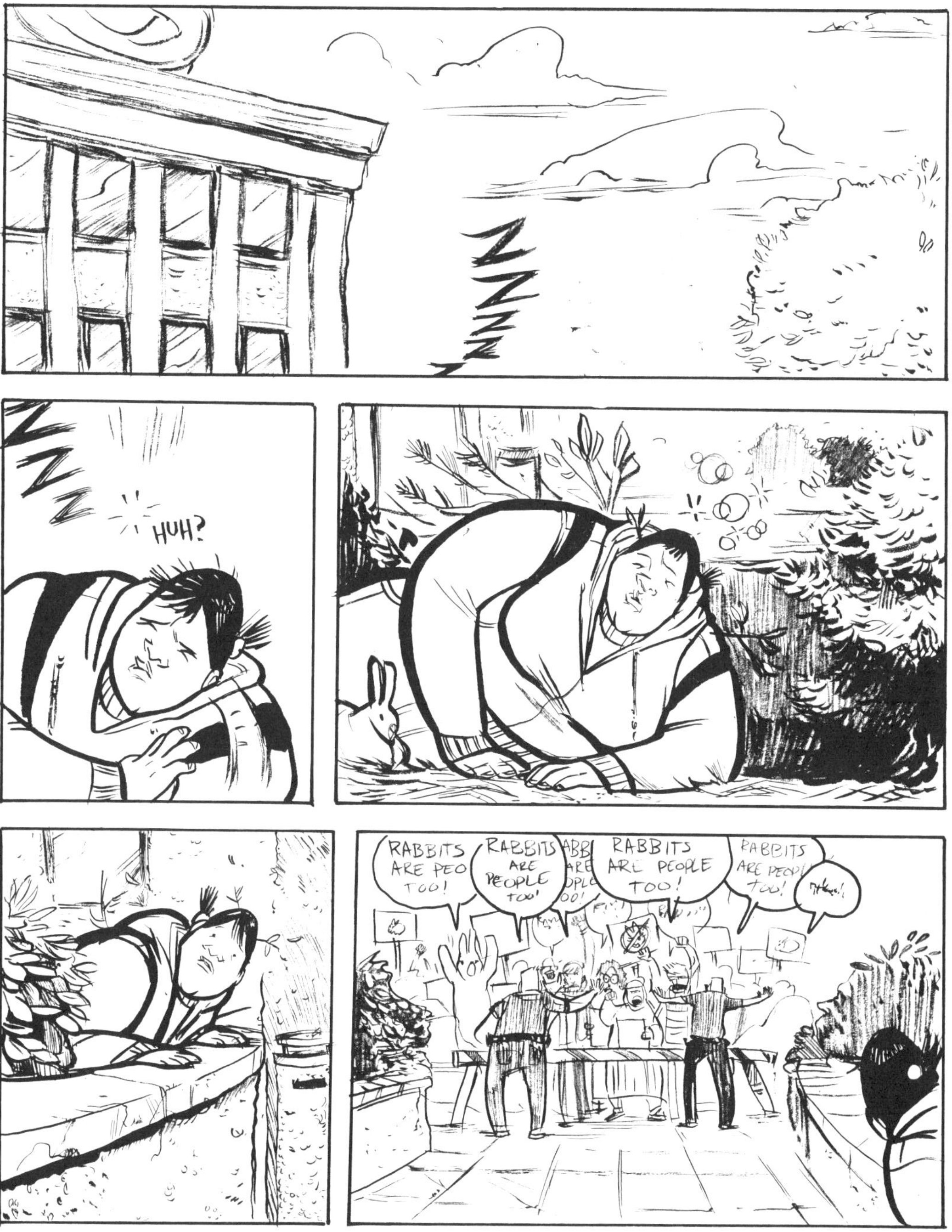

ZZZZZZ
ZZZZ
HUH?
RABBITS ARE PEO TOO!
RABBITS ARE PEOPLE TOO!
RABBITS ARE PEOPLE TOO!
RABBITS ARE PEOPLE TOO!
RABBITS ARE PEOP TOO!

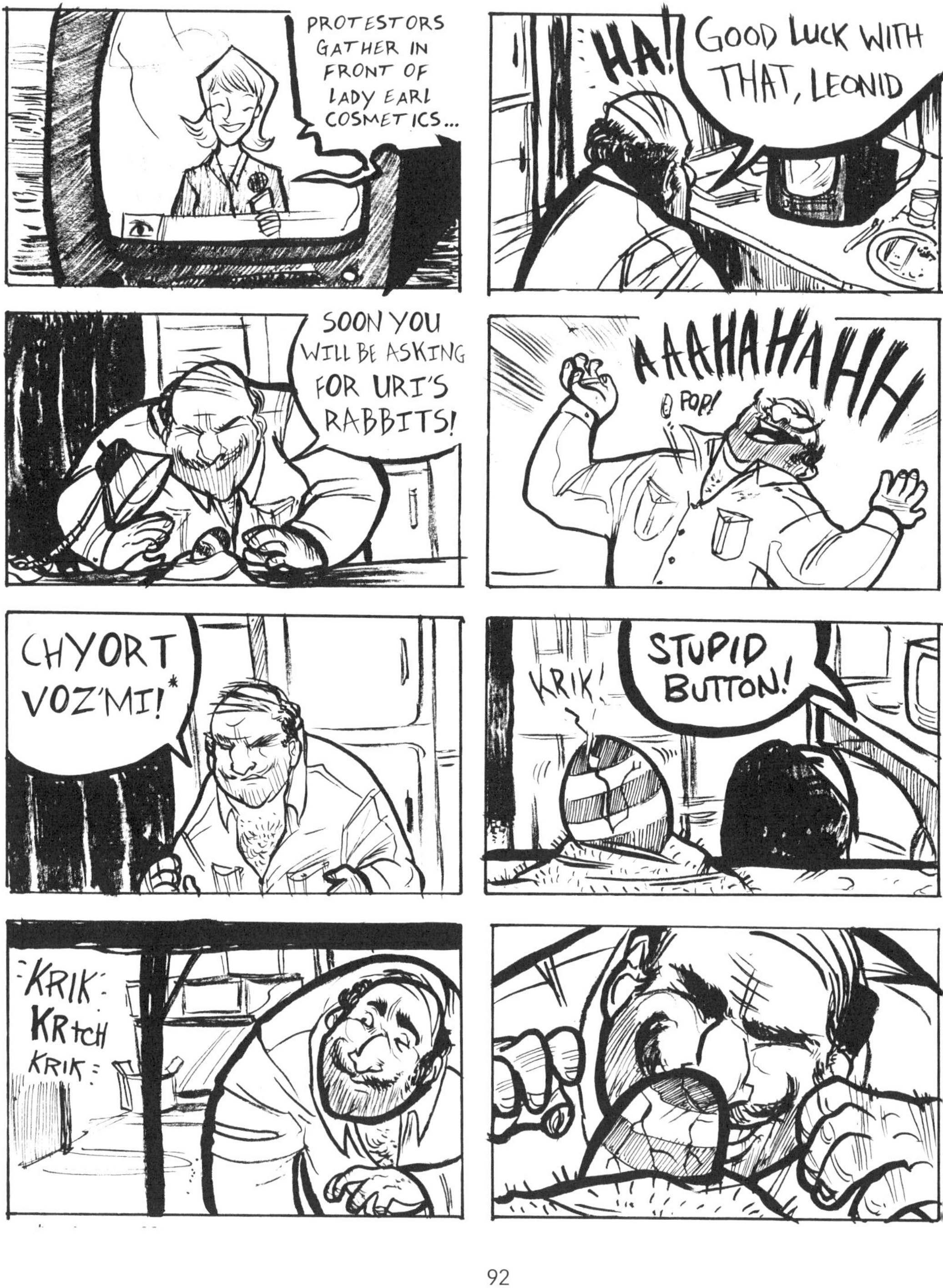
PROTESTORS GATHER IN FRONT OF LADY EARL COSMETICS...
HA!
GOOD LUCK WITH THAT, LEONID
SOON YOU WILL BE ASKING FOR URI'S RABBITS!
AAAHAHAHH
POP!
CHYORT VOZ'MI!*
KRIK!
STUPID BUTTON!
KRIK
KRTCH
KRIK

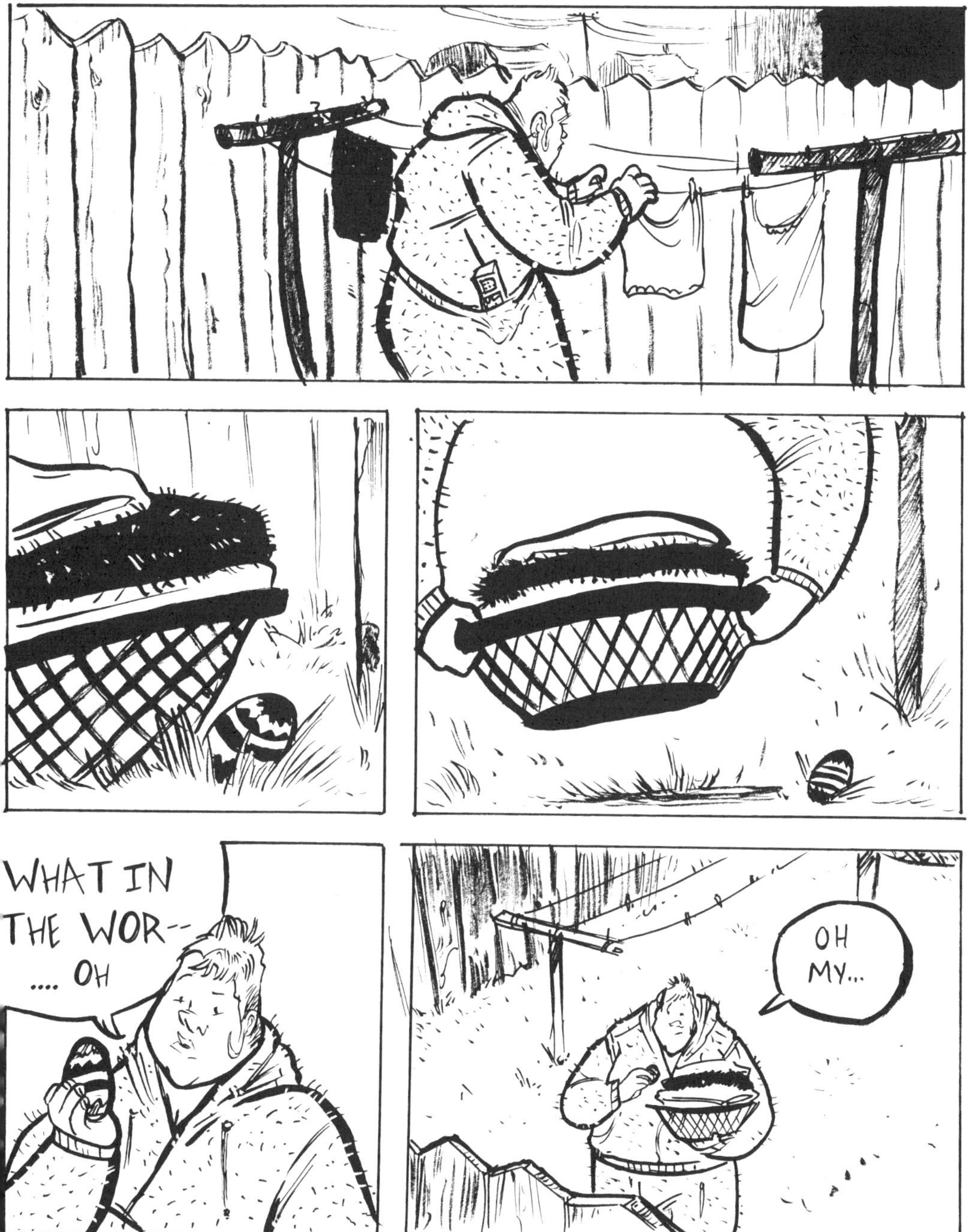
WHAT IN THE WOR-- .... OH
OH MY...

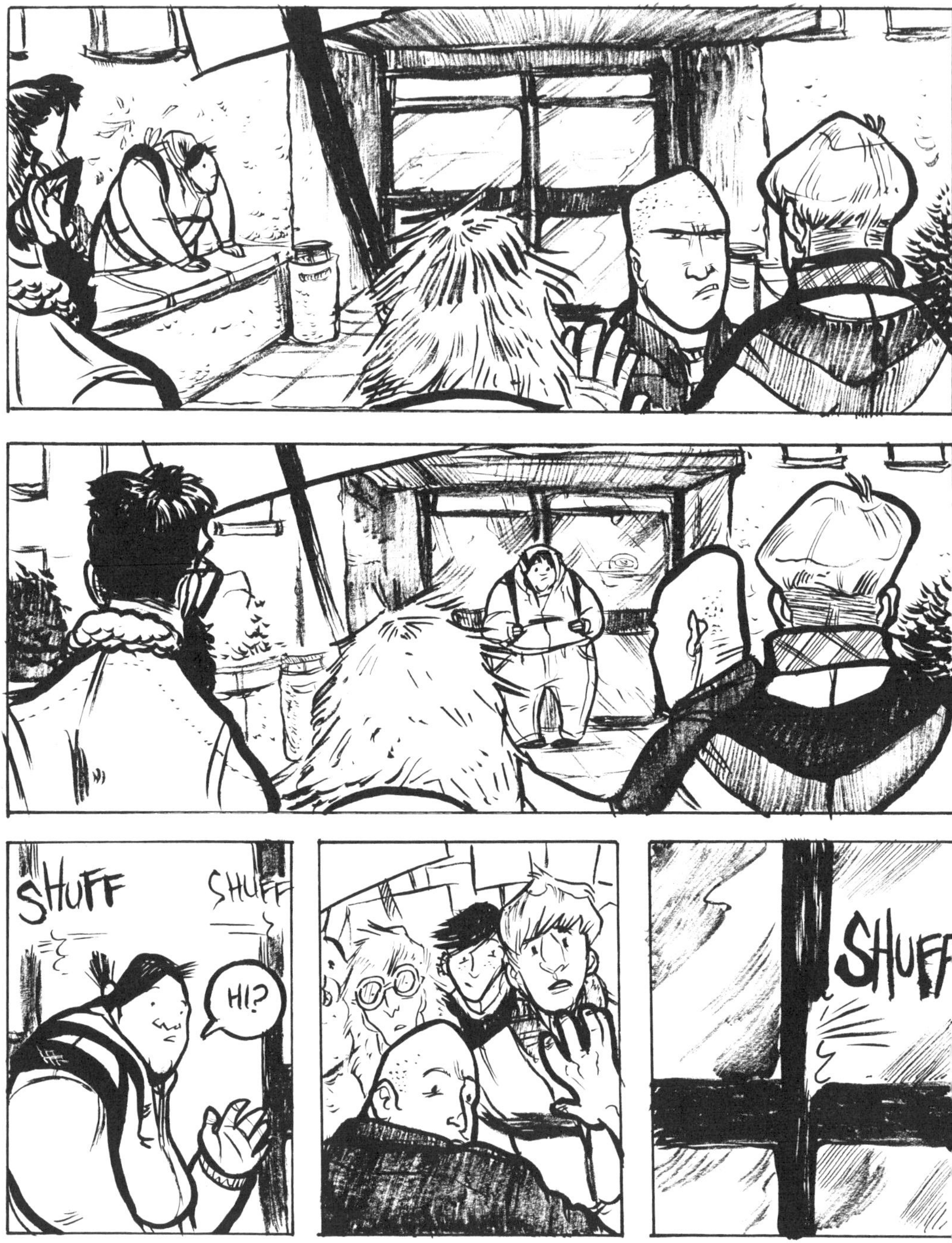
SHUFF
SHUFF
HI?
SHUFF

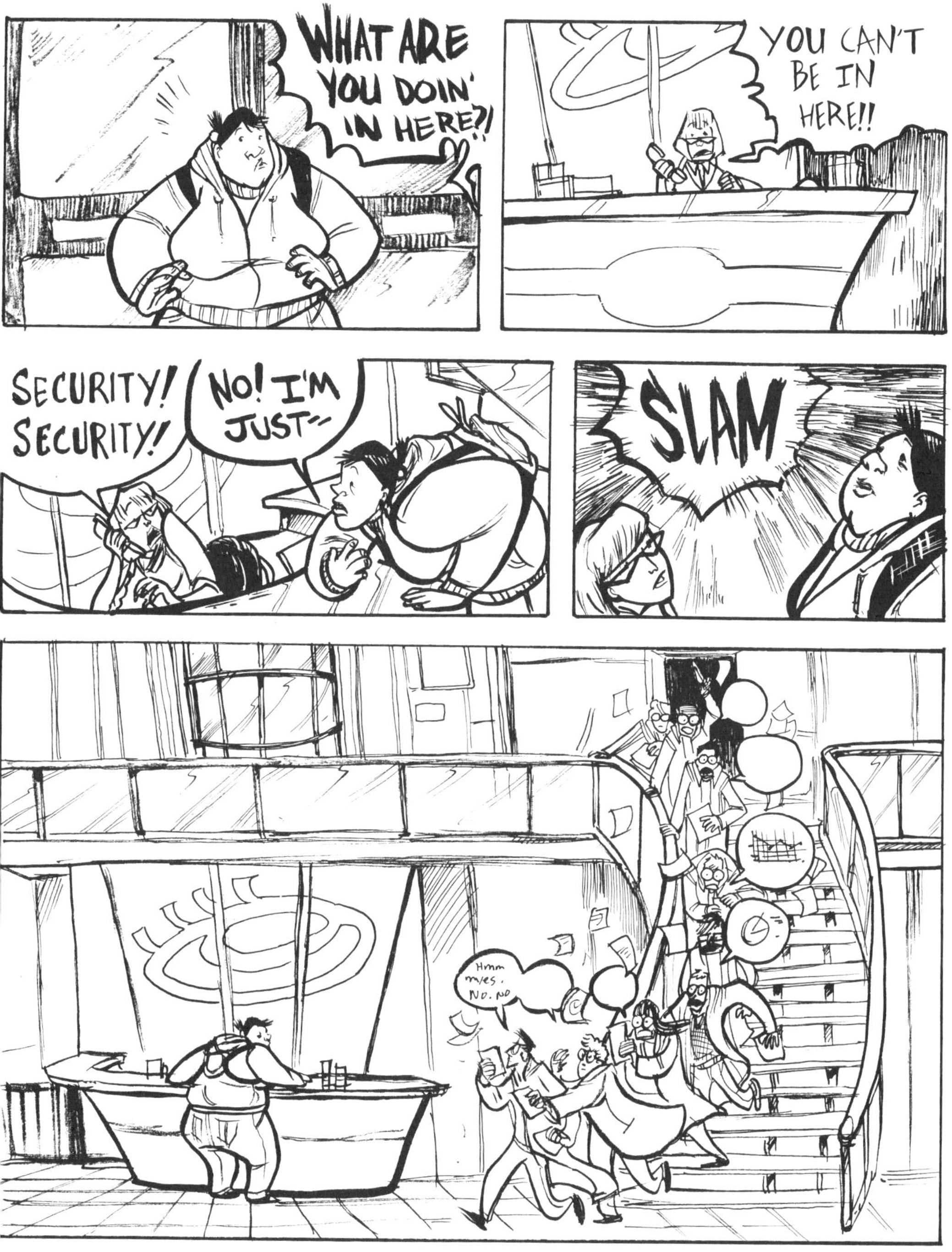
WHAT ARE YOU DOIN' IN HERE?!
YOU CAN'T BE IN HERE!!
SECURITY! SECURITY!
NO! I'M JUST--
SLAM
Hmm m/es. No. No

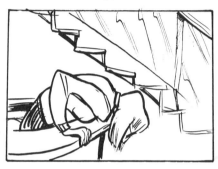

MA'AM?!
WHERE DID
SHE--?!

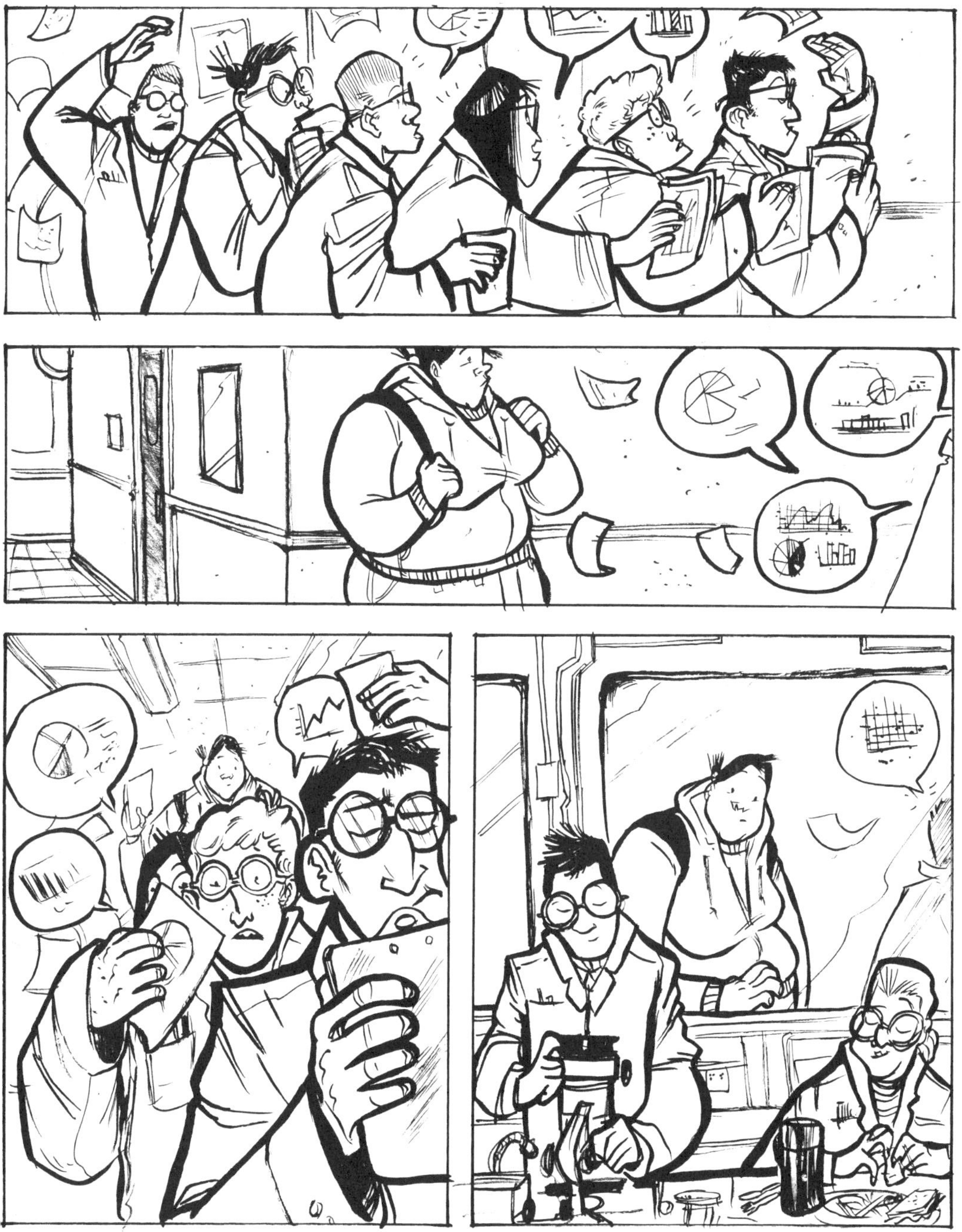

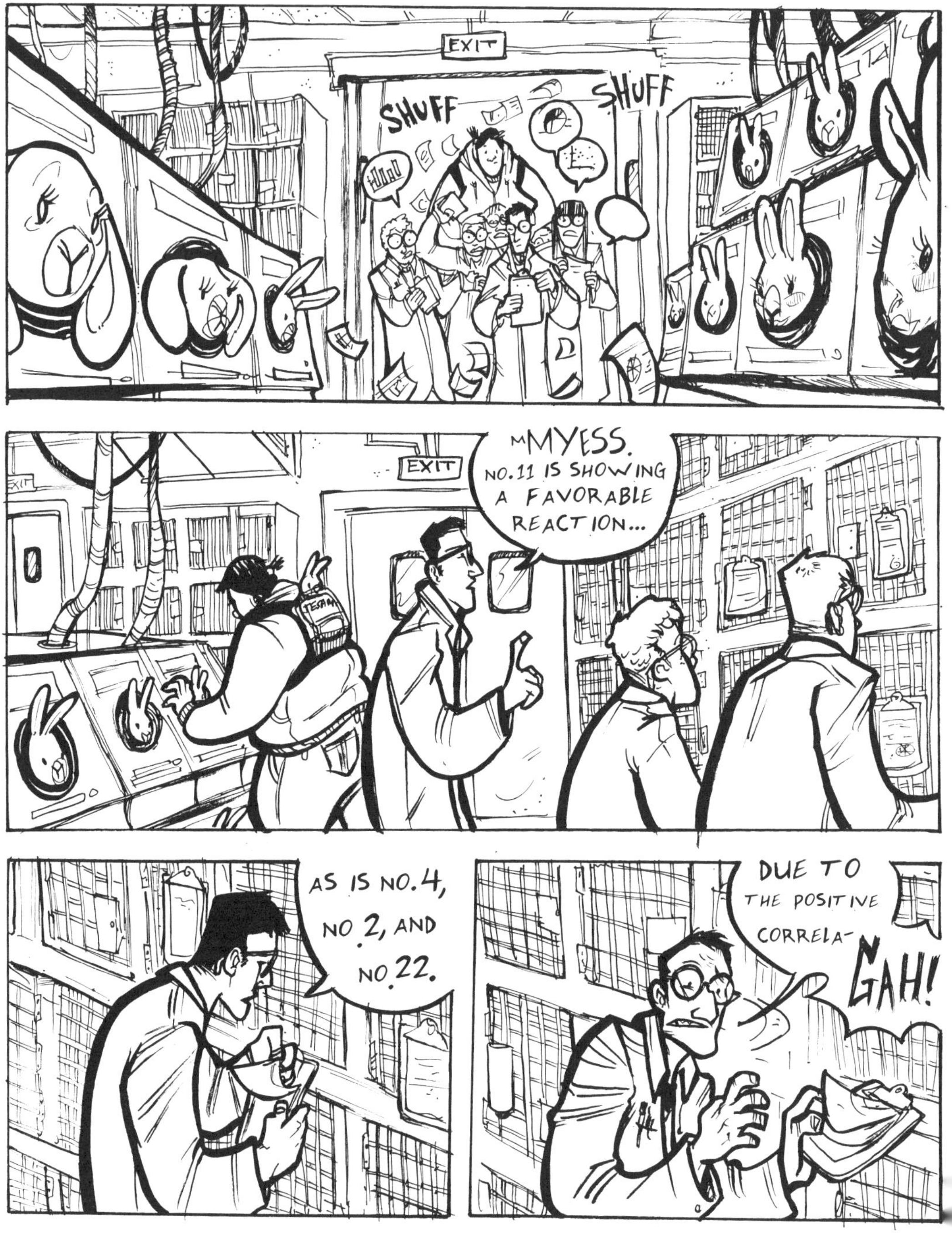
EXIT
SHUFF
SHUFF
EXIT
mMYESS. NO. 11 IS SHOWING A FAVORABLE REACTION...
AS IS NO. 4, NO. 2, AND NO. 22.
DUE TO THE POSITIVE CORRELA-
GAH!

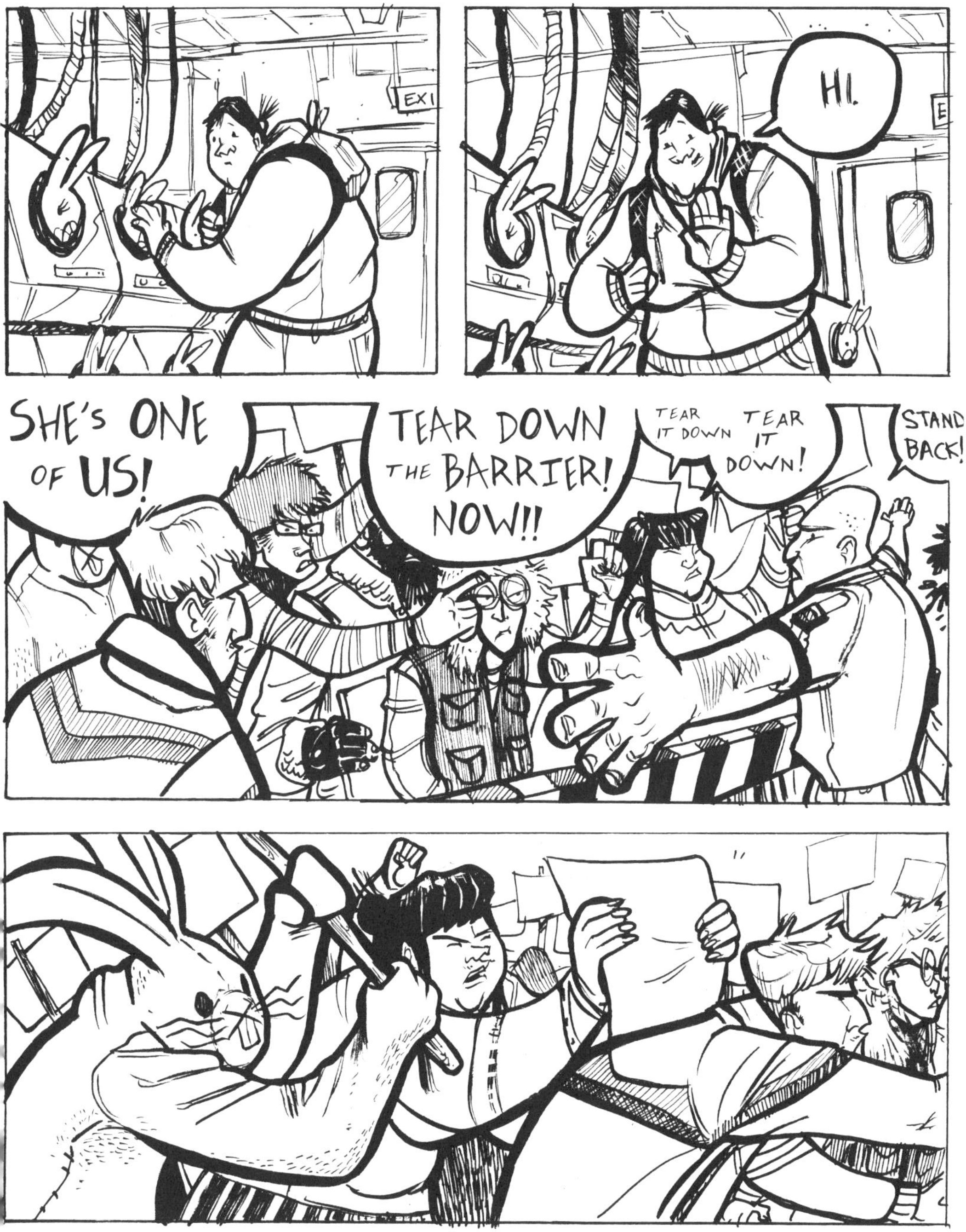
EXI
HI.
E
SHE'S ONE OF US!
TEAR DOWN THE BARRIER! NOW!!
TEAR IT DOWN
TEAR IT DOWN!
STAND BACK!

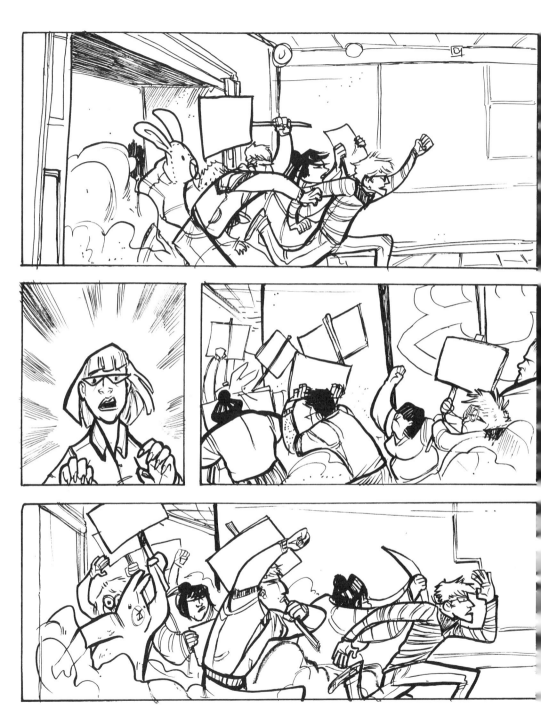

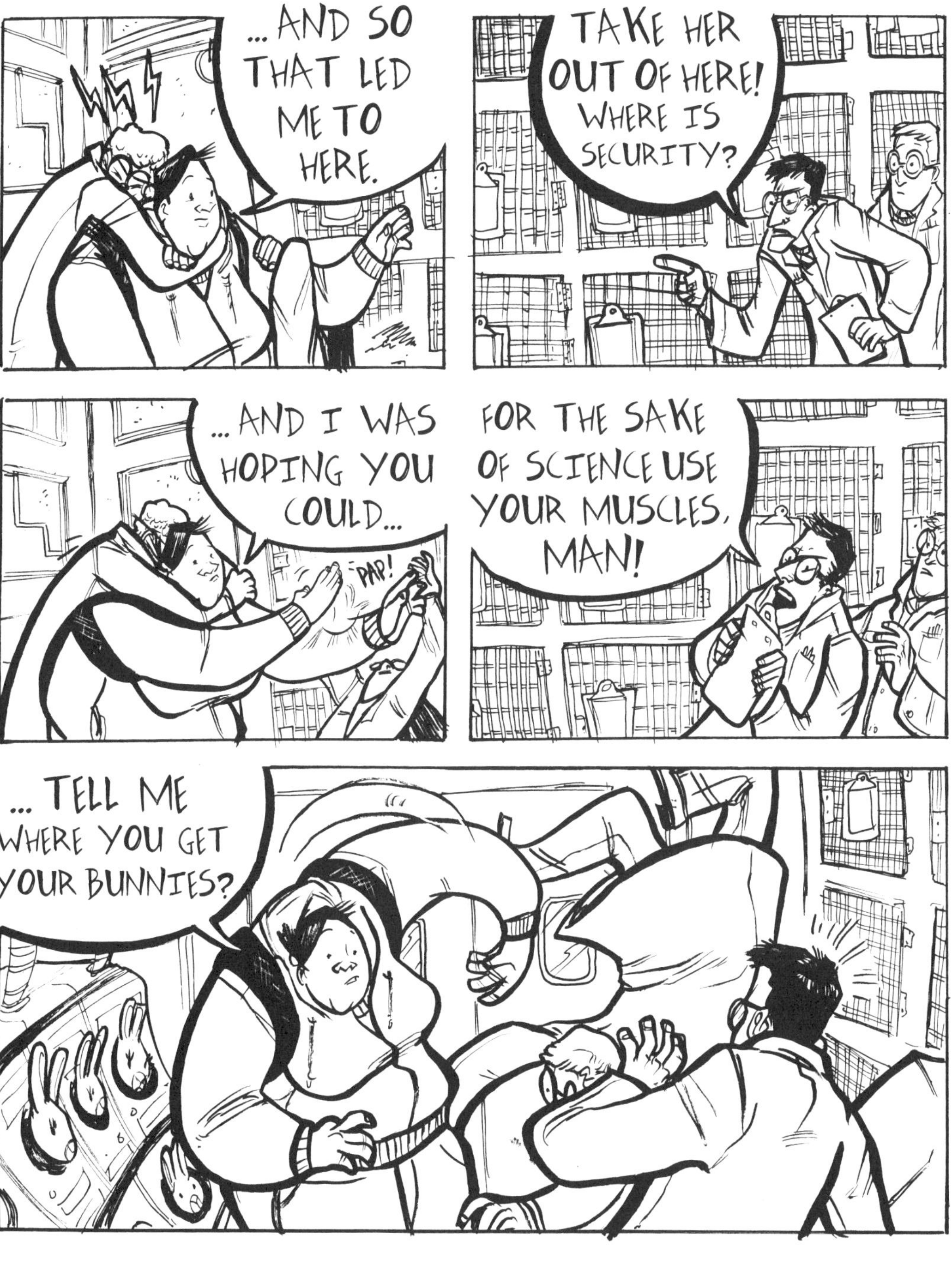
... AND SO THAT LED ME TO HERE.
TAKE HER OUT OF HERE! WHERE IS SECURITY?
... AND I WAS HOPING YOU COULD...
PAP!
FOR THE SAKE OF SCIENCE USE YOUR MUSCLES, MAN!
... TELL ME WHERE YOU GET YOUR BUNNIES?

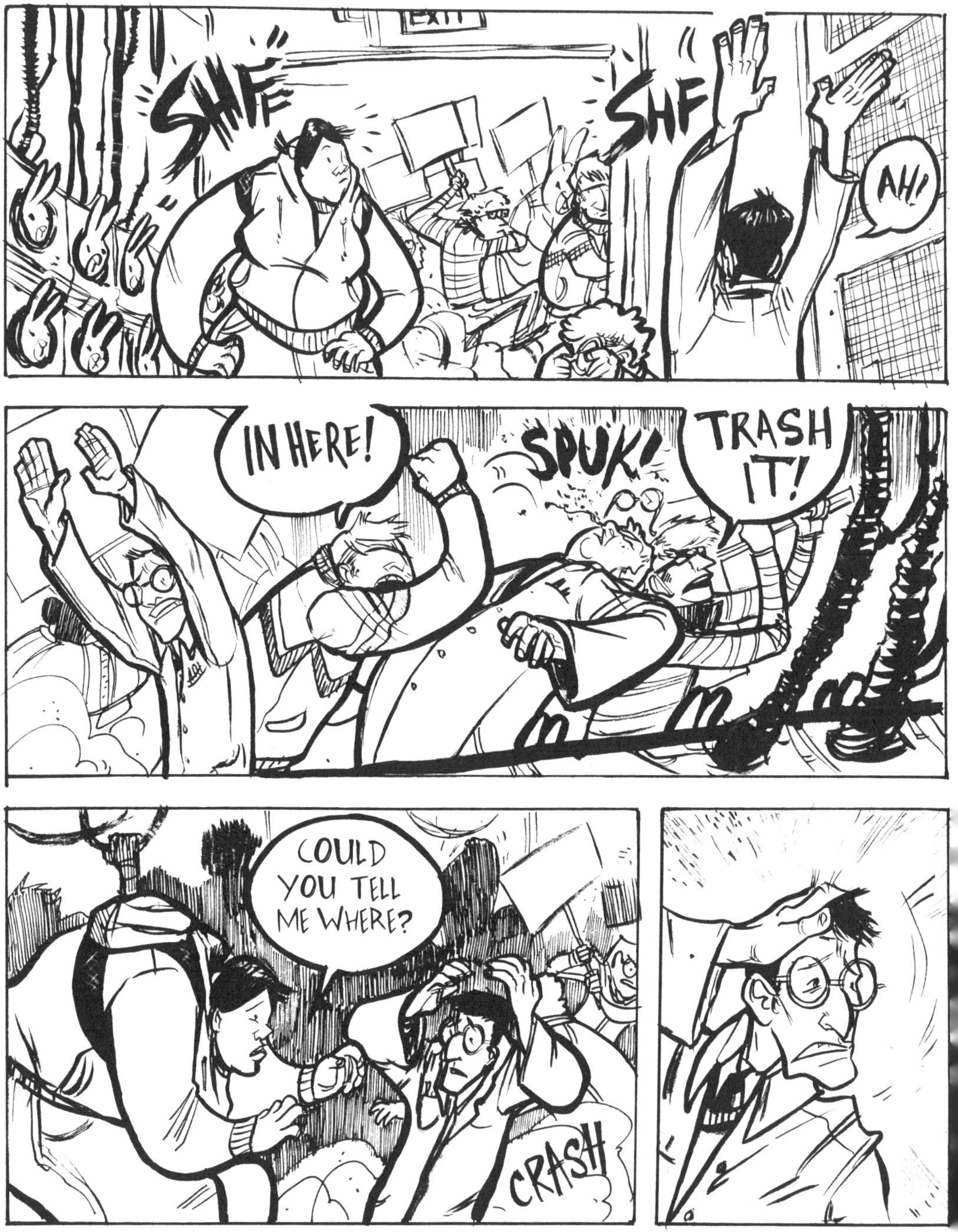
EXIT
SHF
SHF
AH!
IN HERE!
SPUK!
TRASH IT!
COULD YOU TELL ME WHERE?
CRASH

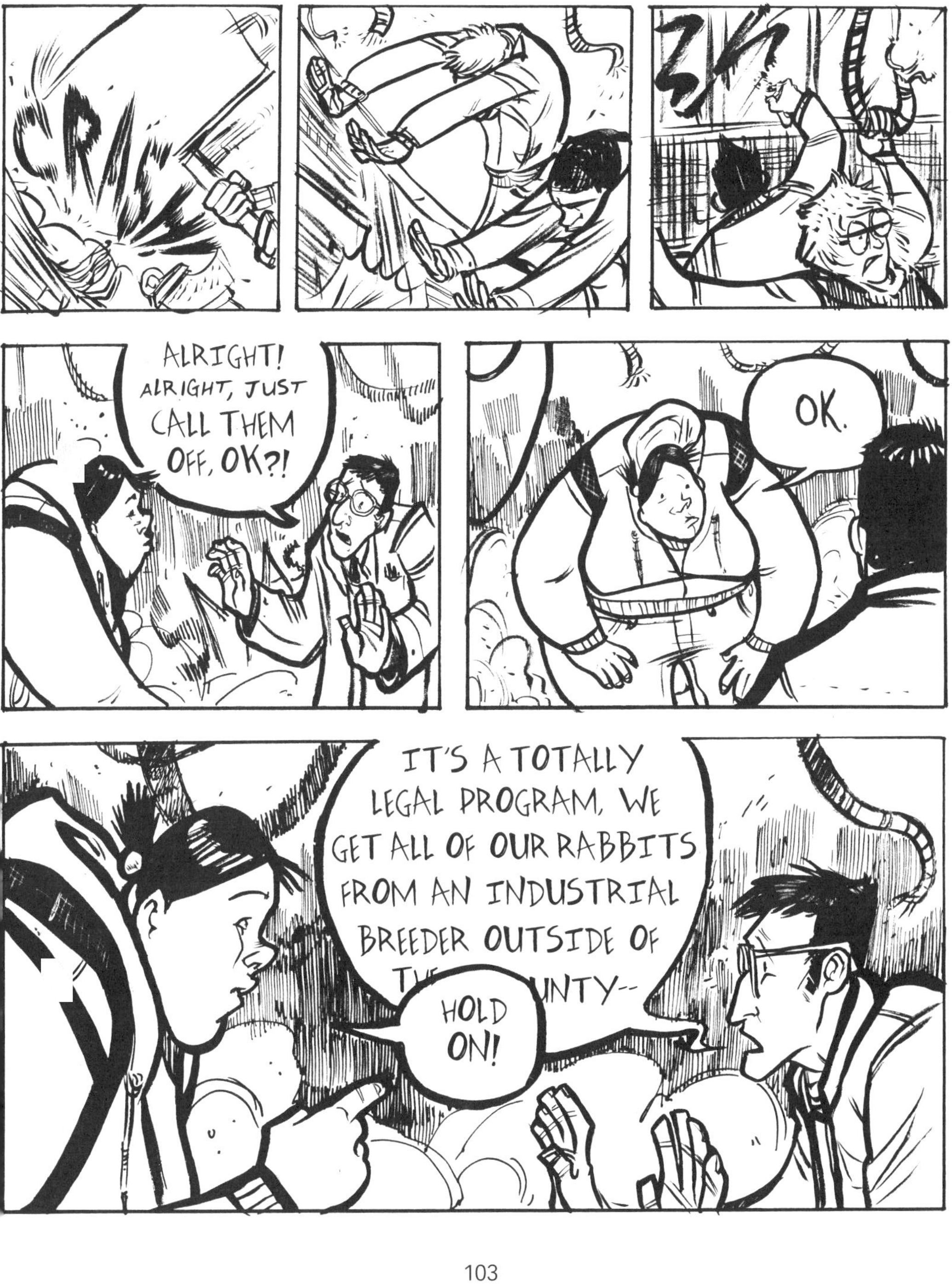
ALRIGHT! ALRIGHT, JUST CALL THEM OFF, OK?!
OK.
IT'S A TOTALLY LEGAL PROGRAM, WE GET ALL OF OUR RABBITS FROM AN INDUSTRIAL BREEDER OUTSIDE OF
HOLD ON!

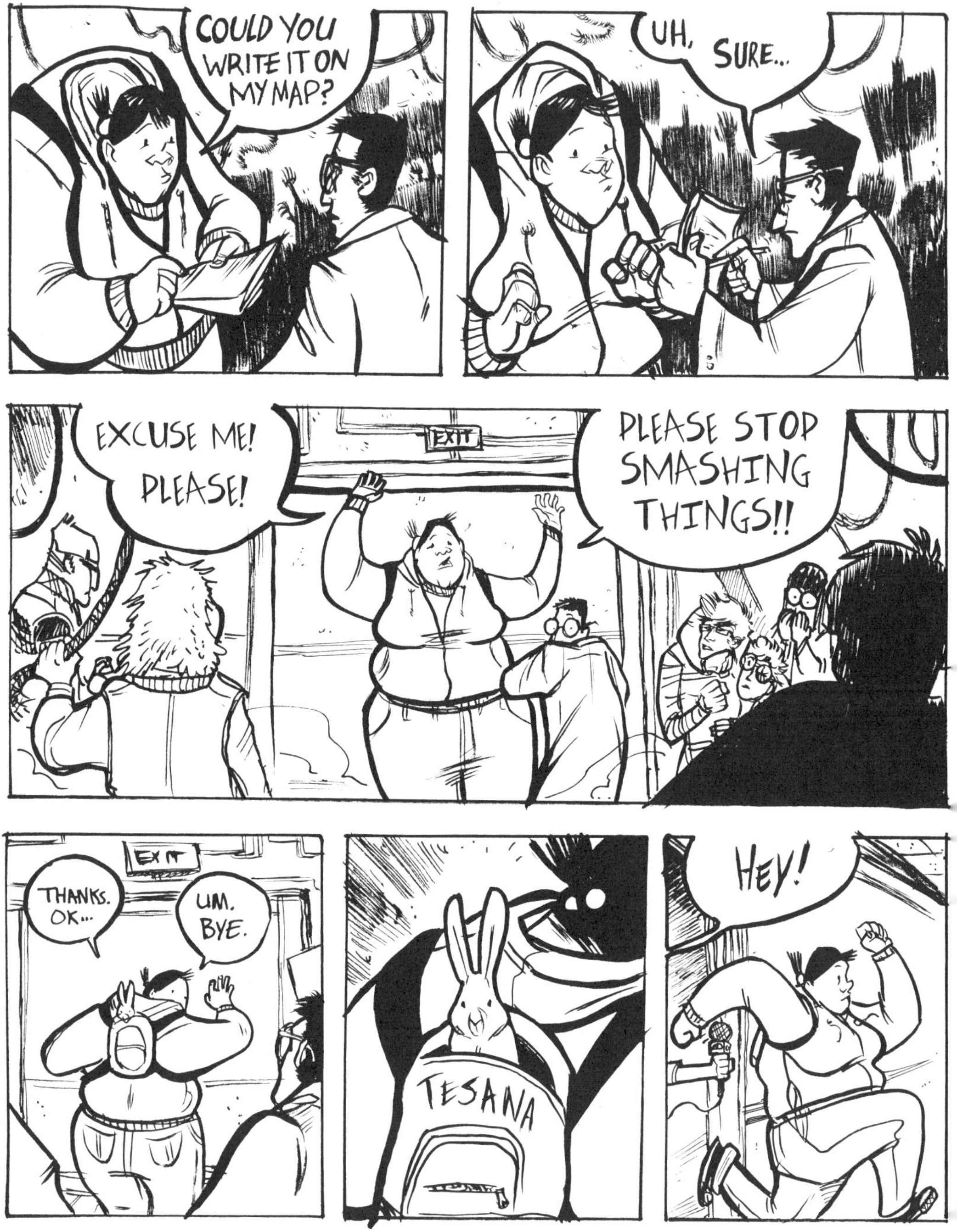
COULD YOU WRITE IT ON MY MAP?
UH, SURE...
EXCUSE ME! PLEASE!
EXIT
PLEASE STOP SMASHING THINGS!!
EXIT
THANKS. OK...
UM. BYE.
TESANA
HEY!

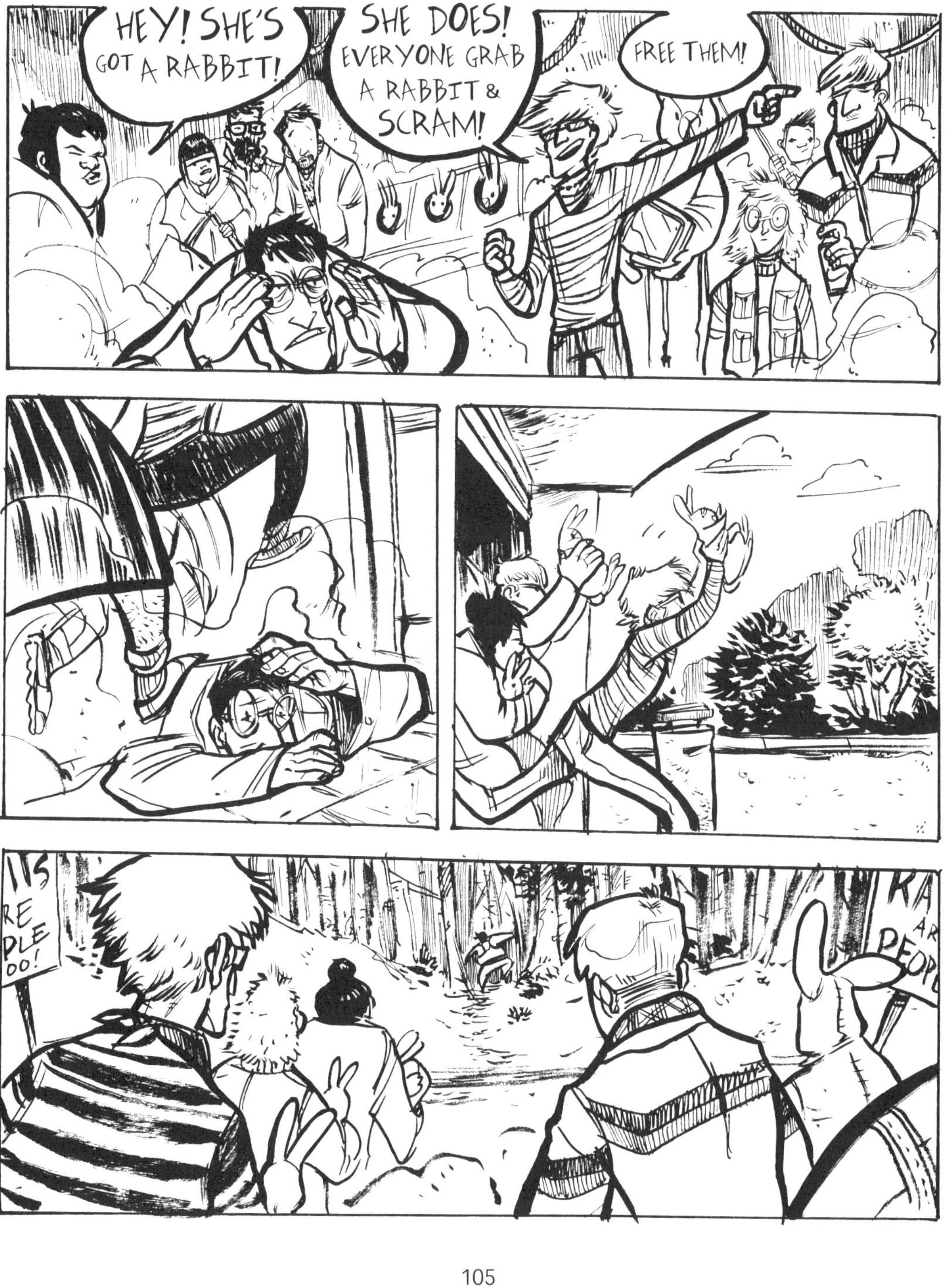
HEY! SHE'S GOT A RABBIT!
SHE DOES! EVERYONE GRAB A RABBIT & SCRAM!
FREE THEM!

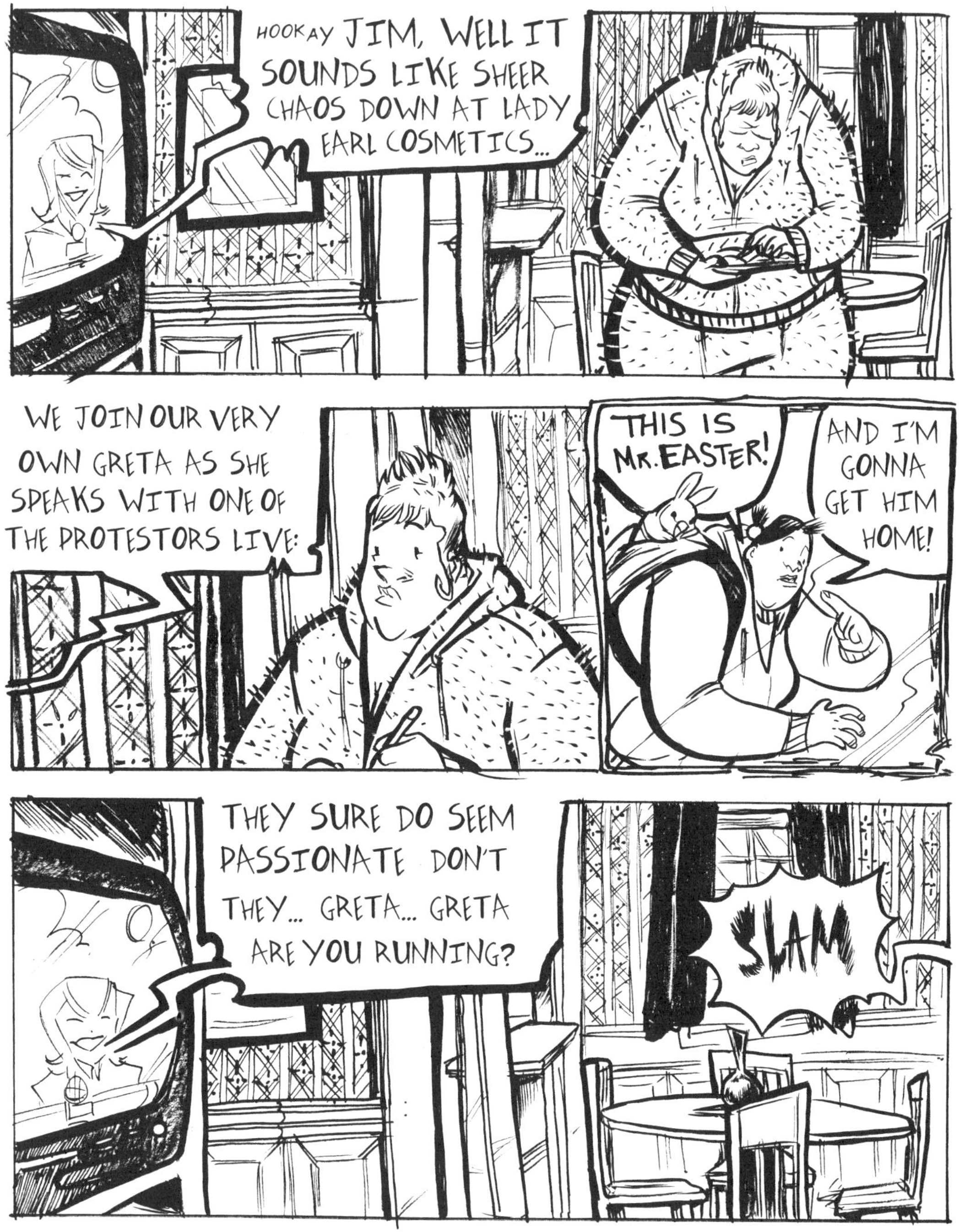
HOOKAY JIM, WELL IT SOUNDS LIKE SHEER CHAOS DOWN AT LADY EARL COSMETICS...
WE JOIN OUR VERY OWN GRETA AS SHE SPEAKS WITH ONE OF THE PROTESTORS LIVE:
THIS IS MR. EASTER!
AND I'M GONNA GET HIM HOME!
THEY SURE DO SEEM PASSIONATE DON'T THEY... GRETA... GRETA ARE YOU RUNNING?
SLAM

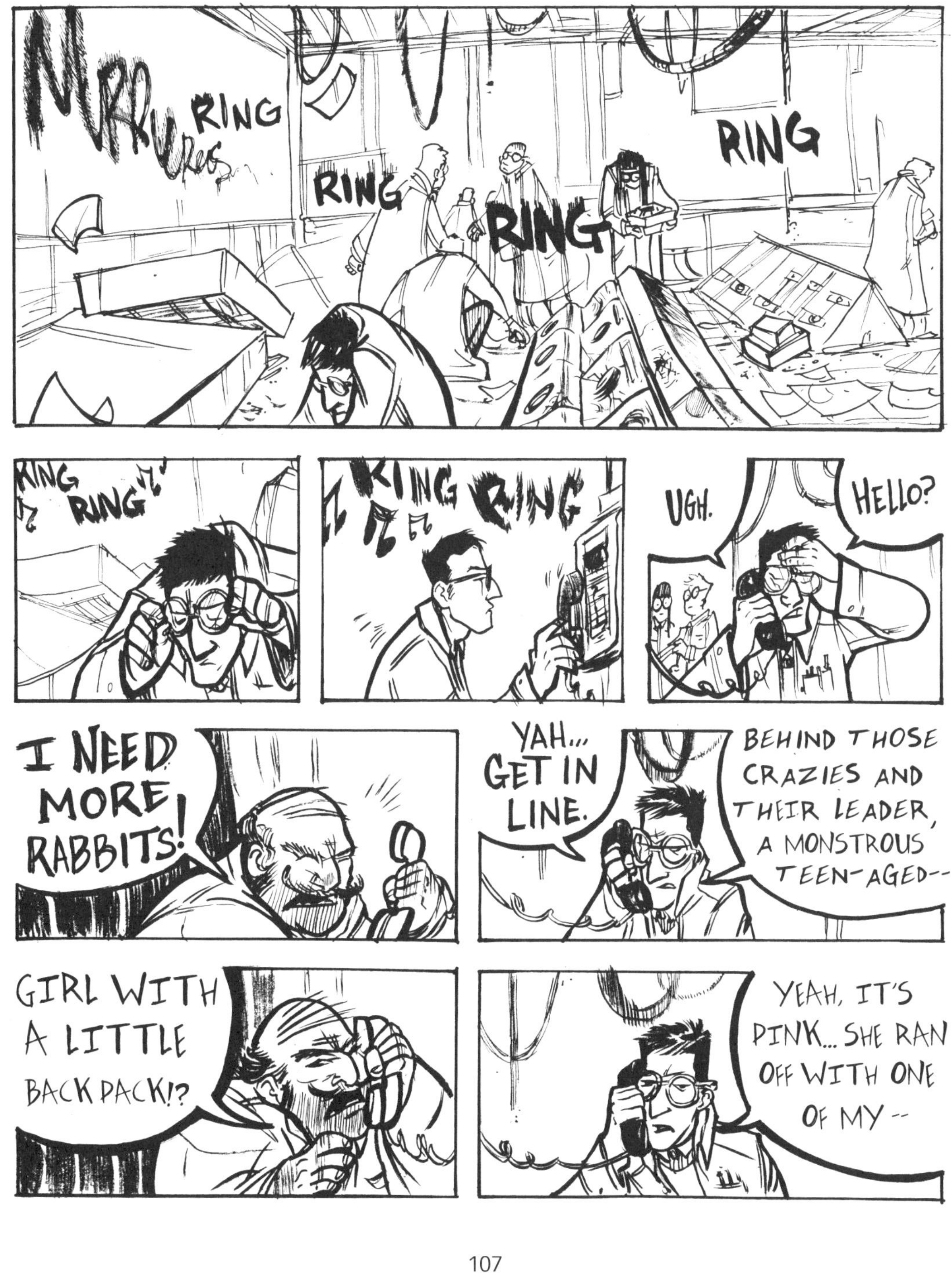
RING
RING
RING
RING
RING
RING
RING
RING
UGH.
HELLO?
I NEED MORE RABBITS!
YAH... GET IN LINE.
BEHIND THOSE CRAZIES AND THEIR LEADER, A MONSTROUS TEEN-AGED--
GIRL WITH A LITTLE BACKPACK!?
YEAH, IT'S PINK... SHE RAN OFF WITH ONE OF MY --

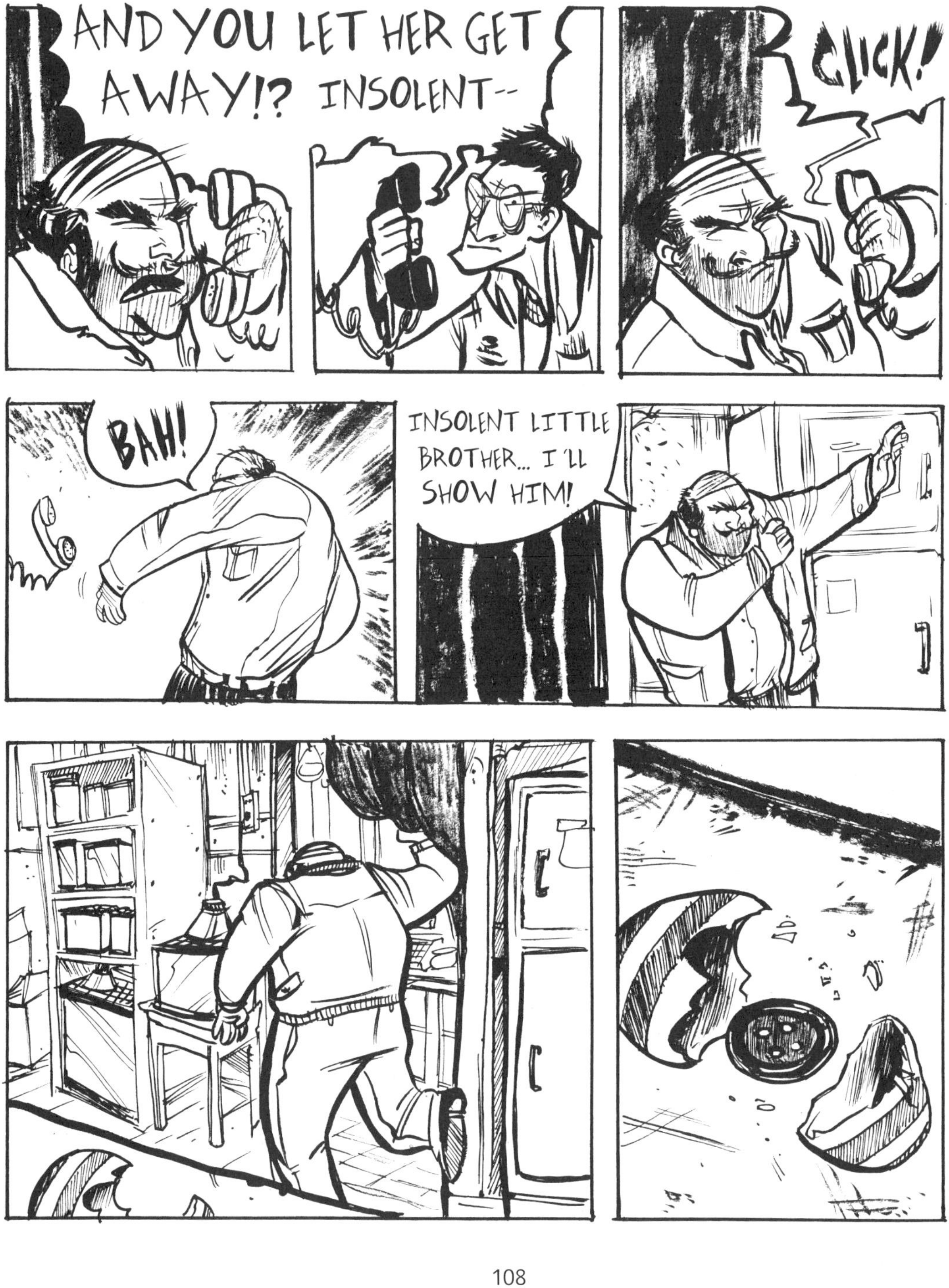
AND YOU LET HER GET AWAY!? INSOLENT--
CLICK!
BAH!
INSOLENT LITTLE BROTHER... I'LL SHOW HIM!

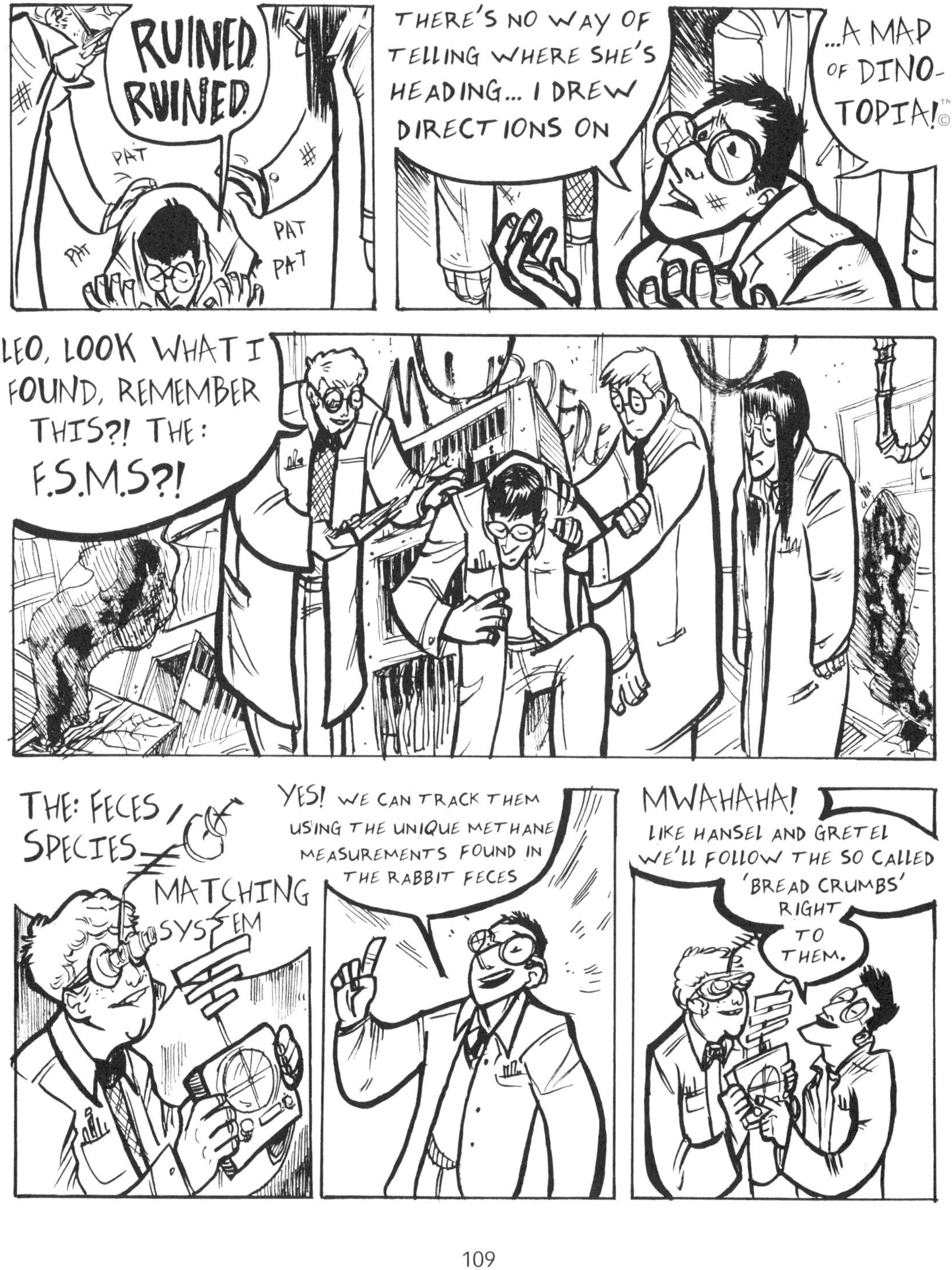
RUINED RUINED.
PAT
PAT
PAT
PAT
THERE'S NO WAY OF TELLING WHERE SHE'S HEADING... I DREW DIRECTIONS ON
...A MAP OF DINO-TOPIA!™©
LEO, LOOK WHAT I FOUND, REMEMBER THIS?! THE: F.S.M.S?!
THE: FECES, SPECIES MATCHING SYSTEM
YES! WE CAN TRACK THEM USING THE UNIQUE METHANE MEASUREMENTS FOUND IN THE RABBIT FECES
MWAHAHA!
LIKE HANSEL AND GRETEL WE'LL FOLLOW THE SO CALLED 'BREAD CRUMBS' RIGHT TO THEM.

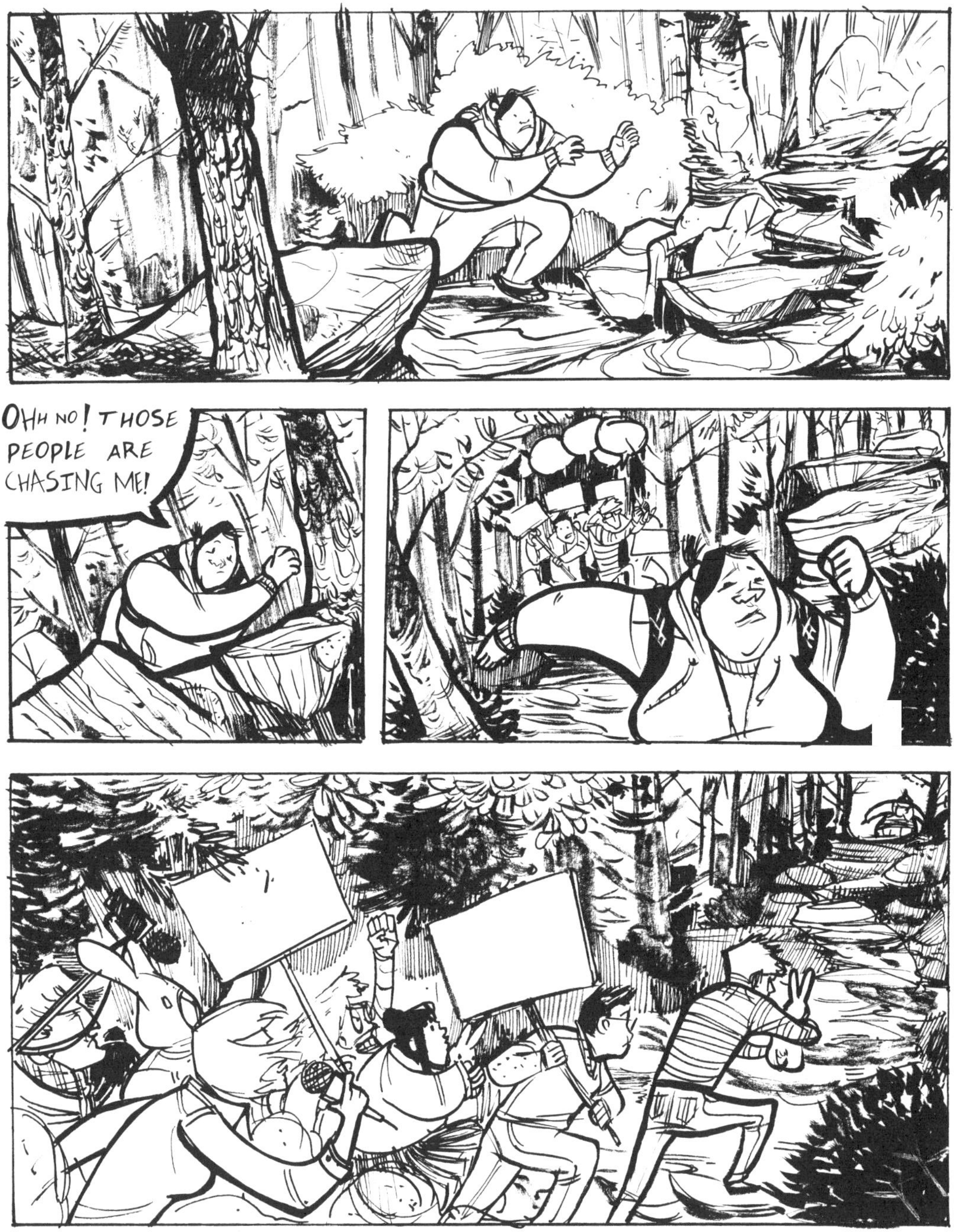
OHH NO! THOSE PEOPLE ARE CHASING ME!

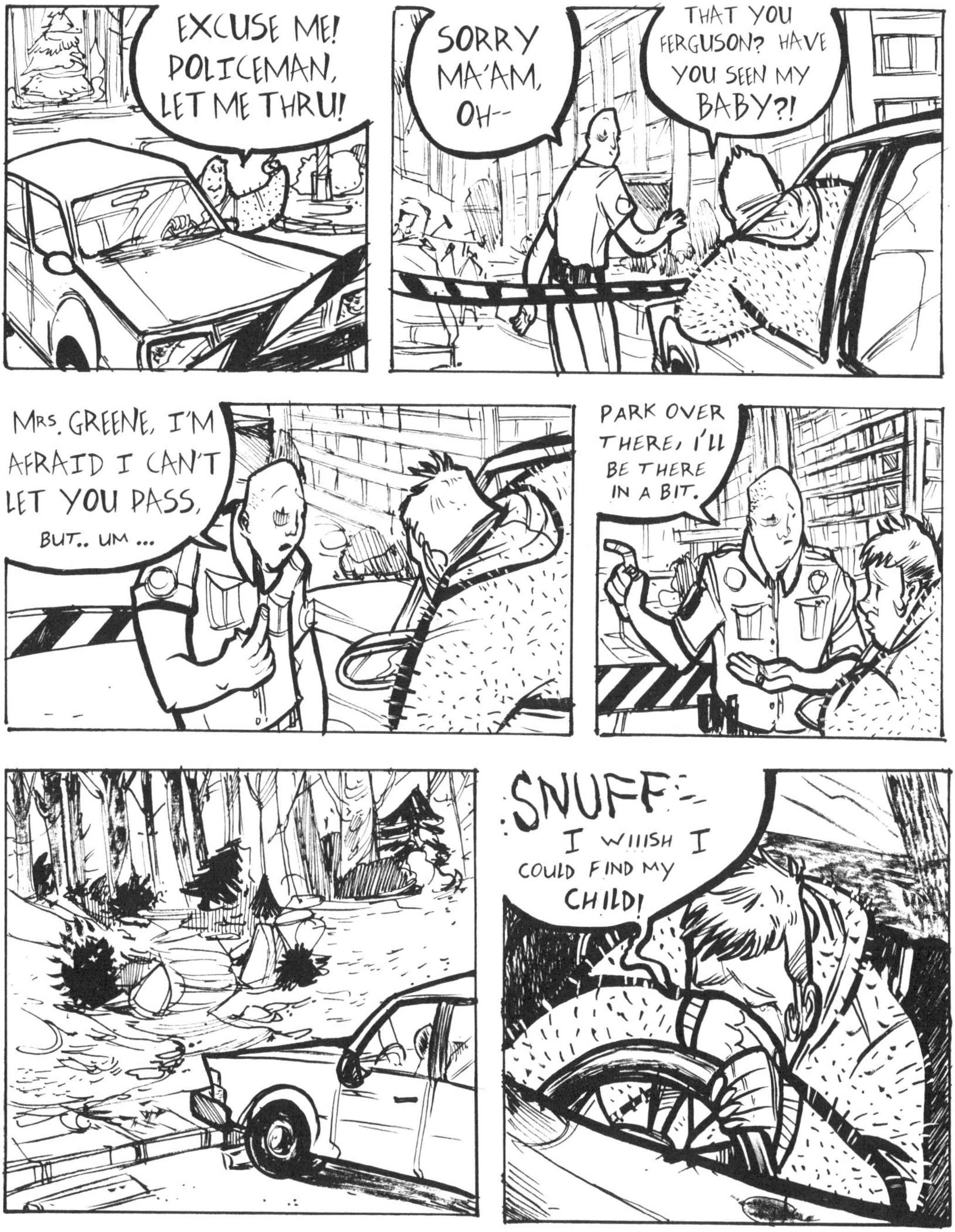
EXCUSE ME! POLICEMAN, LET ME THRU!
SORRY MA'AM, OH--
THAT YOU FERGUSON? HAVE YOU SEEN MY BABY?!
MRS. GREENE, I'M AFRAID I CAN'T LET YOU PASS, BUT.. UM ...
PARK OVER THERE, I'LL BE THERE IN A BIT.
SNUFF
I WIIISH I COULD FIND MY CHILD!

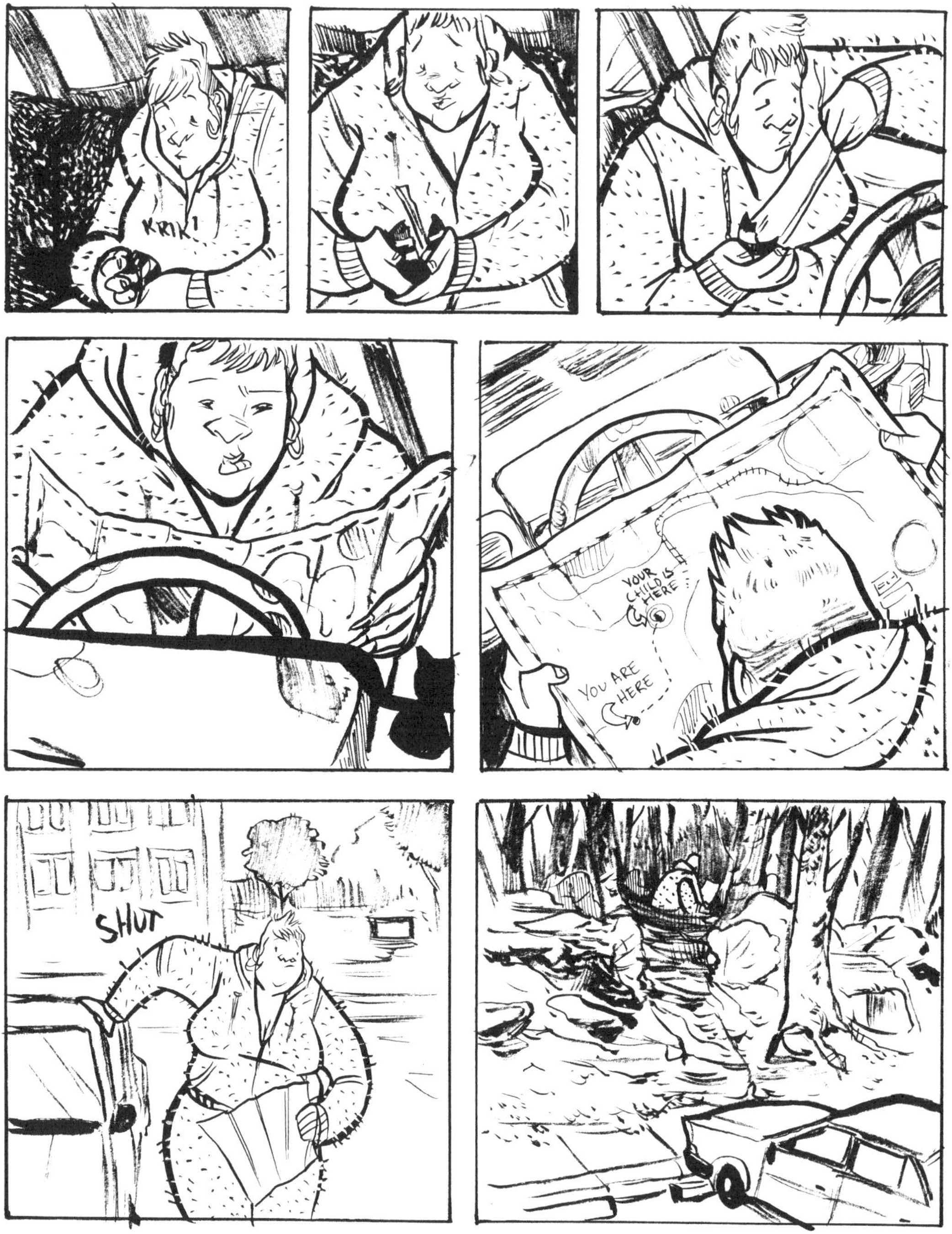
KRIK!
YOUR CHILD IS HERE
YOU ARE HERE
SHUT

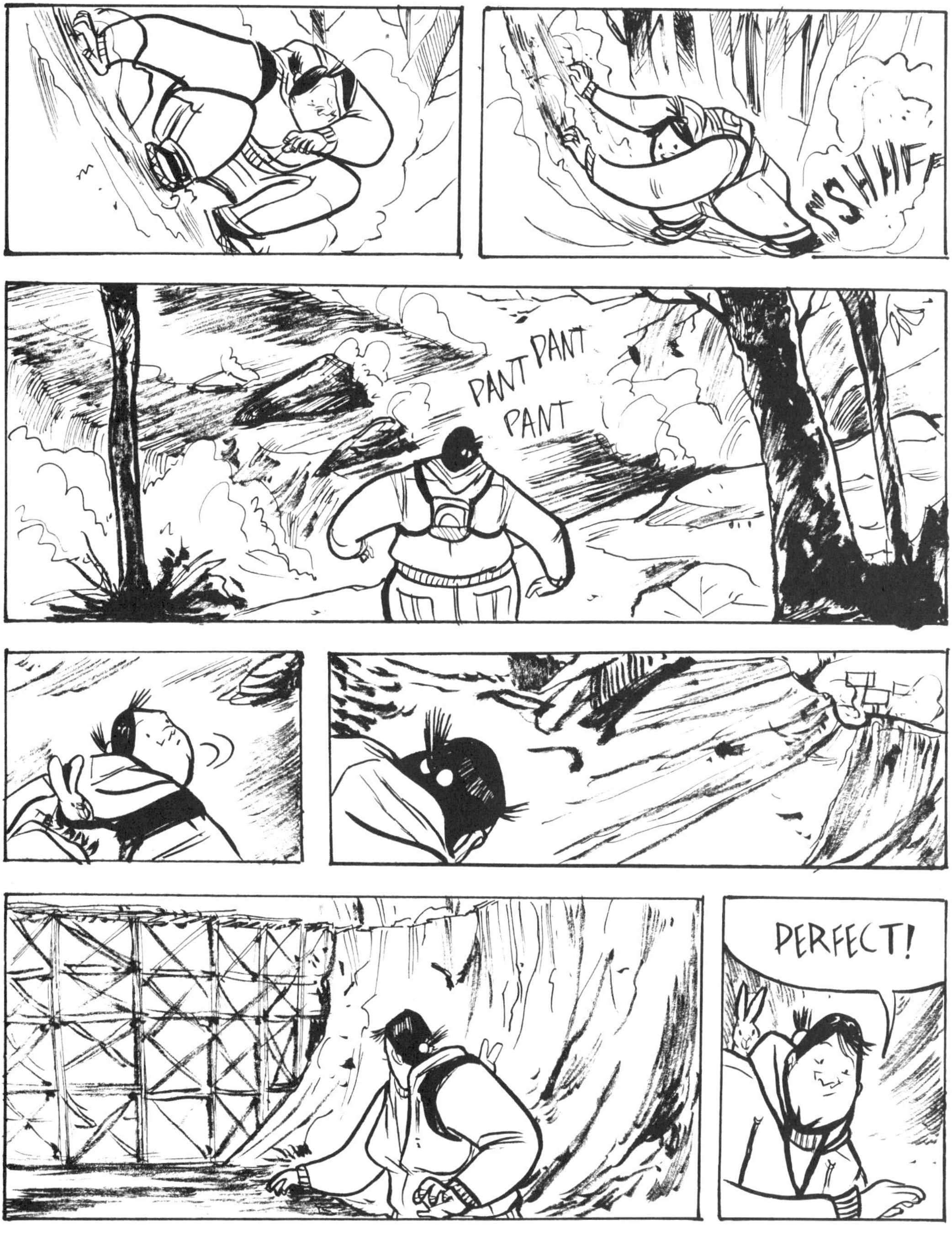
SHHFF
PANT PANT
PANT
PERFECT!

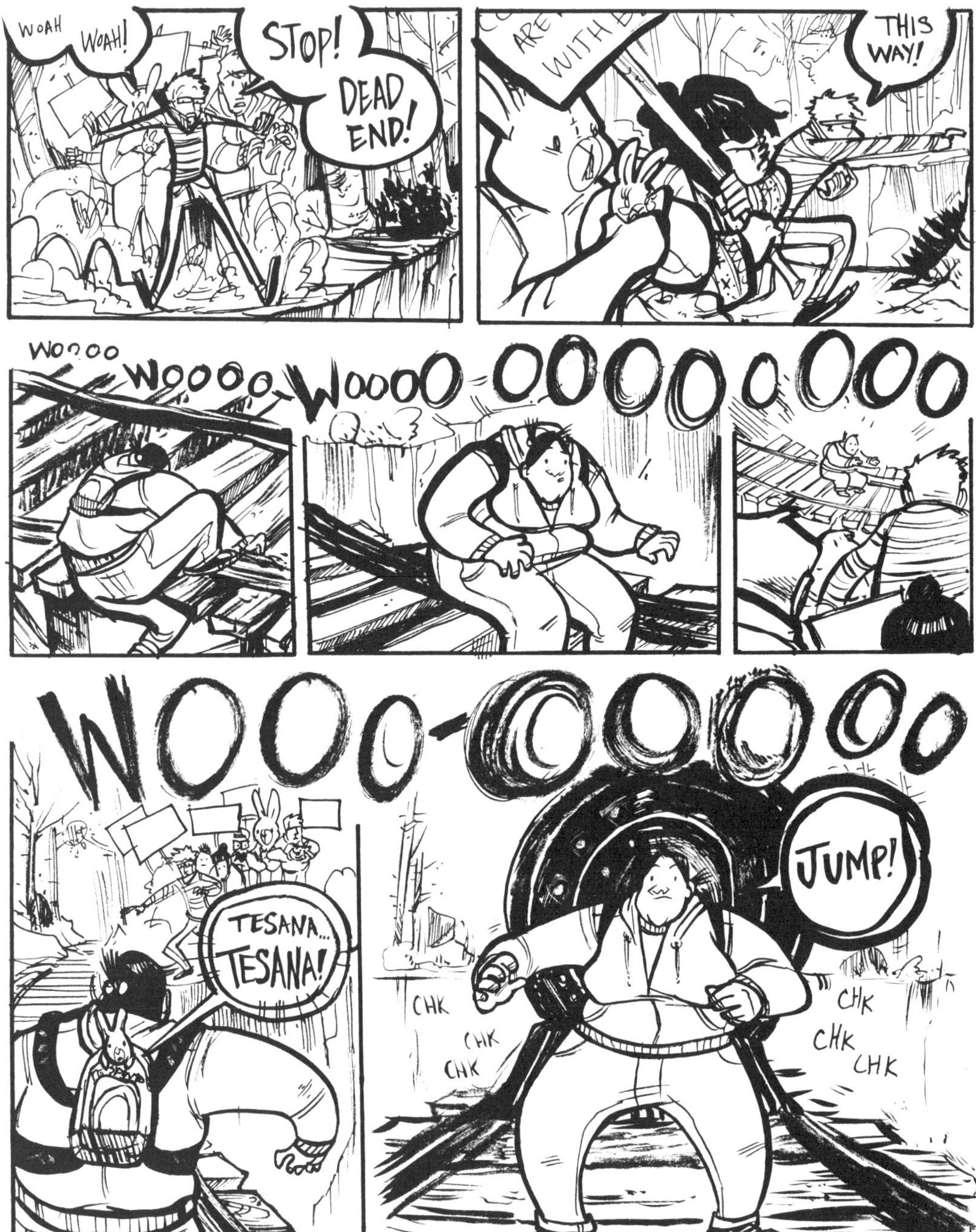
WOAH
WOAH!
STOP!
DEAD END!
THIS WAY!
WOOOO
WOOOO-WOOOO-OOOOOOOOO
WOOO-OOOOOO
TESANA... TESANA!
JUMP!
CHK
CHK
CHK
CHK
CHK
CHK

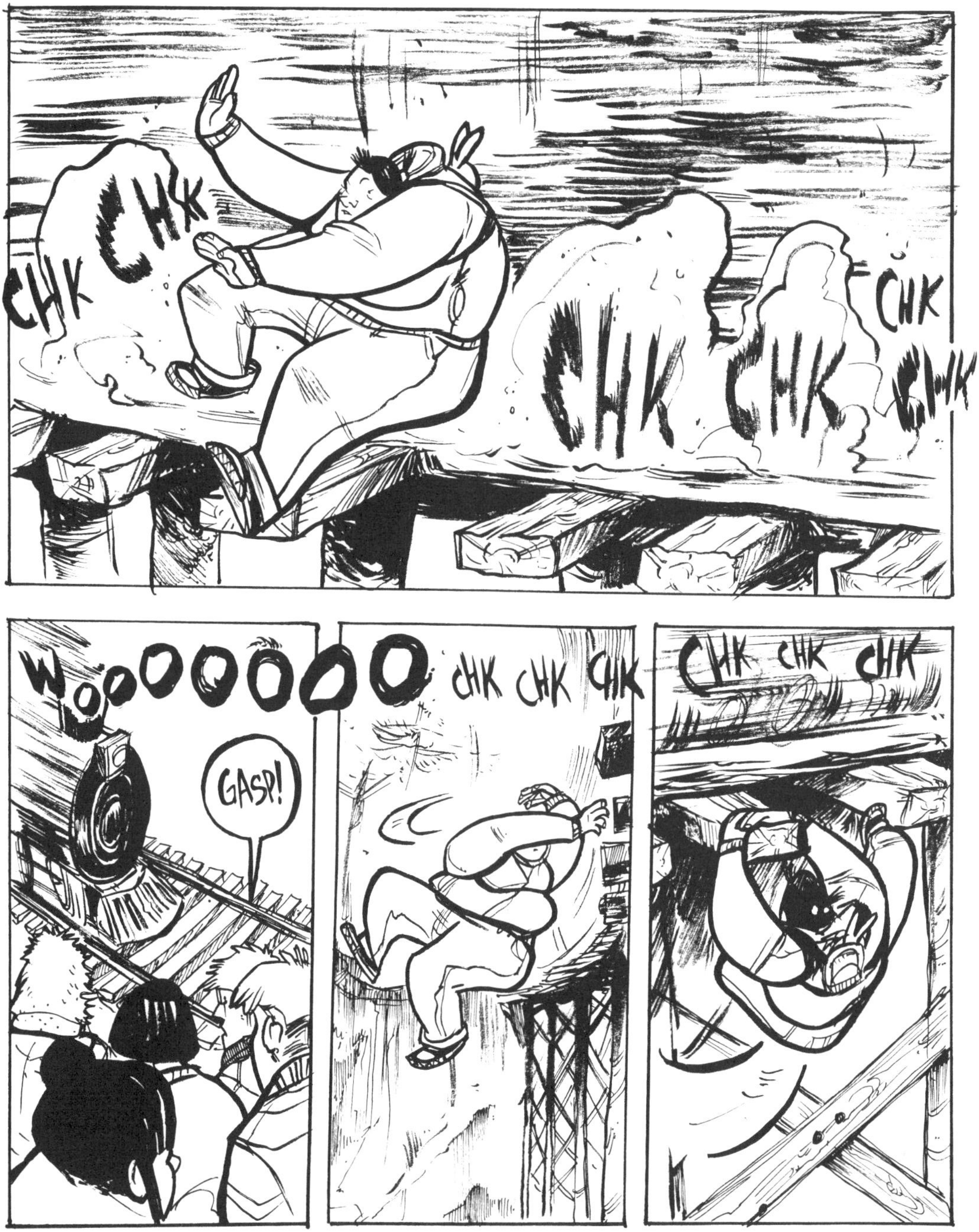
CHK CHK CHK
CHK CHK CHK CHK
WOOOOOOOO
GASP!
CHK CHK CHK
CHK CHK CHK

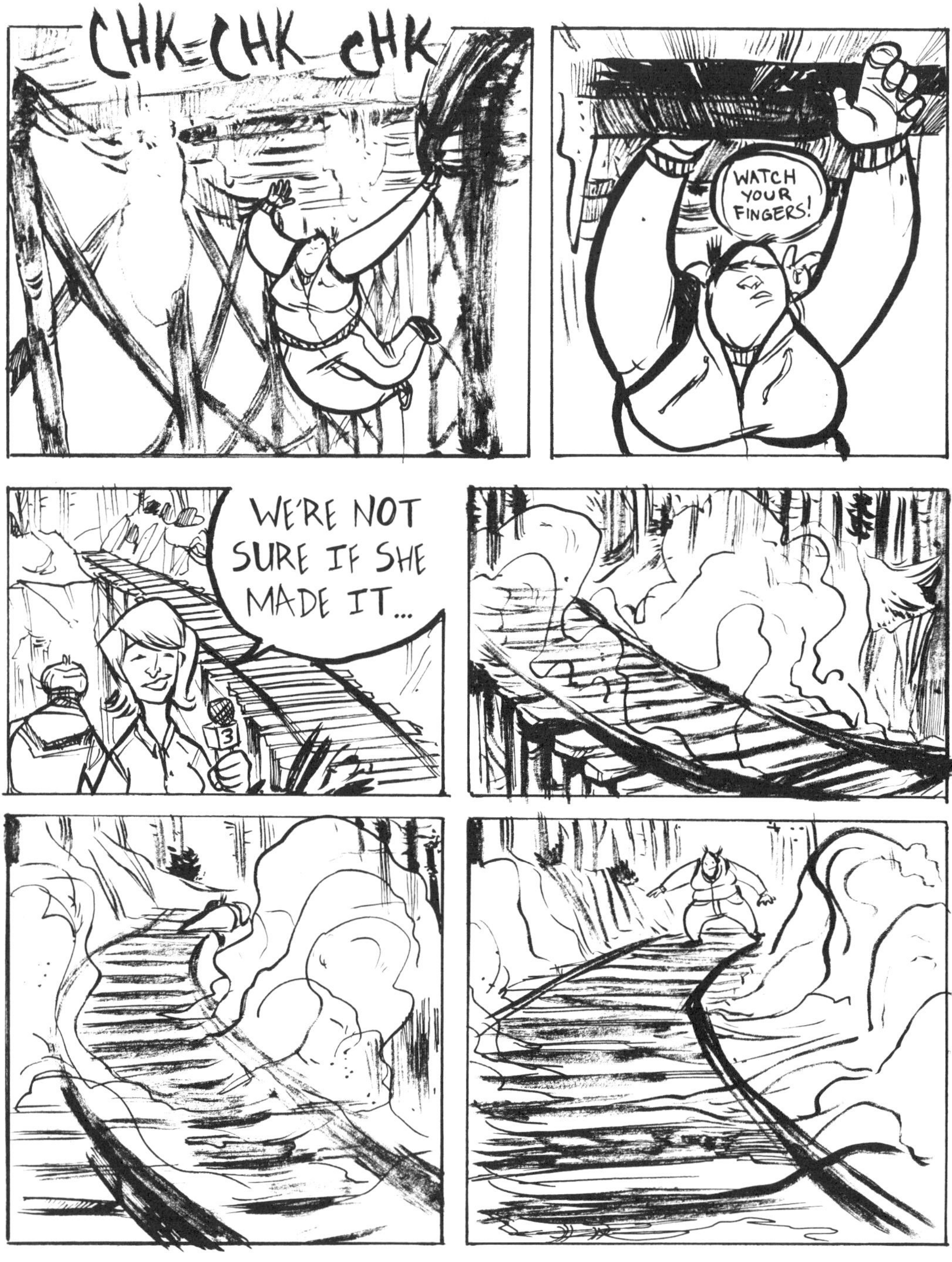
CHK CHK CHK
WATCH YOUR FINGERS!
WE'RE NOT SURE IF SHE MADE IT...

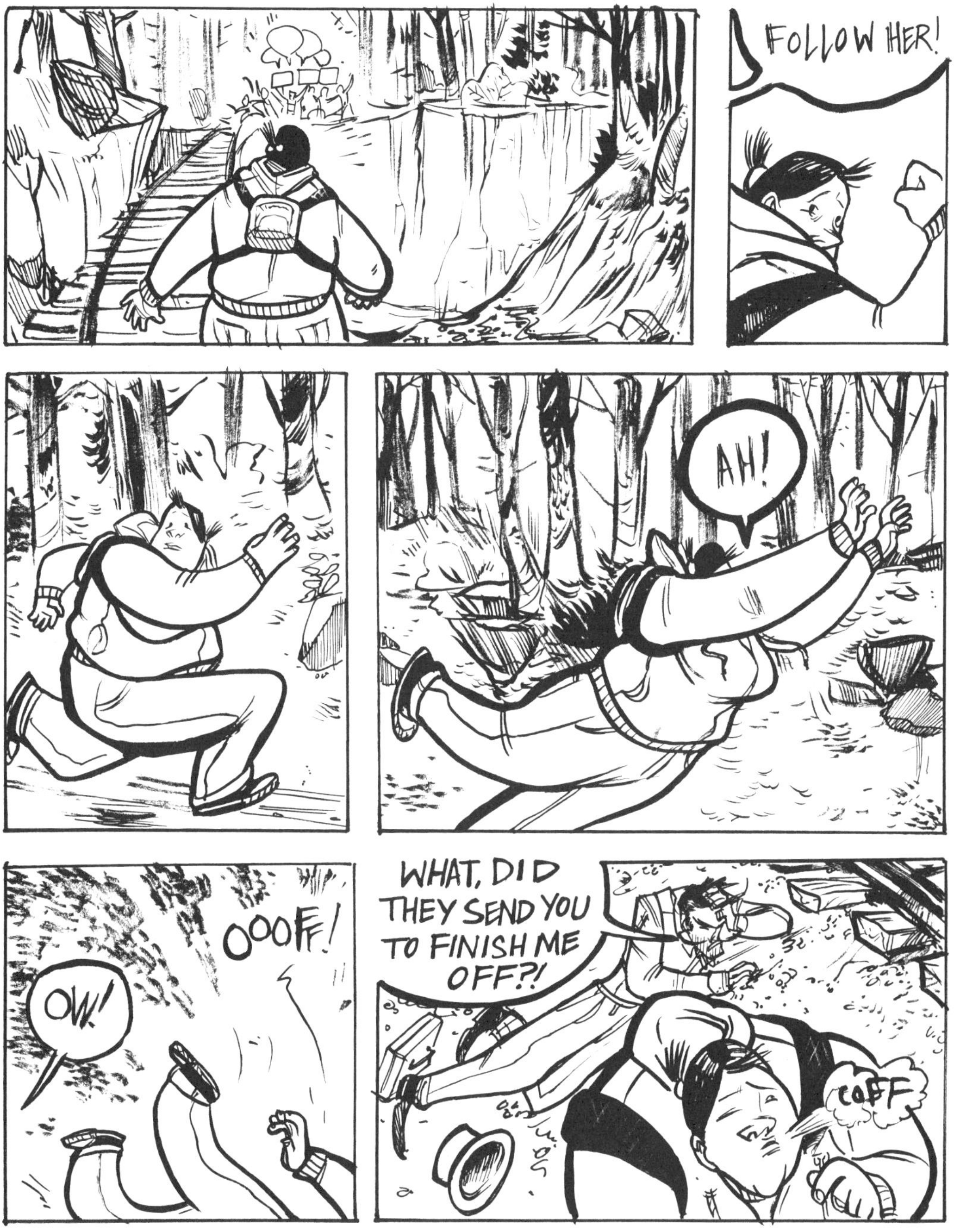
FOLLOW HER!
AH!
OOOFF!
OW!
WHAT, DID THEY SEND YOU TO FINISH ME OFF?!
COFF

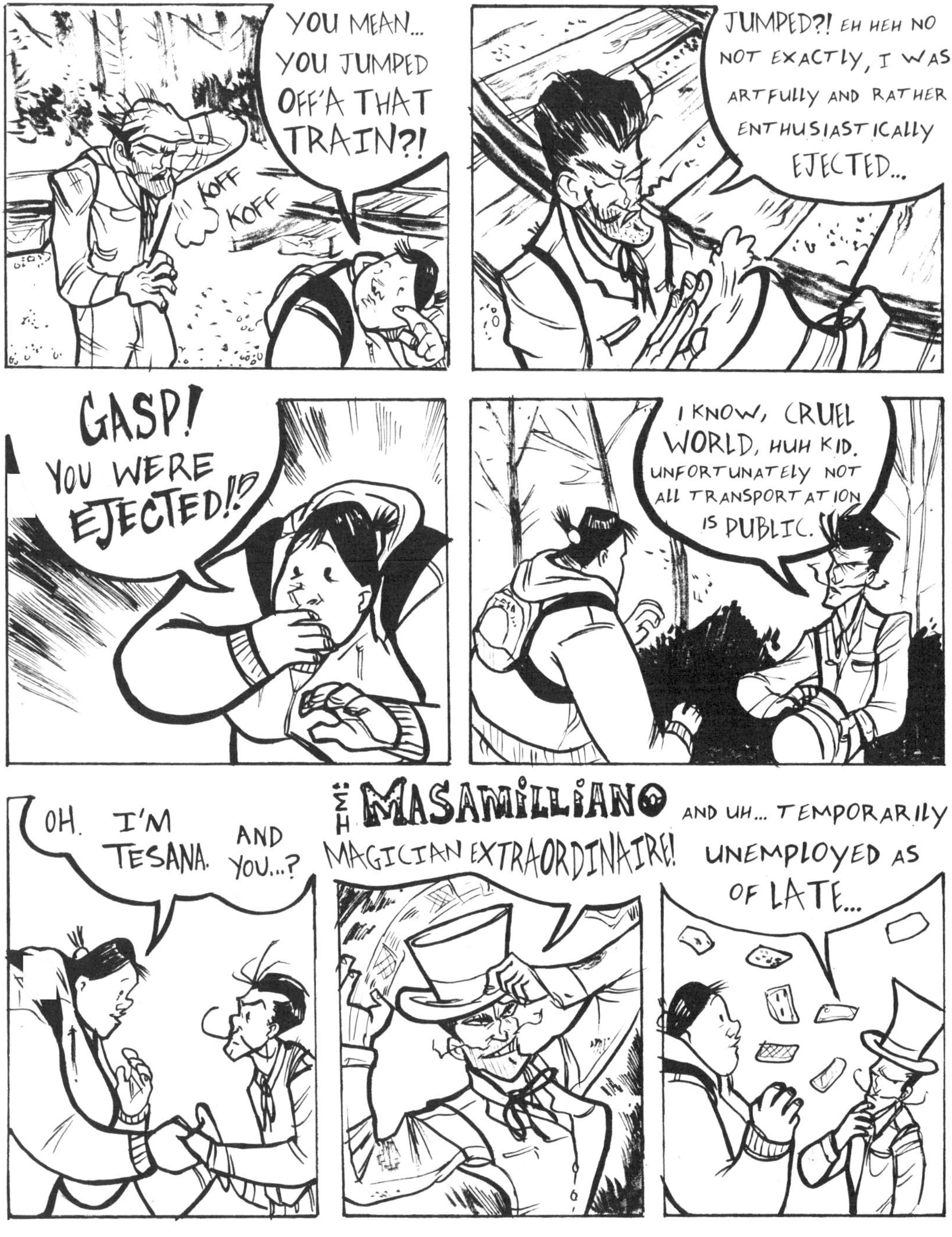
YOU MEAN... YOU JUMPED OFF'A THAT TRAIN?!
KOFF KOFF
JUMPED?! EH HEH NO NOT EXACTLY, I WAS ARTFULLY AND RATHER ENTHUSIASTICALLY EJECTED...
GASP! YOU WERE EJECTED!?
I KNOW, CRUEL WORLD, HUH KID. UNFORTUNATELY NOT ALL TRANSPORTATION IS PUBLIC.
OH. I'M TESANA. AND YOU...?
THE MASAMILLIANO MAGICIAN EXTRAORDINAIRE!
AND UH... TEMPORARILY UNEMPLOYED AS OF LATE...

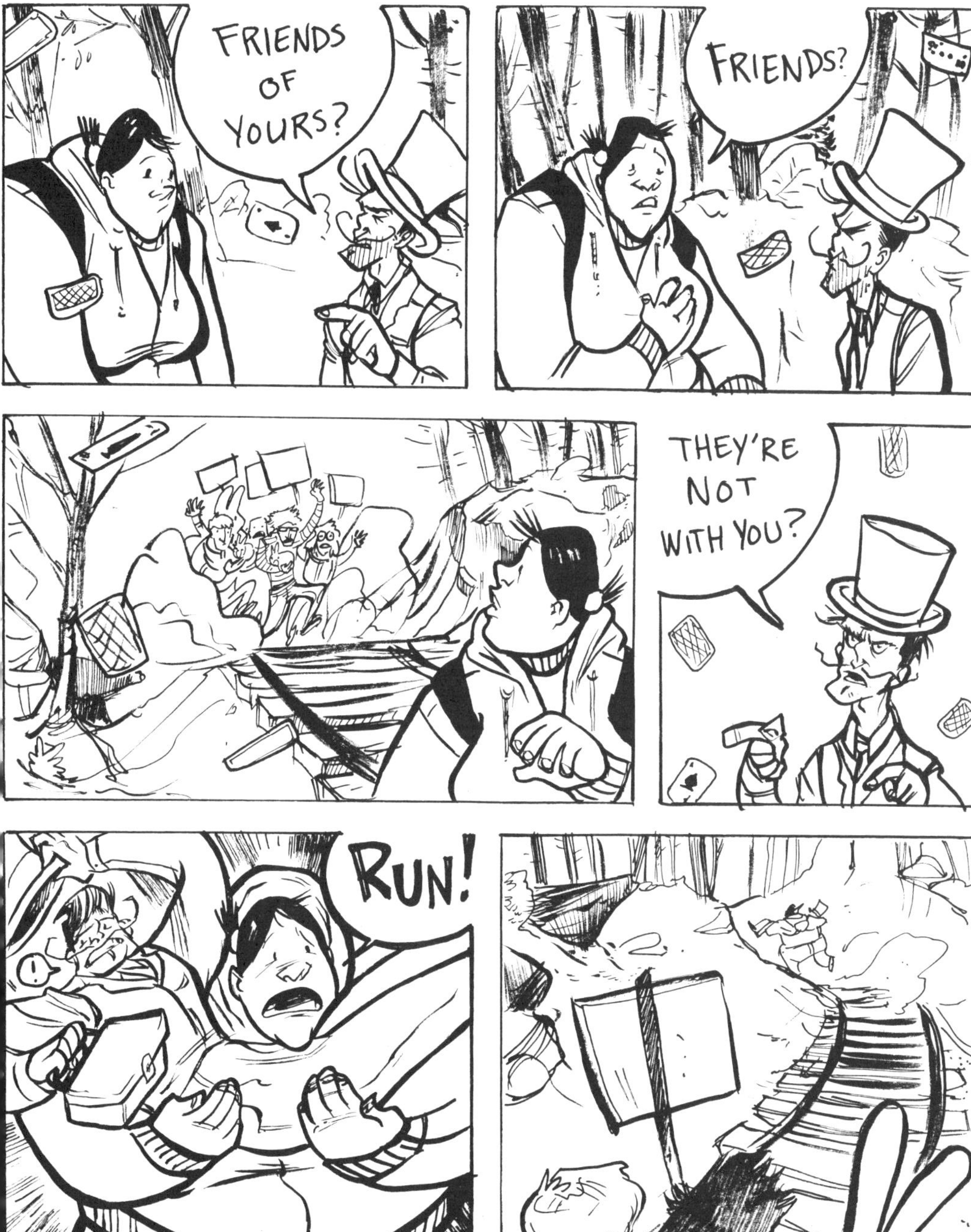
FRIENDS OF YOURS?
FRIENDS?
THEY'RE NOT WITH YOU?
!
RUN!

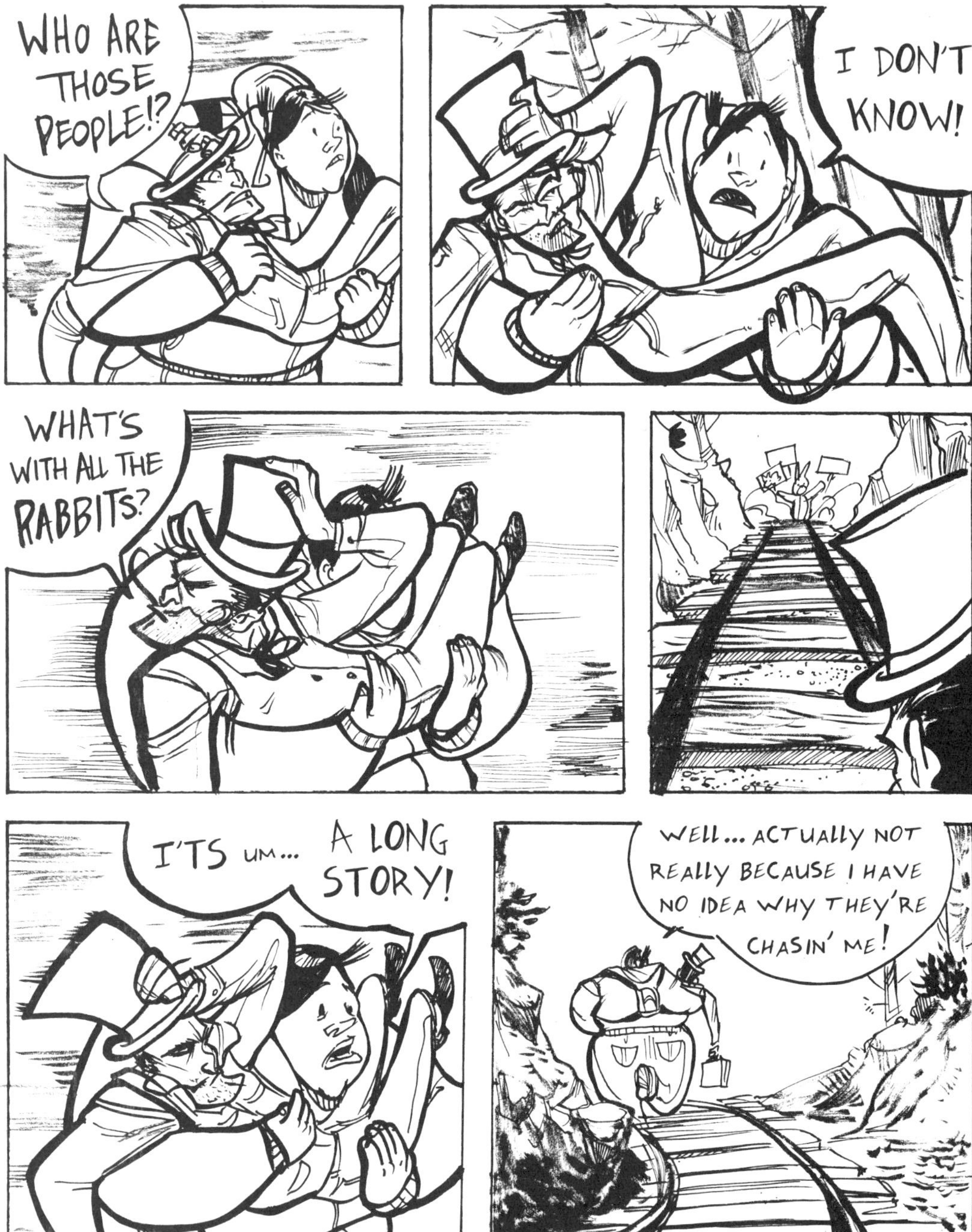

WHO ARE THOSE PEOPLE!?
I DON'T KNOW!
WHAT'S WITH ALL THE RABBITS?
I'TS UM... A LONG STORY!
WELL... ACTUALLY NOT REALLY BECAUSE I HAVE NO IDEA WHY THEY'RE CHASIN' ME!

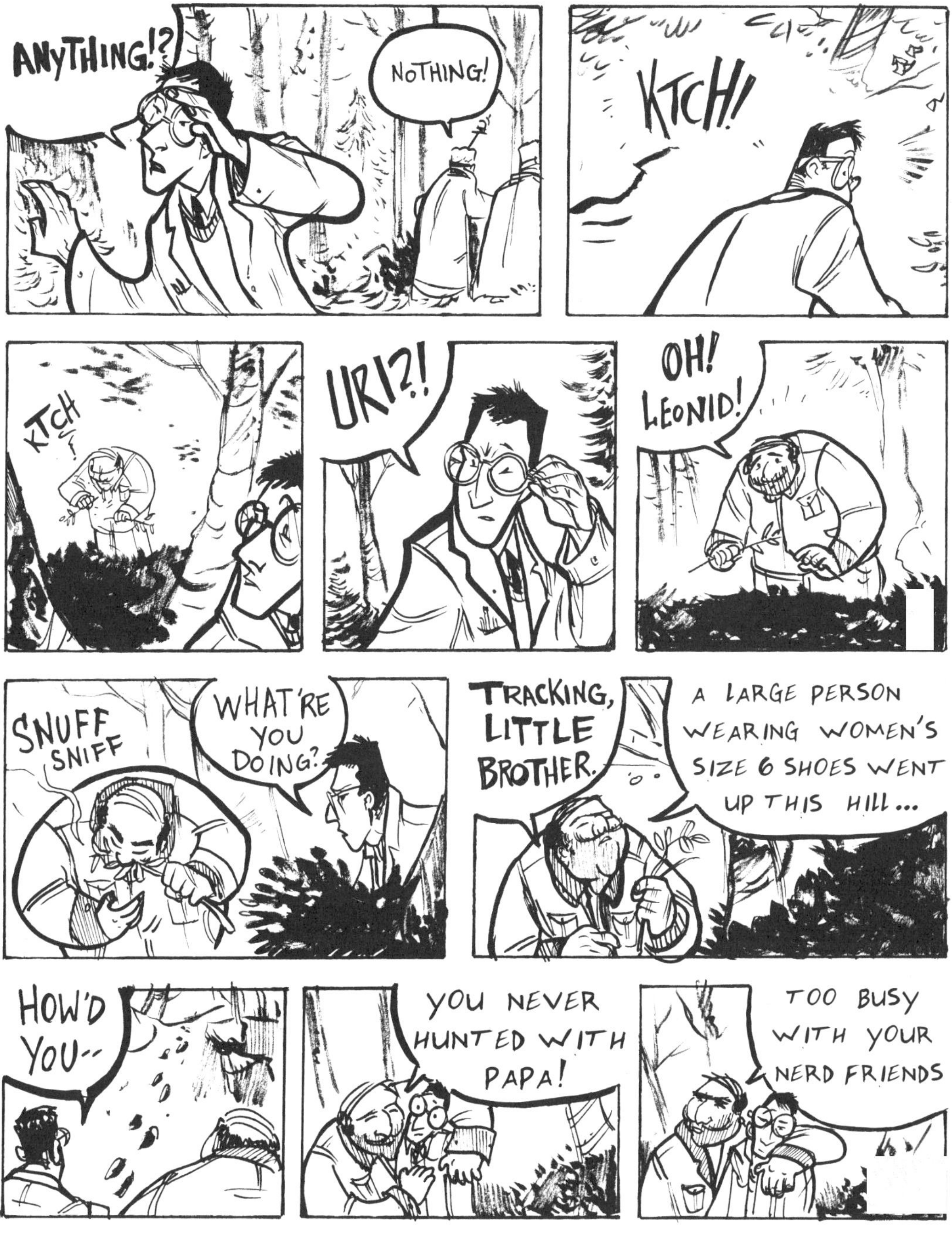

ANYTHING!?
NOTHING!
KTCH!
KTCH
URI?!
OH! LEONID!
SNUFF SNIFF
WHAT'RE YOU DOING?
TRACKING, LITTLE BROTHER.
A LARGE PERSON WEARING WOMEN'S SIZE 6 SHOES WENT UP THIS HILL...
HOW'D YOU--
YOU NEVER HUNTED WITH PAPA!
TOO BUSY WITH YOUR NERD FRIENDS

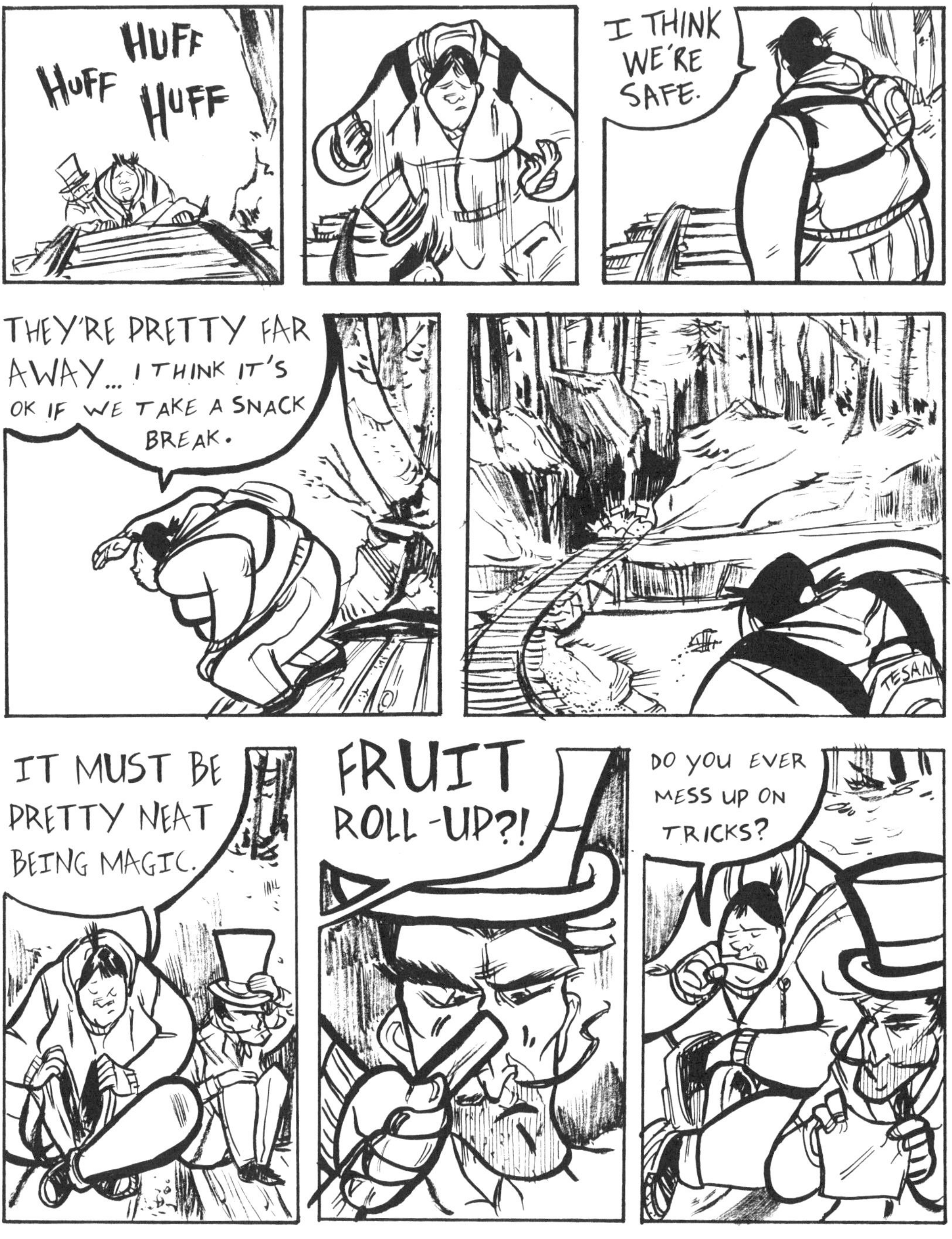
HUFF HUFF
HUFF HUFF
I THINK WE'RE SAFE.
THEY'RE PRETTY FAR AWAY... I THINK IT'S OK IF WE TAKE A SNACK BREAK.
TESAN
IT MUST BE PRETTY NEAT BEING MAGIC.
FRUIT ROLL-UP?!
DO YOU EVER MESS UP ON TRICKS?

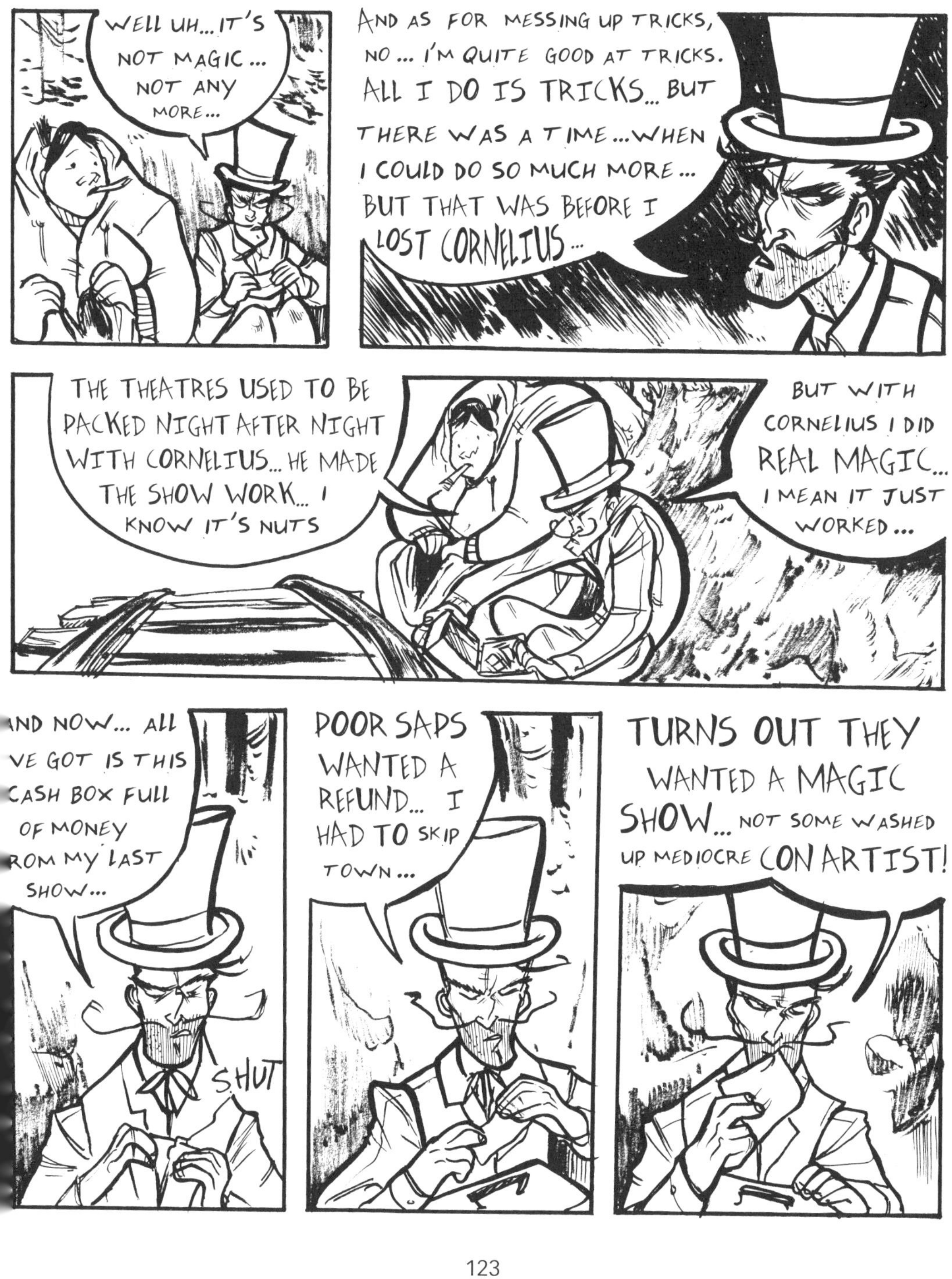
WELL UH... IT'S NOT MAGIC... NOT ANY MORE...
AND AS FOR MESSING UP TRICKS, NO... I'M QUITE GOOD AT TRICKS. ALL I DO IS TRICKS... BUT THERE WAS A TIME... WHEN I COULD DO SO MUCH MORE... BUT THAT WAS BEFORE I LOST CORNELIUS...
THE THEATRES USED TO BE PACKED NIGHT AFTER NIGHT WITH CORNELIUS... HE MADE THE SHOW WORK... I KNOW IT'S NUTS
BUT WITH CORNELIUS I DID REAL MAGIC... I MEAN IT JUST WORKED...
AND NOW... ALL VE GOT IS THIS CASH BOX FULL OF MONEY ROM MY LAST SHOW...
SHUT
POOR SAPS WANTED A REFUND... I HAD TO SKIP TOWN...
TURNS OUT THEY WANTED A MAGIC SHOW... NOT SOME WASHED UP MEDIOCRE CON ARTIST!

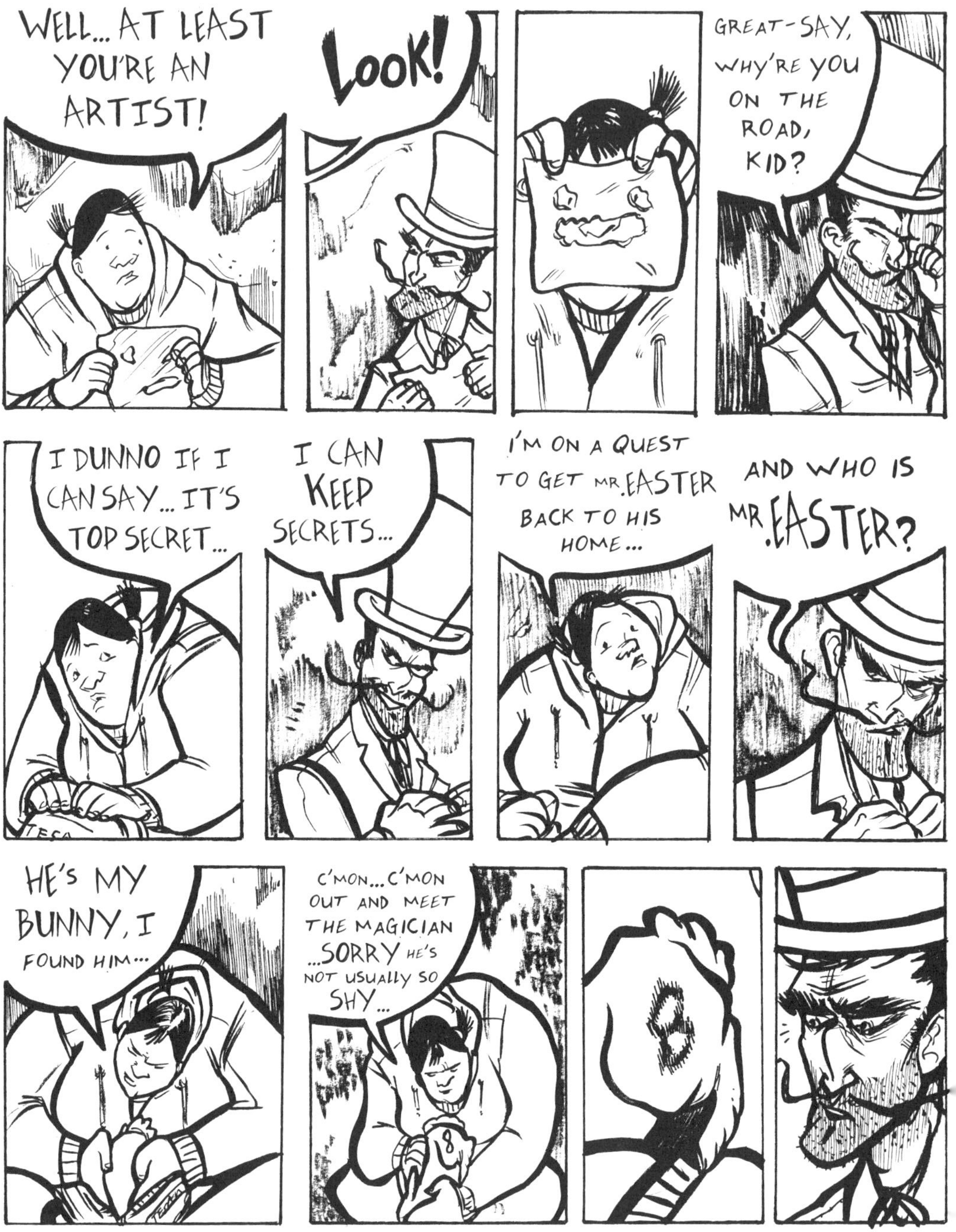
WELL... AT LEAST YOU'RE AN ARTIST!
LOOK!
GREAT-SAY, WHY'RE YOU ON THE ROAD, KID?
I DUNNO IF I CAN SAY... IT'S TOP SECRET...
I CAN KEEP SECRETS...
I'M ON A QUEST TO GET MR.EASTER BACK TO HIS HOME...
AND WHO IS MR.EASTER?
HE'S MY BUNNY, I FOUND HIM...
C'MON... C'MON OUT AND MEET THE MAGICIAN ...SORRY HE'S NOT USUALLY SO SHY...

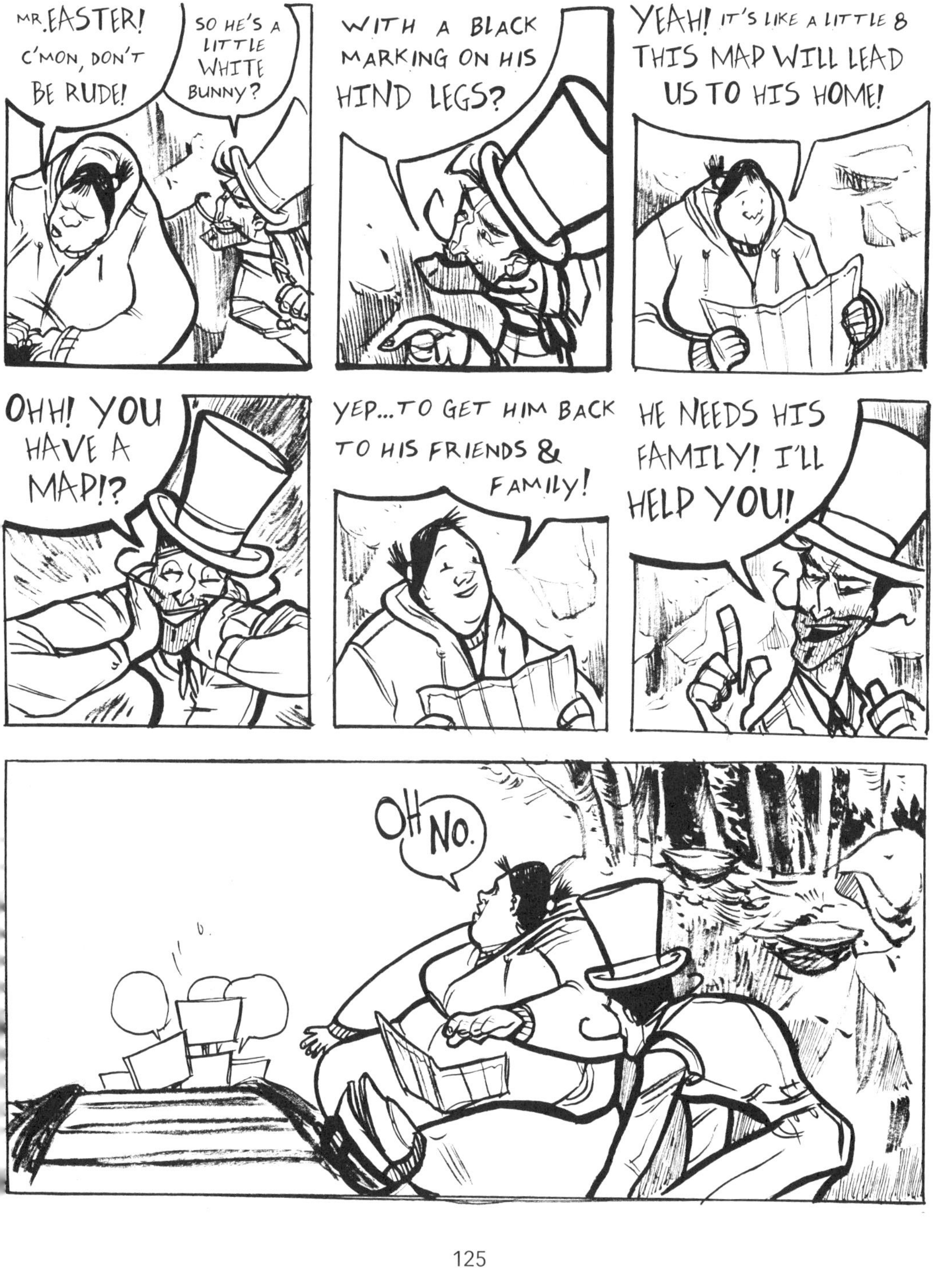
MR. EASTER! C'MON, DON'T BE RUDE!
SO HE'S A LITTLE WHITE BUNNY?
WITH A BLACK MARKING ON HIS HIND LEGS?
YEAH! IT'S LIKE A LITTLE 8 THIS MAP WILL LEAD US TO HIS HOME!
OHH! YOU HAVE A MAP!?
YEP...TO GET HIM BACK TO HIS FRIENDS & FAMILY!
HE NEEDS HIS FAMILY! I'LL HELP YOU!
OH NO.

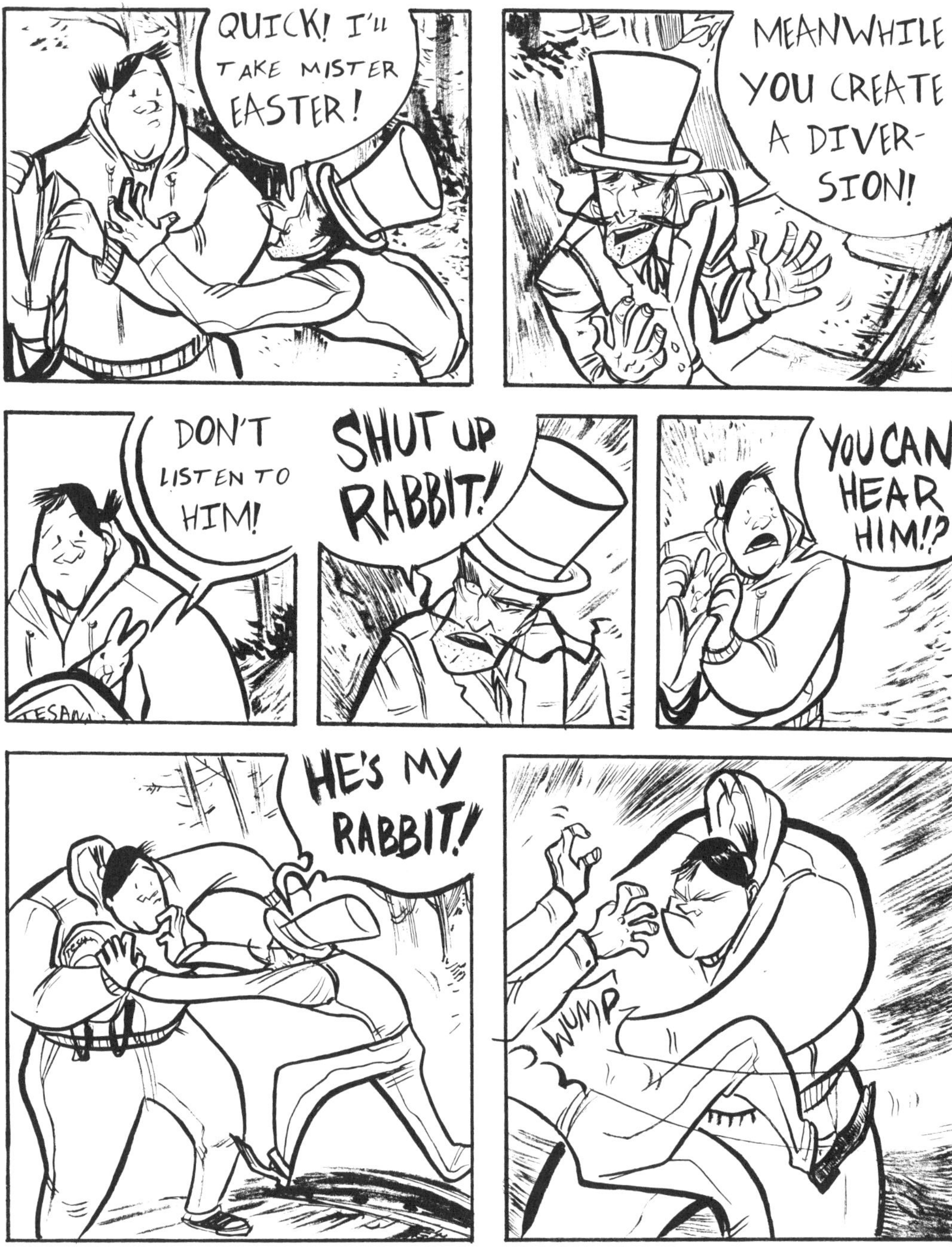
QUICK! I'LL TAKE MISTER EASTER!
MEANWHILE YOU CREATE A DIVERSION!
DON'T LISTEN TO HIM!
SHUT UP RABBIT!
YOU CAN HEAR HIM!?
HE'S MY RABBIT!
WUMP

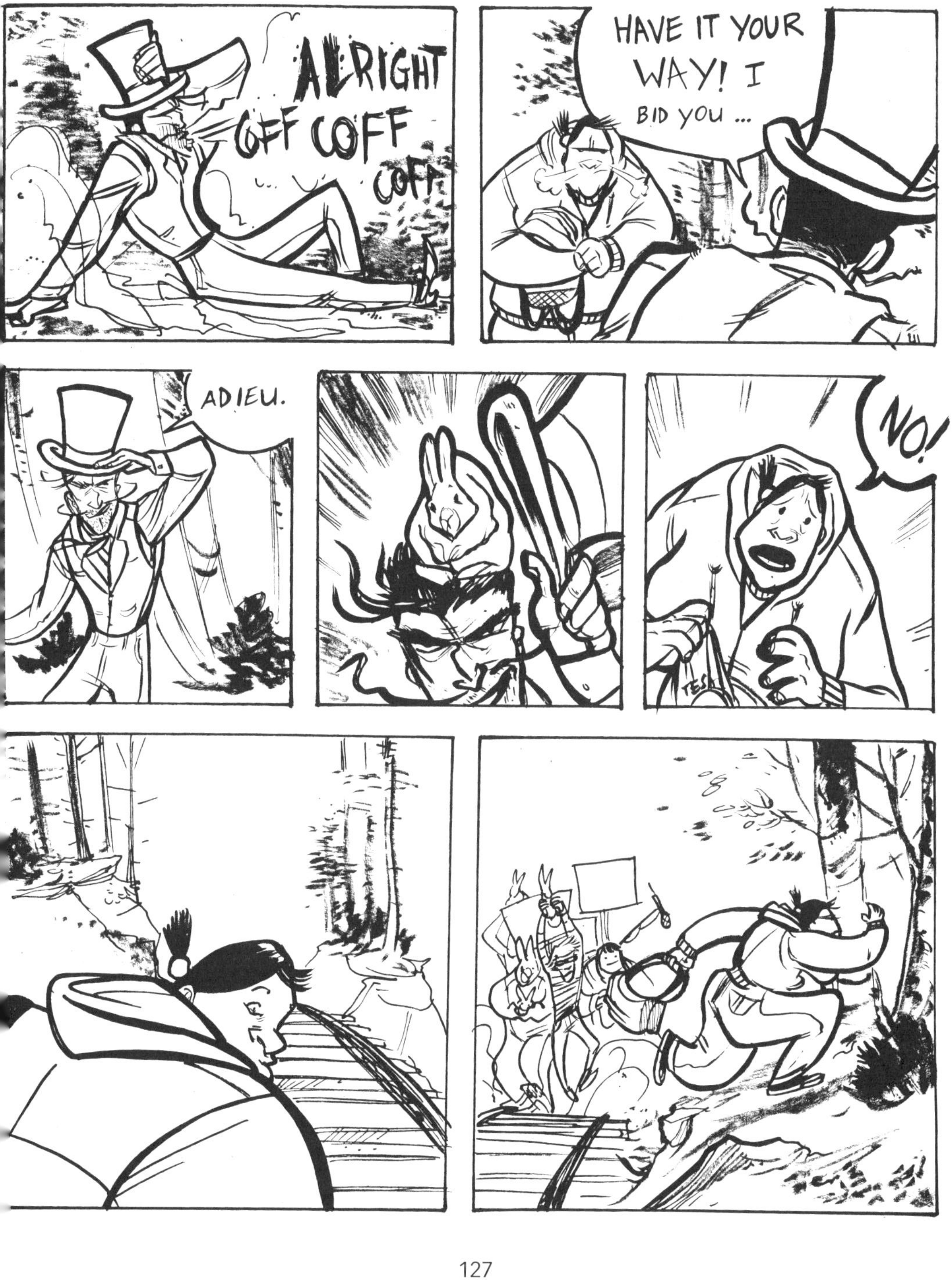
ALRIGHT
COFF COFF
COFF
HAVE IT YOUR WAY! I BID YOU ...
ADIEU.
NO!

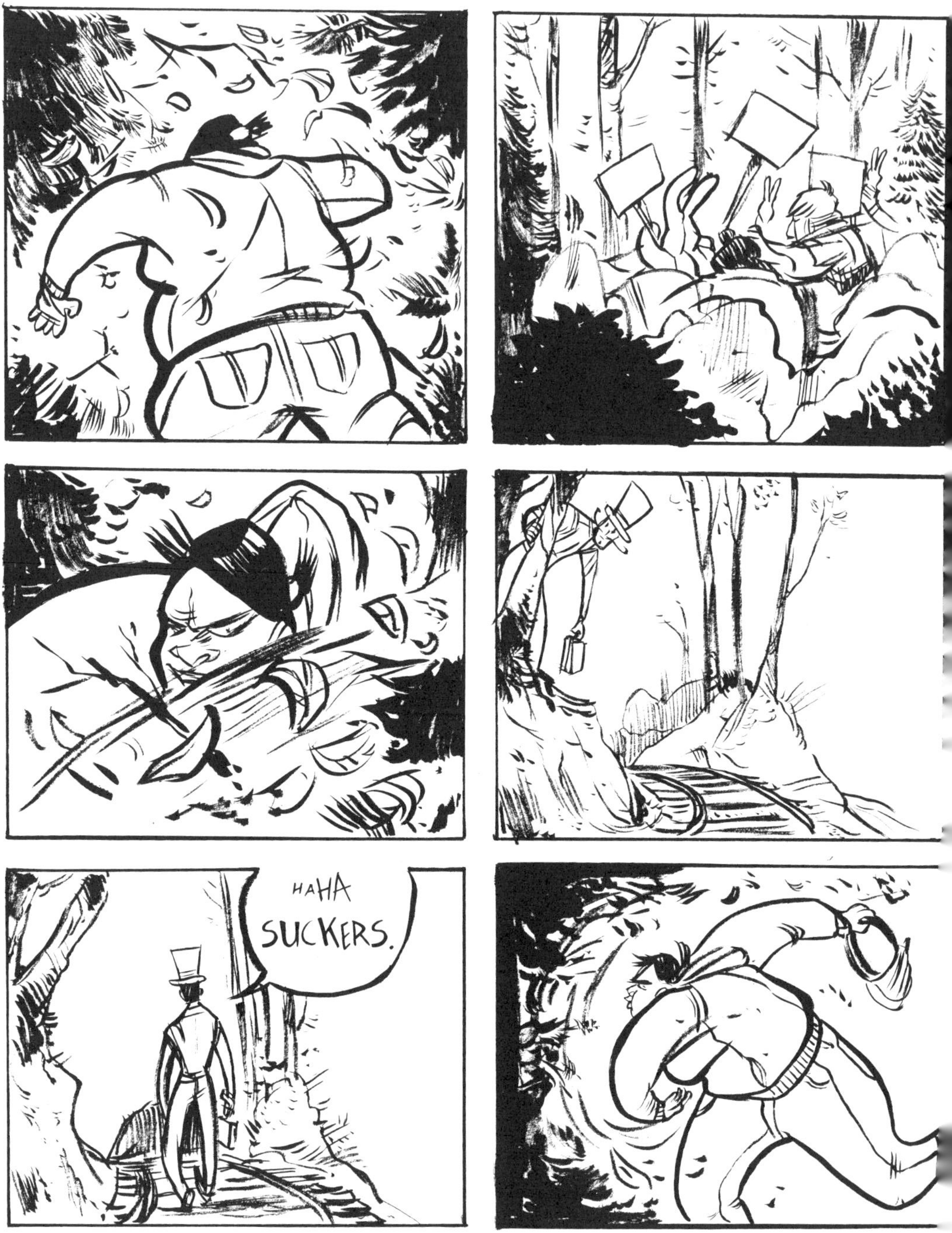
HAHA
SUCKERS.

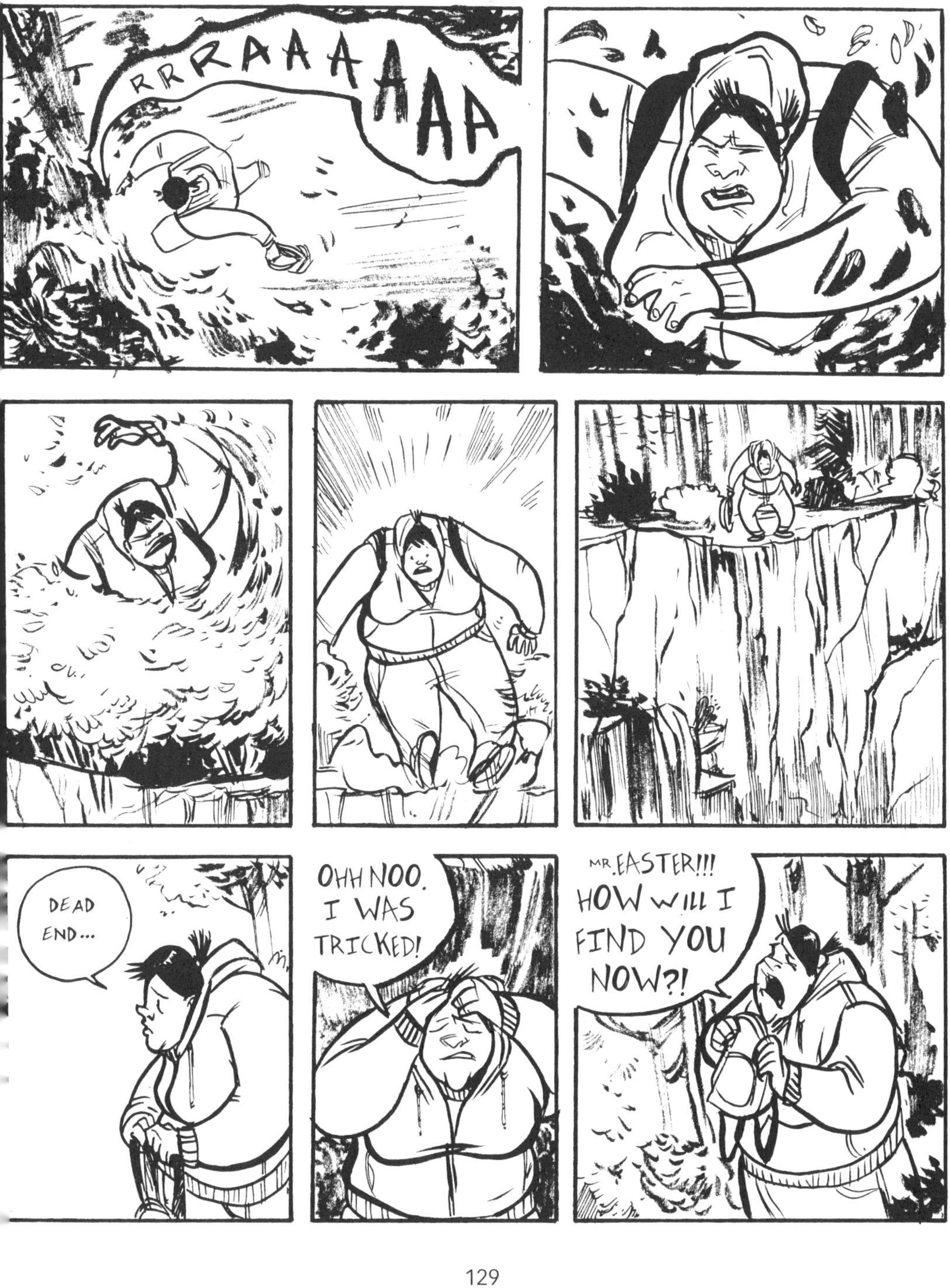
RRRAAAAAAA
DEAD END...
OHH NOO. I WAS TRICKED!
MR. EASTER!!! HOW WILL I FIND YOU NOW?!

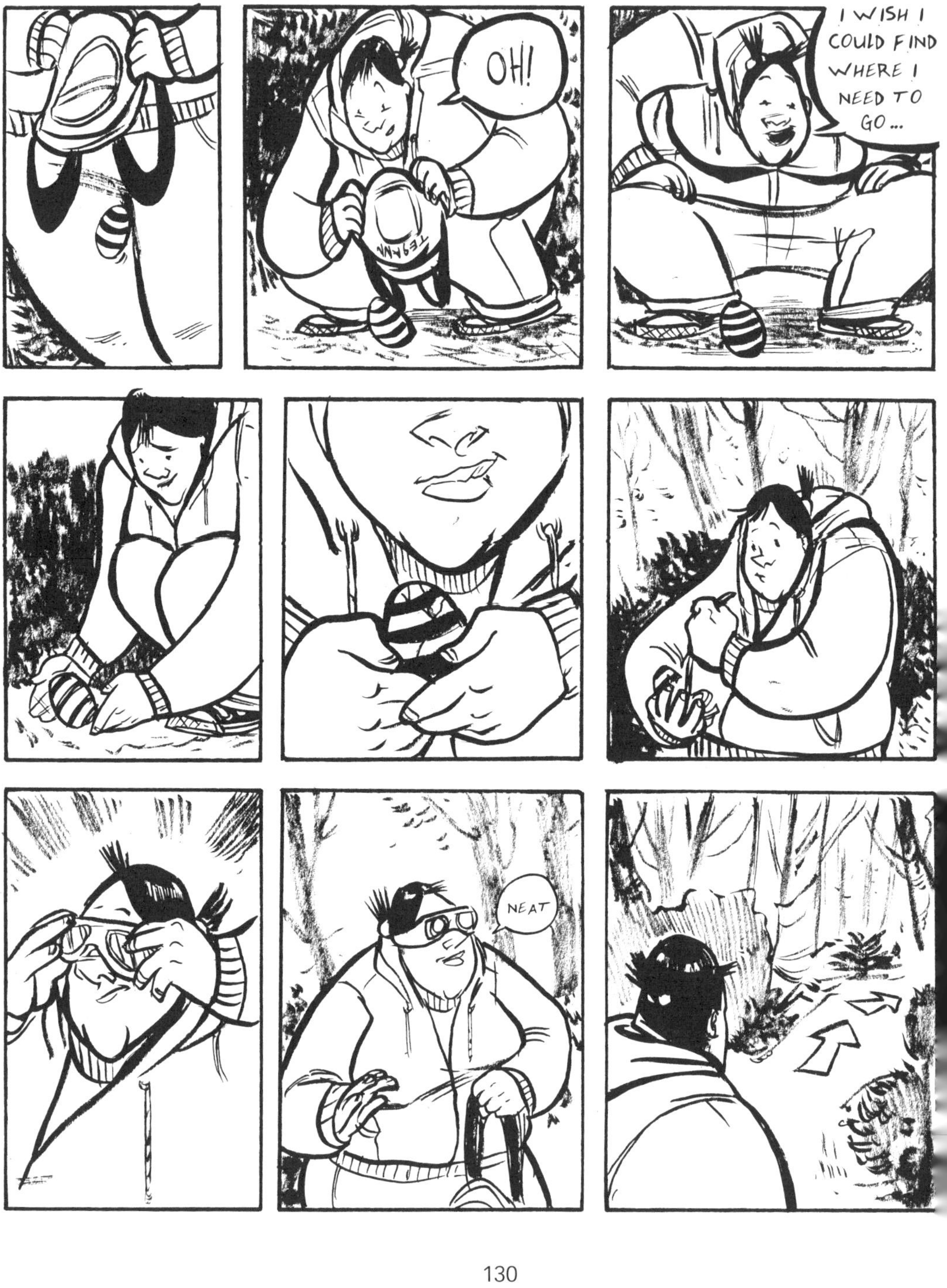
OH!
I WISH I COULD FIND WHERE I NEED TO GO...
NEAT

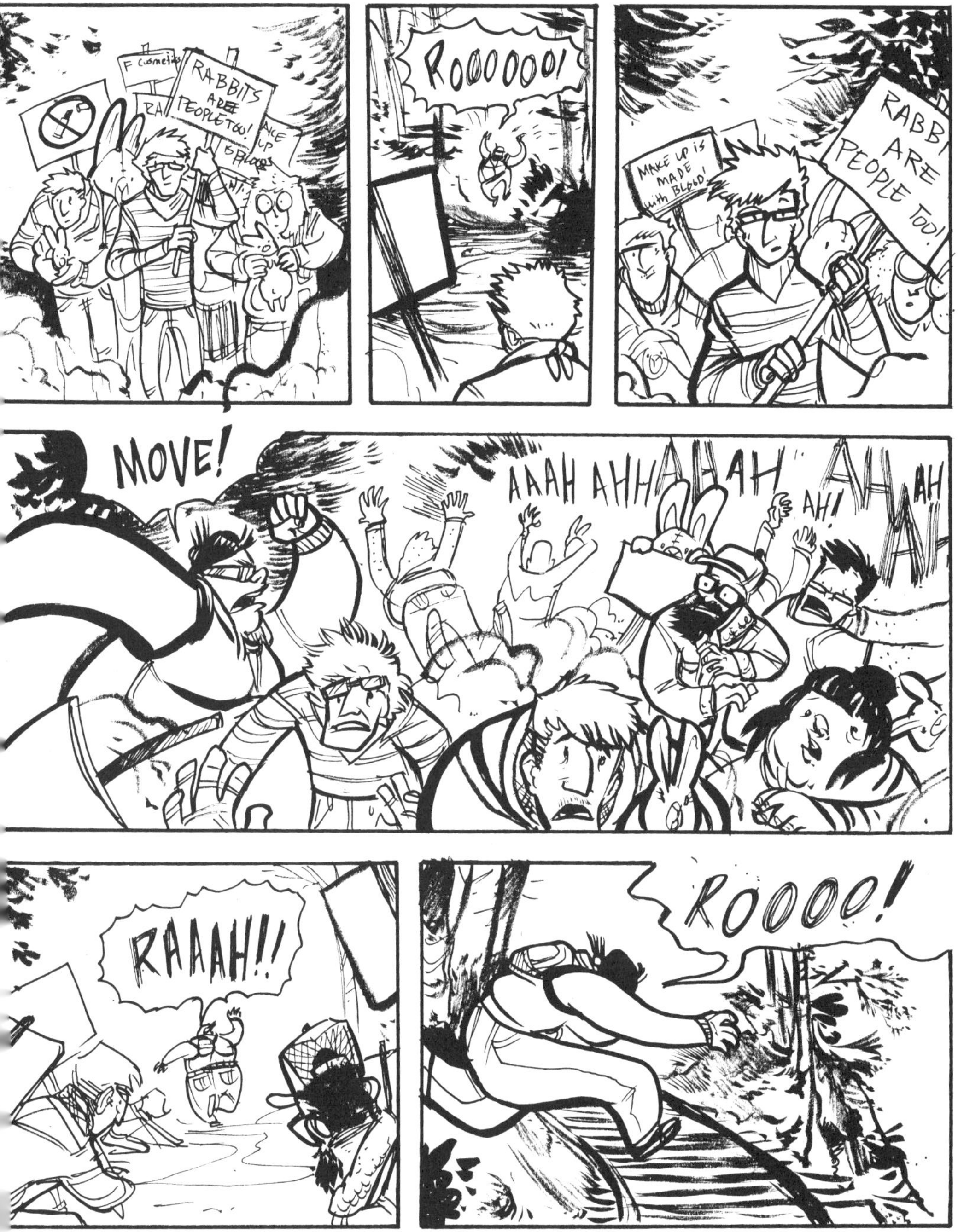
RABBITS ARE PEOPLE TOO!
ROOOOOO!
MAKE UP IS MADE with BLOOD!
RABB ARE PEOPLE TOO!
MOVE!
AAAH AHH AH AH AH
AH!
AH
RAAAH!!
ROOOO!

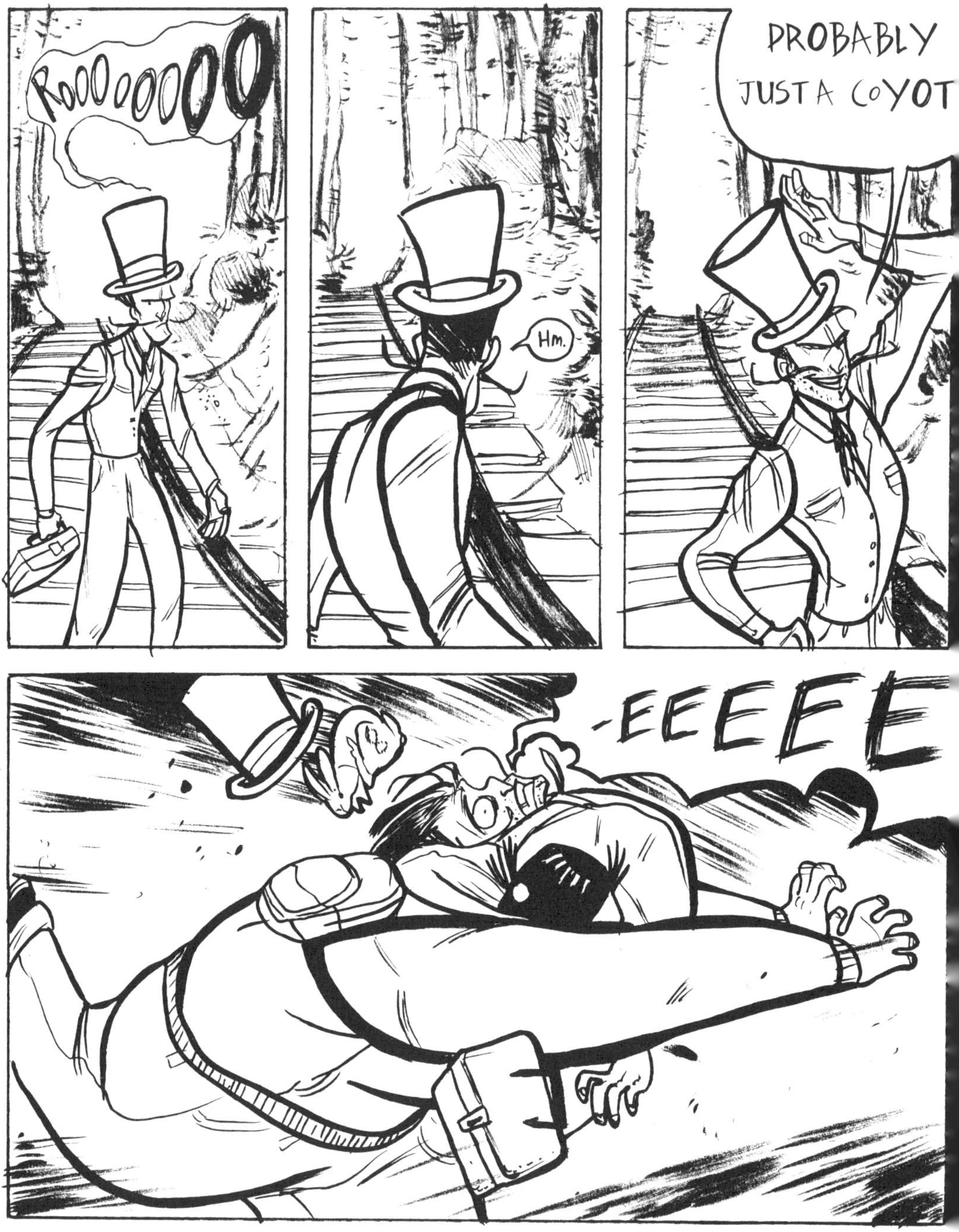

ROOOOOOOOO
Hm.
PROBABLY JUST A COYOT
-EEEEE

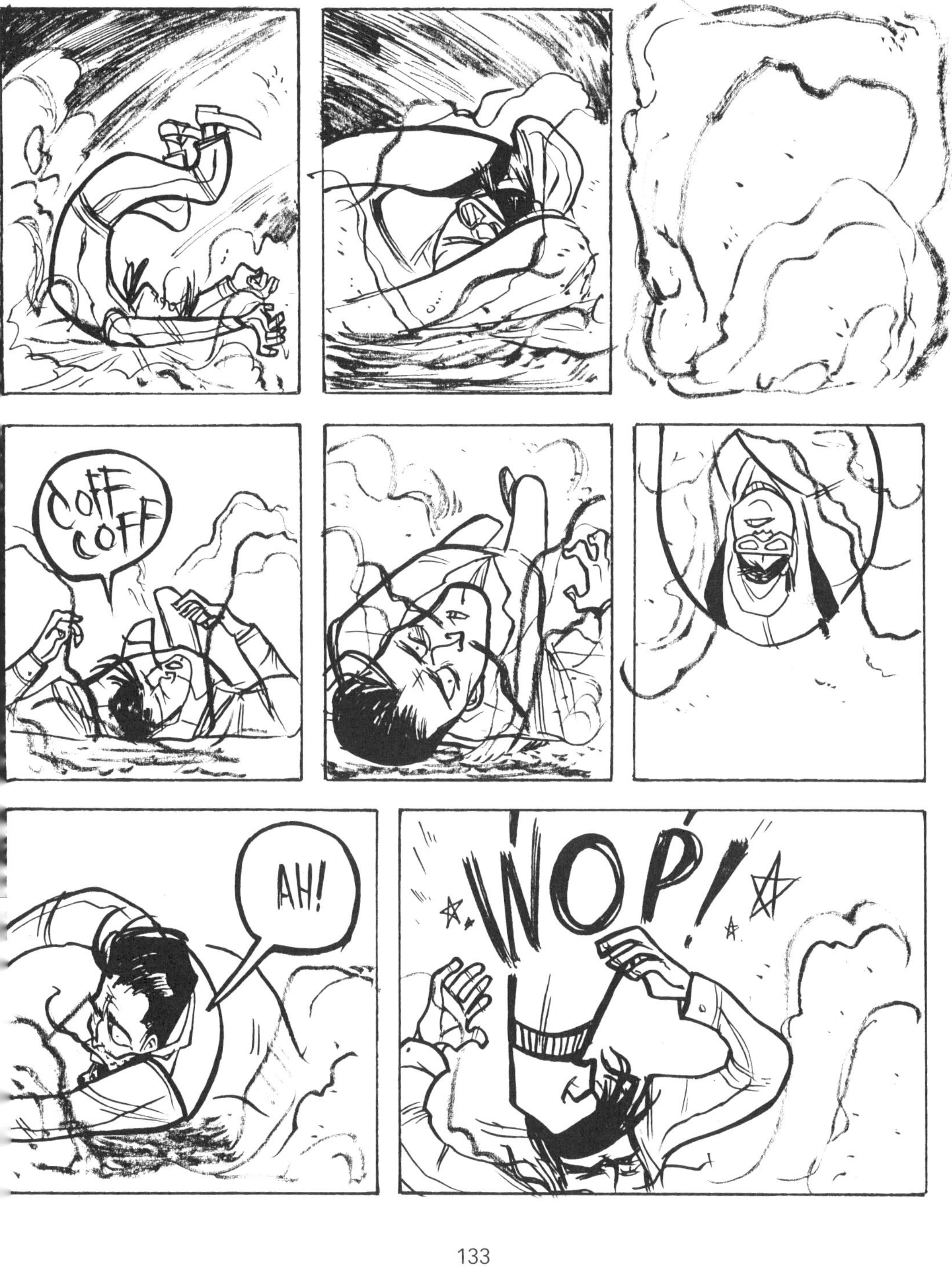
COFF COFF
AH!
WOP!

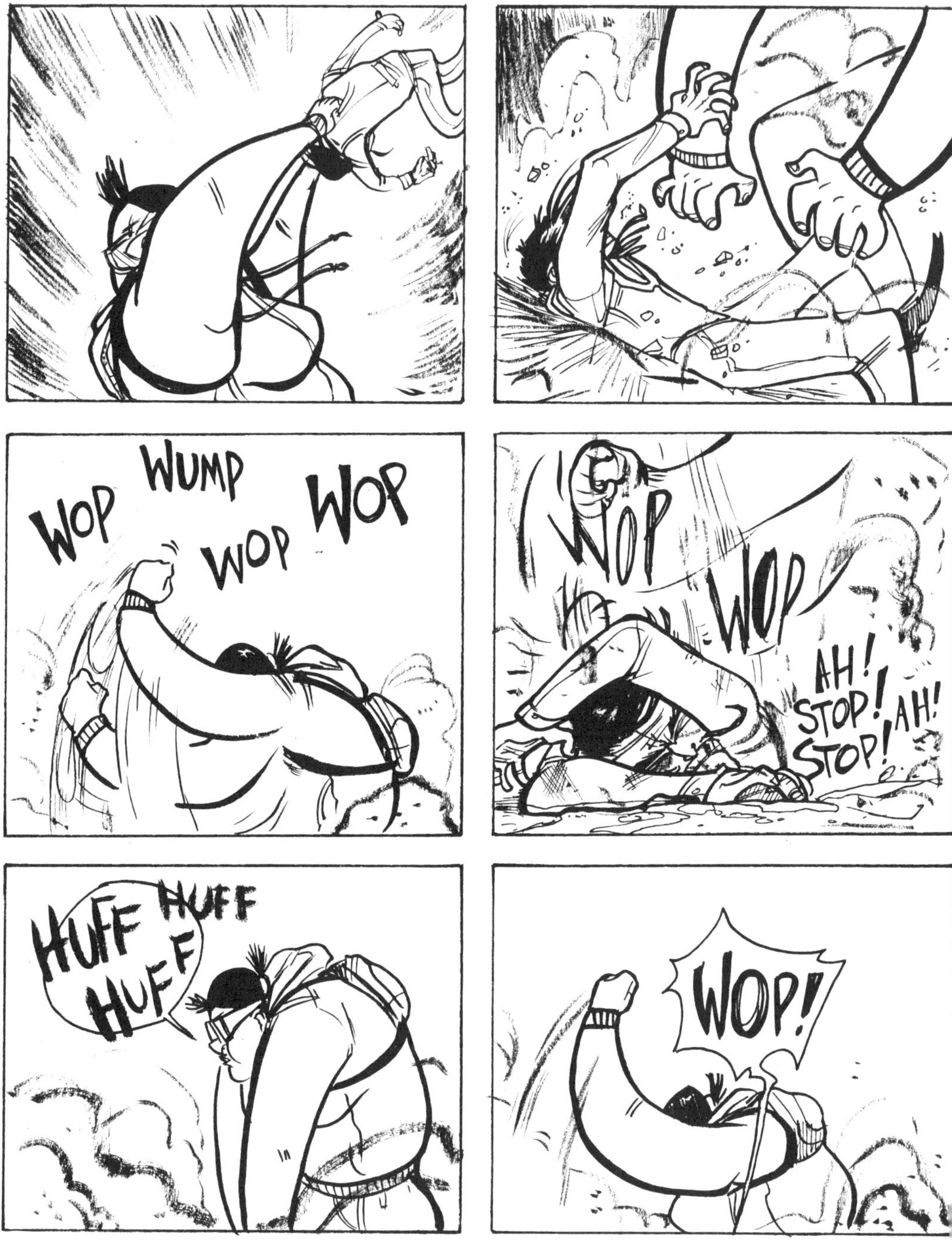
WOP
WUMP
WOP
WOP
WOP
WOP
AH! STOP! STOP! AH!
HUFF HUFF HUFF HUFF
WOP!

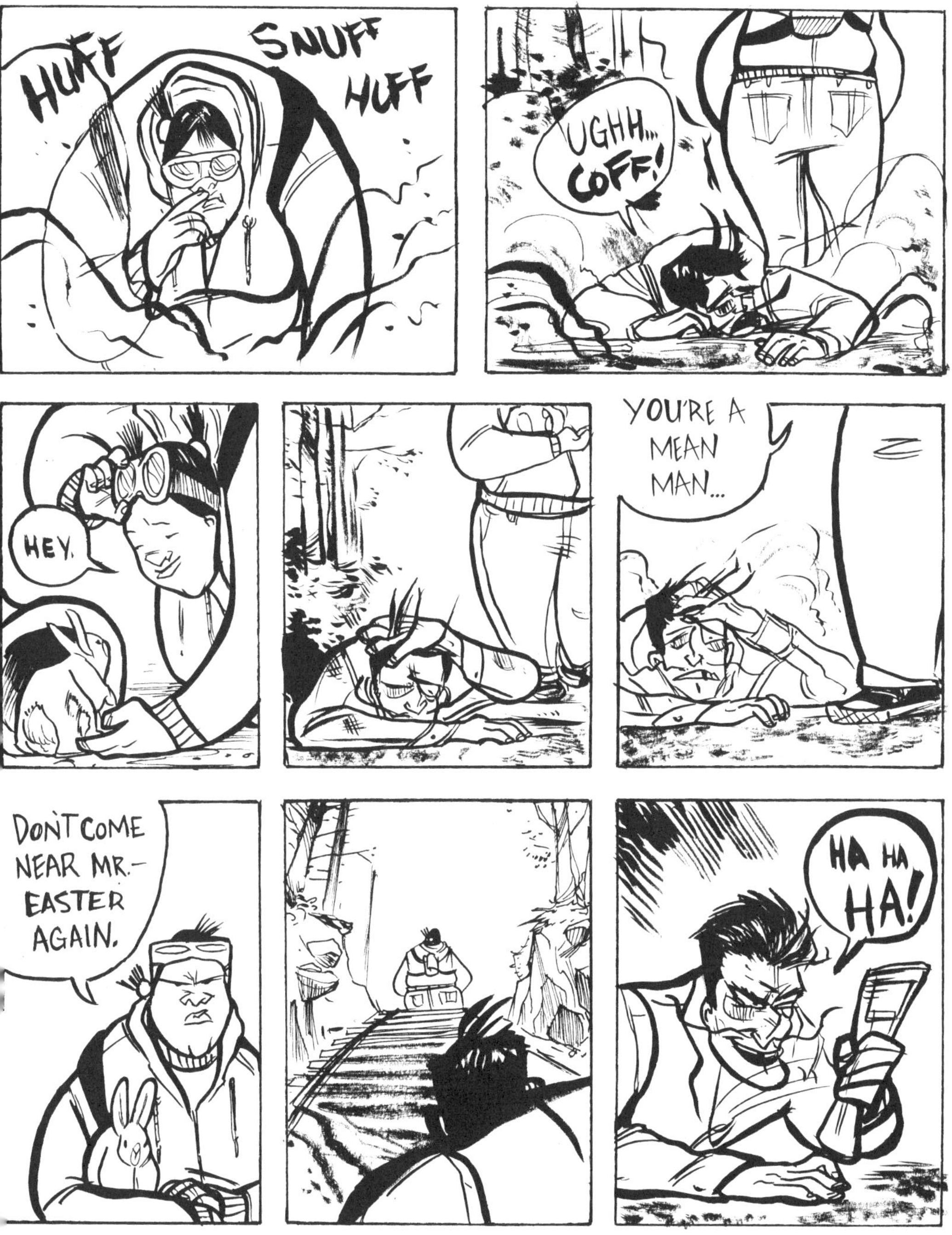
HUFF
SNUFF
HUFF
UGHH... COFF!
HEY.
YOU'RE A MEAN MAN...
DON'T COME NEAR MR. EASTER AGAIN.
HA HA HA!

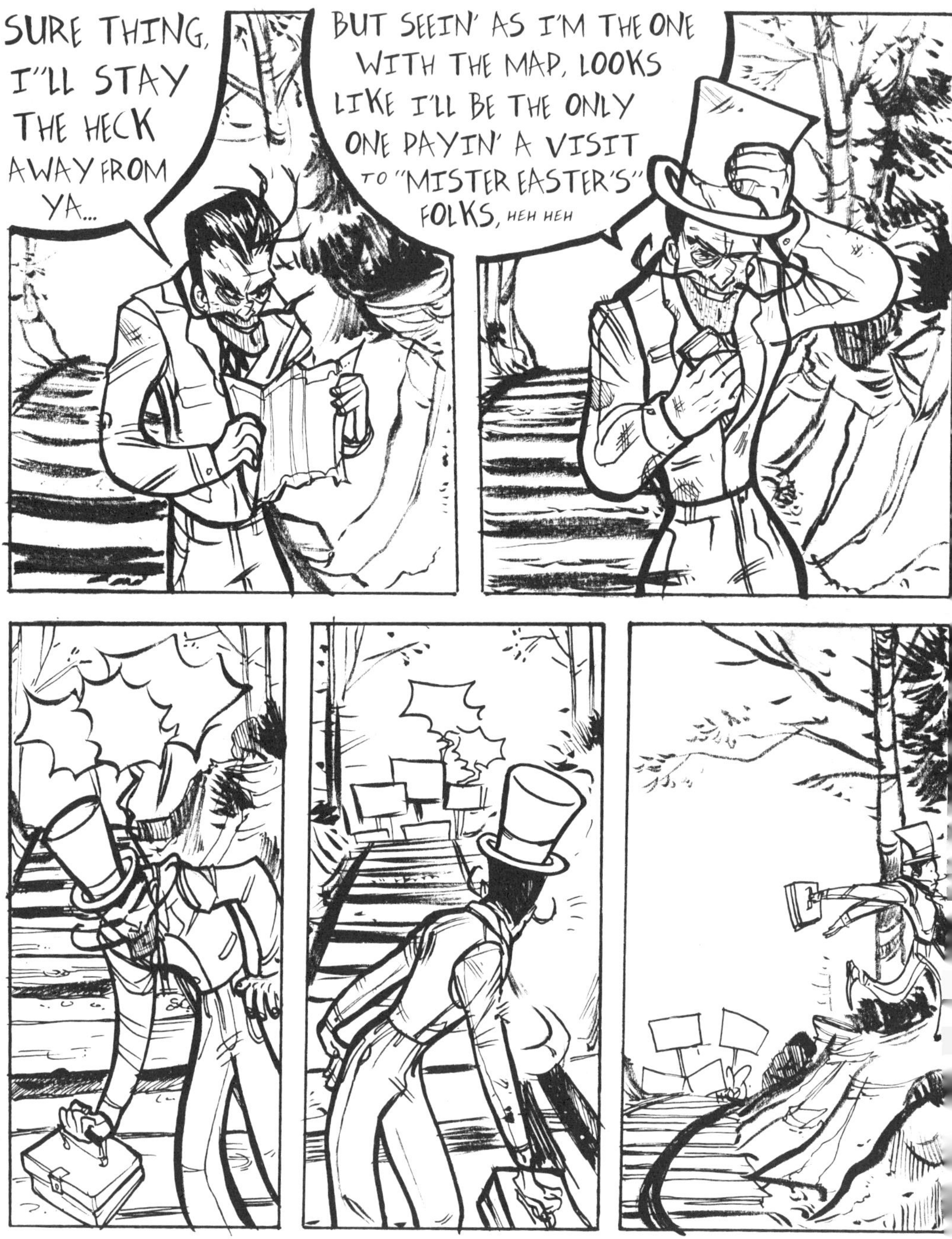
SURE THING, I'LL STAY THE HECK AWAY FROM YA...
BUT SEEIN' AS I'M THE ONE WITH THE MAP, LOOKS LIKE I'LL BE THE ONLY ONE PAYIN' A VISIT TO "MISTER EASTER'S" FOLKS, HEH HEH

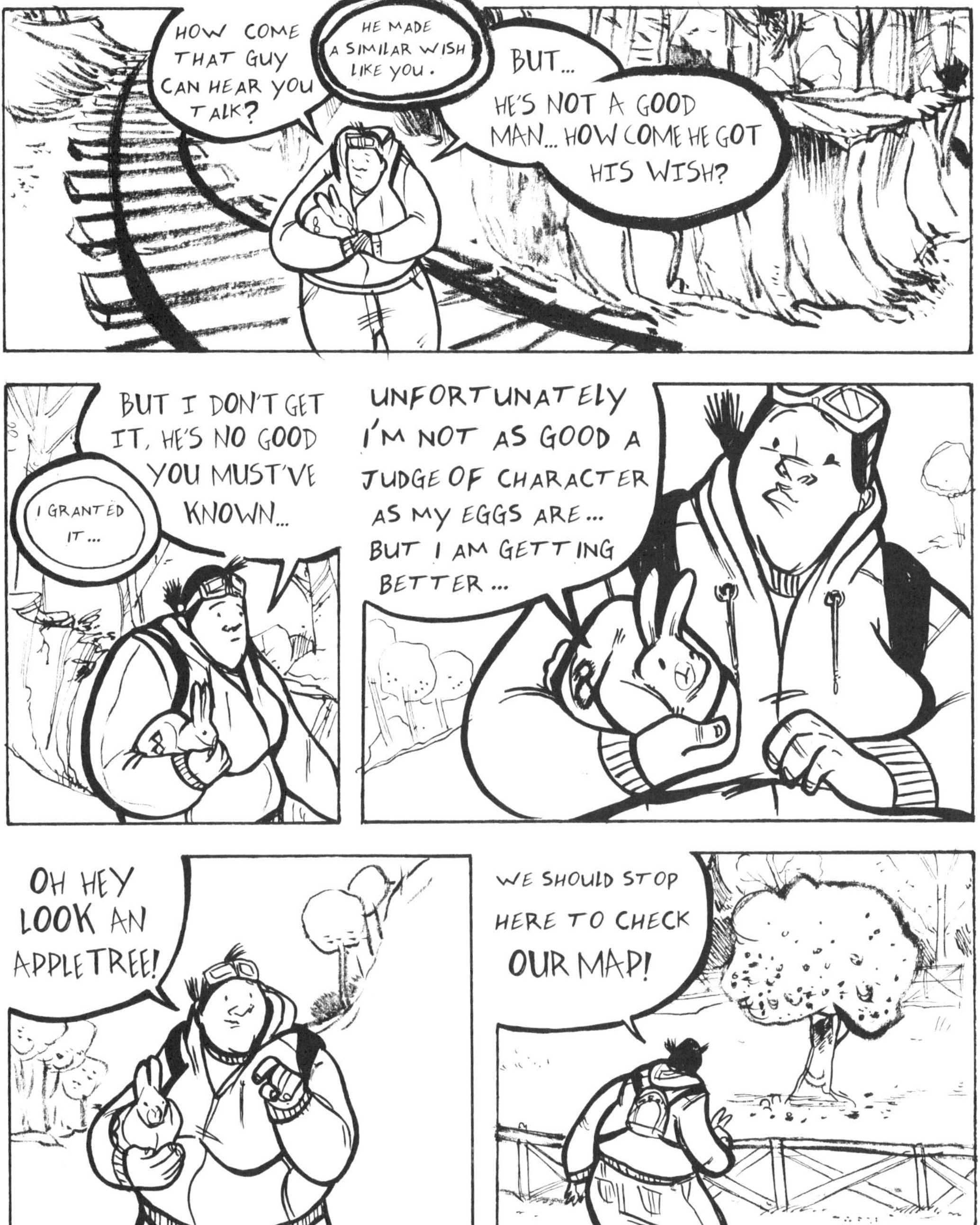
HOW COME THAT GUY CAN HEAR YOU TALK?
HE MADE A SIMILAR WISH LIKE YOU.
BUT...
HE'S NOT A GOOD MAN... HOW COME HE GOT HIS WISH?
BUT I DON'T GET IT, HE'S NO GOOD YOU MUST'VE KNOWN...
I GRANTED IT...
UNFORTUNATELY I'M NOT AS GOOD A JUDGE OF CHARACTER AS MY EGGS ARE... BUT I AM GETTING BETTER...
OH HEY LOOK AN APPLETREE!
WE SHOULD STOP HERE TO CHECK OUR MAP!

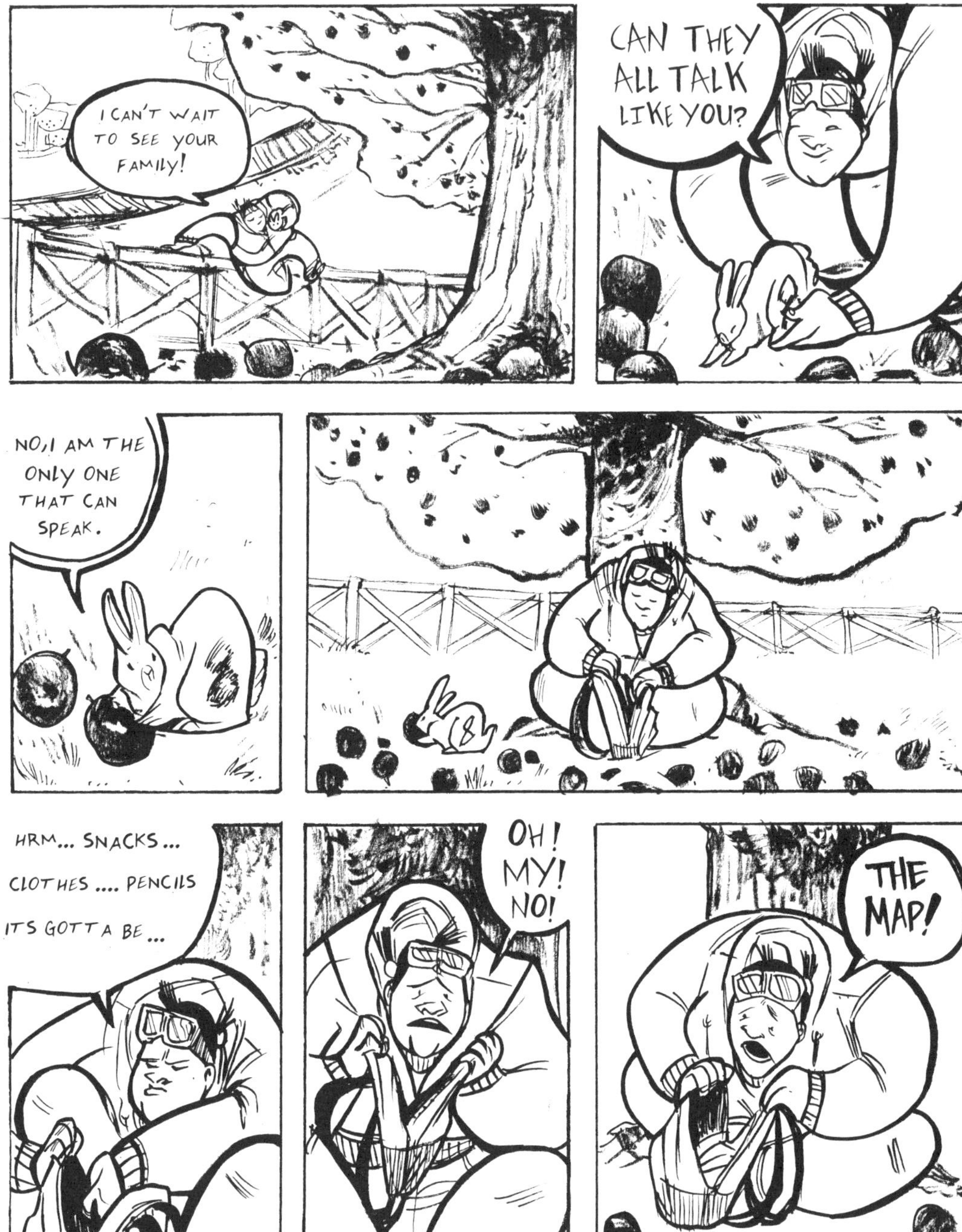
I CAN'T WAIT TO SEE YOUR FAMILY!
CAN THEY ALL TALK LIKE YOU?
NO, I AM THE ONLY ONE THAT CAN SPEAK.
HRM... SNACKS... CLOTHES .... PENCILS ITS GOTTA BE...
OH! MY! NO!
THE MAP!

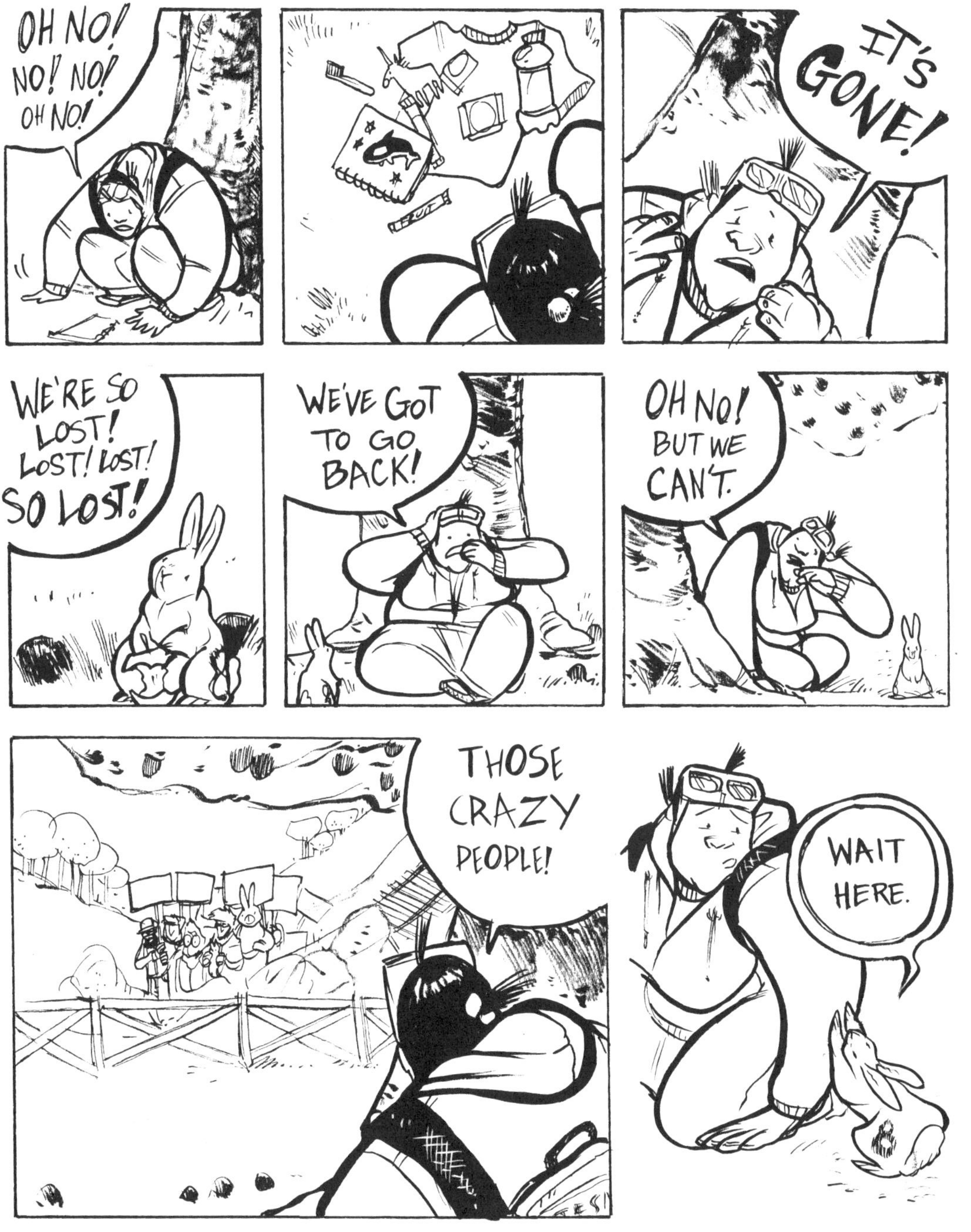
OH NO! NO! NO! OH NO!
IT'S GONE!
WE'RE SO LOST! LOST! LOST! SO LOST!
WE'VE GOT TO GO BACK!
OH NO! BUT WE CAN'T.
THOSE CRAZY PEOPLE!
WAIT HERE.

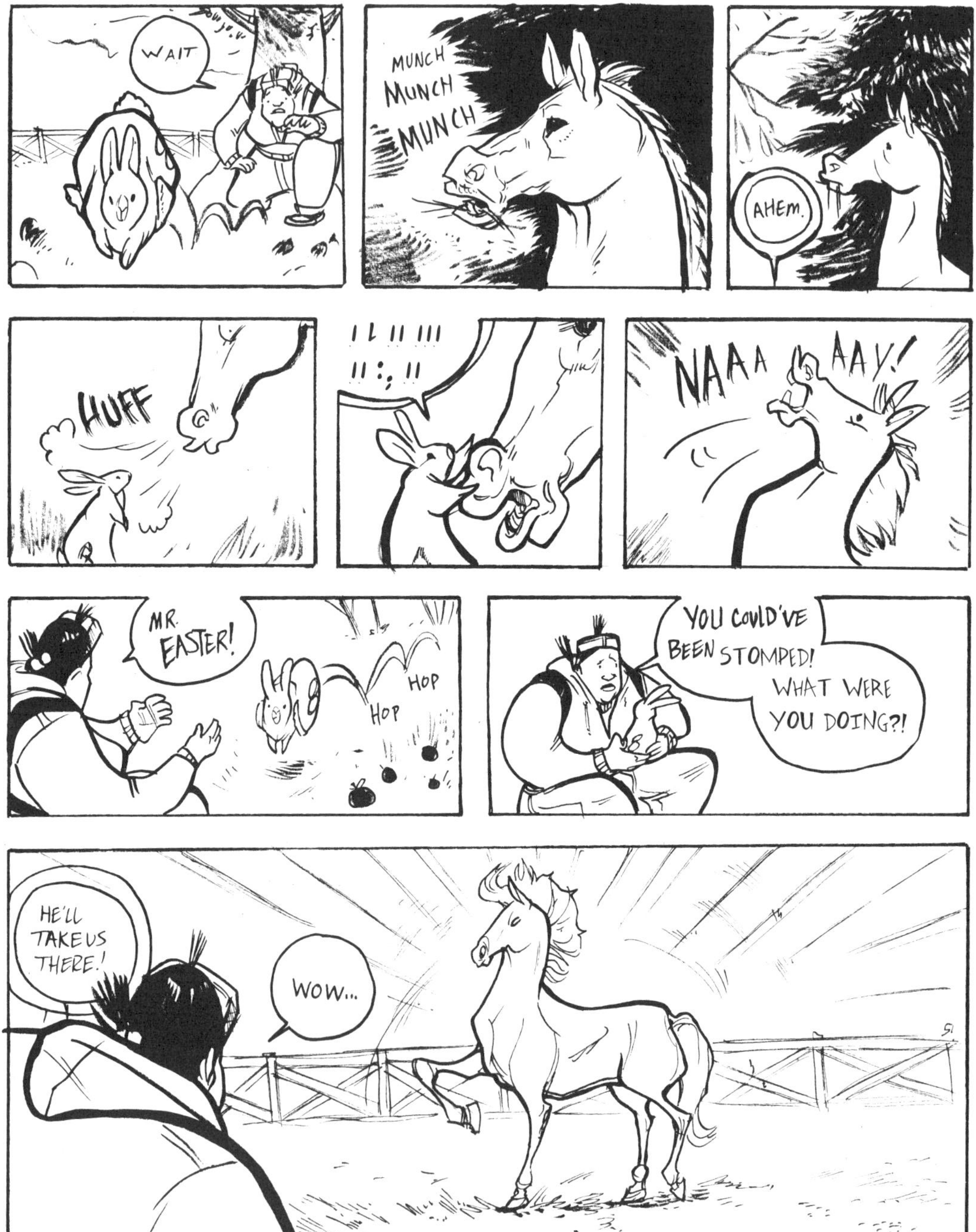
WAIT
MUNCH MUNCH MUNCH
AHEM.
HUFF
!! !! !!! !!! !!:; !!
NAAA AAAY!
MR. EASTER!
HOP HOP
YOU COULD'VE BEEN STOMPED!
WHAT WERE YOU DOING?!
HE'LL TAKE US THERE!
WOW...

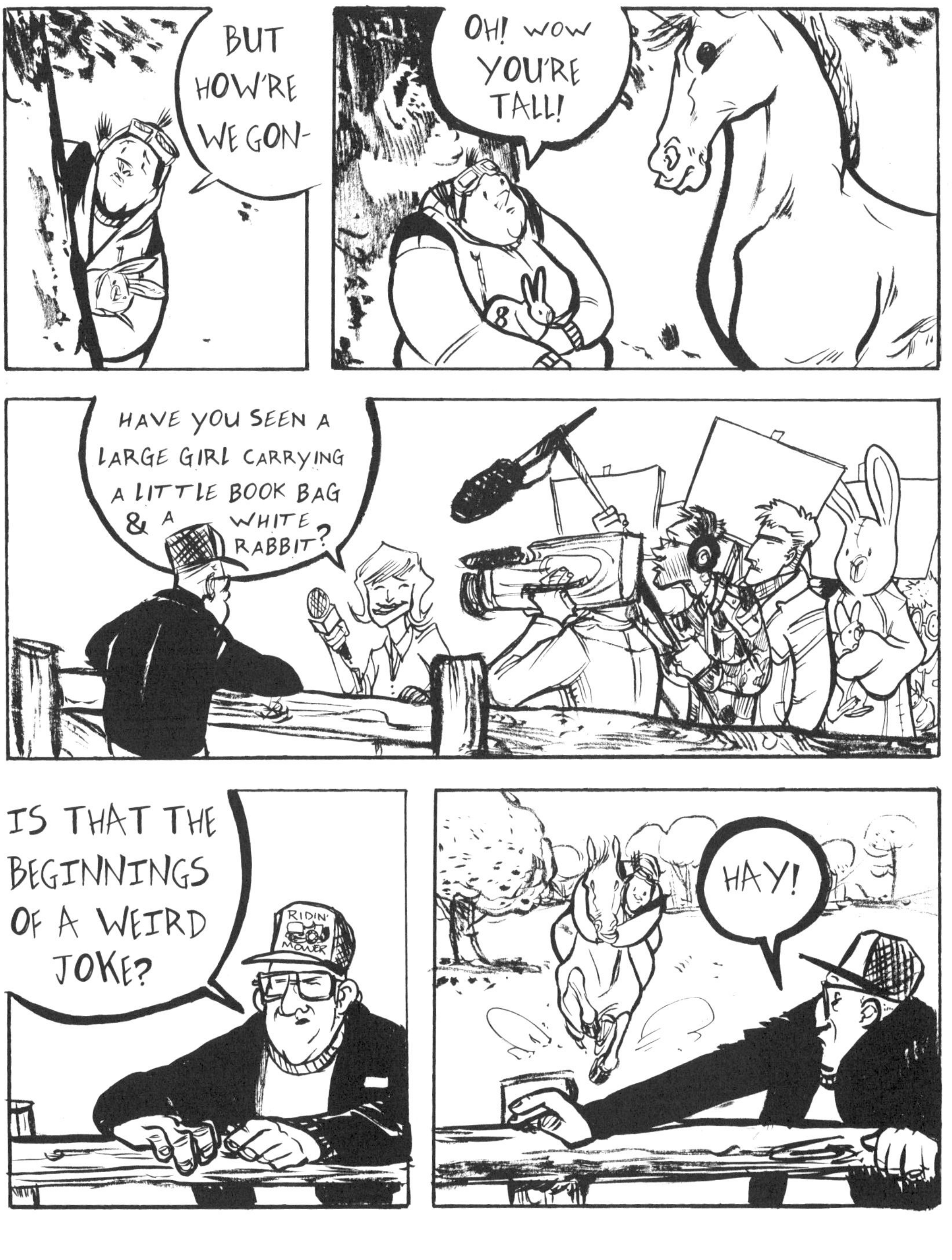
BUT HOW'RE WE GON-
OH! WOW YOU'RE TALL!
HAVE YOU SEEN A LARGE GIRL CARRYING A LITTLE BOOK BAG & A WHITE RABBIT?
IS THAT THE BEGINNINGS OF A WEIRD JOKE?
RIDIN' MOWER
HAY!

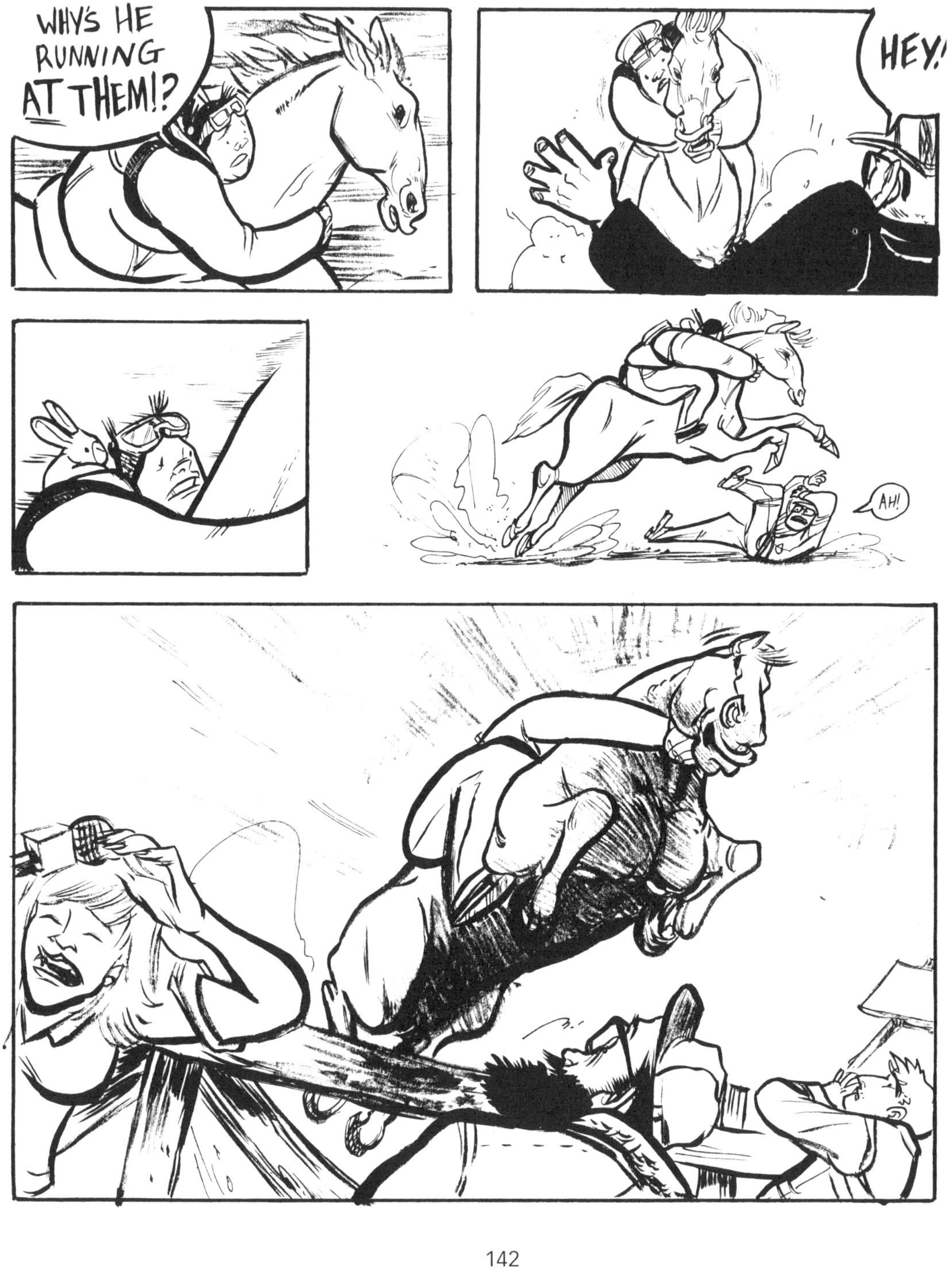
WHY'S HE RUNNING AT THEM!?
HEY!
AH!

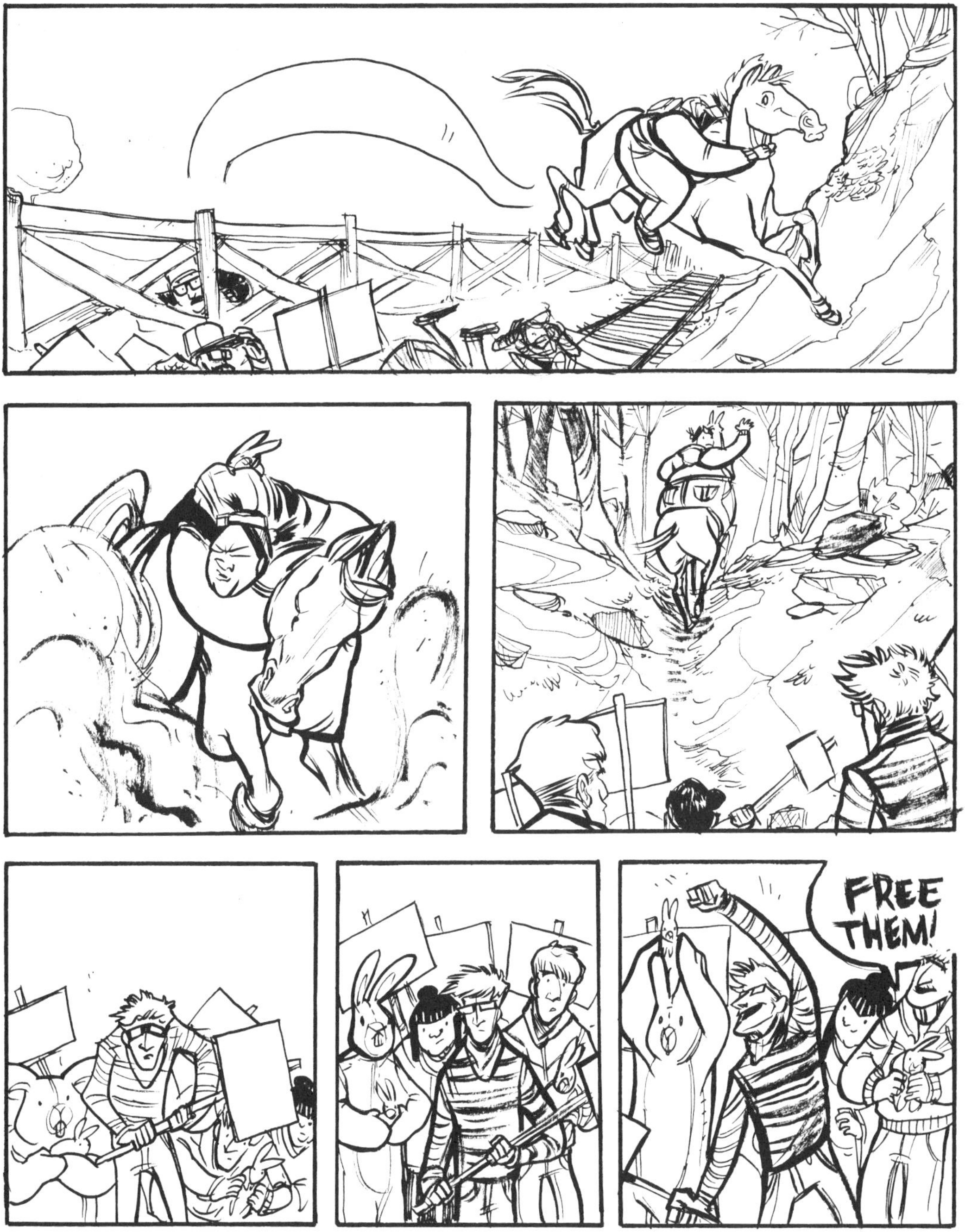
FREE THEM!

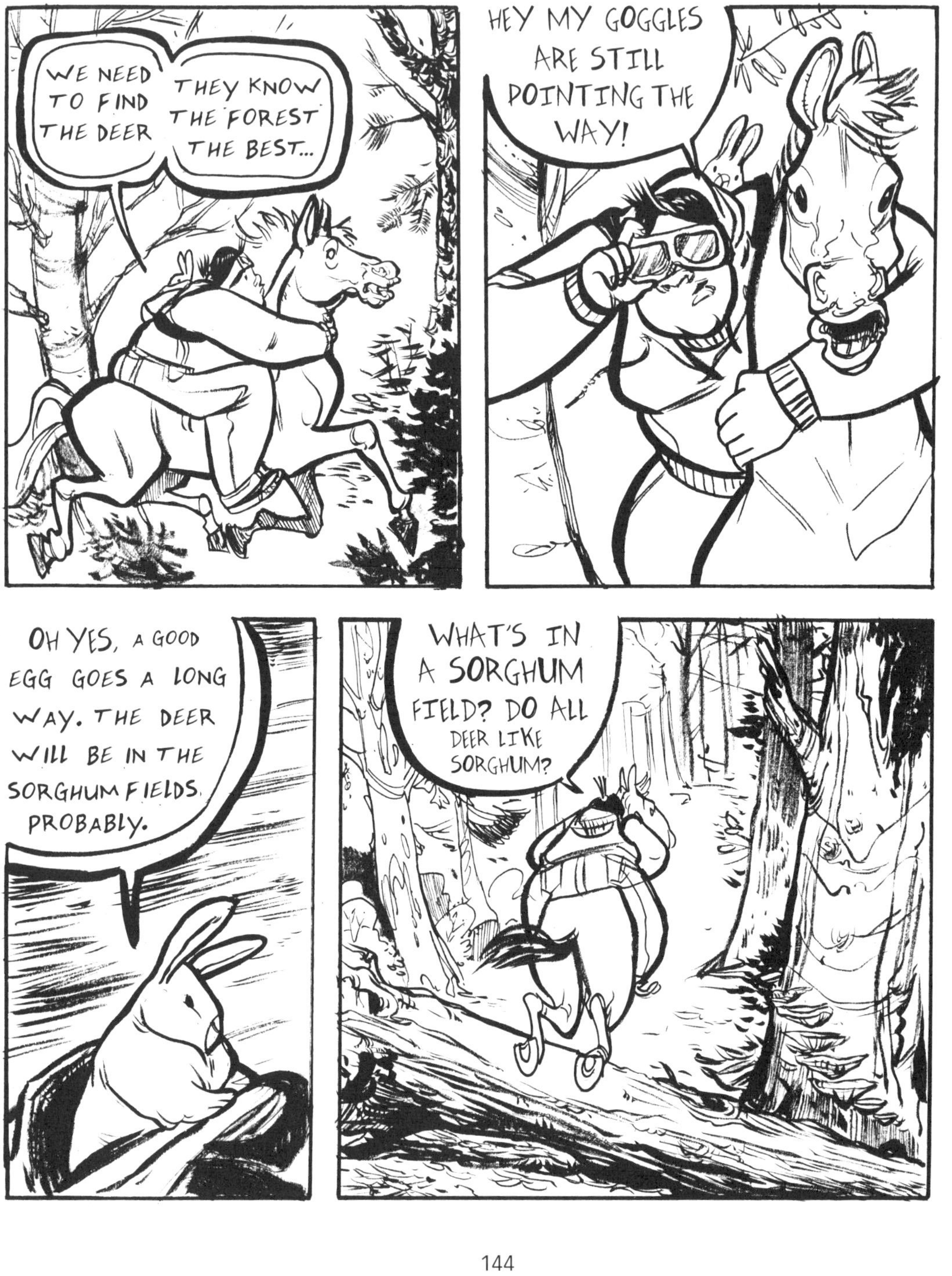
WE NEED TO FIND THE DEER
THEY KNOW THE FOREST THE BEST...
HEY MY GOGGLES ARE STILL POINTING THE WAY!
OH YES, A GOOD EGG GOES A LONG WAY. THE DEER WILL BE IN THE SORGHUM FIELDS, PROBABLY.
WHAT'S IN A SORGHUM FIELD? DO ALL DEER LIKE SORGHUM?

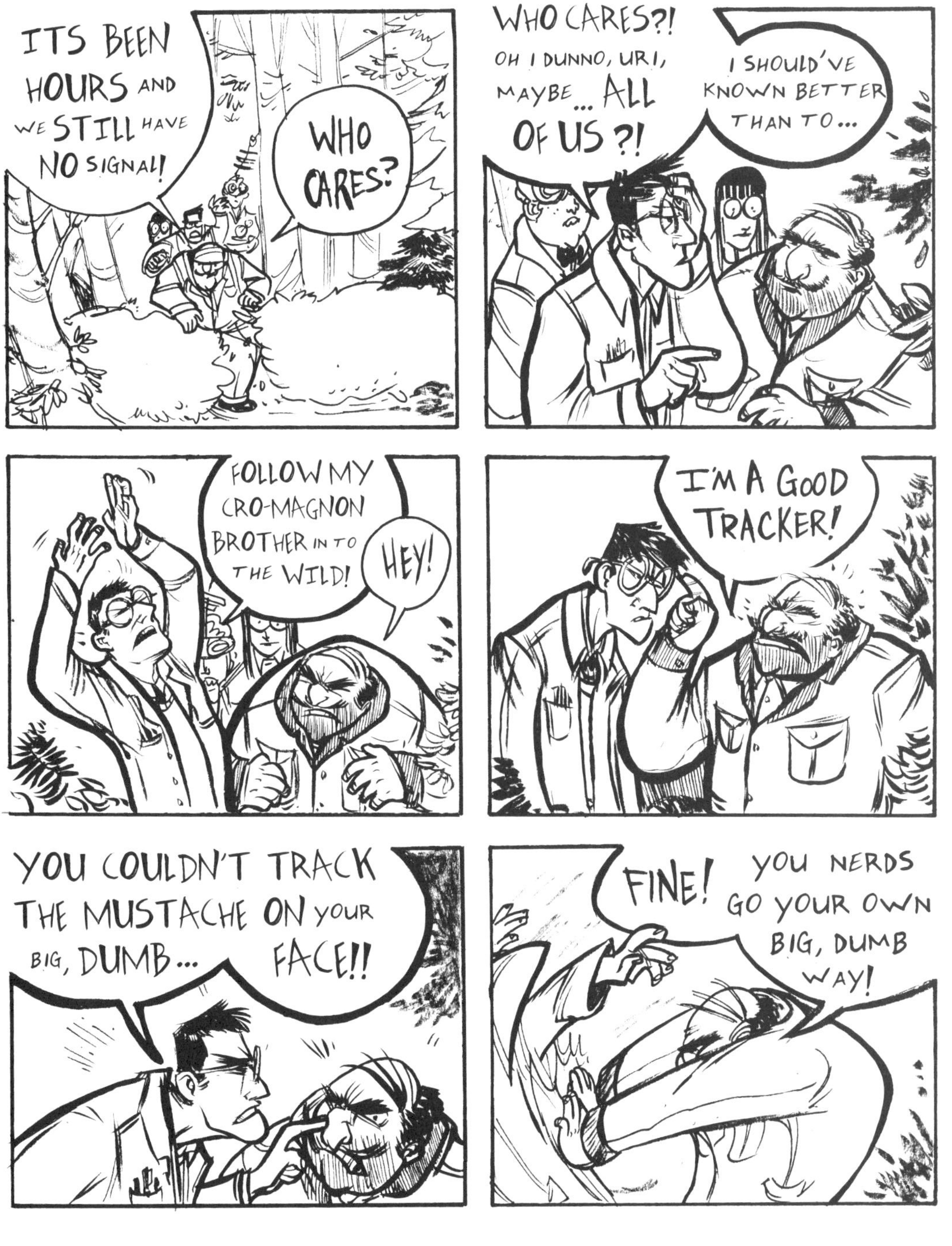
ITS BEEN HOURS AND WE STILL HAVE NO SIGNAL!
WHO CARES?
WHO CARES?! OH I DUNNO, URI, MAYBE ... ALL OF US?!
I SHOULD'VE KNOWN BETTER THAN TO...
FOLLOW MY CRO-MAGNON BROTHER IN TO THE WILD!
HEY!
I'M A GOOD TRACKER!
YOU COULDN'T TRACK THE MUSTACHE ON YOUR BIG, DUMB... FACE!!
FINE!
YOU NERDS GO YOUR OWN BIG, DUMB WAY!

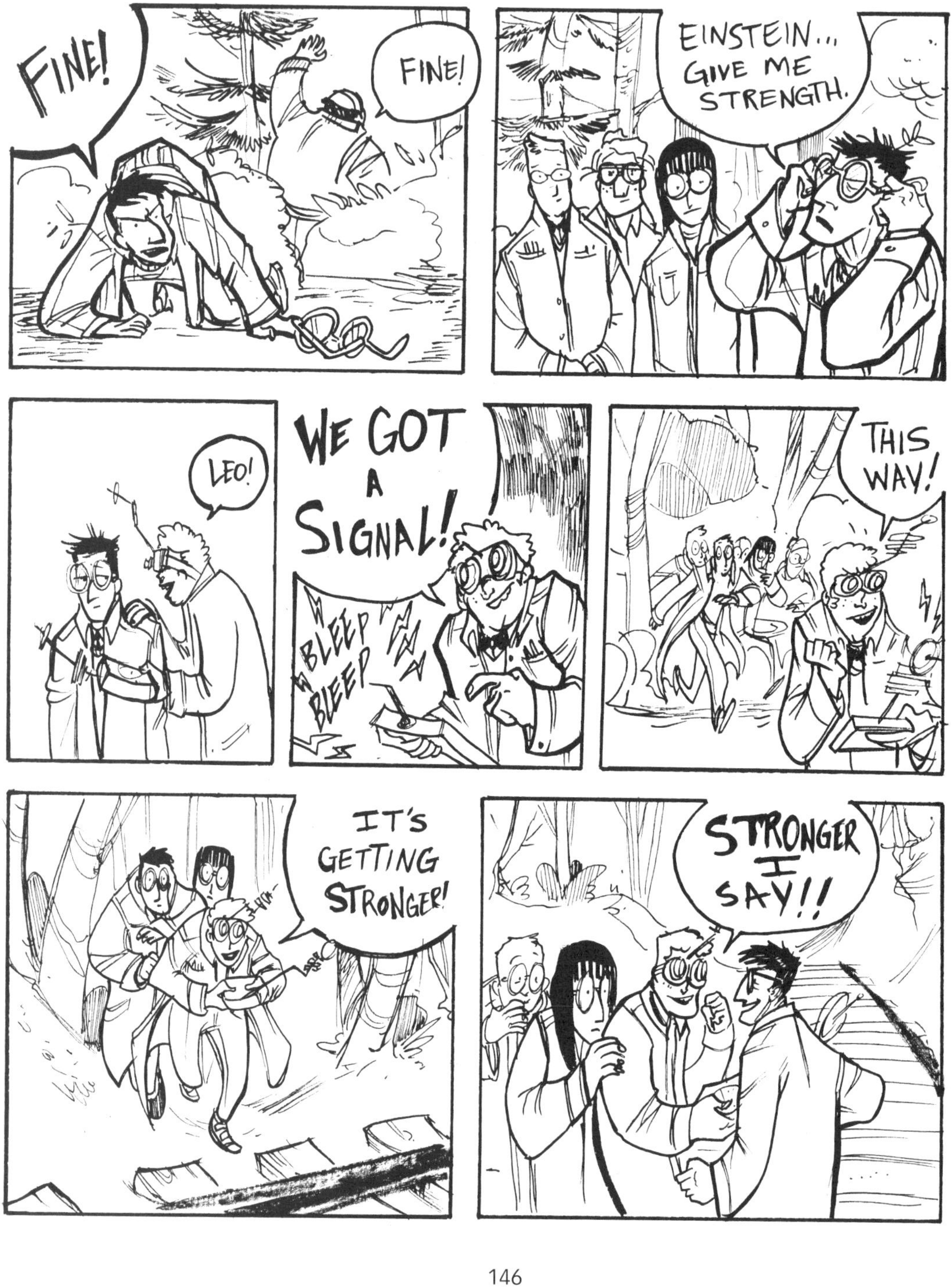
FINE!
FINE!
EINSTEIN... GIVE ME STRENGTH.
LEO!
WE GOT A SIGNAL!
BLEEP BLEEP
THIS WAY!
IT'S GETTING STRONGER!
STRONGER I SAY!!

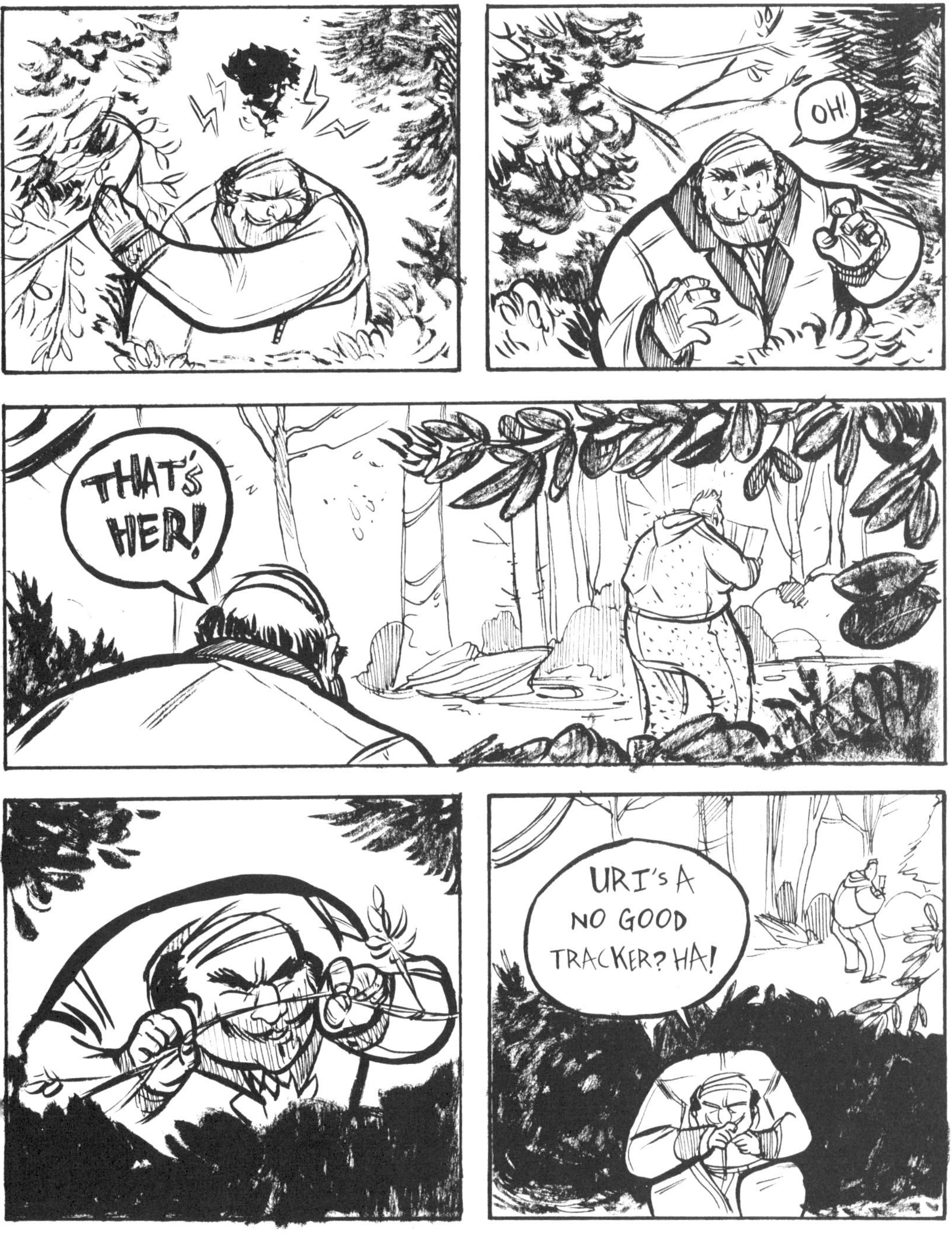
OH!
THAT'S HER!
URI'S A NO GOOD TRACKER? HA!

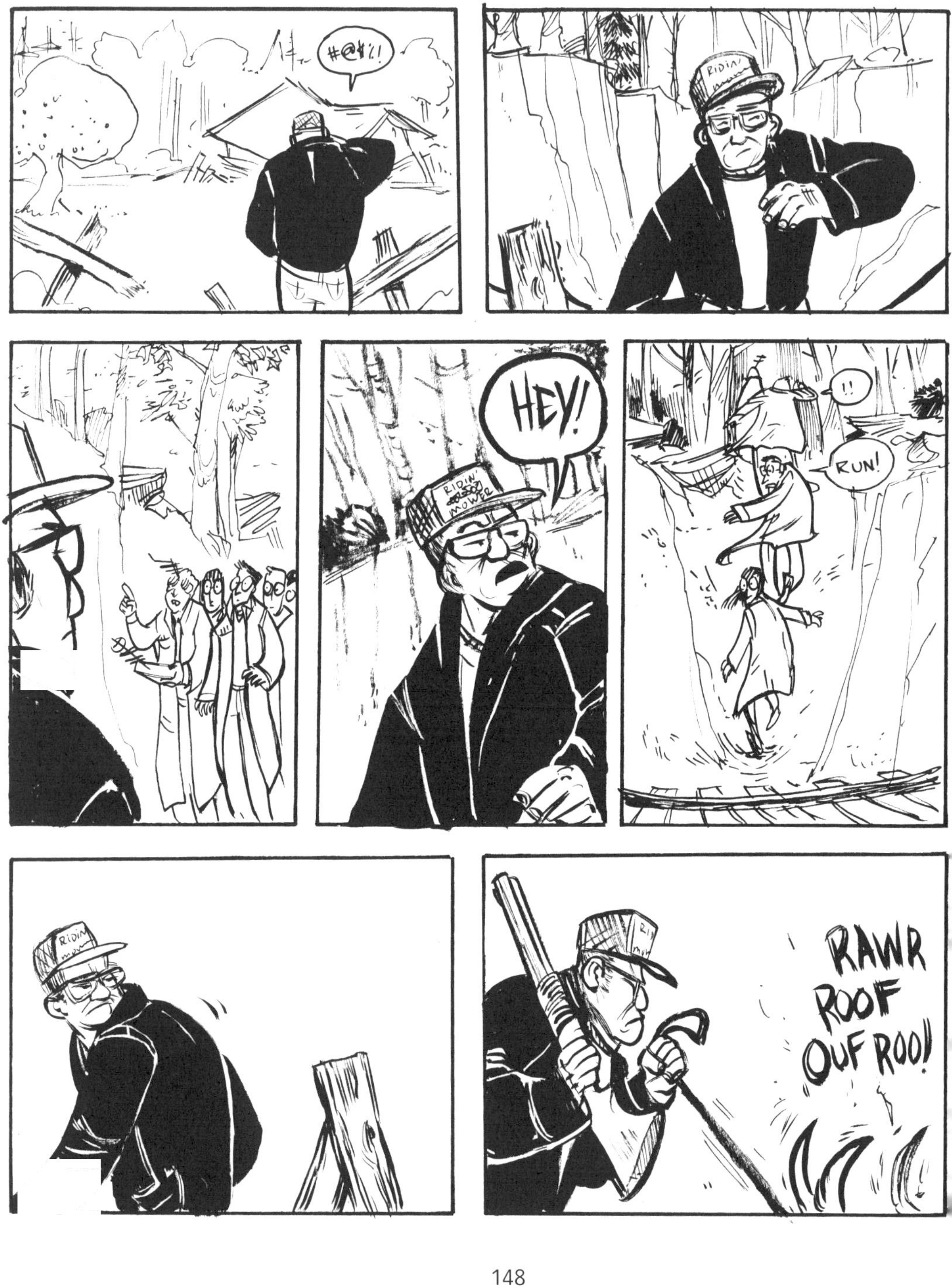
HEY!
RIDIN' MOWER
!!
RUN!
RAWR
ROOF
OUF ROO!

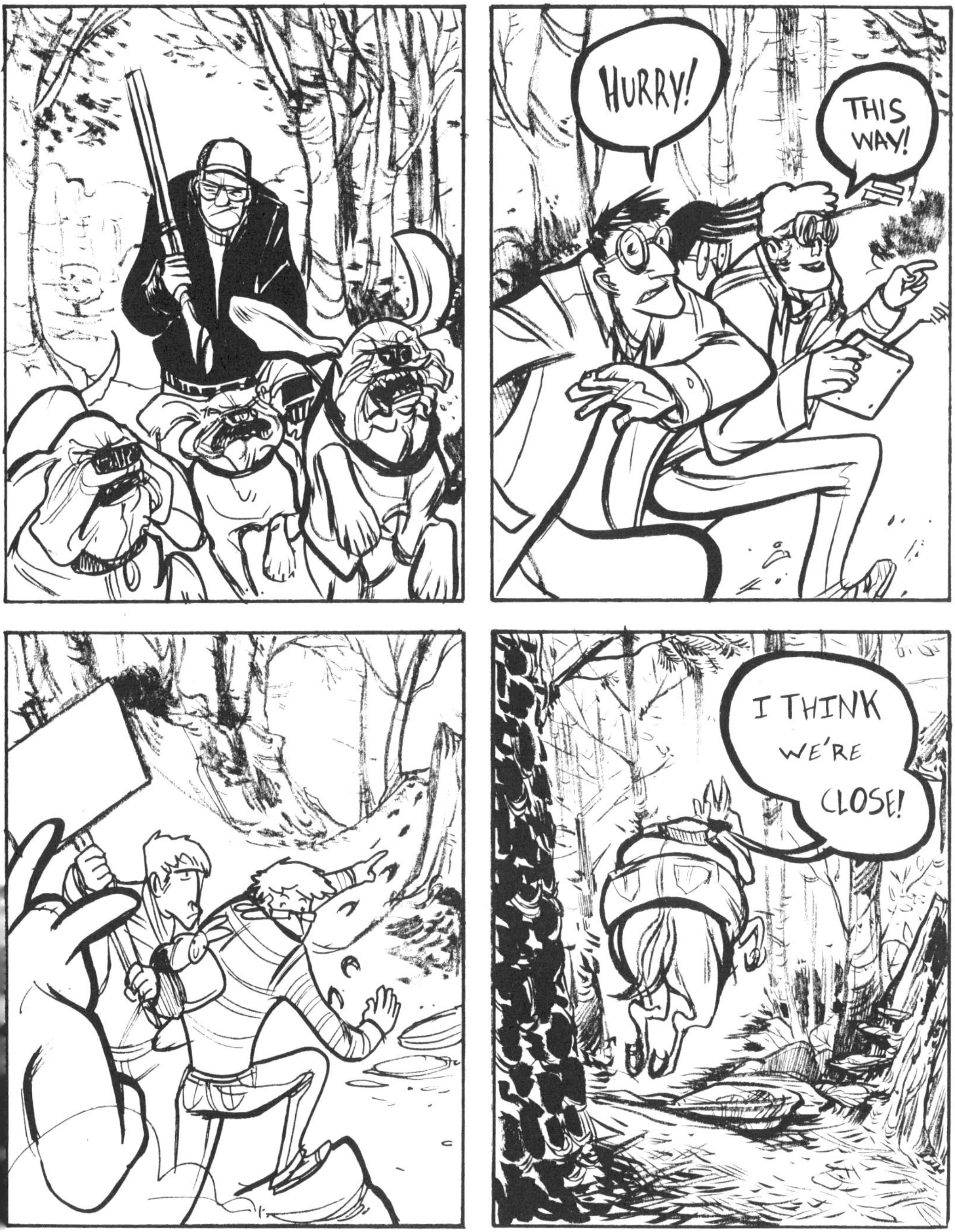
HURRY!
THIS WAY!
I THINK WE'RE CLOSE!

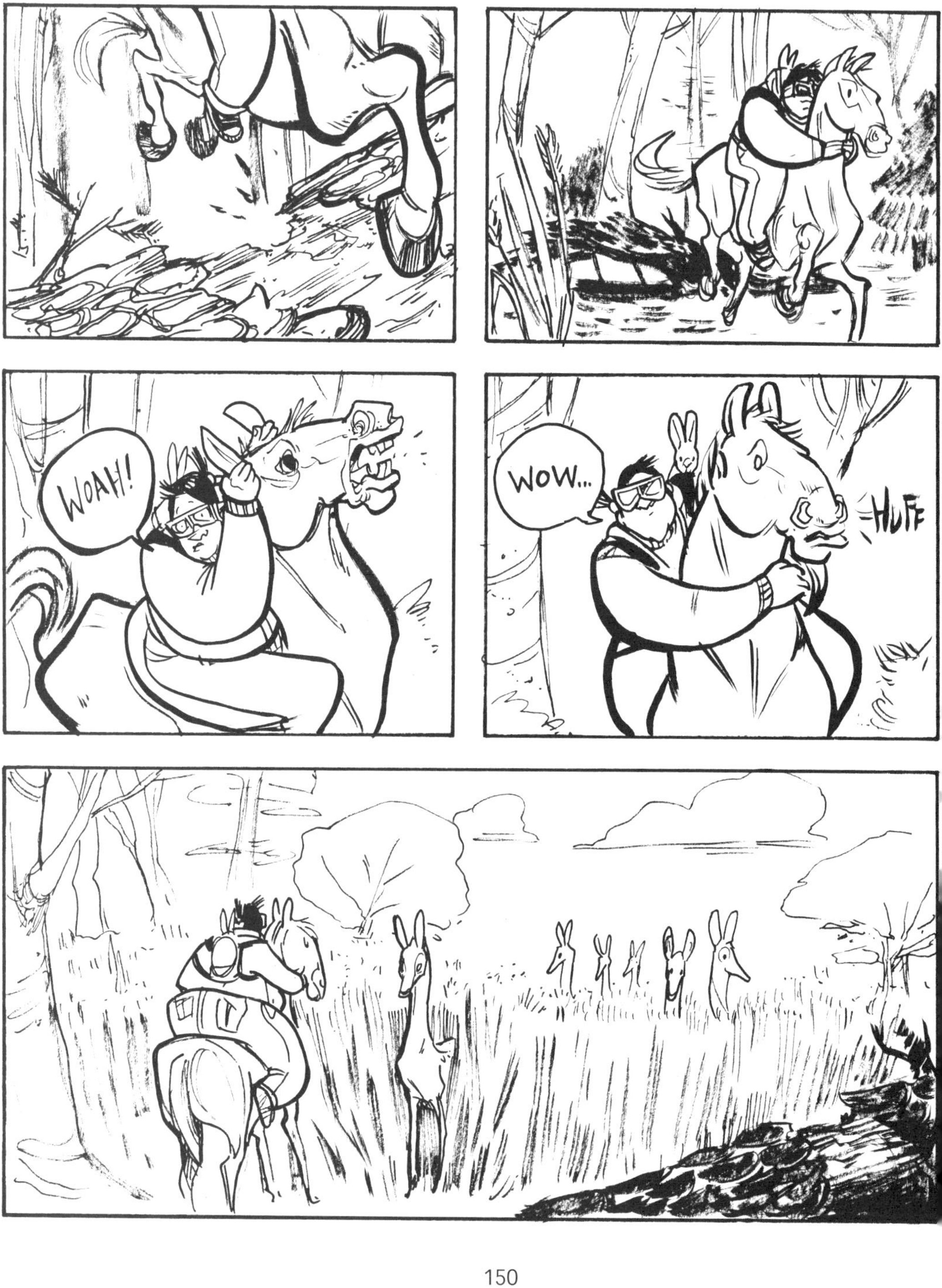
WOAH!
WOW...
HUFF

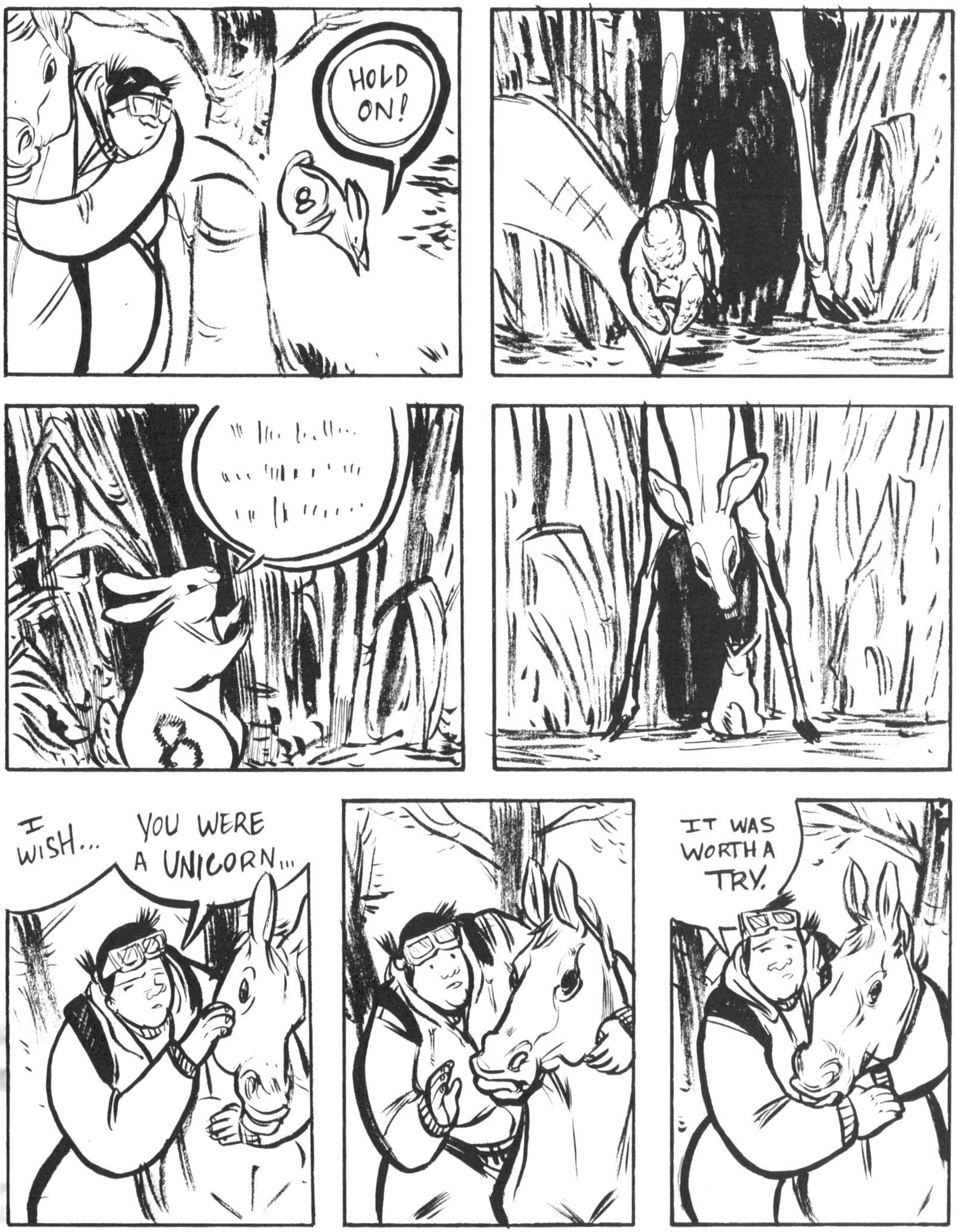
HOLD ON!
I WISH... YOU WERE A UNICORN...
IT WAS WORTH A TRY.

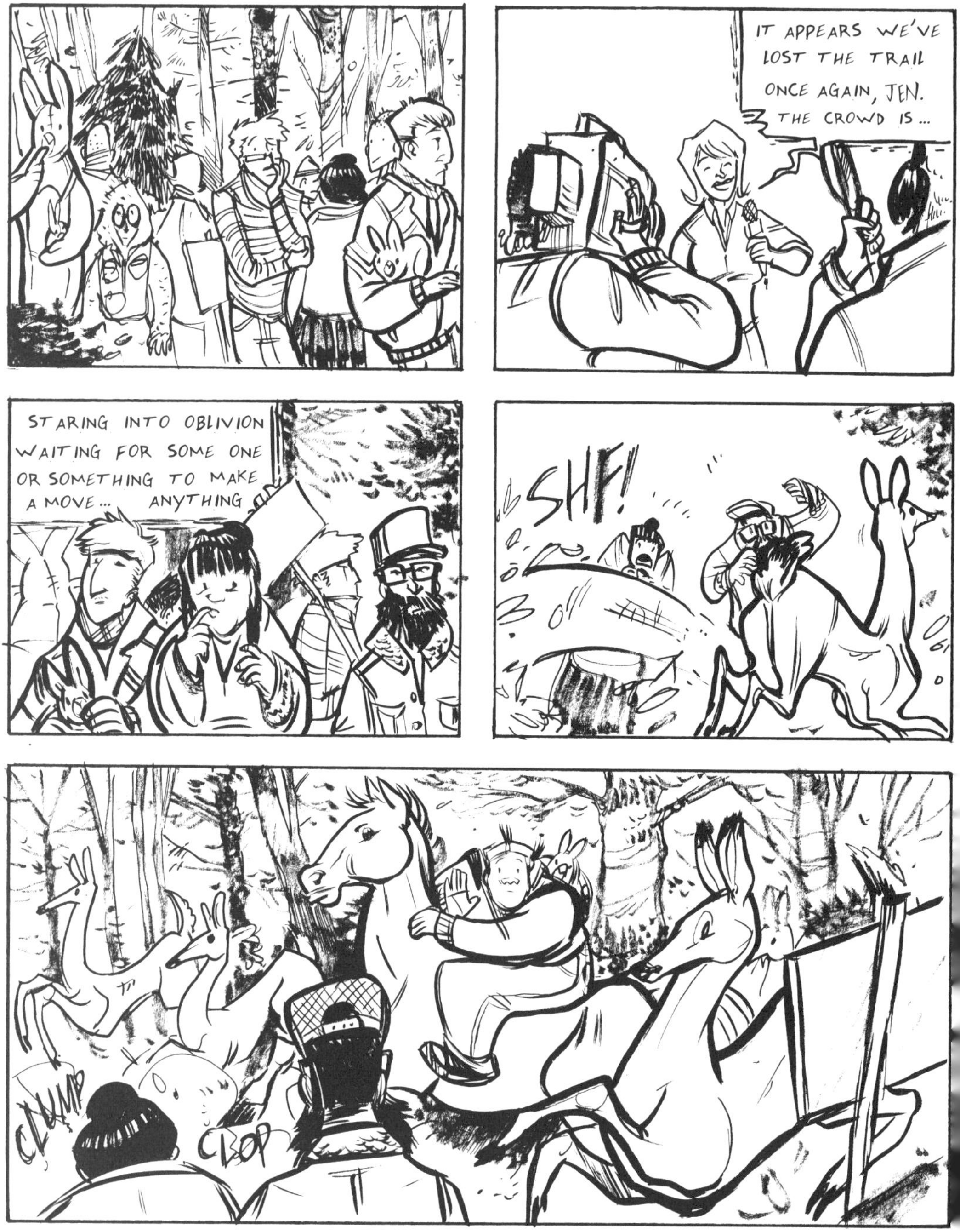
IT APPEARS WE'VE LOST THE TRAIL ONCE AGAIN, JEN. THE CROWD IS...
STARING INTO OBLIVION WAITING FOR SOME ONE OR SOMETHING TO MAKE A MOVE... ANYTHING
SHF!
CLOMP
CLOP

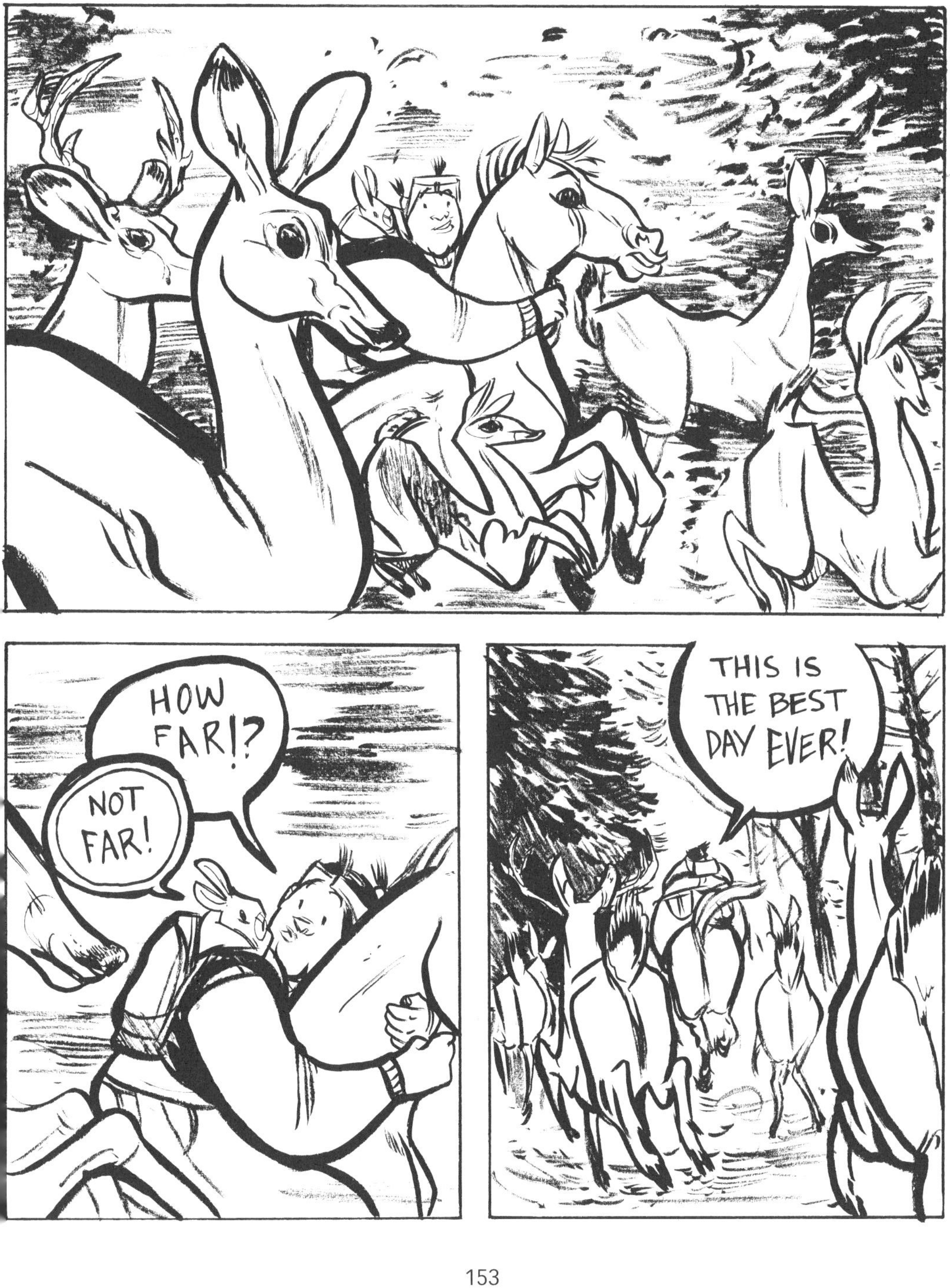
HOW FAR!?
NOT FAR!
THIS IS THE BEST DAY EVER!

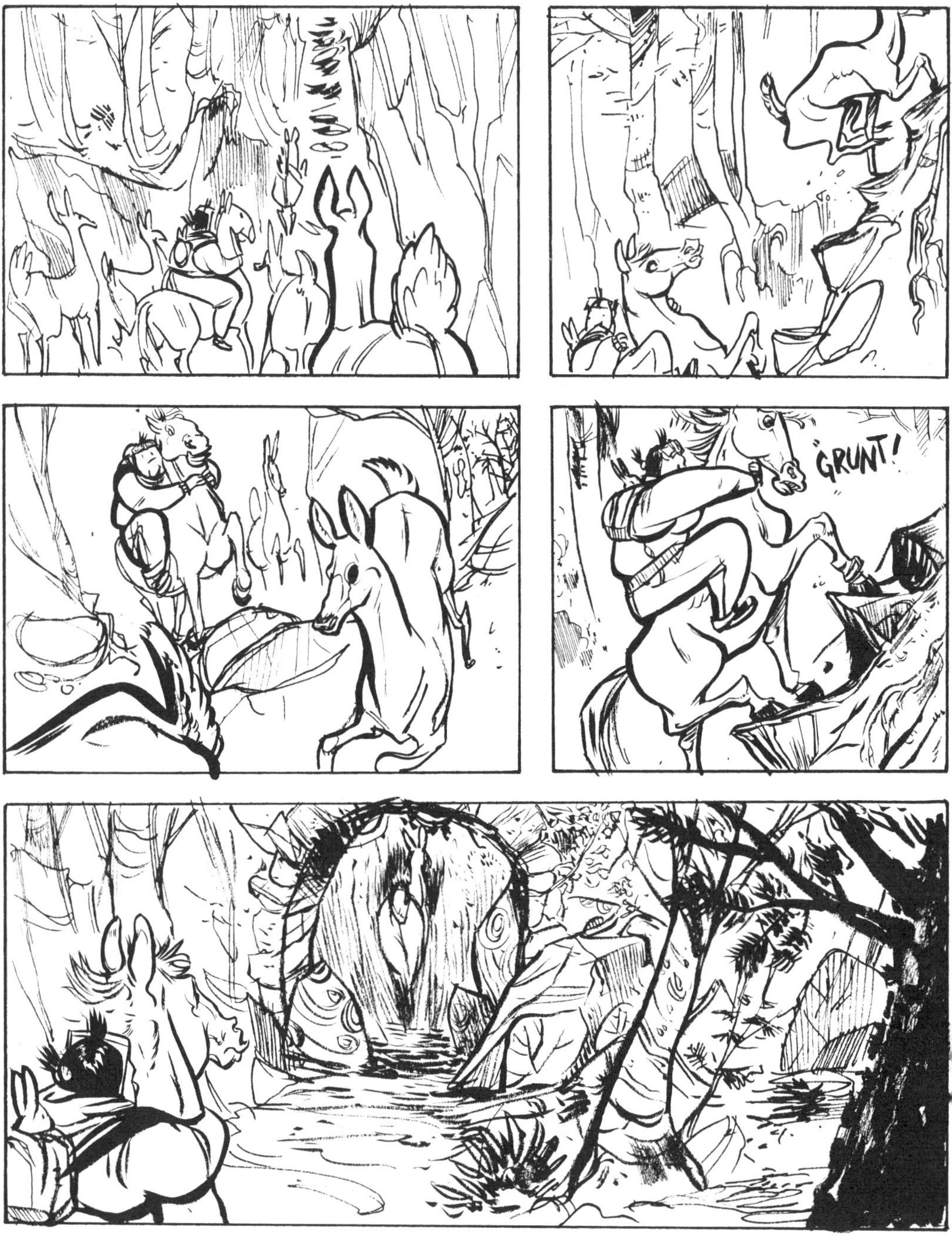
GRUNT!

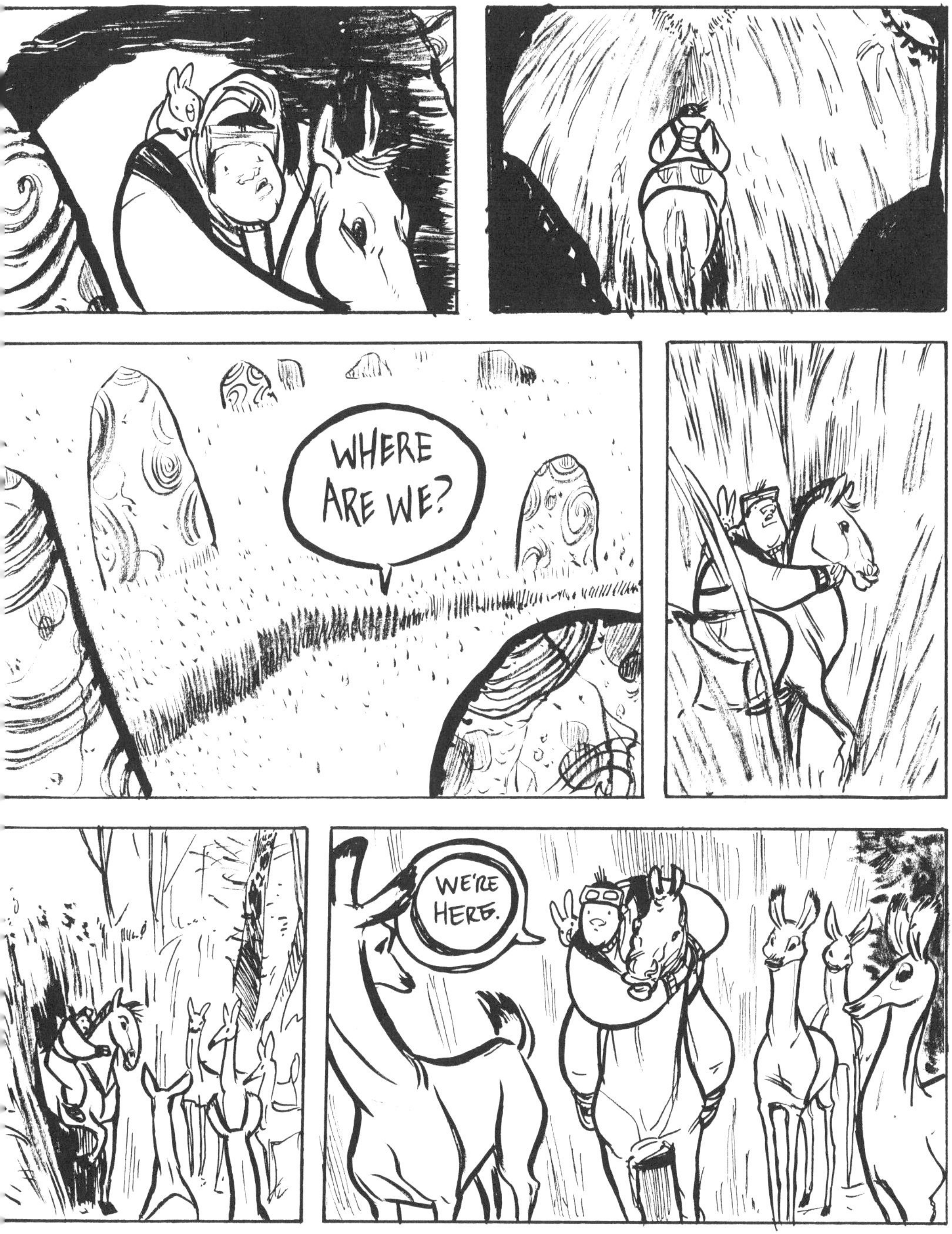
WHERE ARE WE?
WE'RE HERE.

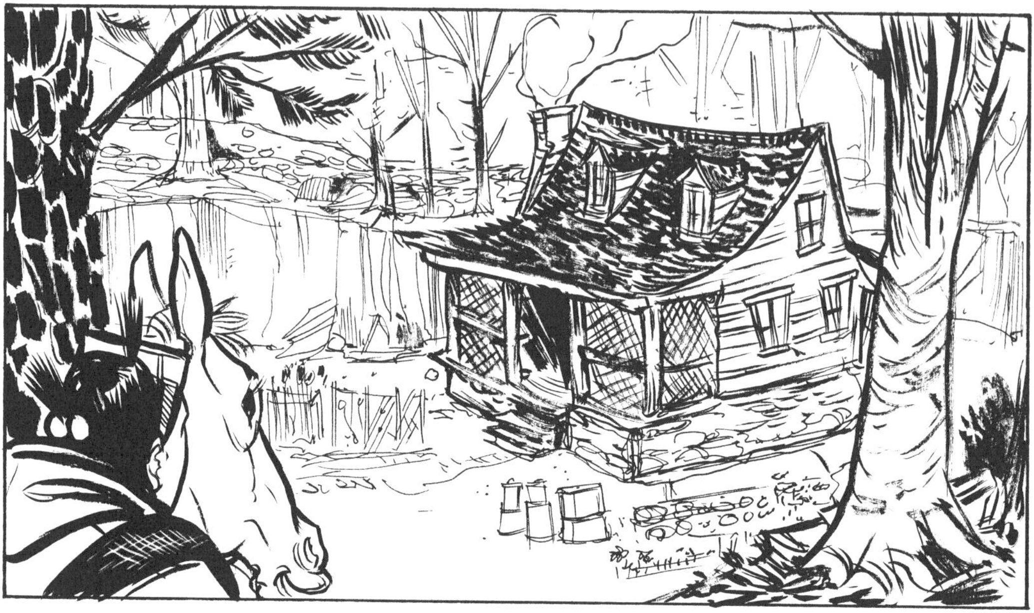

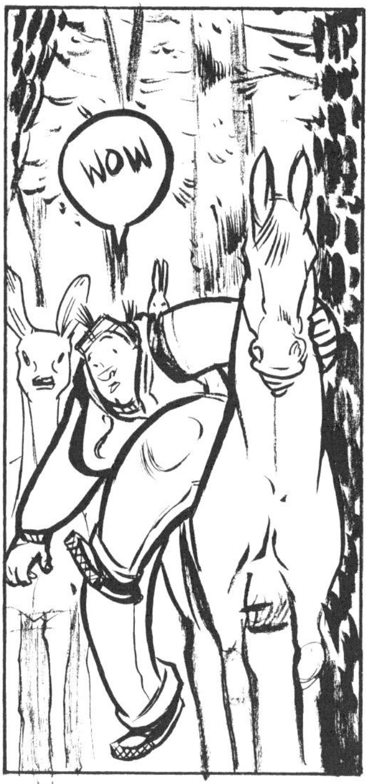
WOW

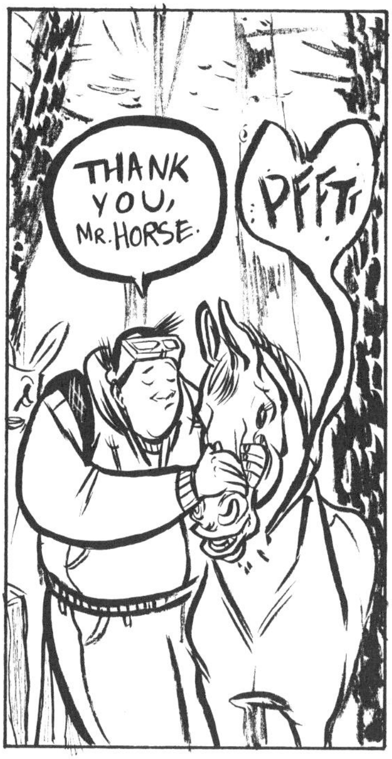
THANK YOU, MR. HORSE.
PFFTT

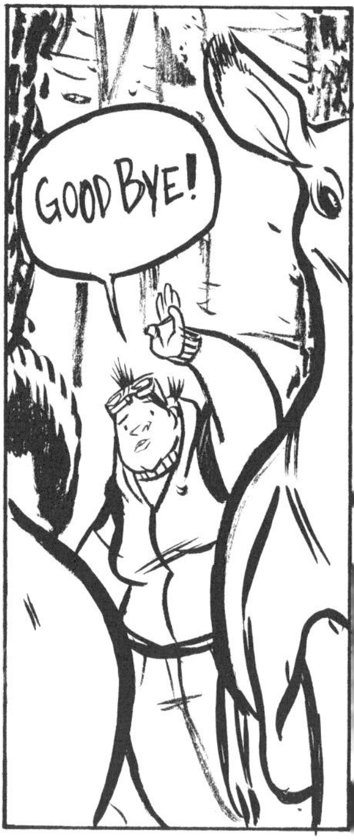
GOOD BYE!

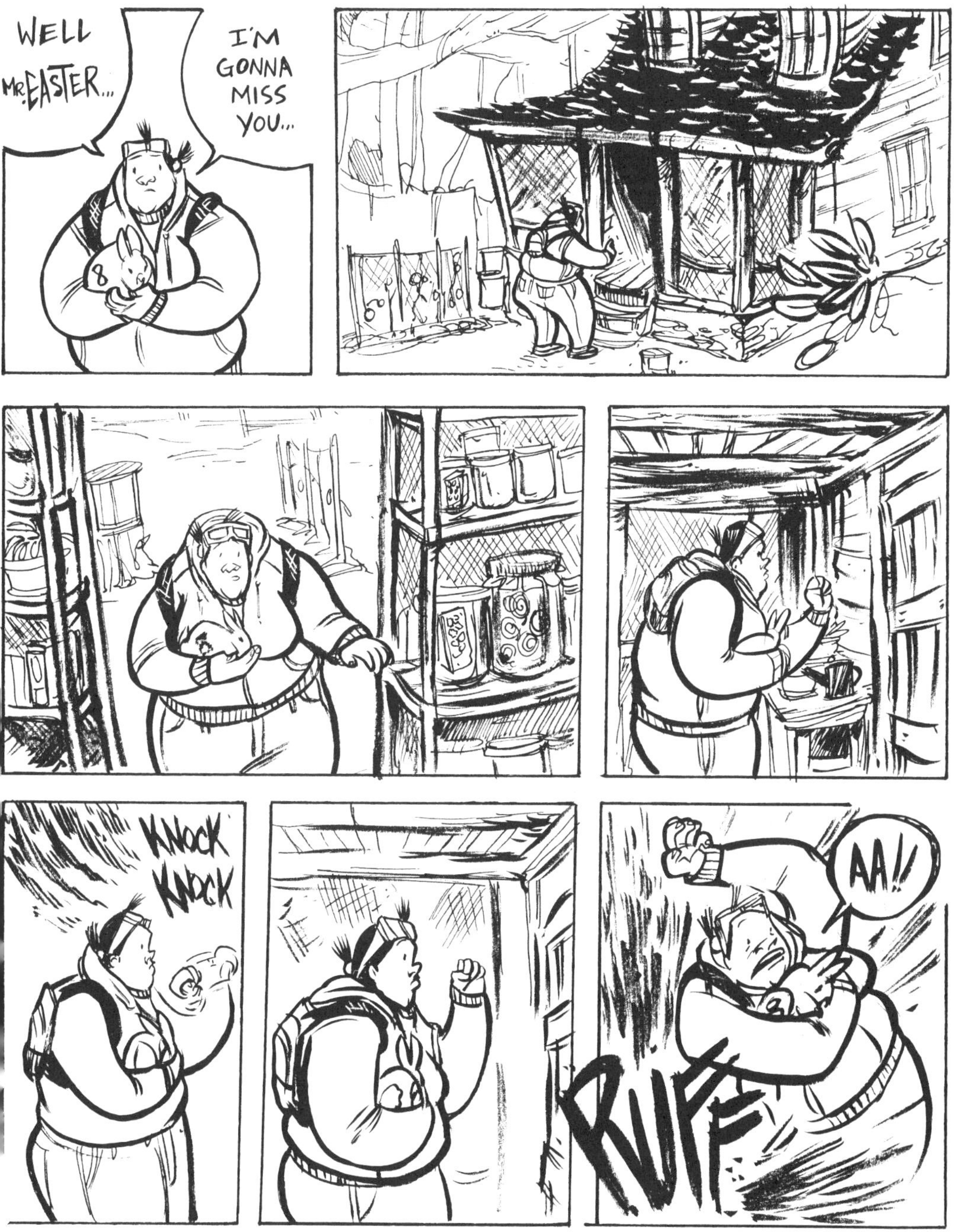
WELL MR. EASTER...
I'M GONNA MISS YOU...
KNOCK KNOCK
AA!!
RUFF

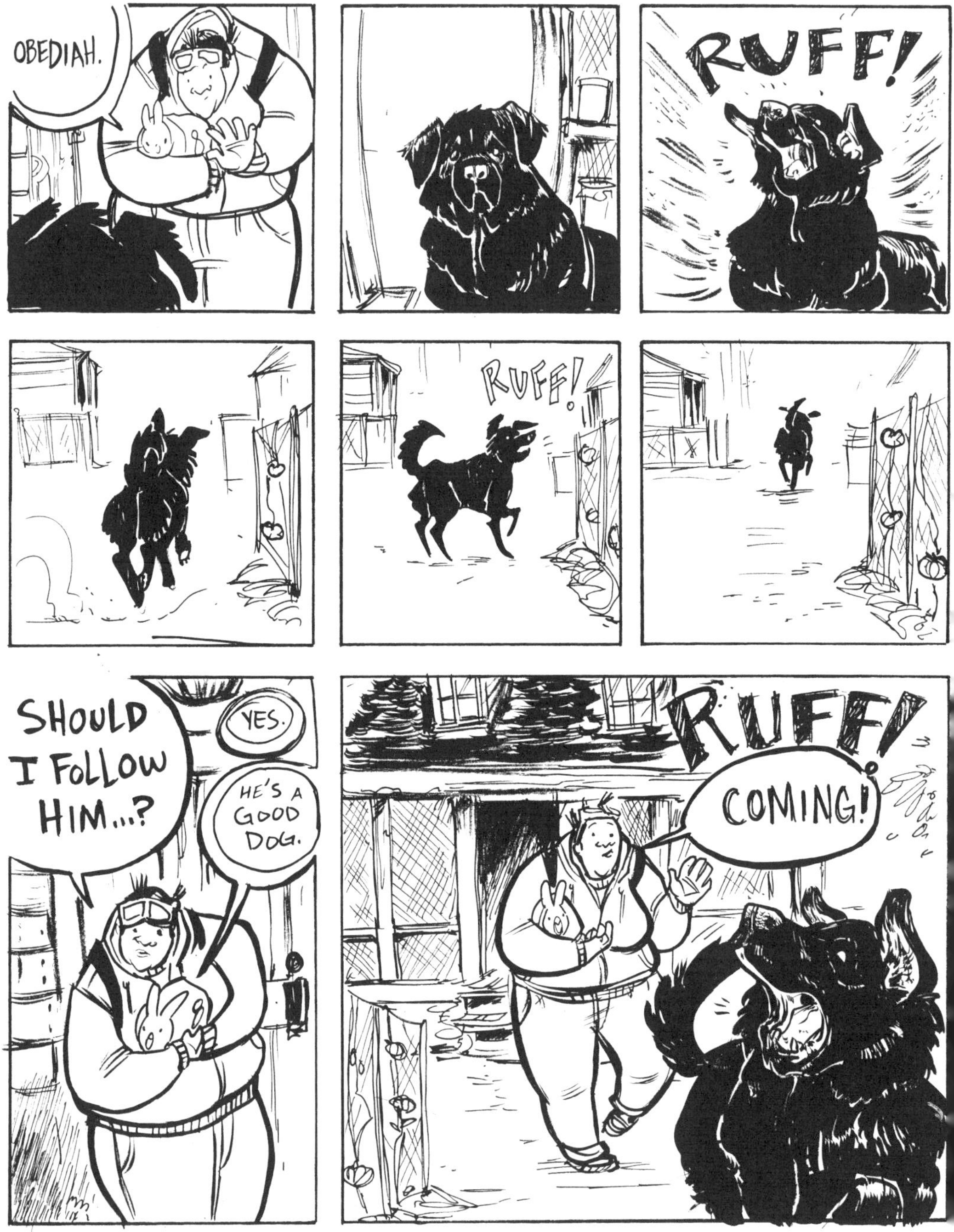

OBEDIAH.
RUFF!
RUFF!
SHOULD I FOLLOW HIM...?
YES.
HE'S A GOOD DOG.
RUFF!
COMING!

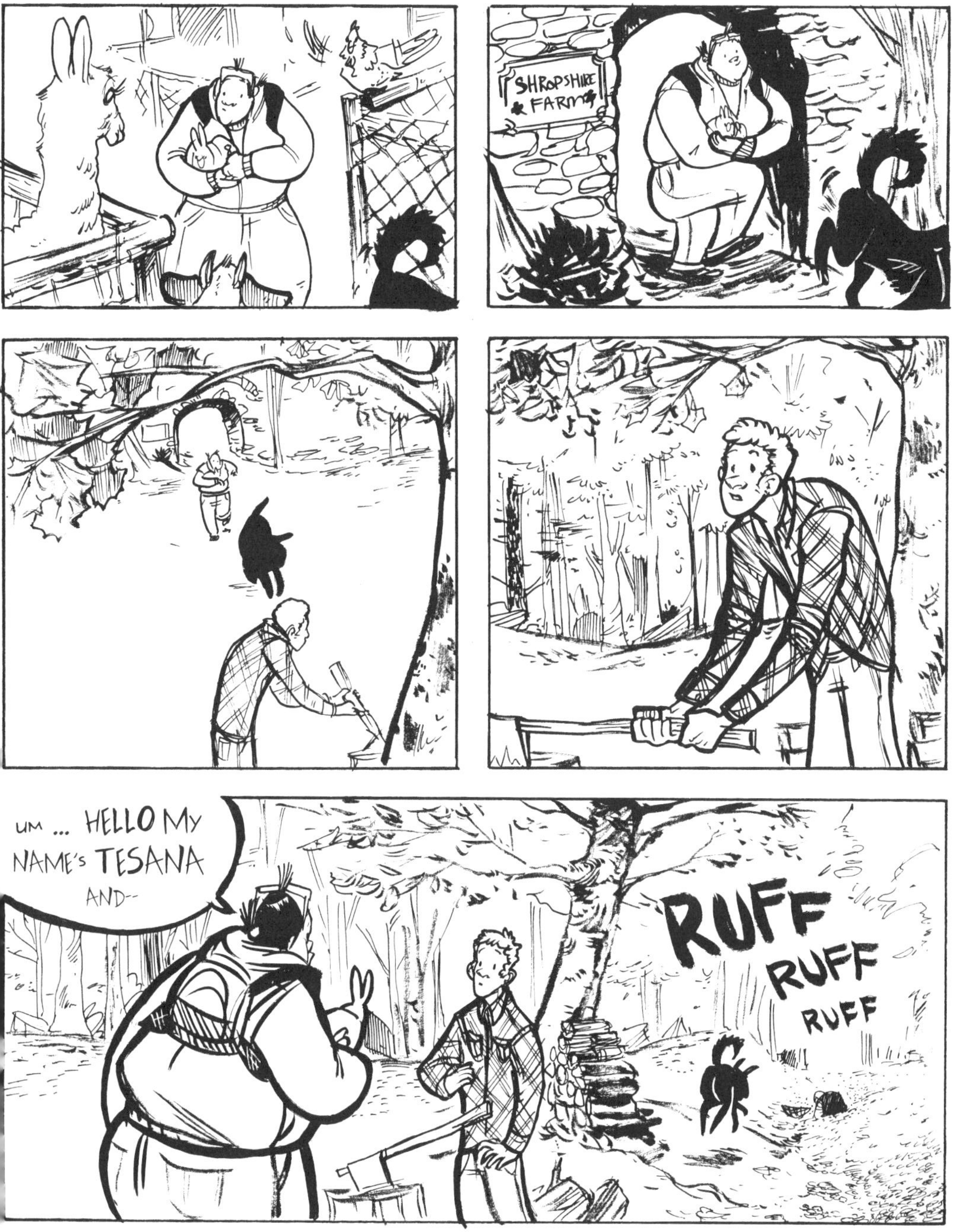
SHROPSHIRE FARM
UM ... HELLO MY NAME'S TESANA AND--
RUFF
RUFF
RUFF

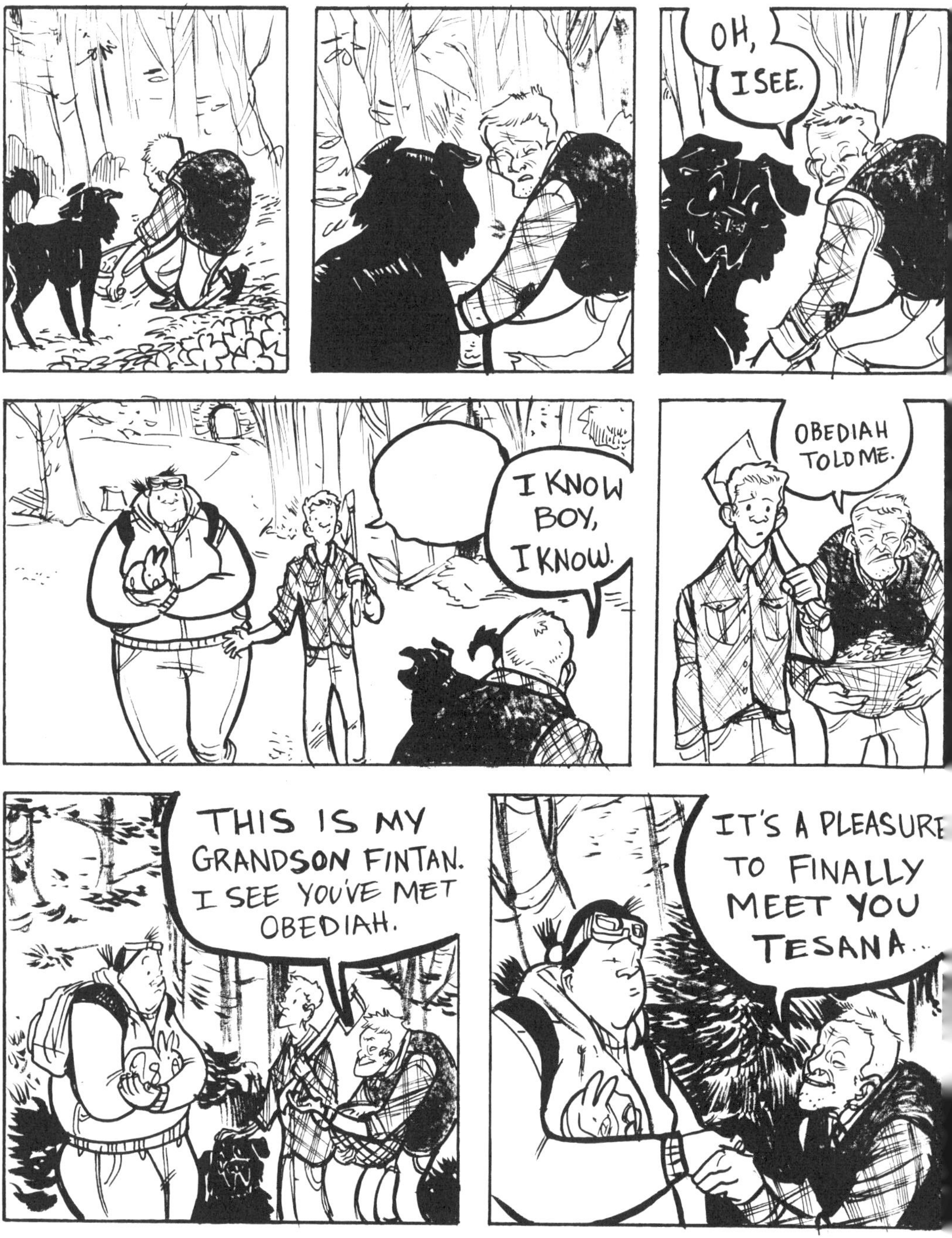
OH, I SEE.
I KNOW BOY, I KNOW.
OBEDIAH TOLD ME.
THIS IS MY GRANDSON FINTAN. I SEE YOU'VE MET OBEDIAH.
IT'S A PLEASURE TO FINALLY MEET YOU TESANA...

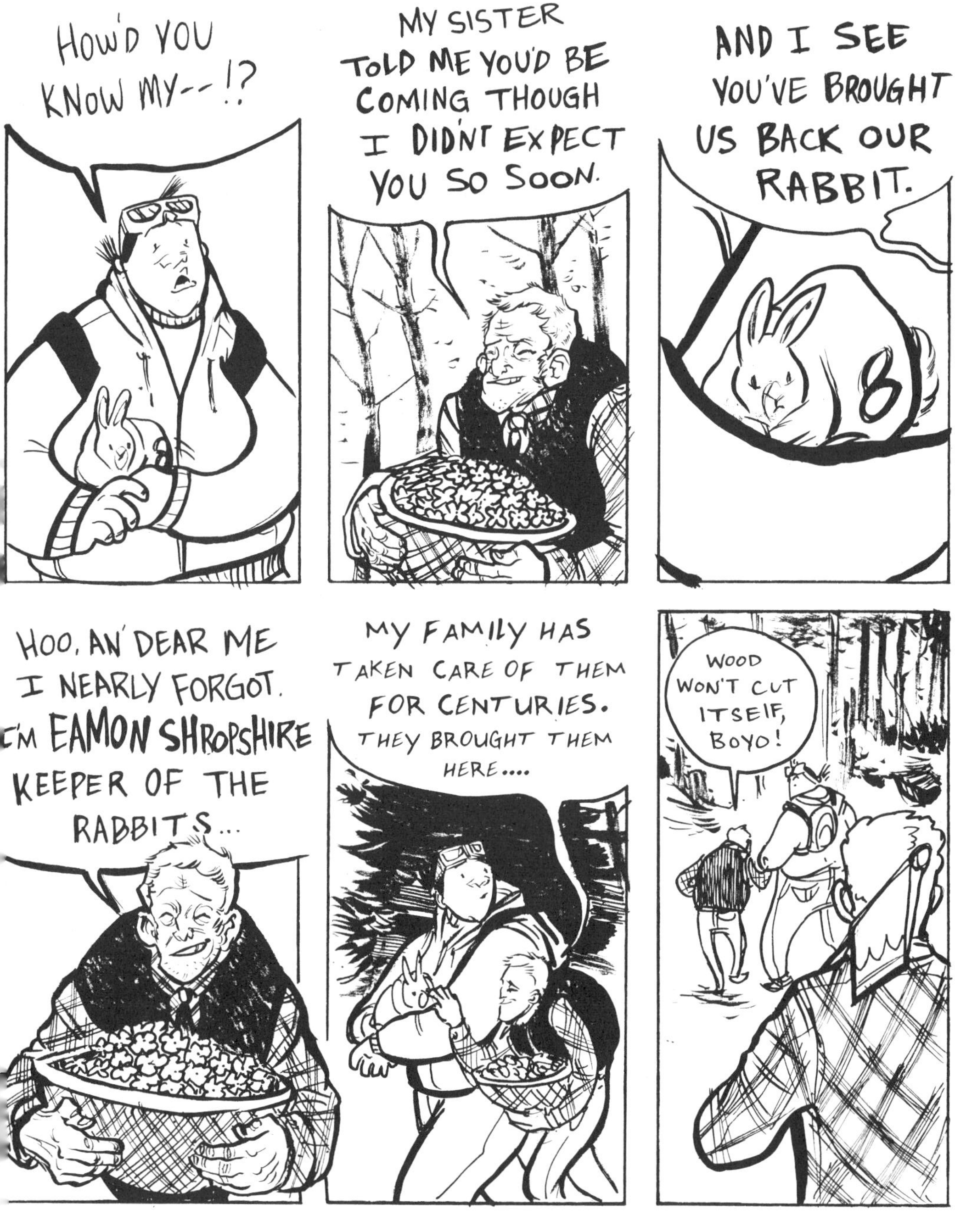
HOW'D YOU KNOW MY--!?
MY SISTER TOLD ME YOU'D BE COMING THOUGH I DIDN'T EXPECT YOU SO SOON.
AND I SEE YOU'VE BROUGHT US BACK OUR RABBIT.
8
HOO, AN' DEAR ME I NEARLY FORGOT. I'M EAMON SHROPSHIRE KEEPER OF THE RABBITS...
MY FAMILY HAS TAKEN CARE OF THEM FOR CENTURIES. THEY BROUGHT THEM HERE....
WOOD WON'T CUT ITSELF, BOYO!

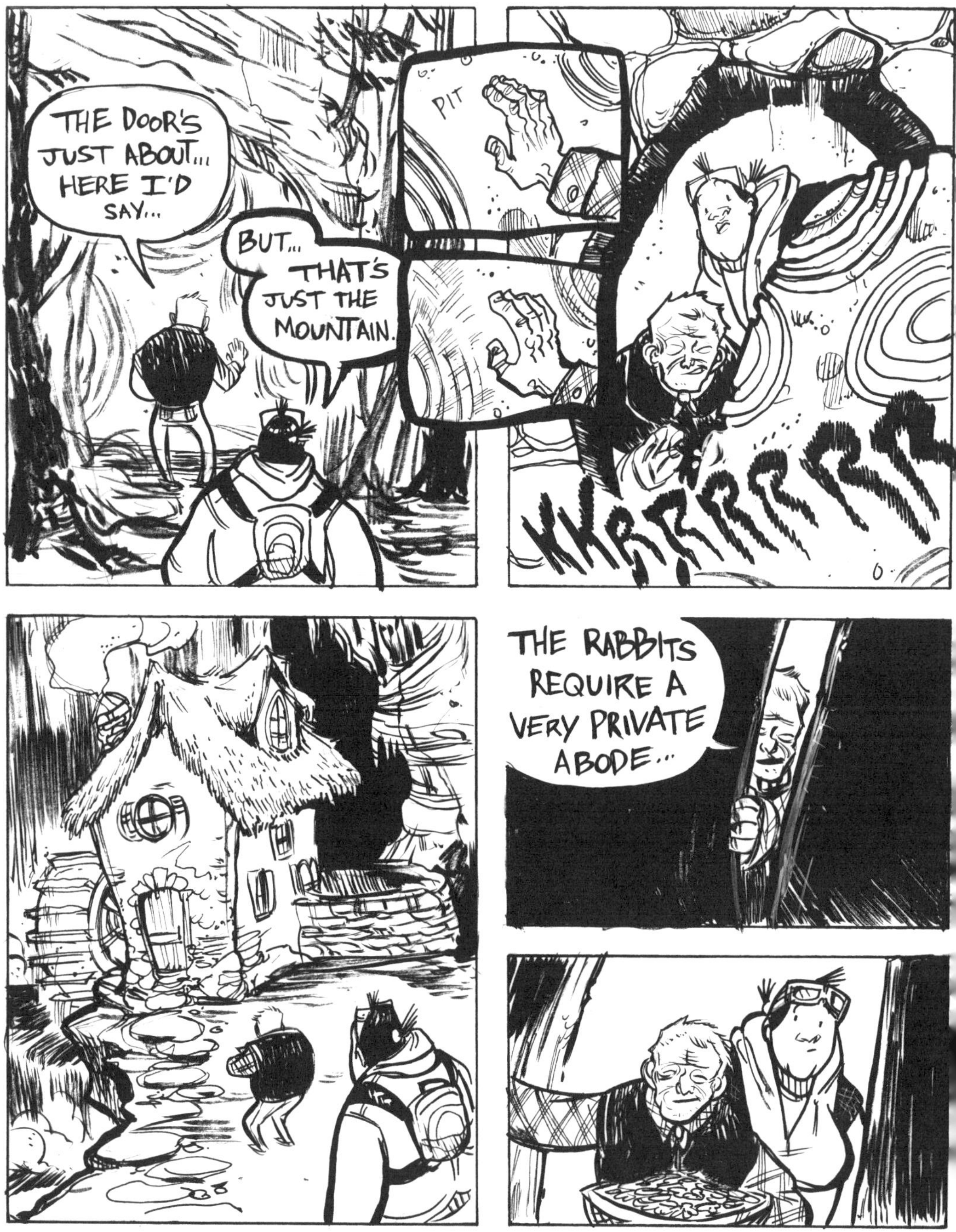
THE DOOR'S JUST ABOUT... HERE I'D SAY...
BUT... THAT'S JUST THE MOUNTAIN.
PIT
KKBBRRRRRR
THE RABBITS REQUIRE A VERY PRIVATE ABODE...

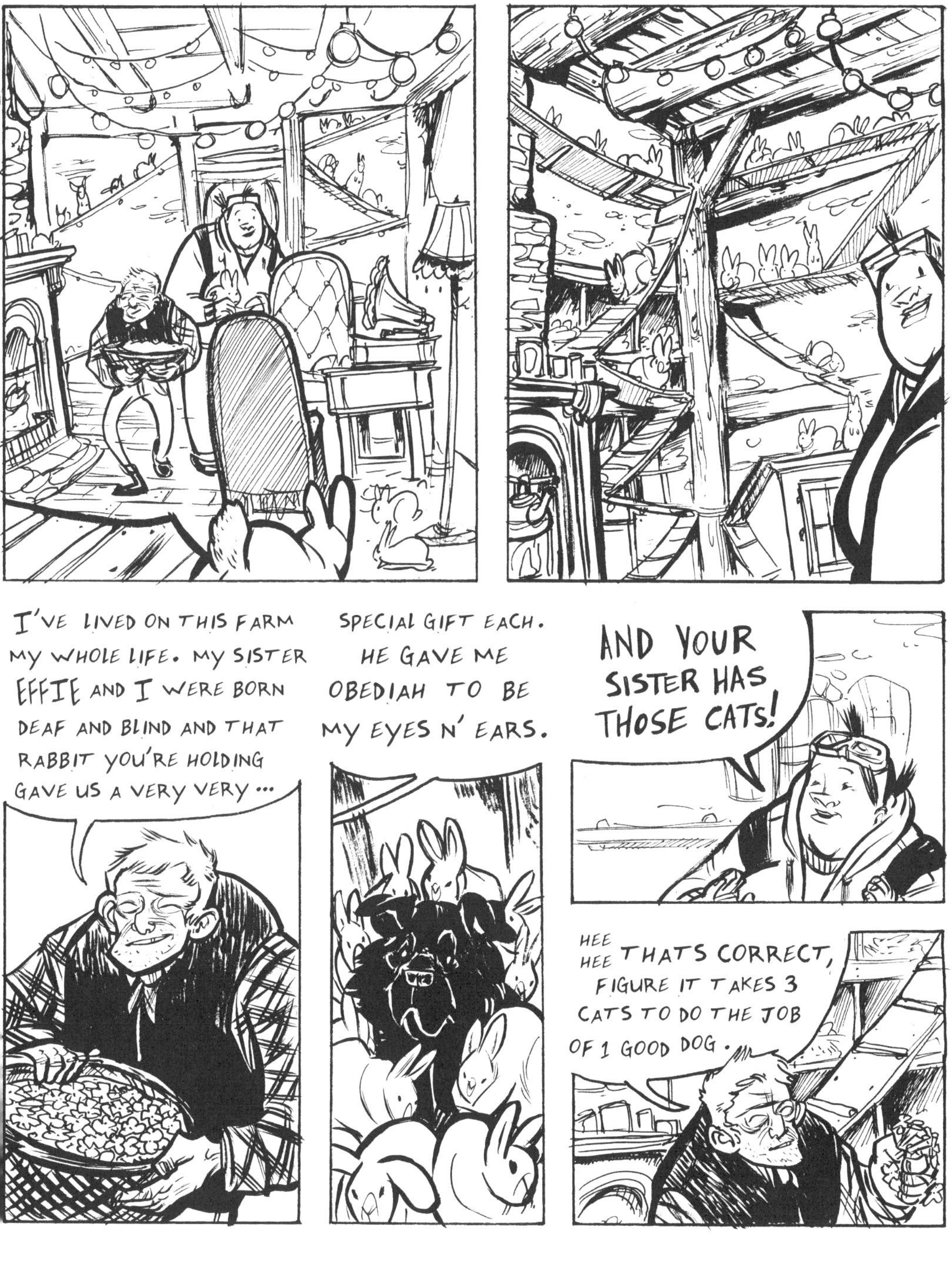
I'VE LIVED ON THIS FARM MY WHOLE LIFE. MY SISTER EFFIE AND I WERE BORN DEAF AND BLIND AND THAT RABBIT YOU'RE HOLDING GAVE US A VERY VERY ...
SPECIAL GIFT EACH. HE GAVE ME OBEDIAH TO BE MY EYES N' EARS.
AND YOUR SISTER HAS THOSE CATS!
HEE HEE
THATS CORRECT, FIGURE IT TAKES 3 CATS TO DO THE JOB OF 1 GOOD DOG.

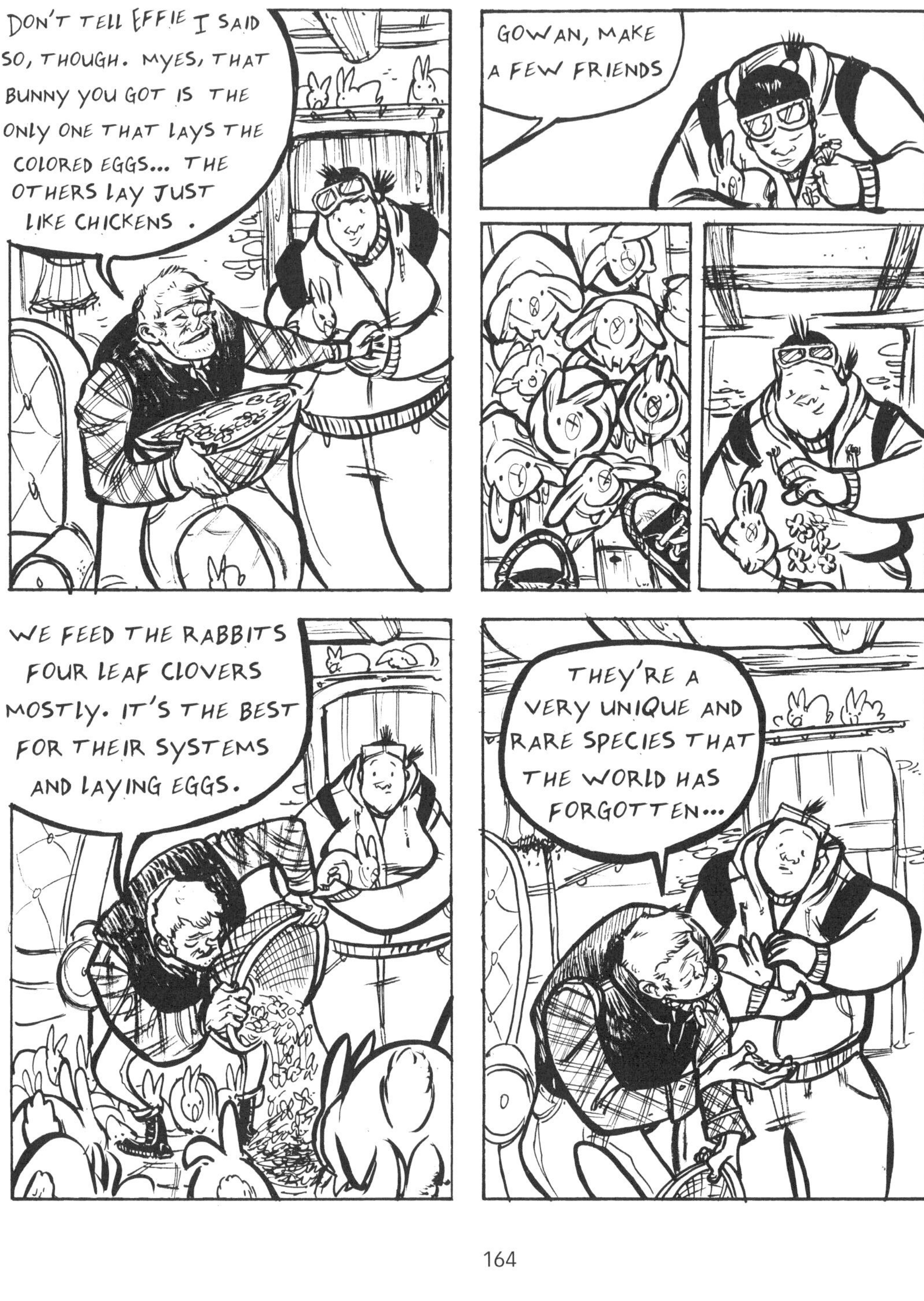
DON'T TELL EFFIE I SAID SO, THOUGH. MYES, THAT BUNNY YOU GOT IS THE ONLY ONE THAT LAYS THE COLORED EGGS... THE OTHERS LAY JUST LIKE CHICKENS.
GOWAN, MAKE A FEW FRIENDS
WE FEED THE RABBITS FOUR LEAF CLOVERS MOSTLY. IT'S THE BEST FOR THEIR SYSTEMS AND LAYING EGGS.
THEY'RE A VERY UNIQUE AND RARE SPECIES THAT THE WORLD HAS FORGOTTEN...

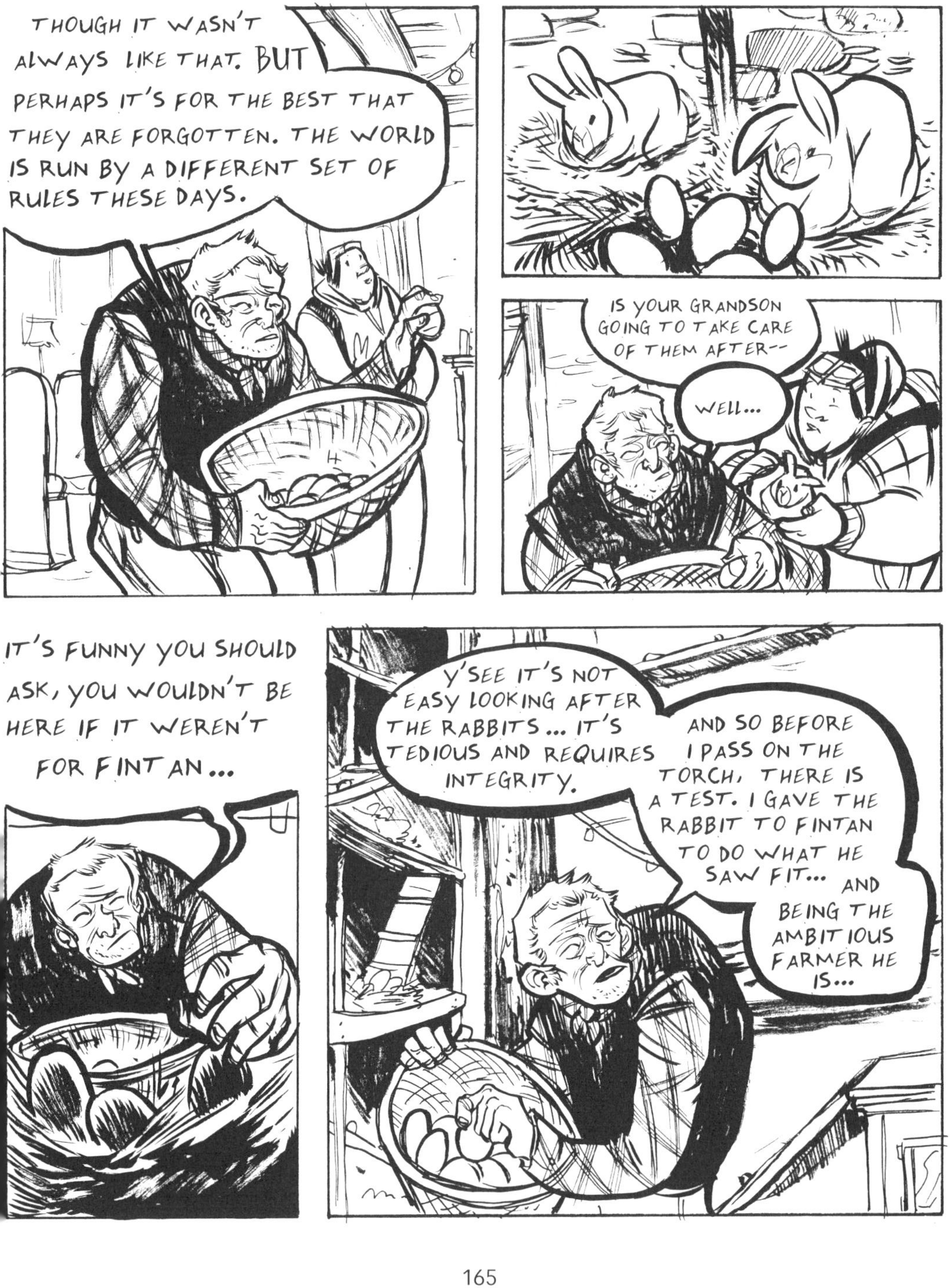
THOUGH IT WASN'T ALWAYS LIKE THAT. BUT PERHAPS IT'S FOR THE BEST THAT THEY ARE FORGOTTEN. THE WORLD IS RUN BY A DIFFERENT SET OF RULES THESE DAYS.
IS YOUR GRANDSON GOING TO TAKE CARE OF THEM AFTER--
WELL...
IT'S FUNNY YOU SHOULD ASK, YOU WOULDN'T BE HERE IF IT WEREN'T FOR FINTAN...
Y'SEE IT'S NOT EASY LOOKING AFTER THE RABBITS... IT'S TEDIOUS AND REQUIRES INTEGRITY.
AND SO BEFORE I PASS ON THE TORCH, THERE IS A TEST. I GAVE THE RABBIT TO FINTAN TO DO WHAT HE SAW FIT...
AND BEING THE AMBITIOUS FARMER HE IS...

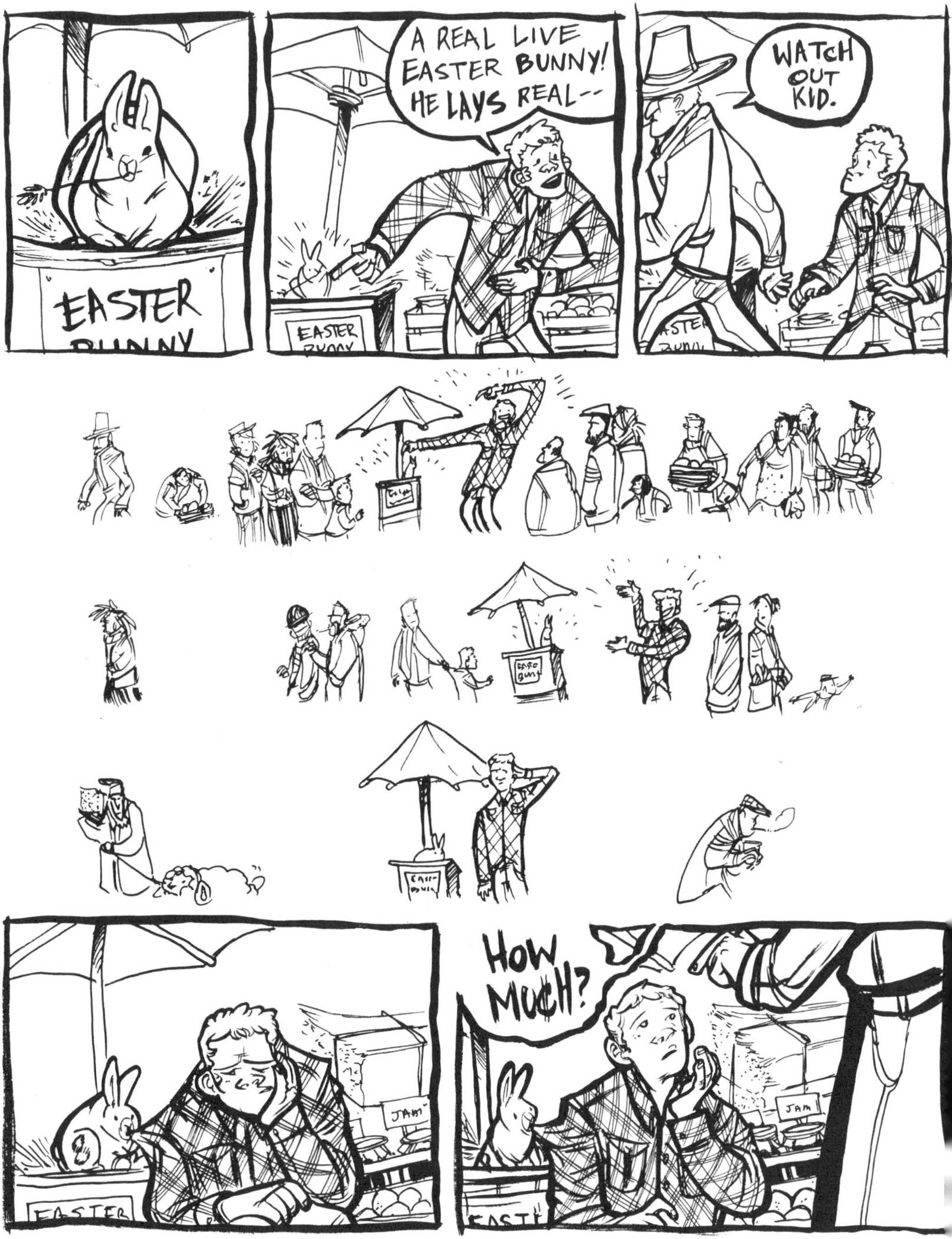
EASTER
A REAL LIVE EASTER BUNNY! HE LAYS REAL--
WATCH OUT KID.
JAM
HOW MUCH?
JAM

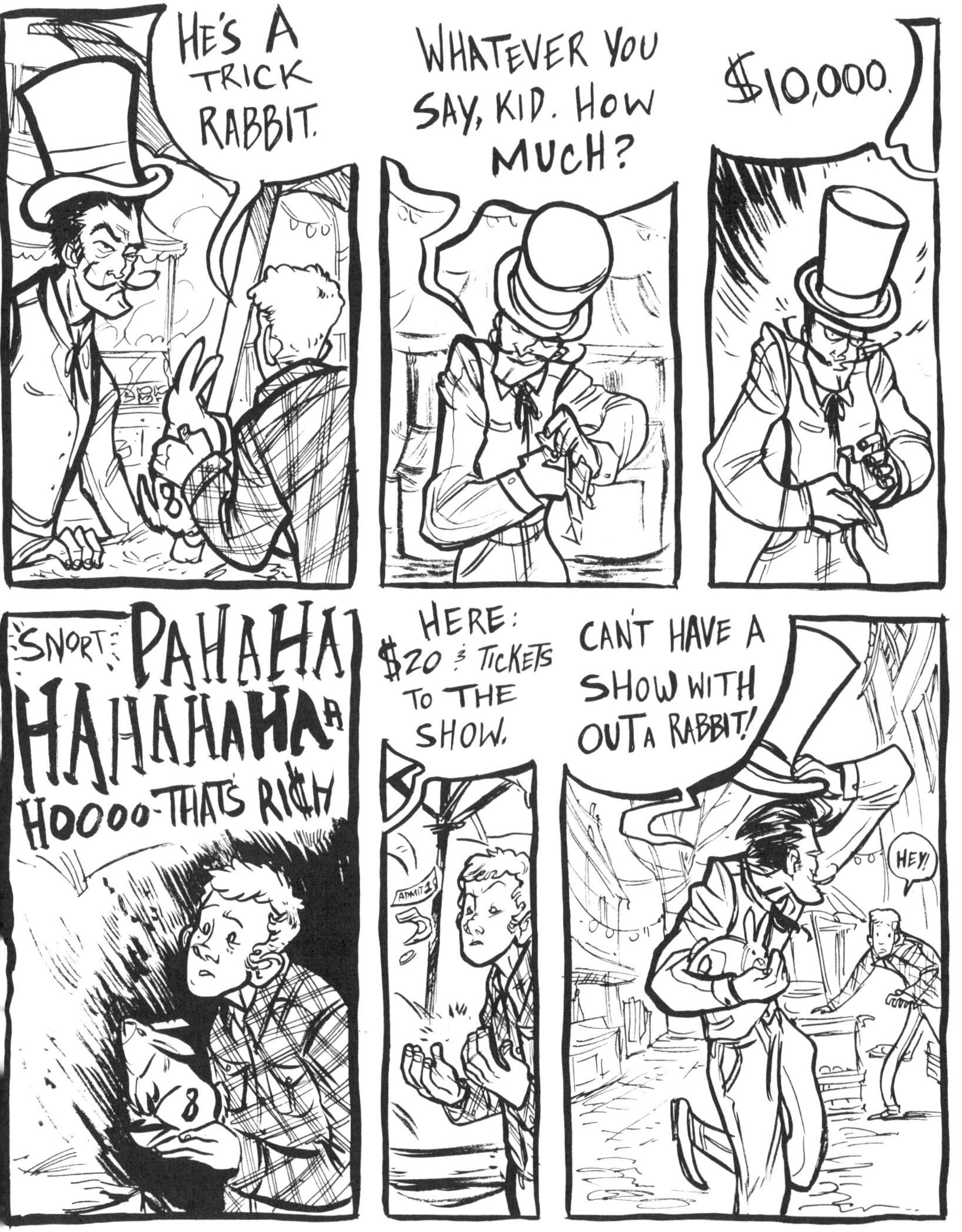
HE'S A TRICK RABBIT.
WHATEVER YOU SAY, KID. HOW MUCH?
$10,000.
SNORT PAHAHA HAHAHAHAHA HOOOO-THAT'S RICH
HERE: $20 & TICKETS TO THE SHOW.
ADMIT 1
CAN'T HAVE A SHOW WITH OUT A RABBIT!
HEY!

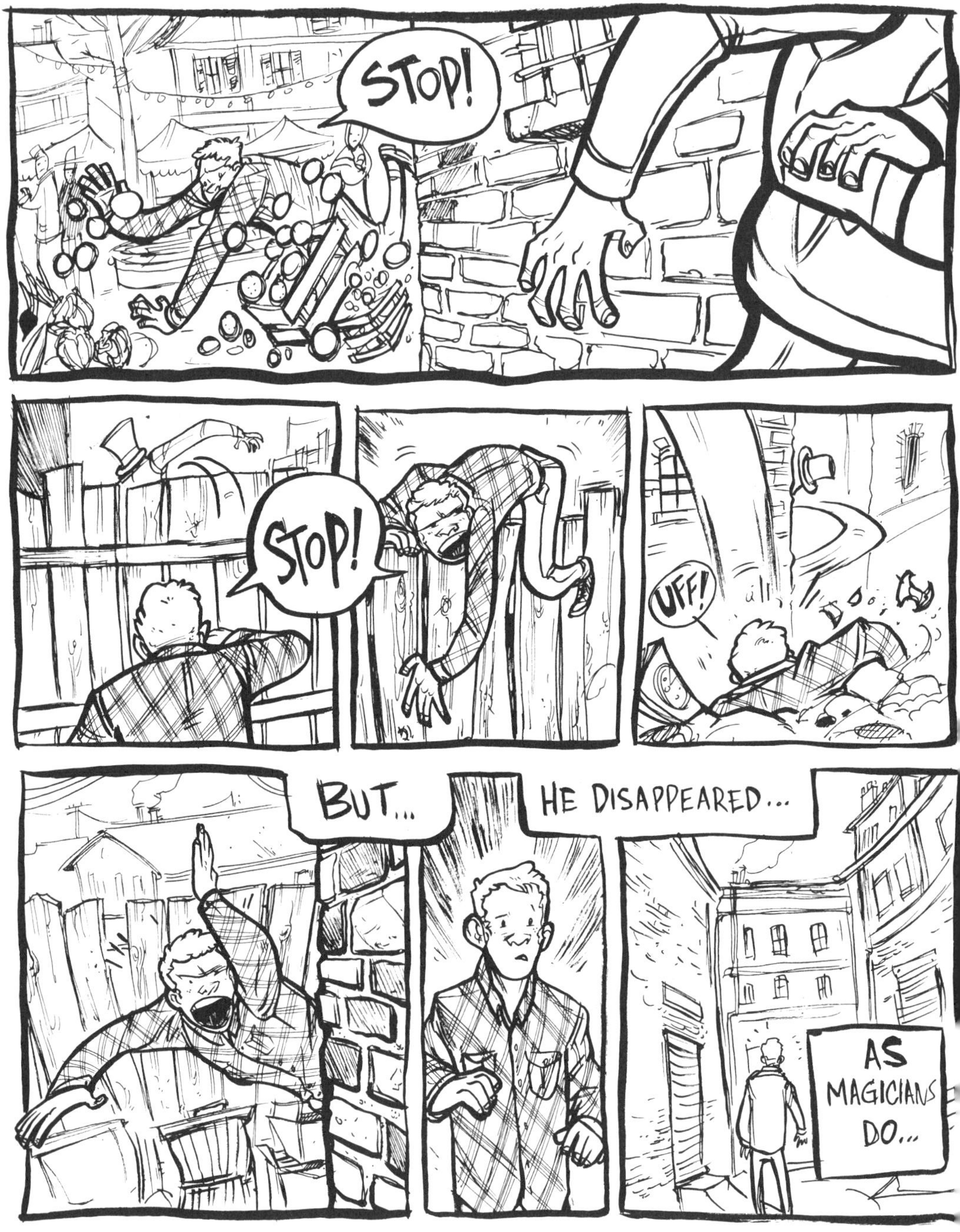
STOP!
STOP!
UFF!
BUT...
HE DISAPPEARED...
AS MAGICIANS DO...

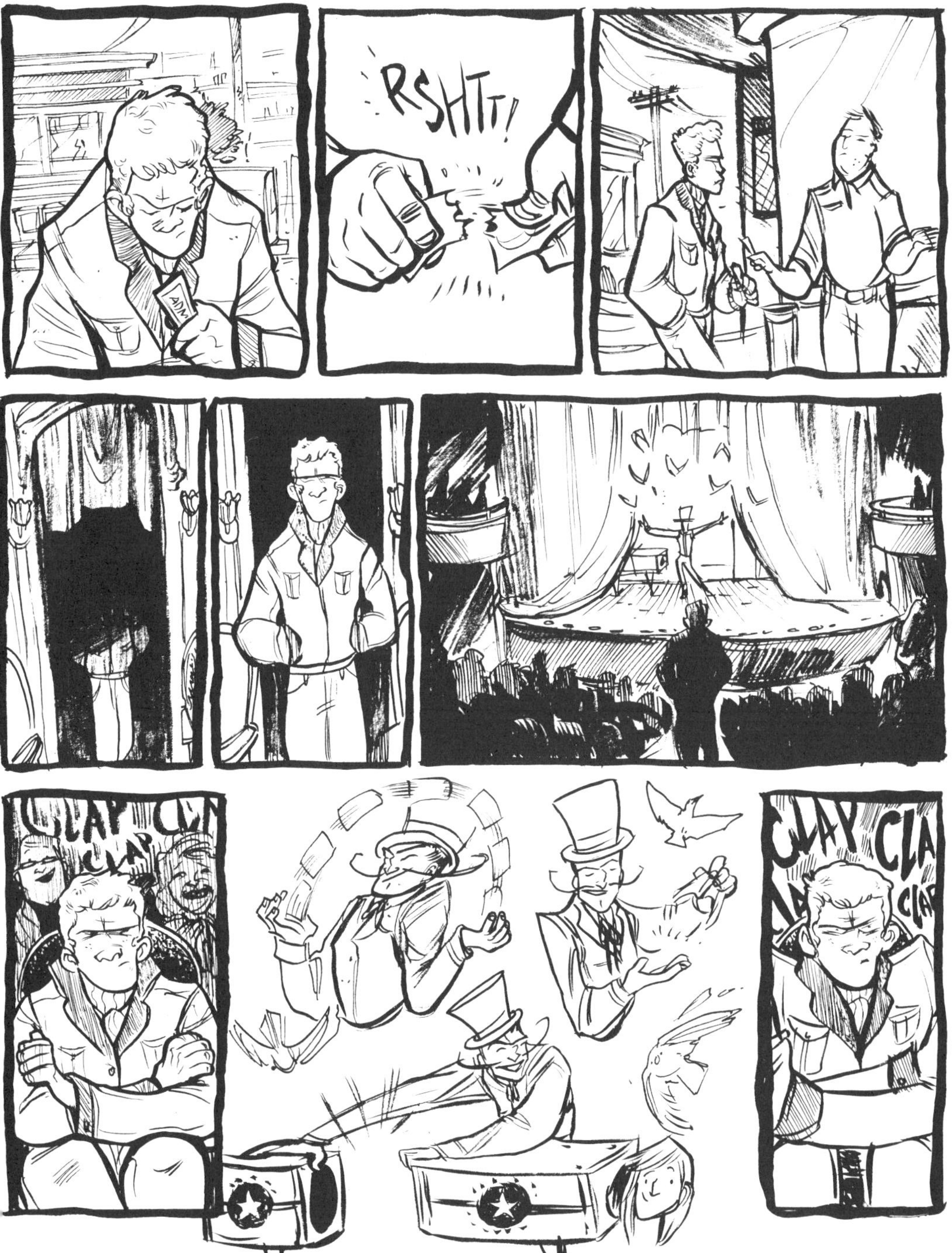
RSHTT!
CLAP
CLAP
CLAP
CLAP

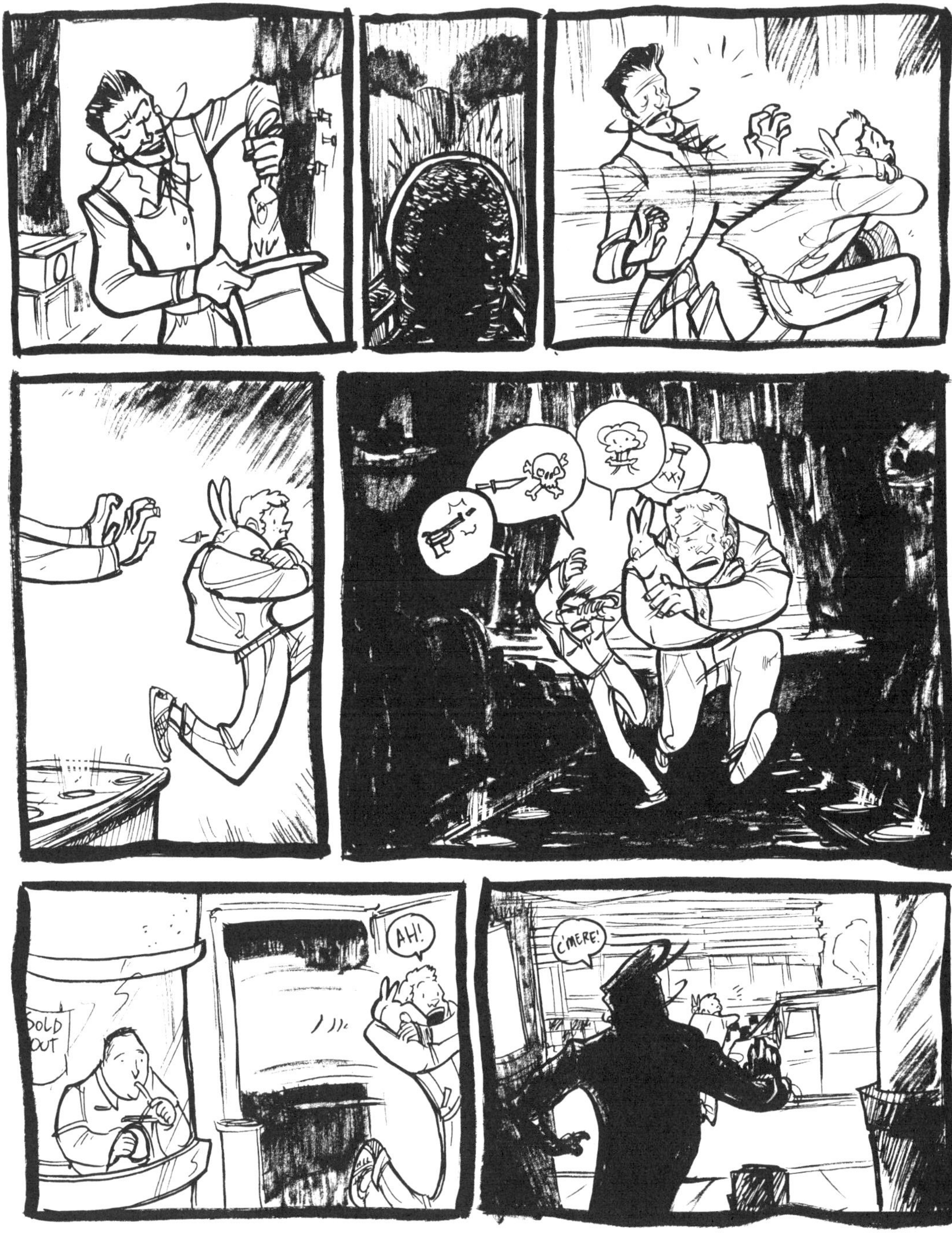
AH!
SOLD OUT
C'MERE!

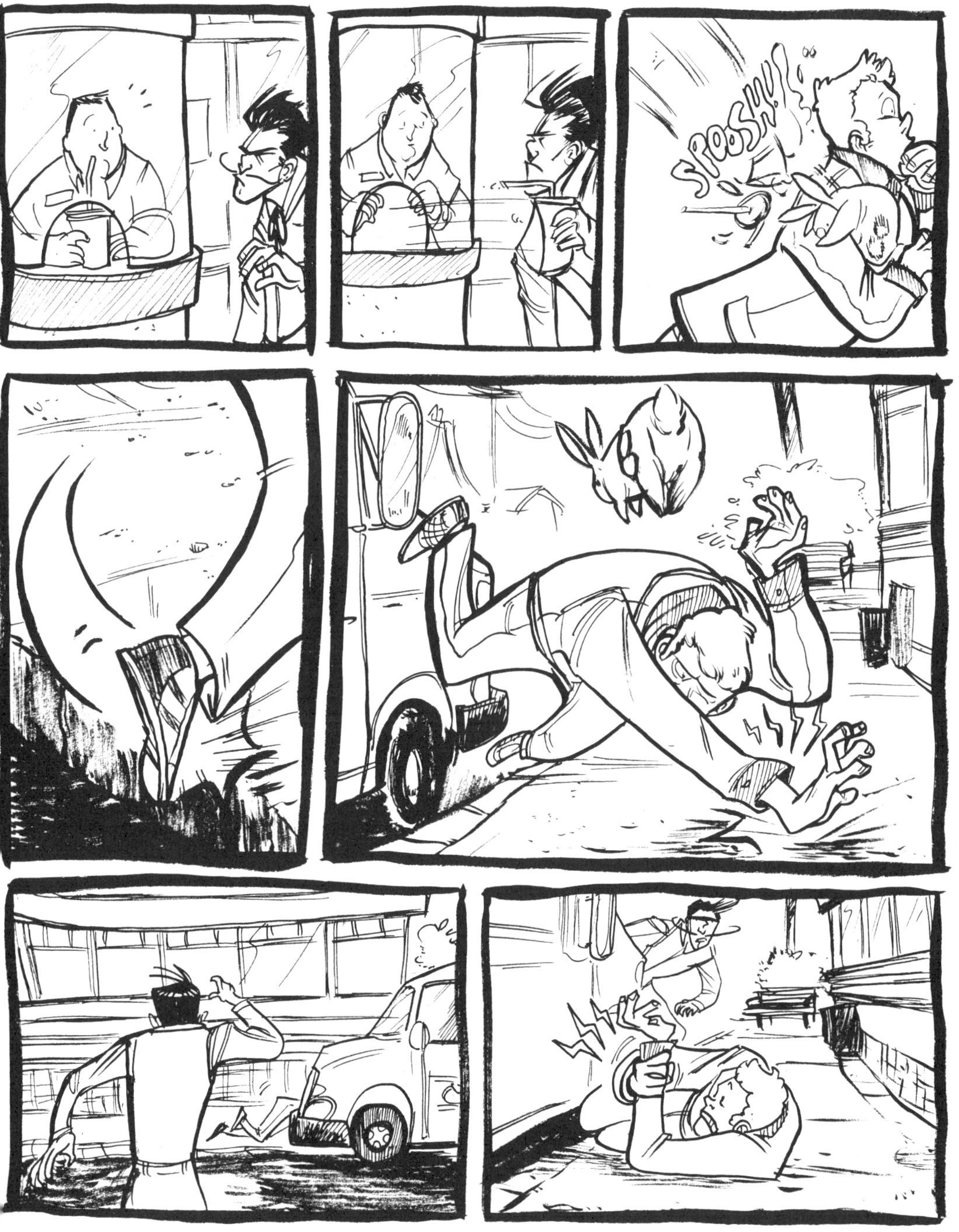
SPOOSH!

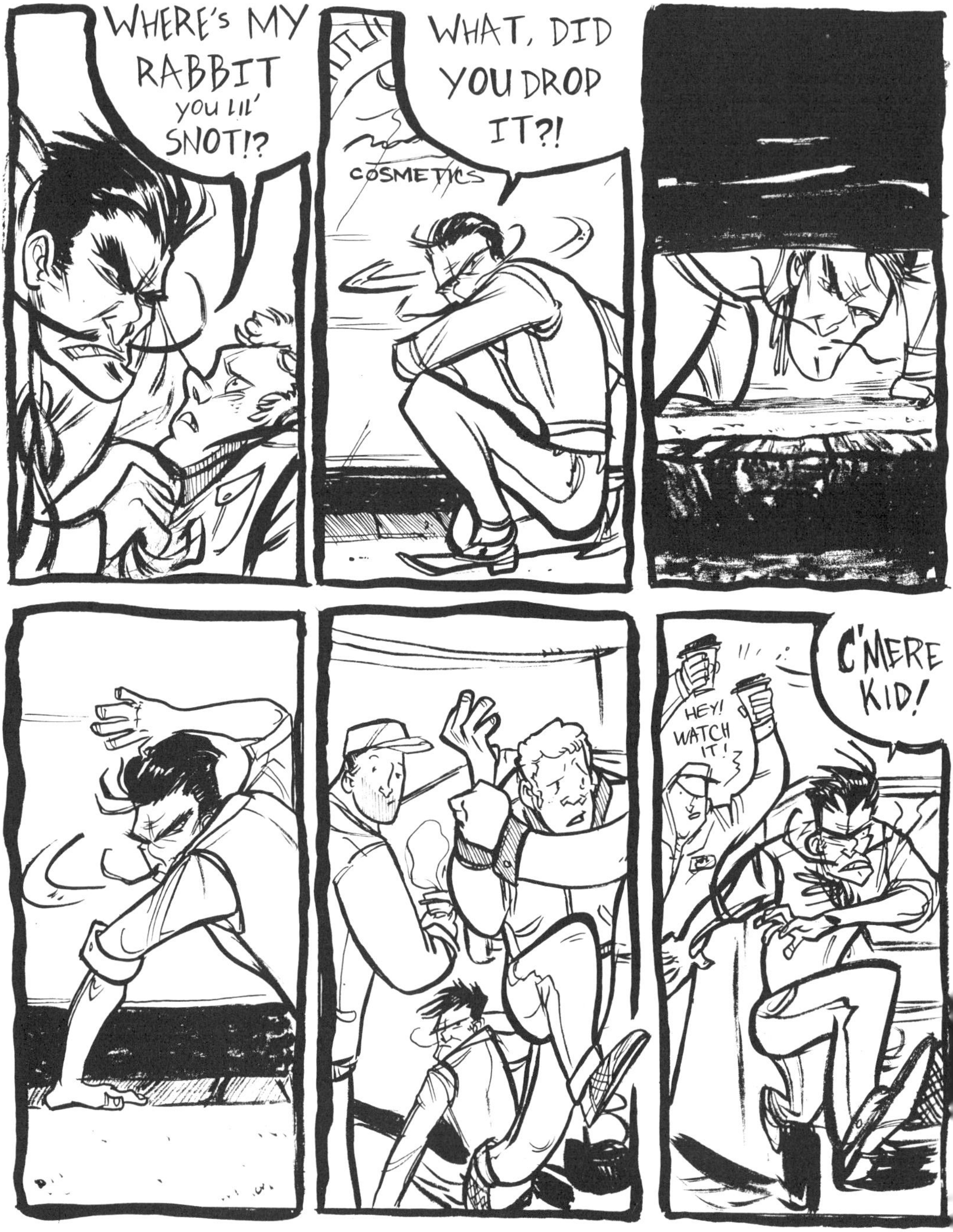
WHERE'S MY RABBIT YOU LIL' SNOT!?
COSMETICS
WHAT, DID YOU DROP IT?!
HEY! WATCH IT!
C'MERE KID!

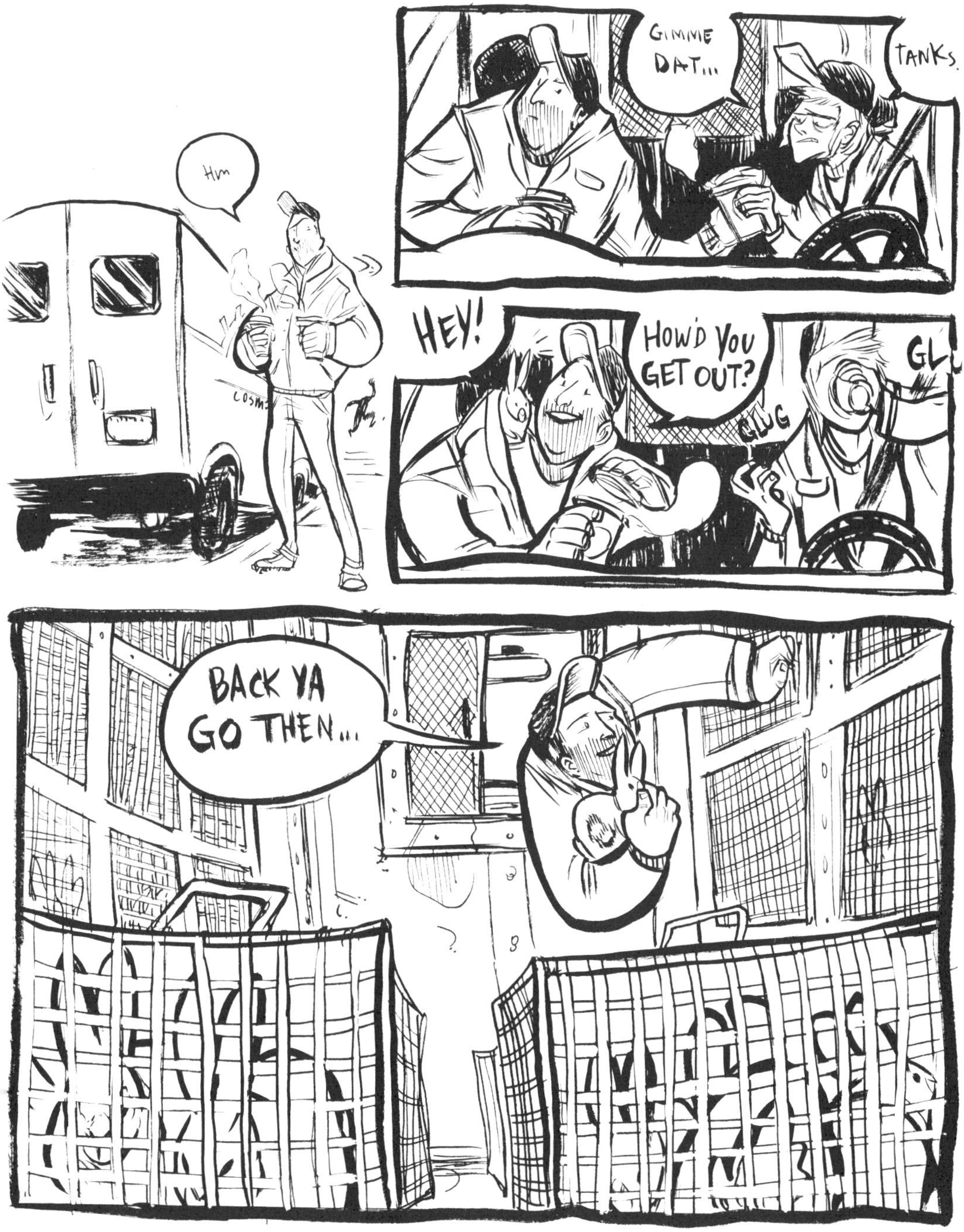

Hm
GIMME DAT...
TANKS.
HEY!
HOW'D YOU GET OUT?
GLUG
BACK YA GO THEN...

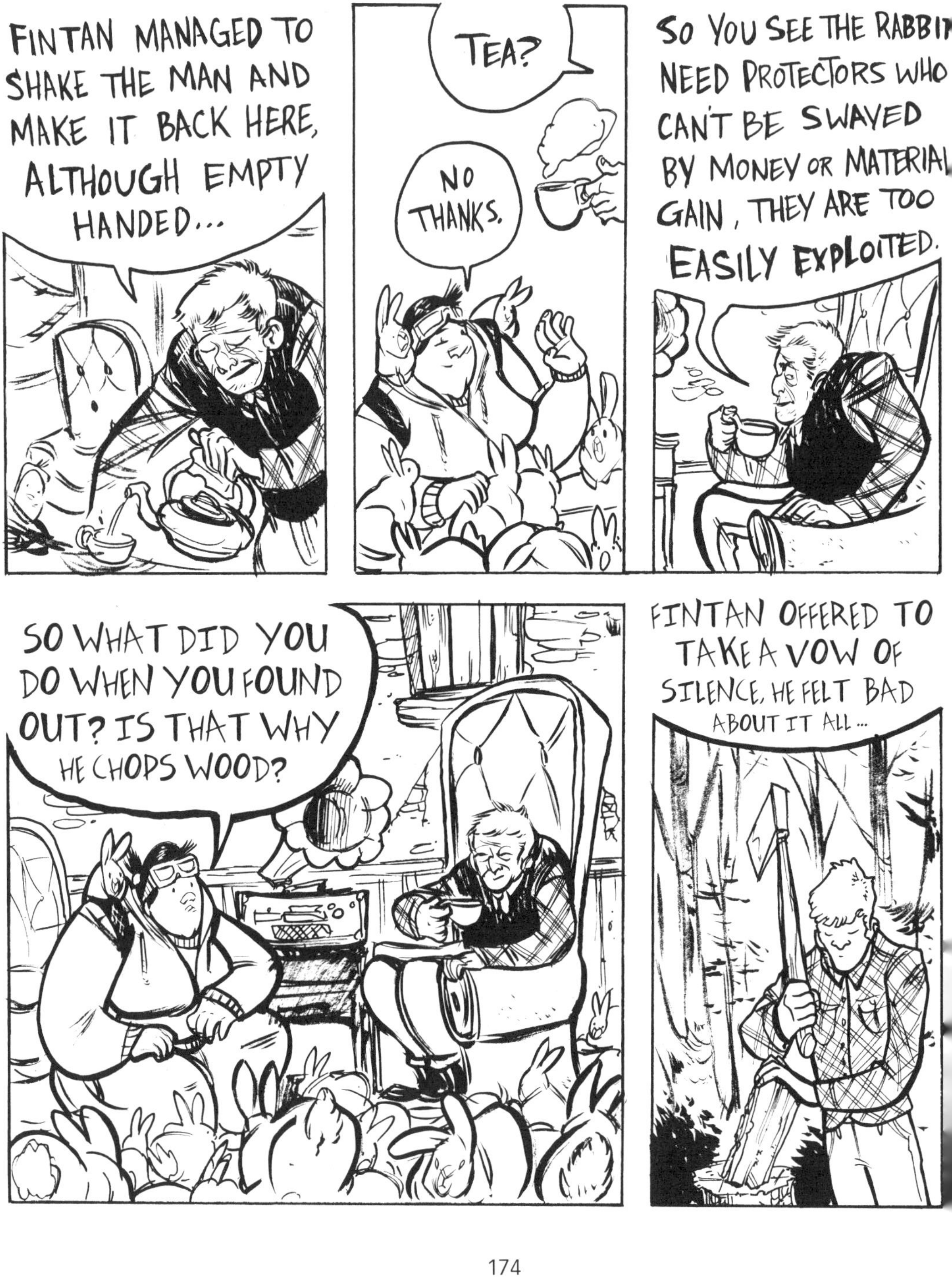
FINTAN MANAGED TO SHAKE THE MAN AND MAKE IT BACK HERE, ALTHOUGH EMPTY HANDED...
TEA?
NO THANKS.
SO YOU SEE THE RABBIT NEED PROTECTORS WHO CAN'T BE SWAYED BY MONEY OR MATERIAL GAIN, THEY ARE TOO EASILY EXPLOITED.
SO WHAT DID YOU DO WHEN YOU FOUND OUT? IS THAT WHY HE CHOPS WOOD?
FINTAN OFFERED TO TAKE A VOW OF SILENCE, HE FELT BAD ABOUT IT ALL...

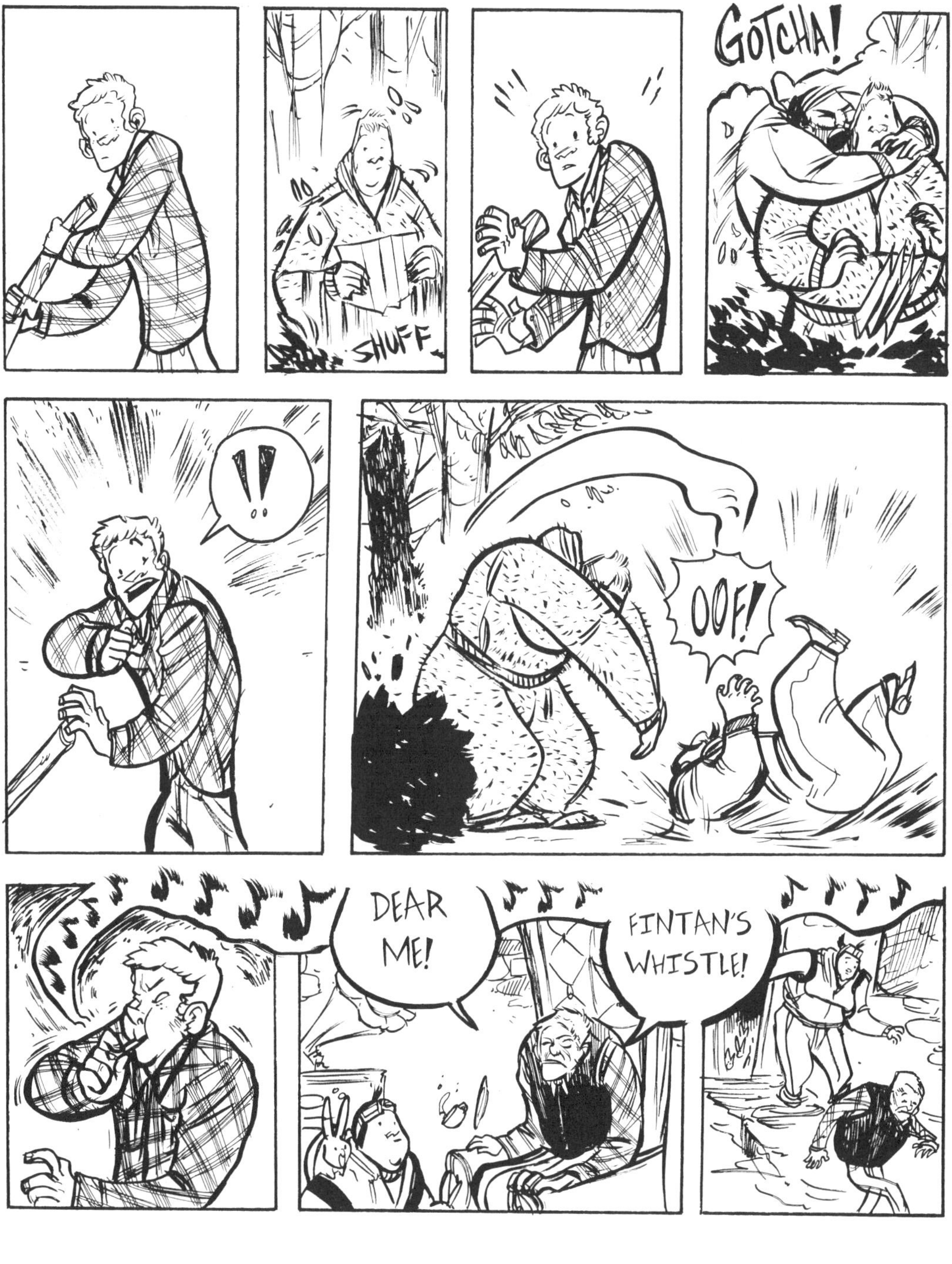
SHUFF
GOTCHA!
!!
OOF!
DEAR ME!
FINTAN'S WHISTLE!

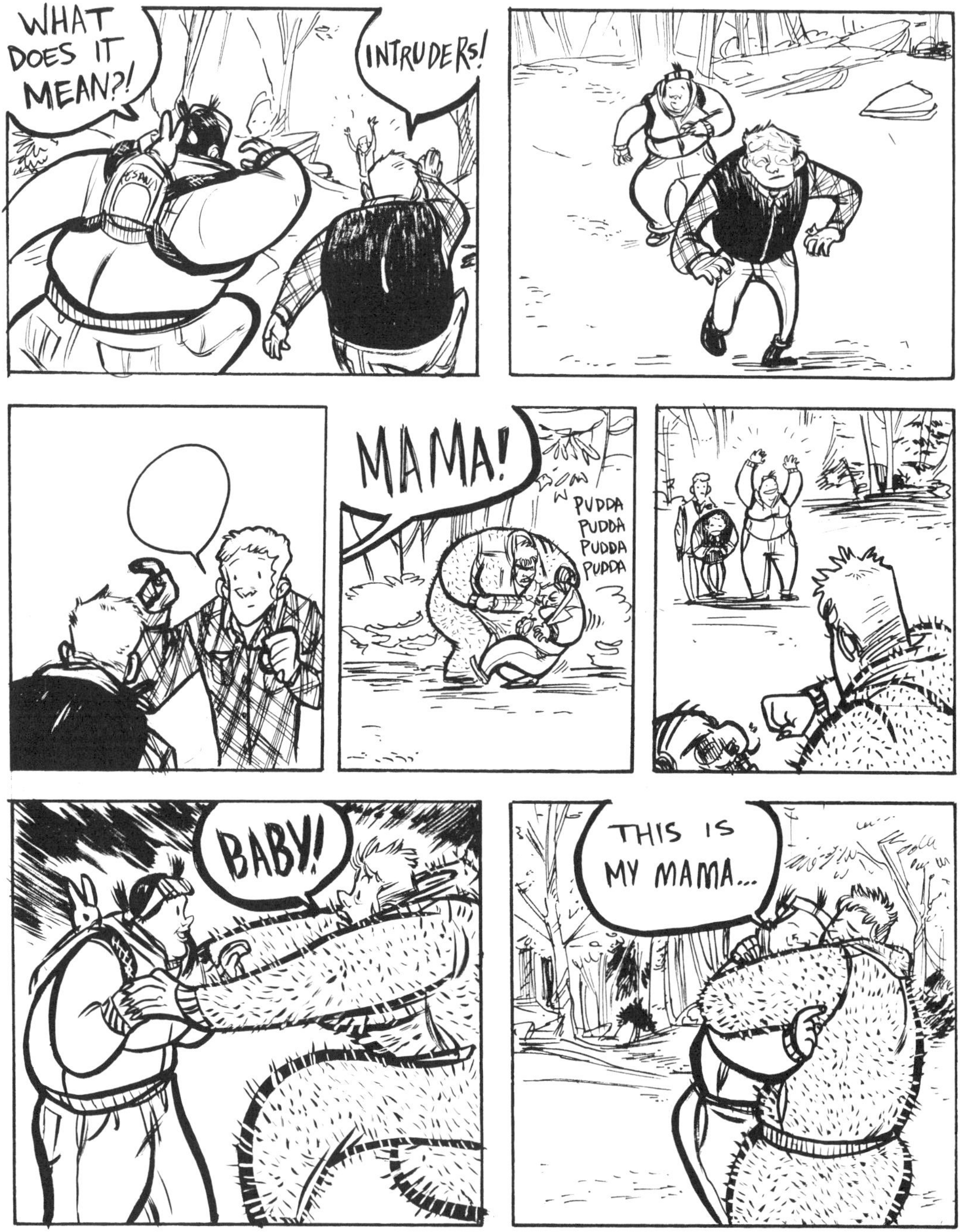
WHAT DOES IT MEAN?!
INTRUDERS!
MAMA!
PUDDA PUDDA PUDDA PUDDA
BABY!
THIS IS MY MAMA...

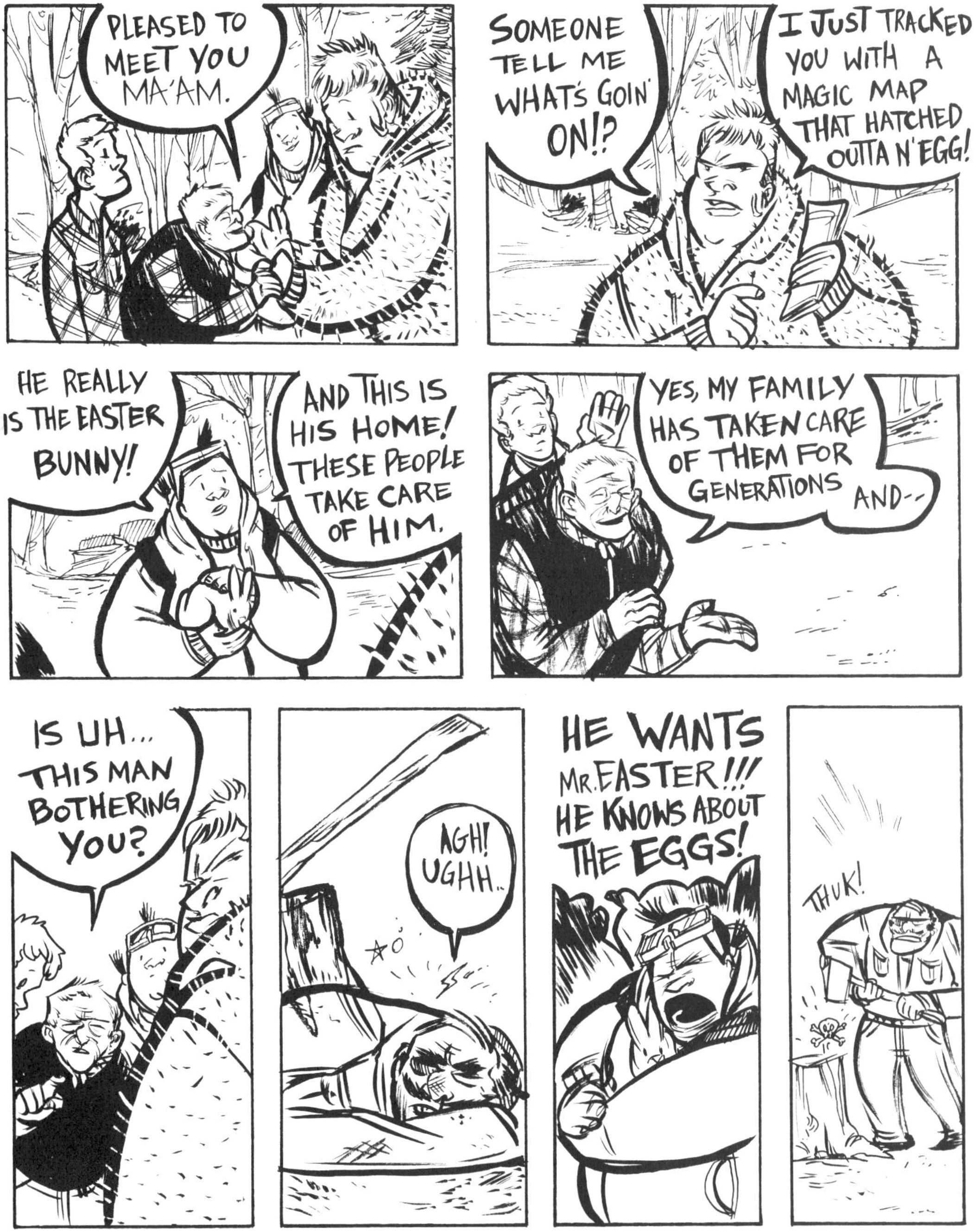
PLEASED TO MEET YOU MA'AM.
SOMEONE TELL ME WHAT'S GOIN' ON!?
I JUST TRACKED YOU WITH A MAGIC MAP THAT HATCHED OUTTA N'EGG!
HE REALLY IS THE EASTER BUNNY!
AND THIS IS HIS HOME! THESE PEOPLE TAKE CARE OF HIM.
YES, MY FAMILY HAS TAKEN CARE OF THEM FOR GENERATIONS AND--
IS UH... THIS MAN BOTHERING YOU?
AGH! UGHH..
HE WANTS MR. EASTER!!! HE KNOWS ABOUT THE EGGS!
THUK!

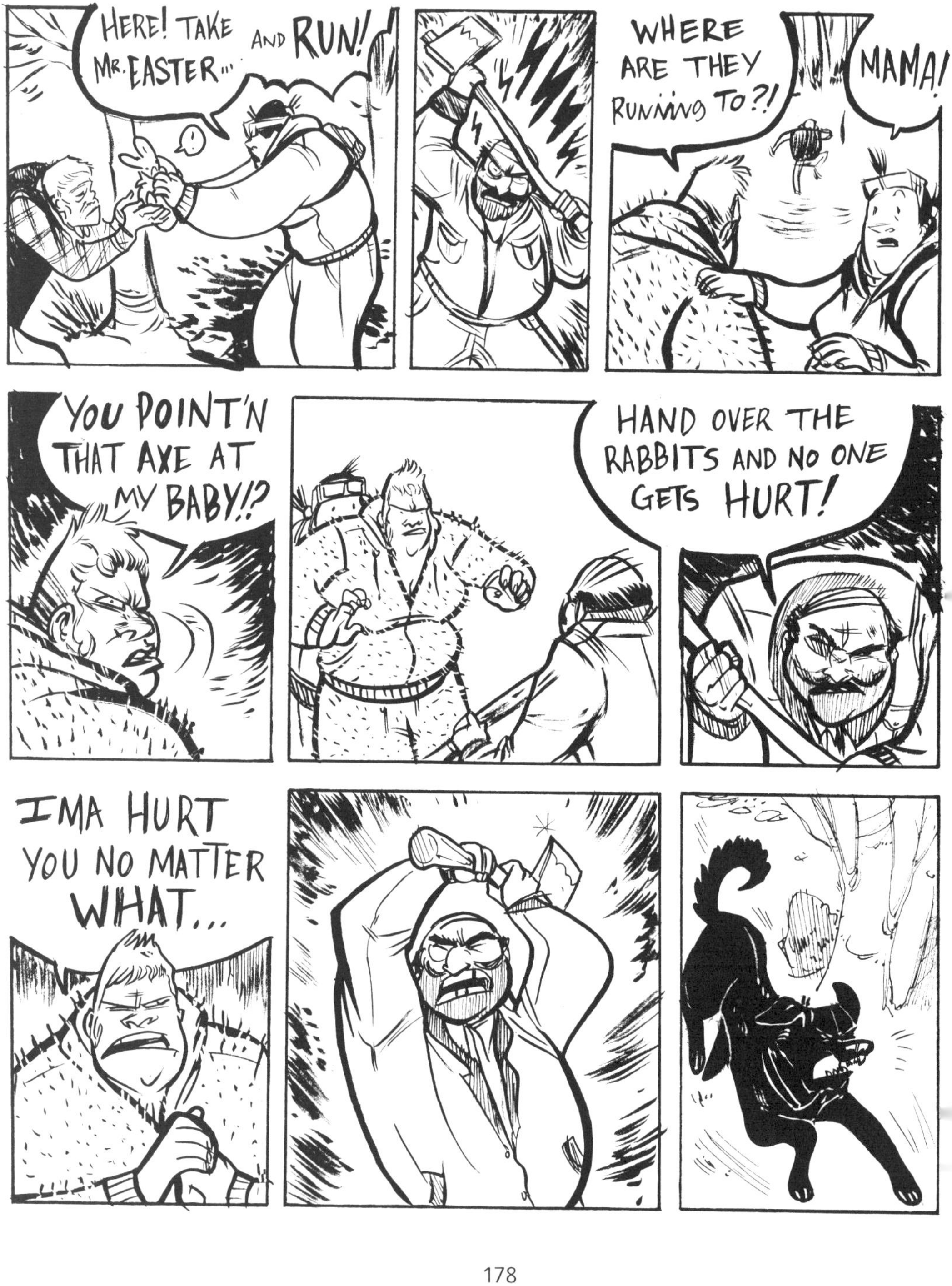
HERE! TAKE MR. EASTER... AND RUN!
!
WHERE ARE THEY RUNNING TO?!
MAMA!
YOU POINT'N THAT AXE AT MY BABY!?
HAND OVER THE RABBITS AND NO ONE GETS HURT!
IMA HURT YOU NO MATTER WHAT...

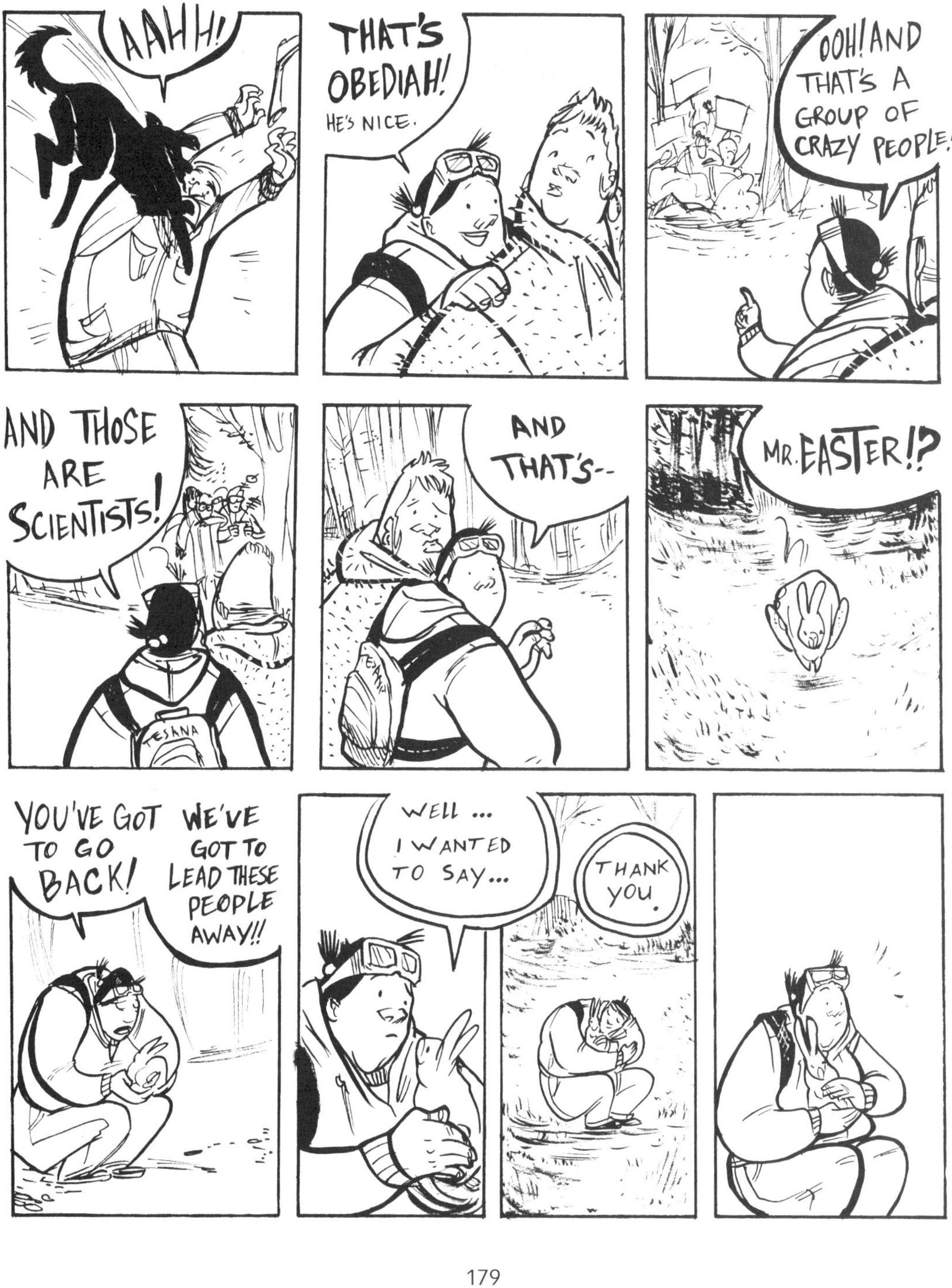
AAHH!
THAT'S OBEDIAH! HE'S NICE.
OOH! AND THAT'S A GROUP OF CRAZY PEOPLE!
AND THOSE ARE SCIENTISTS!
AND THAT'S--
MR. EASTER!?
YOU'VE GOT TO GO BACK!
WE'VE GOT TO LEAD THESE PEOPLE AWAY!!
WELL ... I WANTED TO SAY...
THANK YOU.

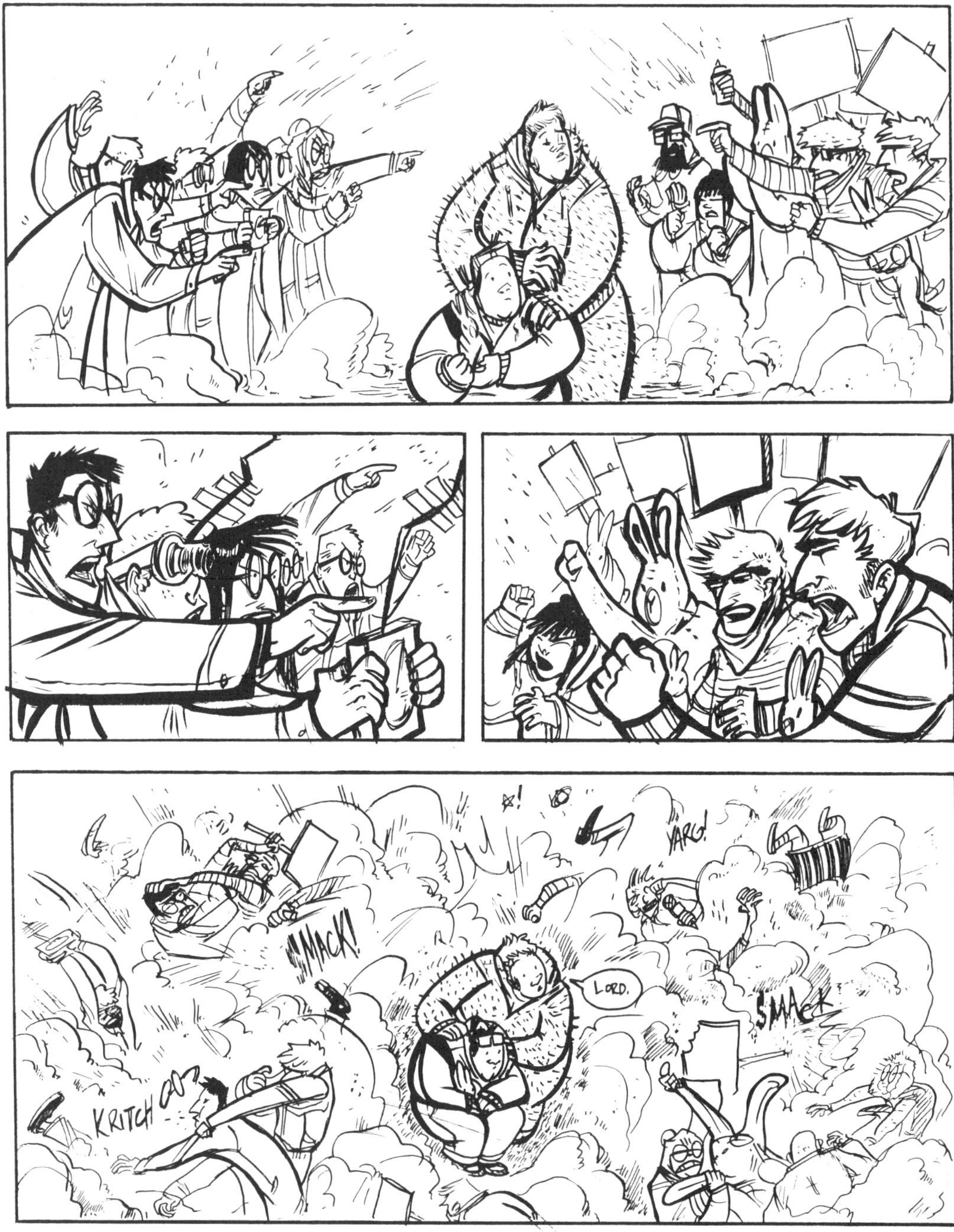
YARG!
SMACK!
LORD.
SMACK
KRITCH

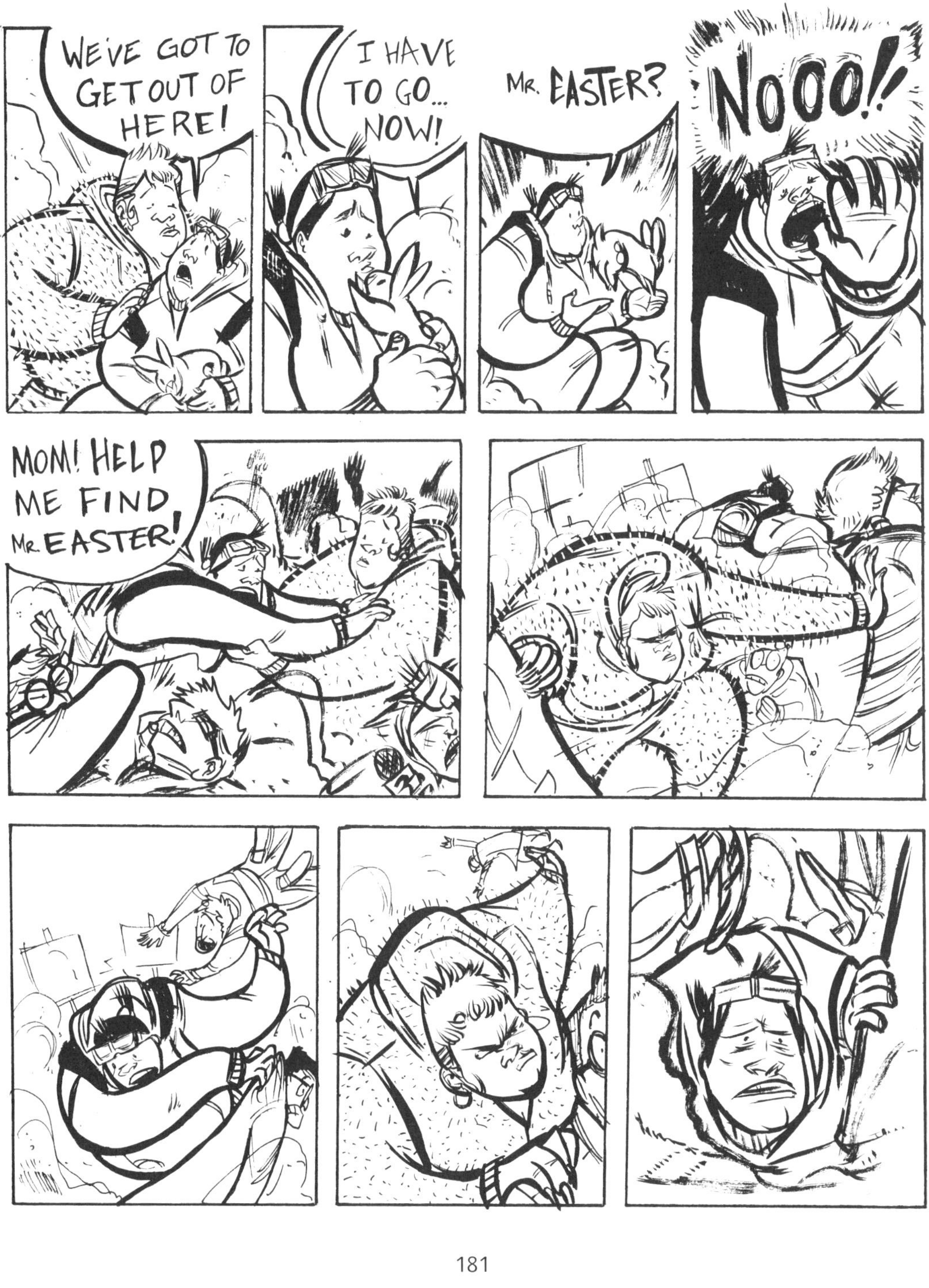
WE'VE GOT TO GET OUT OF HERE!
I HAVE TO GO... NOW!
MR. EASTER?
NOOO!!
MOM! HELP ME FIND MR. EASTER!

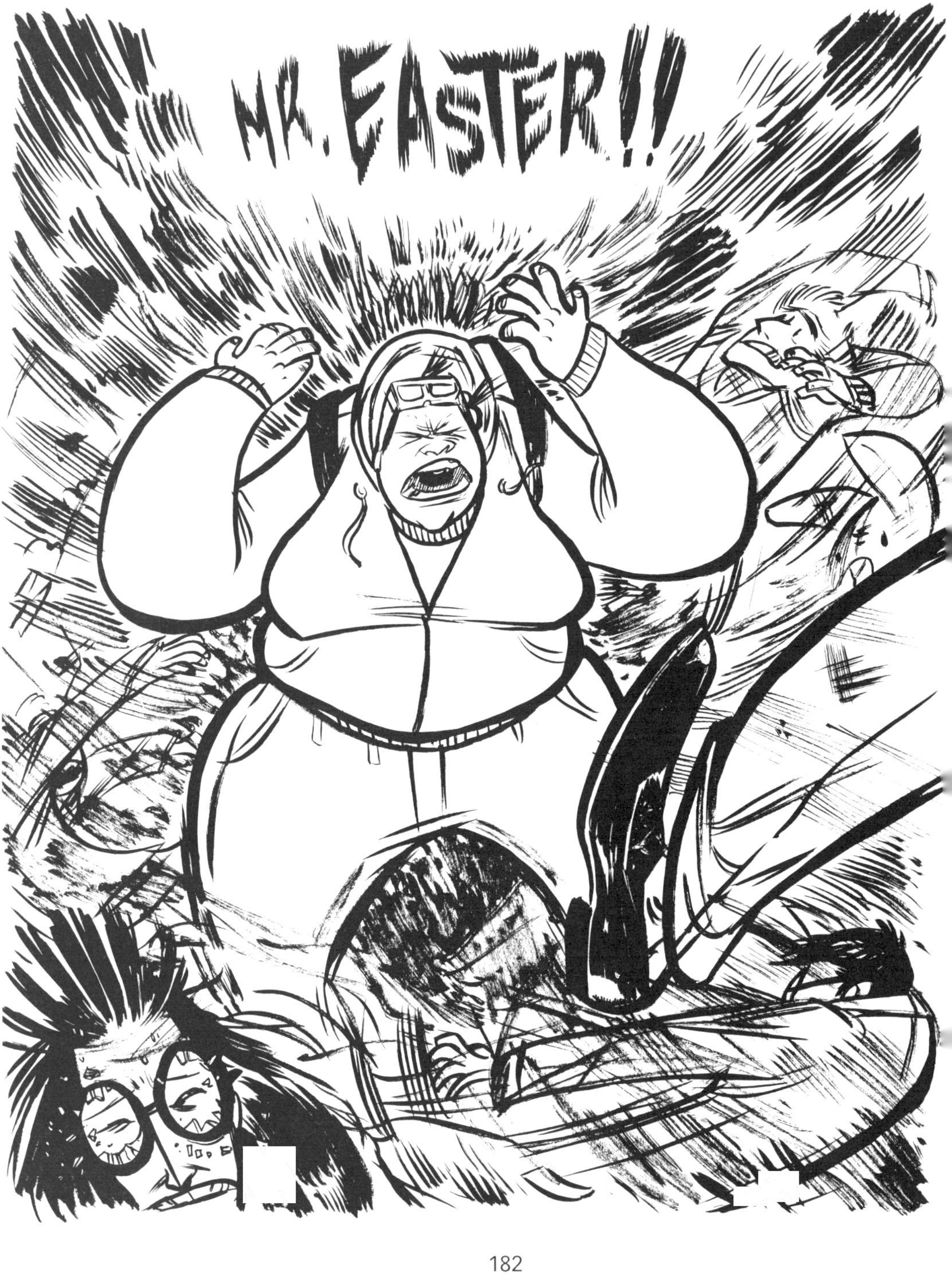
MR. EASTER!!

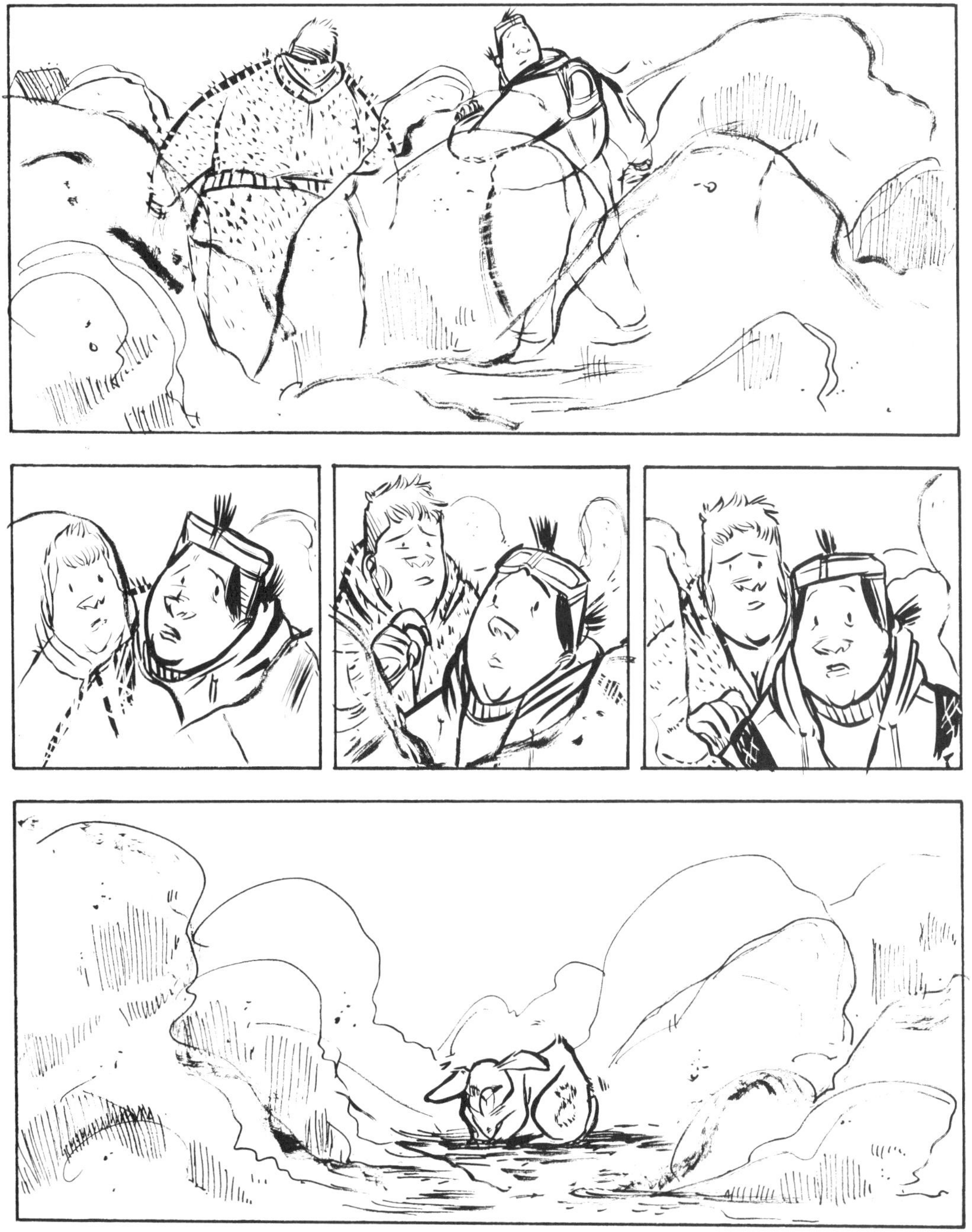

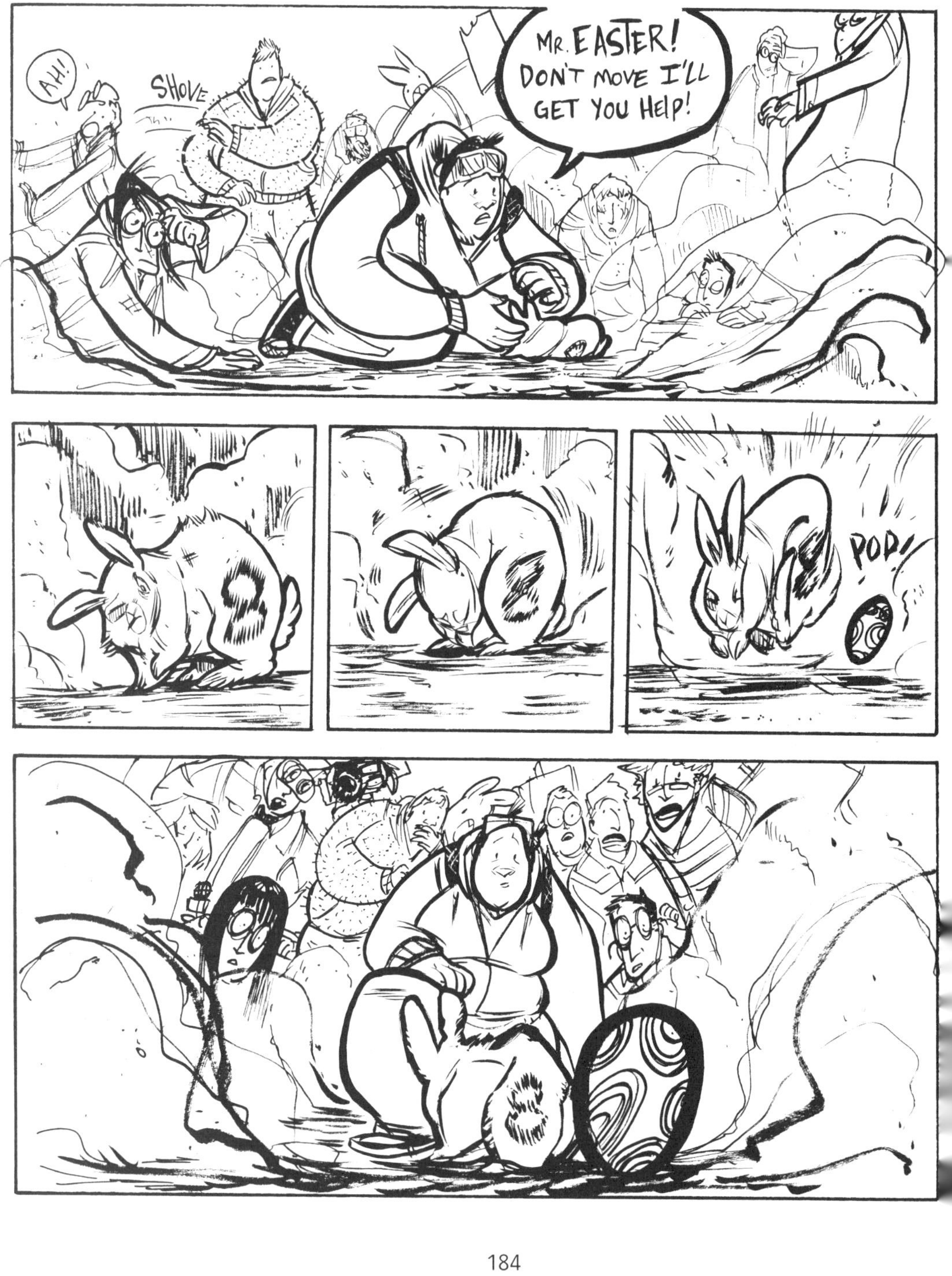
AH!
SHOVE
MR. EASTER! DON'T MOVE I'LL GET YOU HELP!
POP!

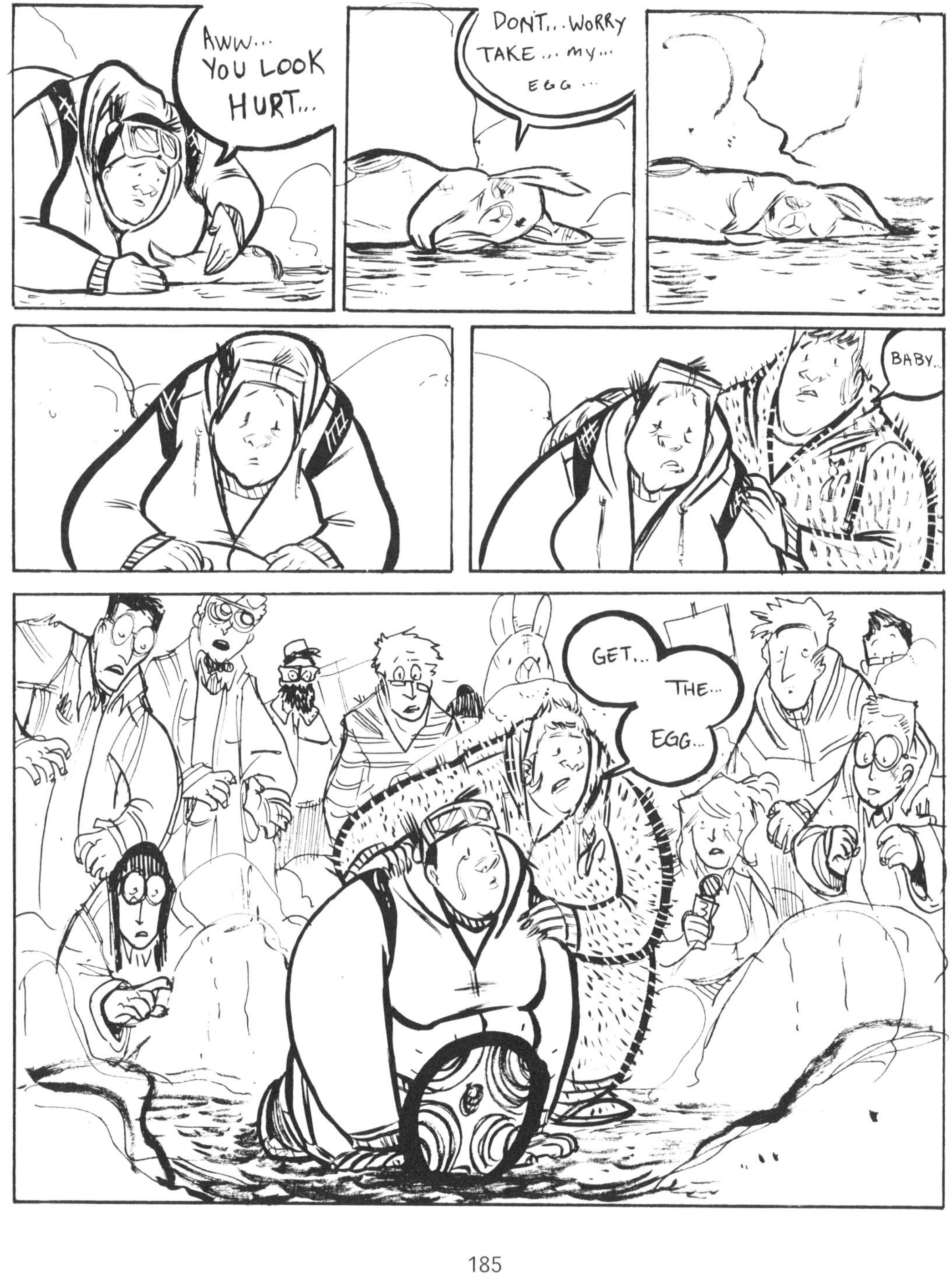
AWW... YOU LOOK HURT...
DON'T... WORRY TAKE... MY... EGG...
BABY...
GET... THE... EGG...

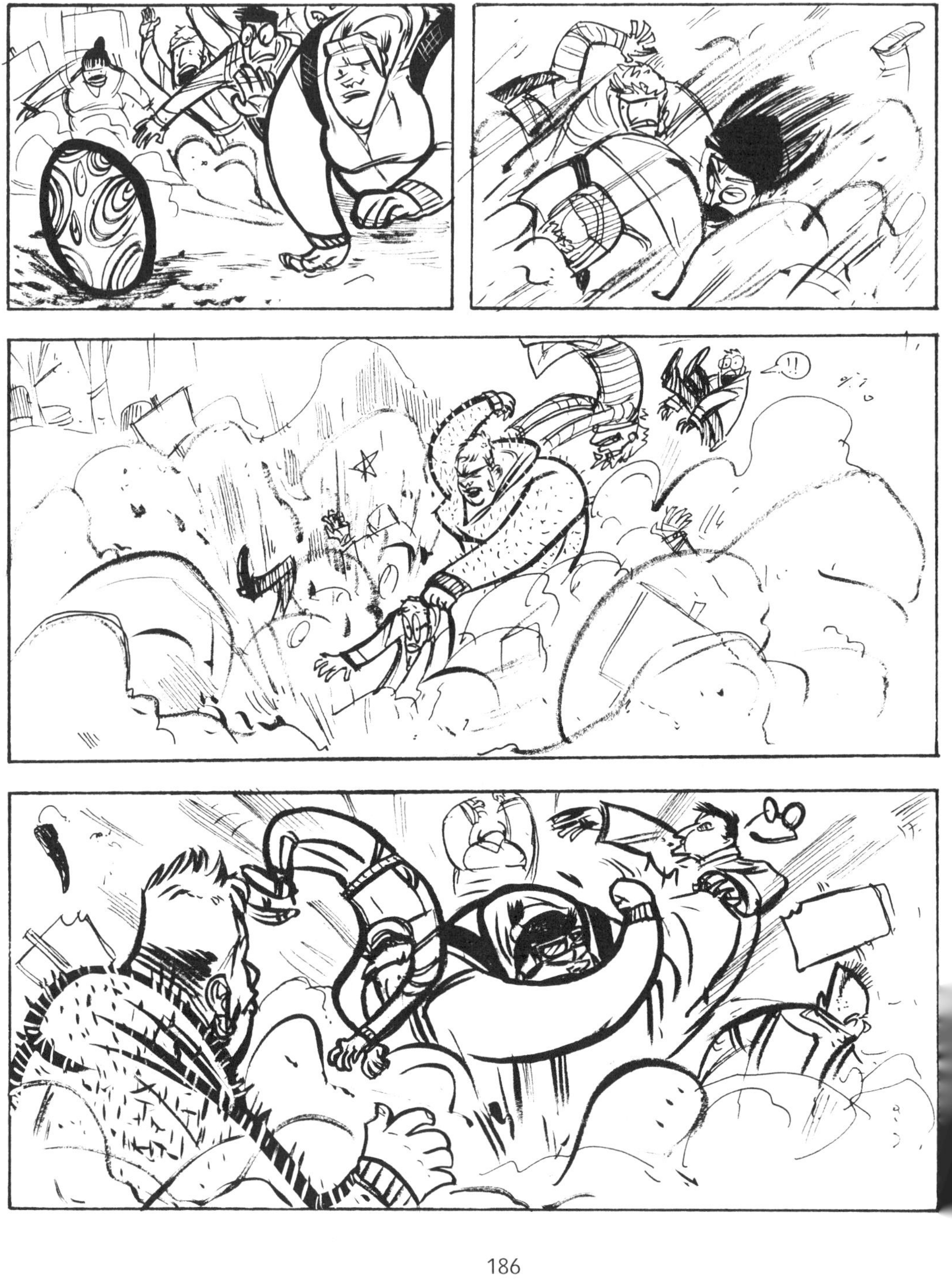
!!

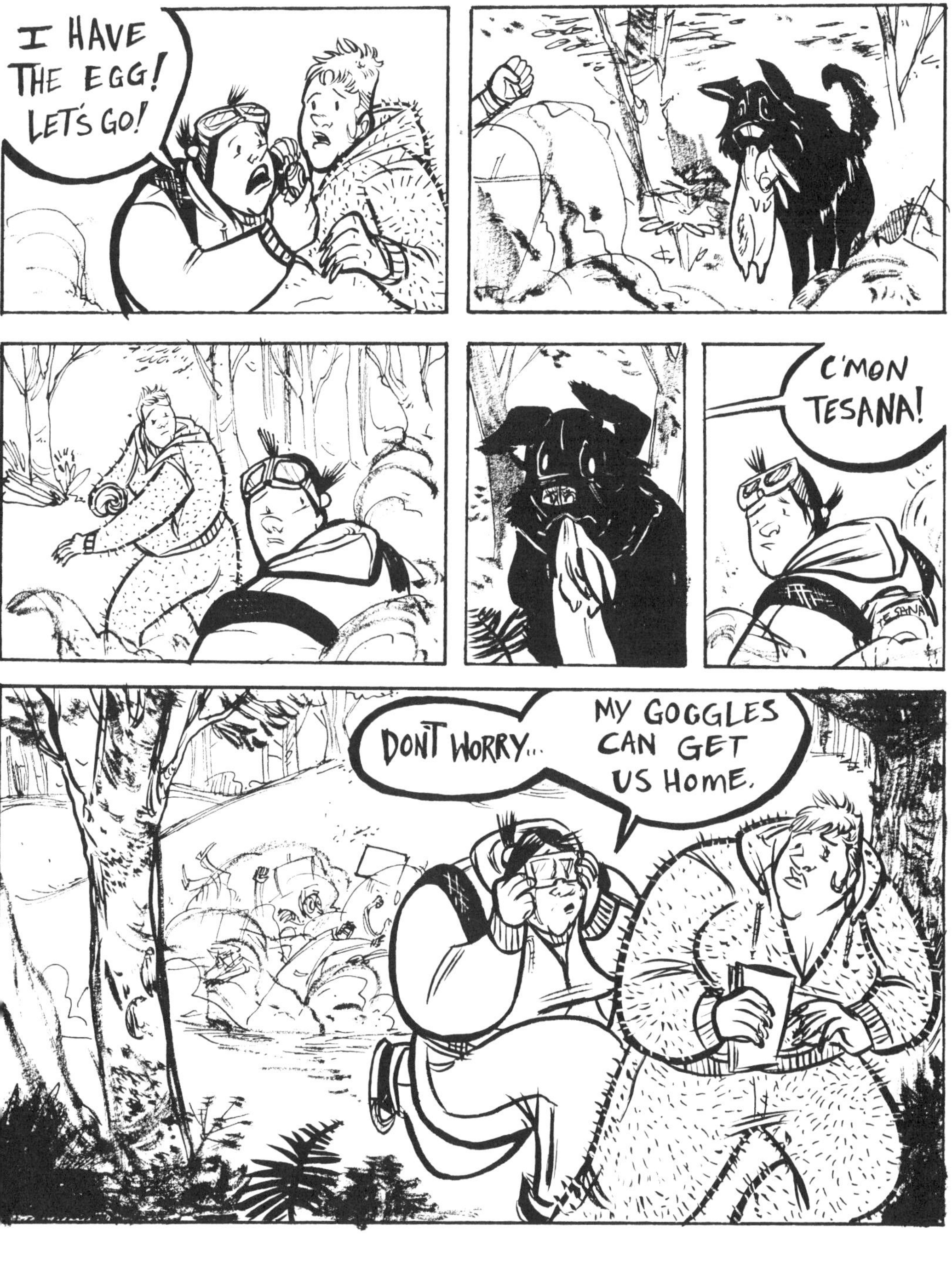
I HAVE THE EGG! LET'S GO!
C'MON TESANA!
TESANA
DON'T WORRY...
MY GOGGLES CAN GET US HOME.

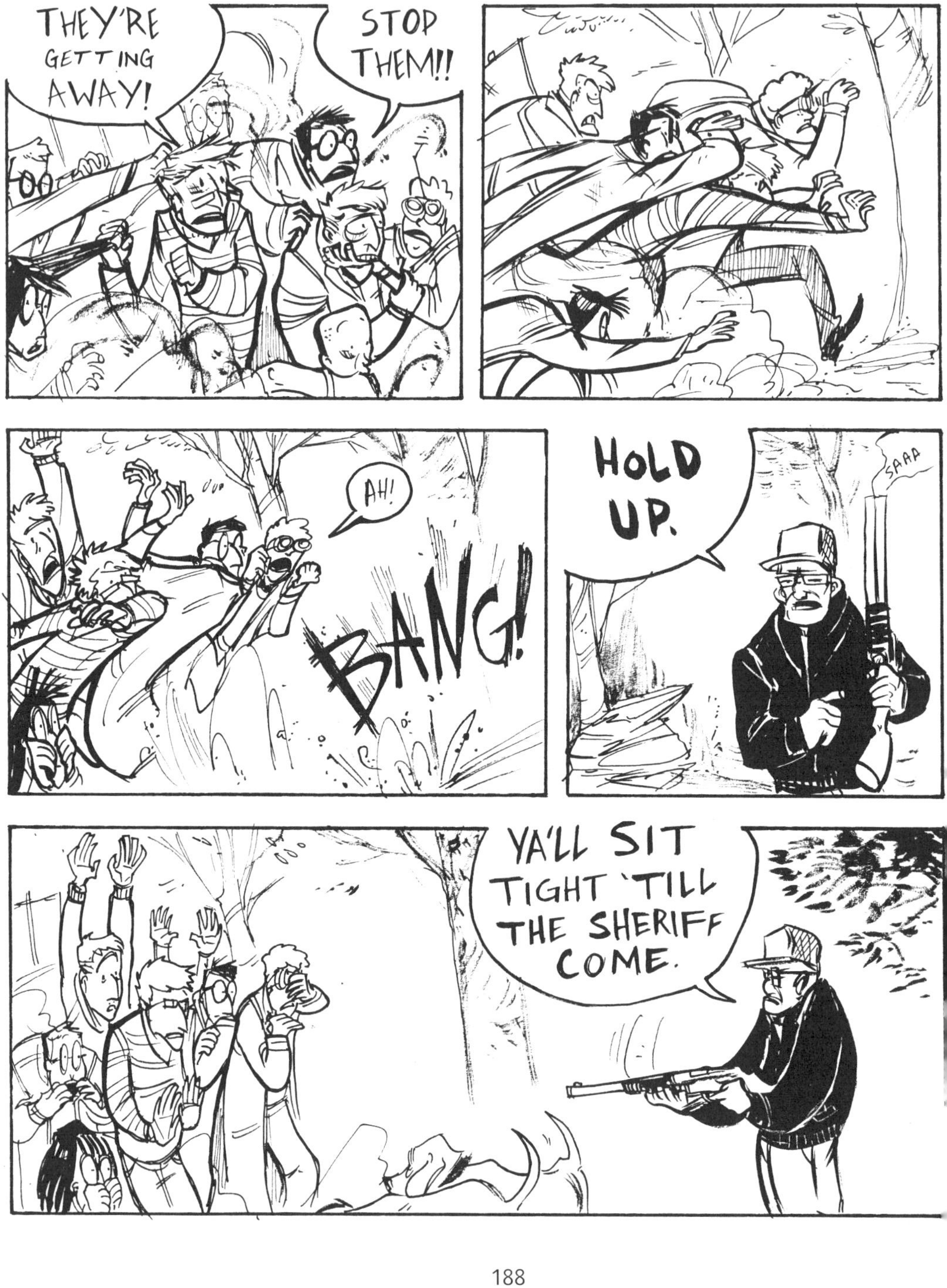
THEY'RE GETTING AWAY!
STOP THEM!!
AH!
BANG!
HOLD UP.
SAAA
YA'LL SIT TIGHT 'TILL THE SHERIFF COME.

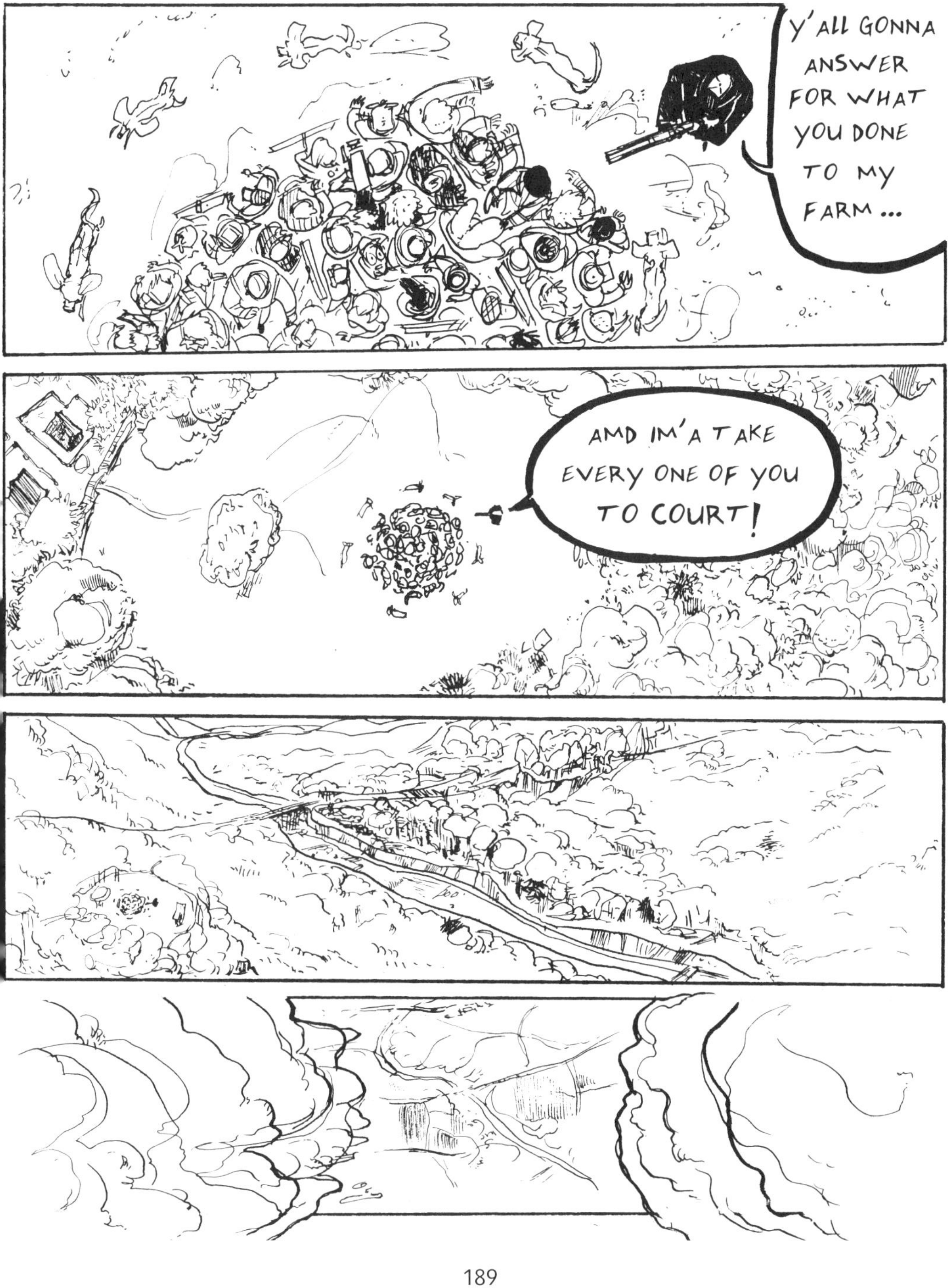
Y'ALL GONNA ANSWER FOR WHAT YOU DONE TO MY FARM...
AMD IM'A TAKE EVERY ONE OF YOU TO COURT!

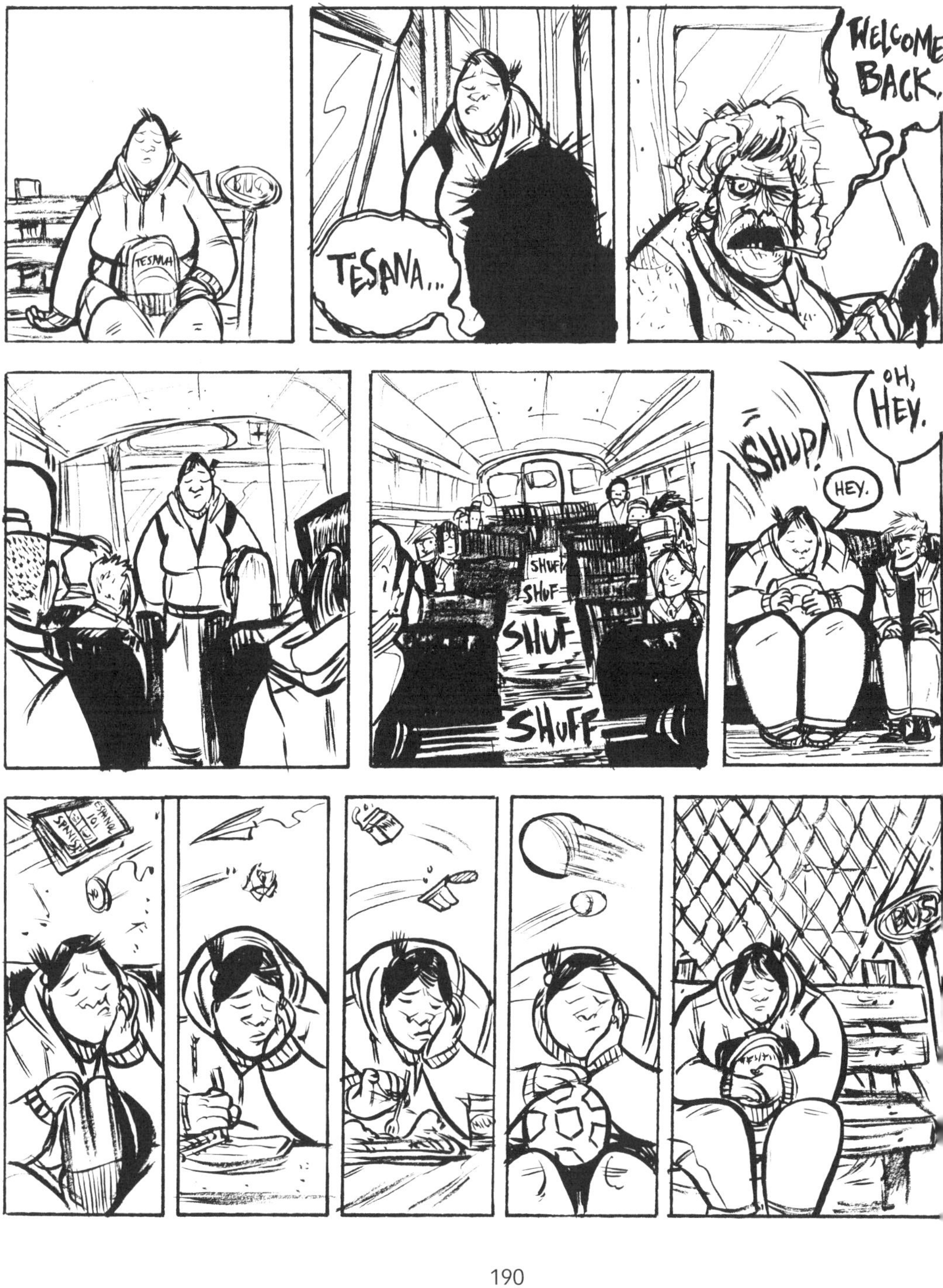
BUS
TESANA
TESANA...
WELCOME BACK.
SHUF
SHUF
SHUF
SHUFF
SHUP!
OH, HEY.
HEY.
ESPAÑOL 101
SPANISH
BUS

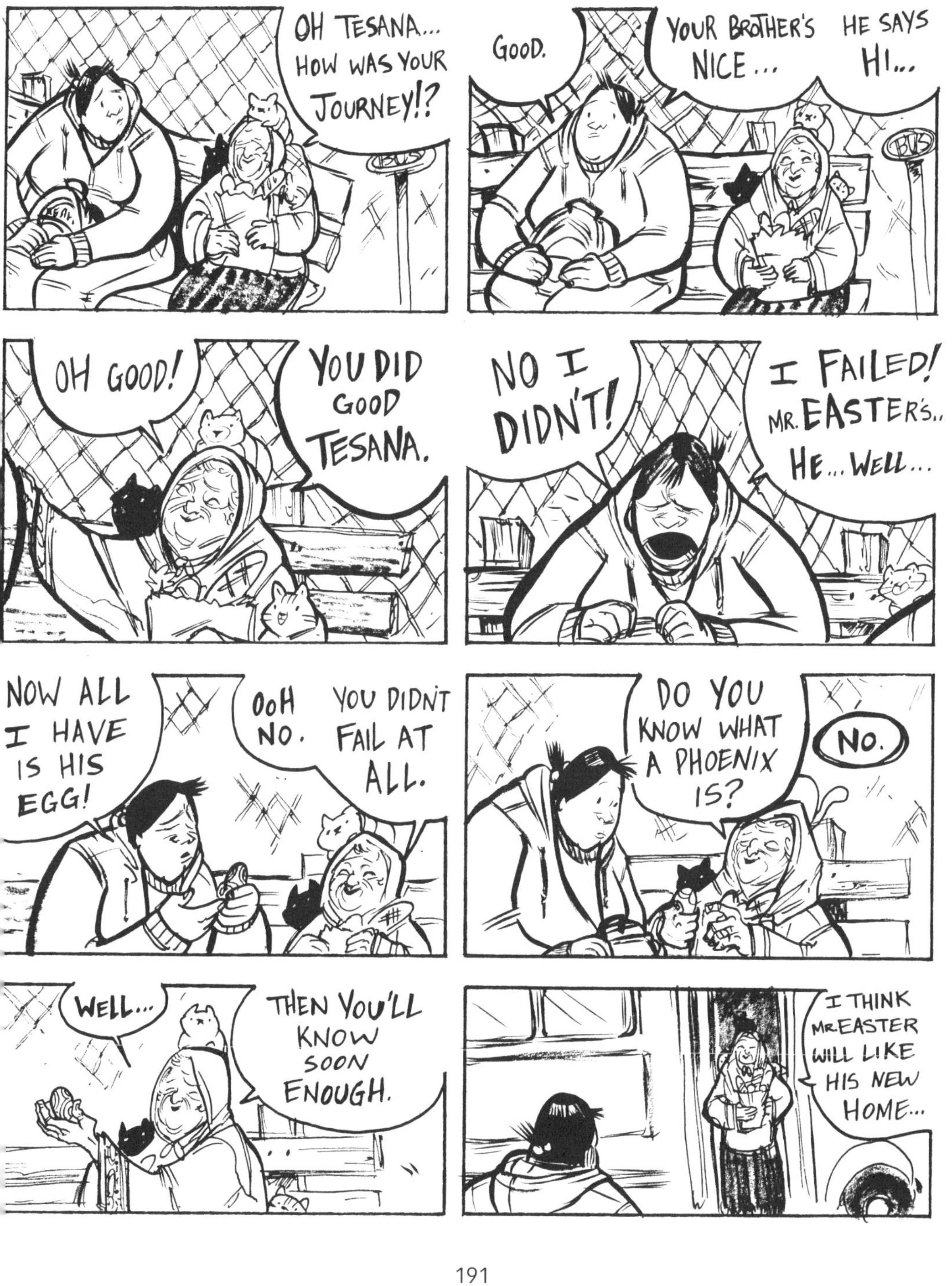
OH TESANA... HOW WAS YOUR JOURNEY!?
GOOD.
YOUR BROTHER'S NICE...
HE SAYS HI...
OH GOOD!
YOU DID GOOD TESANA.
NO I DIDN'T!
I FAILED! MR. EASTER'S.. HE... WELL...
NOW ALL I HAVE IS HIS EGG!
OOH NO.
YOU DIDN'T FAIL AT ALL.
DO YOU KNOW WHAT A PHOENIX IS?
NO.
WELL...
THEN YOU'LL KNOW SOON ENOUGH.
I THINK MR. EASTER WILL LIKE HIS NEW HOME...

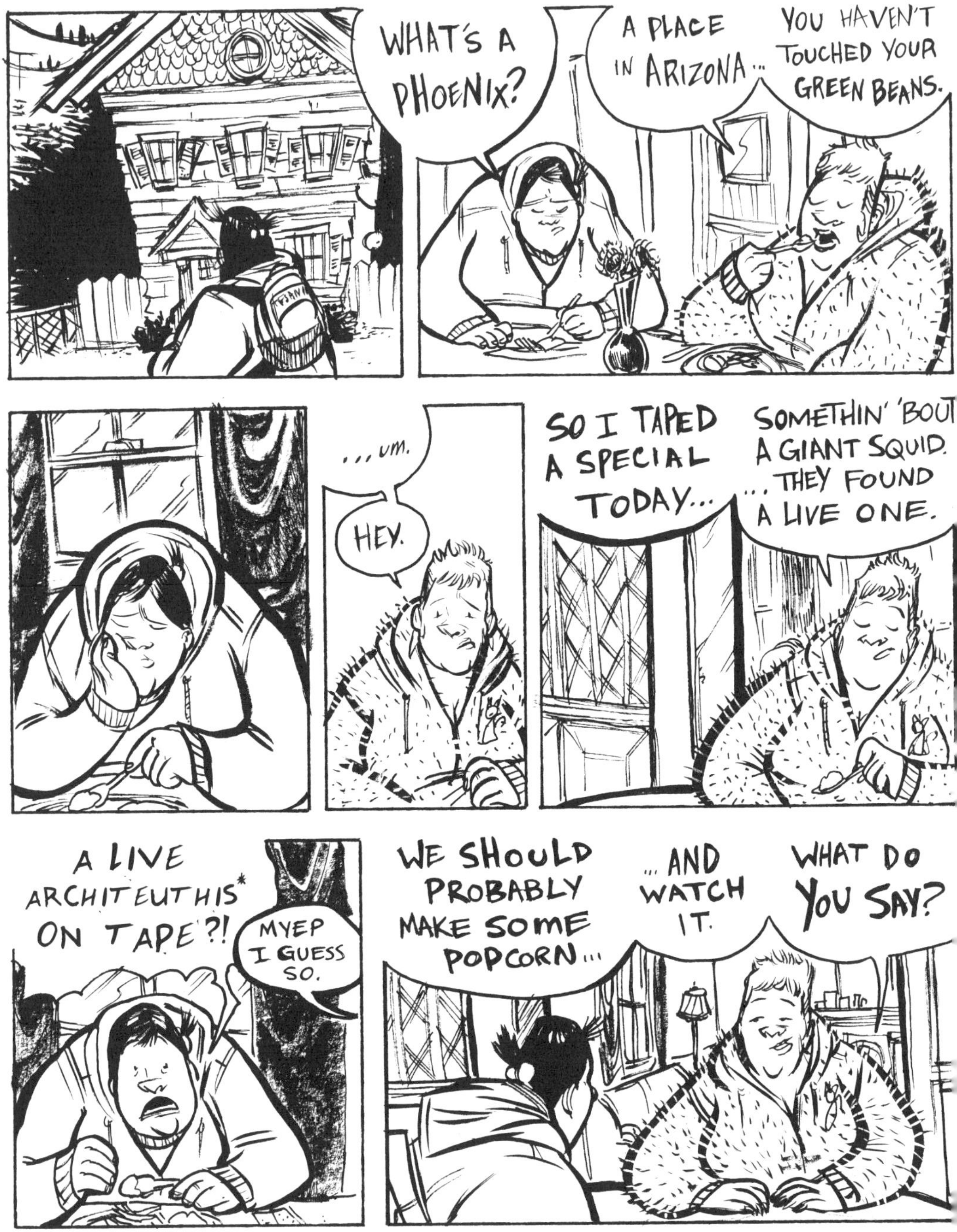
WHAT'S A PHOENIX?
A PLACE IN ARIZONA...
YOU HAVEN'T TOUCHED YOUR GREEN BEANS.
...UM.
HEY.
SO I TAPED A SPECIAL TODAY...
SOMETHIN' 'BOUT A GIANT SQUID. ...THEY FOUND A LIVE ONE.
A LIVE ARCHITEUTHIS* ON TAPE?!
MYEP I GUESS SO.
WE SHOULD PROBABLY MAKE SOME POPCORN...
...AND WATCH IT.
WHAT DO YOU SAY?

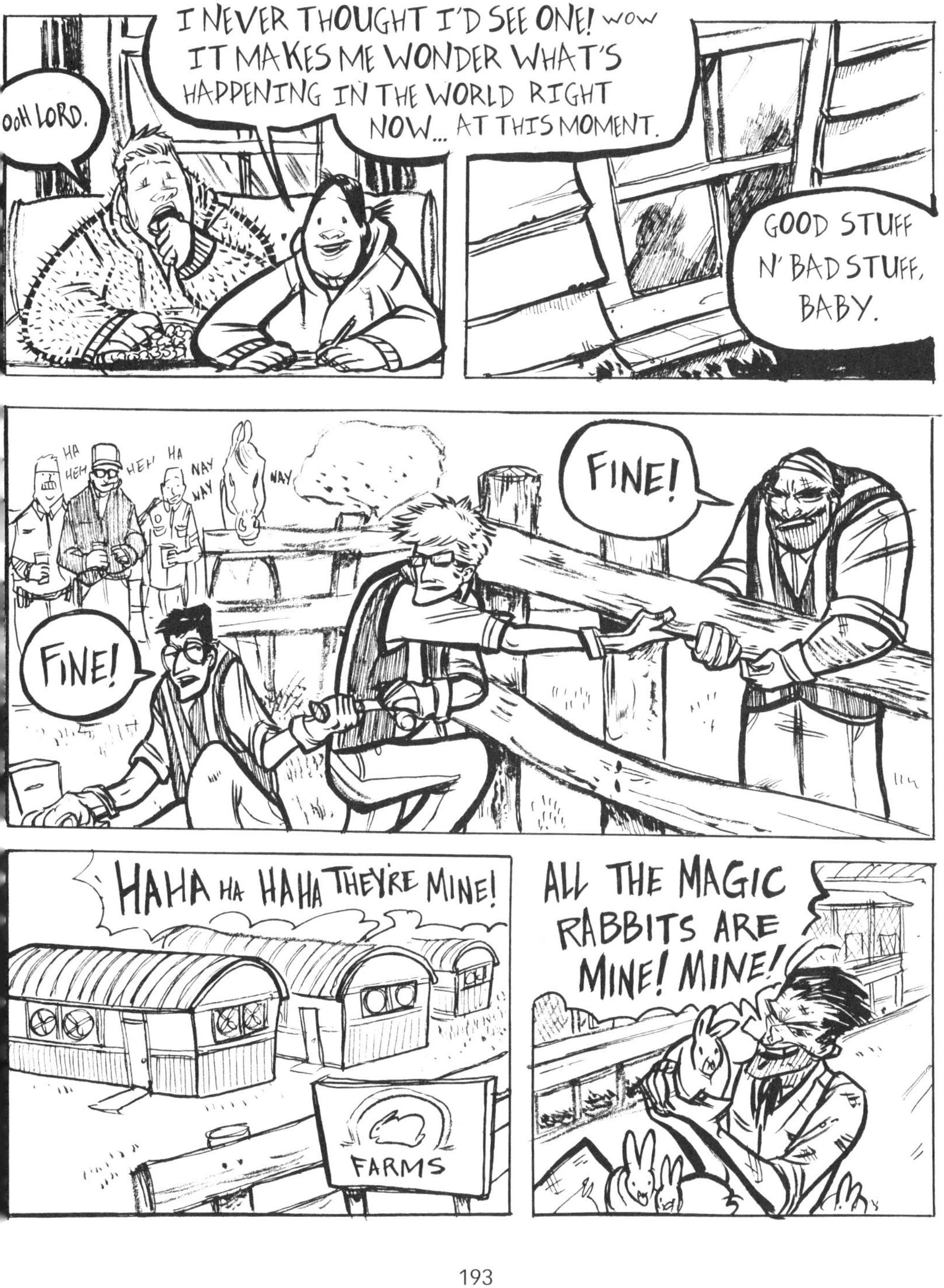
OOH LORD.
I NEVER THOUGHT I'D SEE ONE! WOW IT MAKES ME WONDER WHAT'S HAPPENING IN THE WORLD RIGHT NOW... AT THIS MOMENT.
GOOD STUFF N' BAD STUFF, BABY.
HA HEH HEH HA
NAY NAY NAY
FINE!
FINE!
HAHA HA HAHA THEY'RE MINE!
FARMS
ALL THE MAGIC RABBITS ARE MINE! MINE!

CLICK
I WISH...
...YOU GROW UP TO BE THE HAPPIEST BUNNY EVER.
GOODNIGHT EGG.
TESANA...

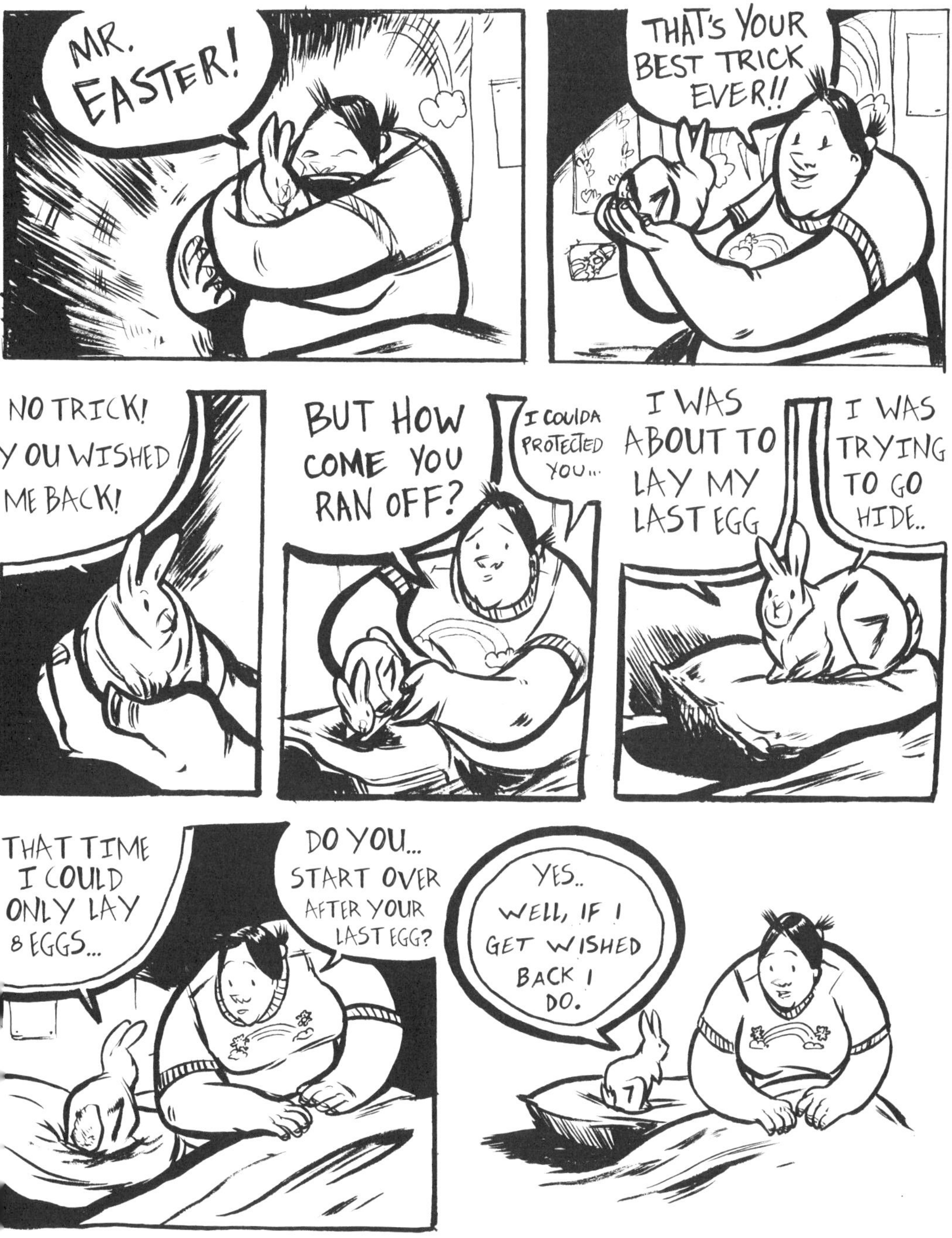
MR. EASTER!
THAT'S YOUR BEST TRICK EVER!!
NO TRICK! YOU WISHED ME BACK!
BUT HOW COME YOU RAN OFF?
I COULDA PROTECTED YOU...
I WAS ABOUT TO LAY MY LAST EGG
I WAS TRYING TO GO HIDE..
THAT TIME I COULD ONLY LAY 8 EGGS...
DO YOU... START OVER AFTER YOUR LAST EGG?
YES.. WELL, IF I GET WISHED BACK I DO.

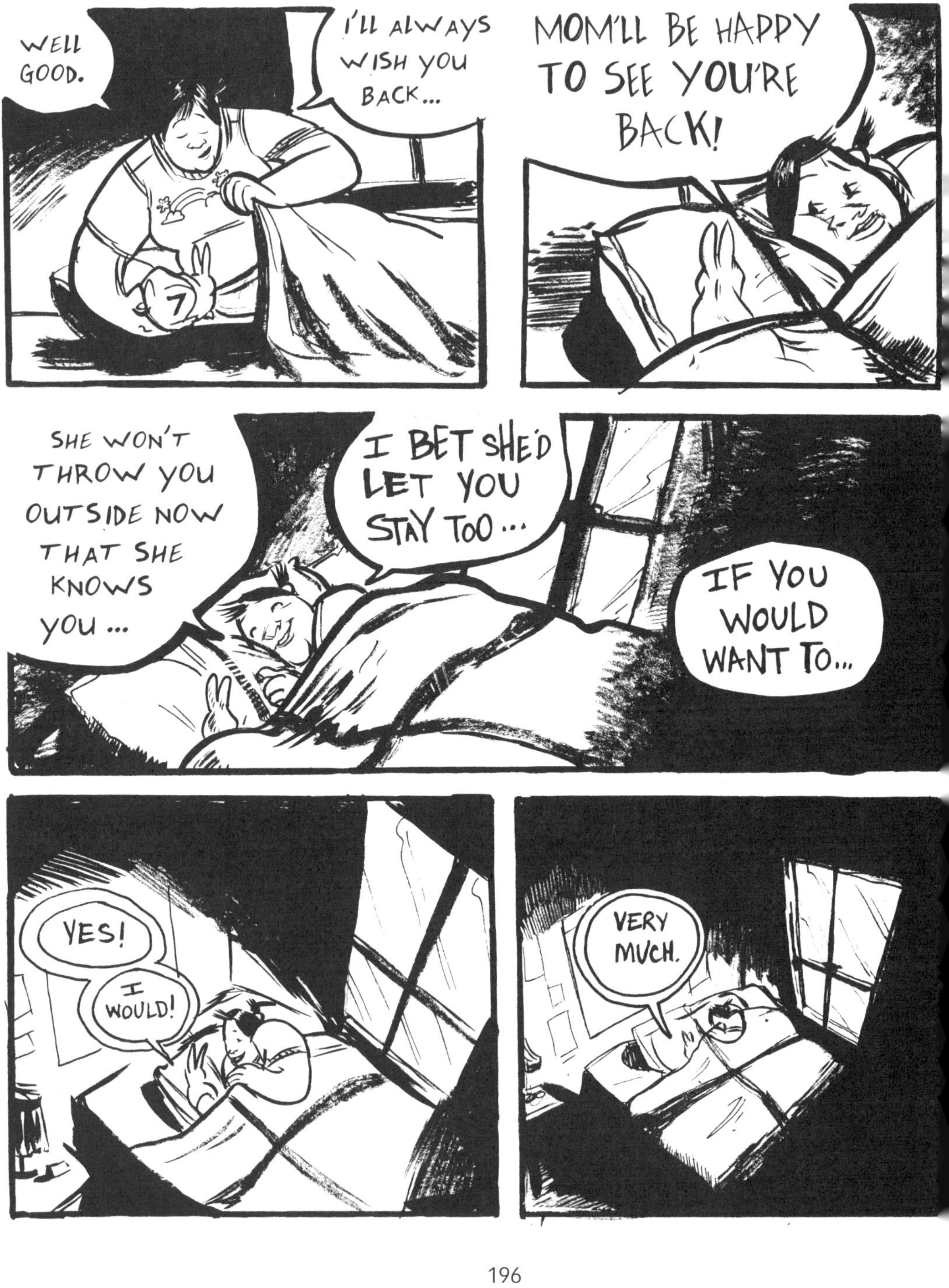
WELL GOOD.
I'LL ALWAYS WISH YOU BACK...
MOM'LL BE HAPPY TO SEE YOU'RE BACK!
SHE WON'T THROW YOU OUTSIDE NOW THAT SHE KNOWS YOU...
I BET SHE'D LET YOU STAY TOO...
IF YOU WOULD WANT TO...
YES!
I WOULD!
VERY MUCH.

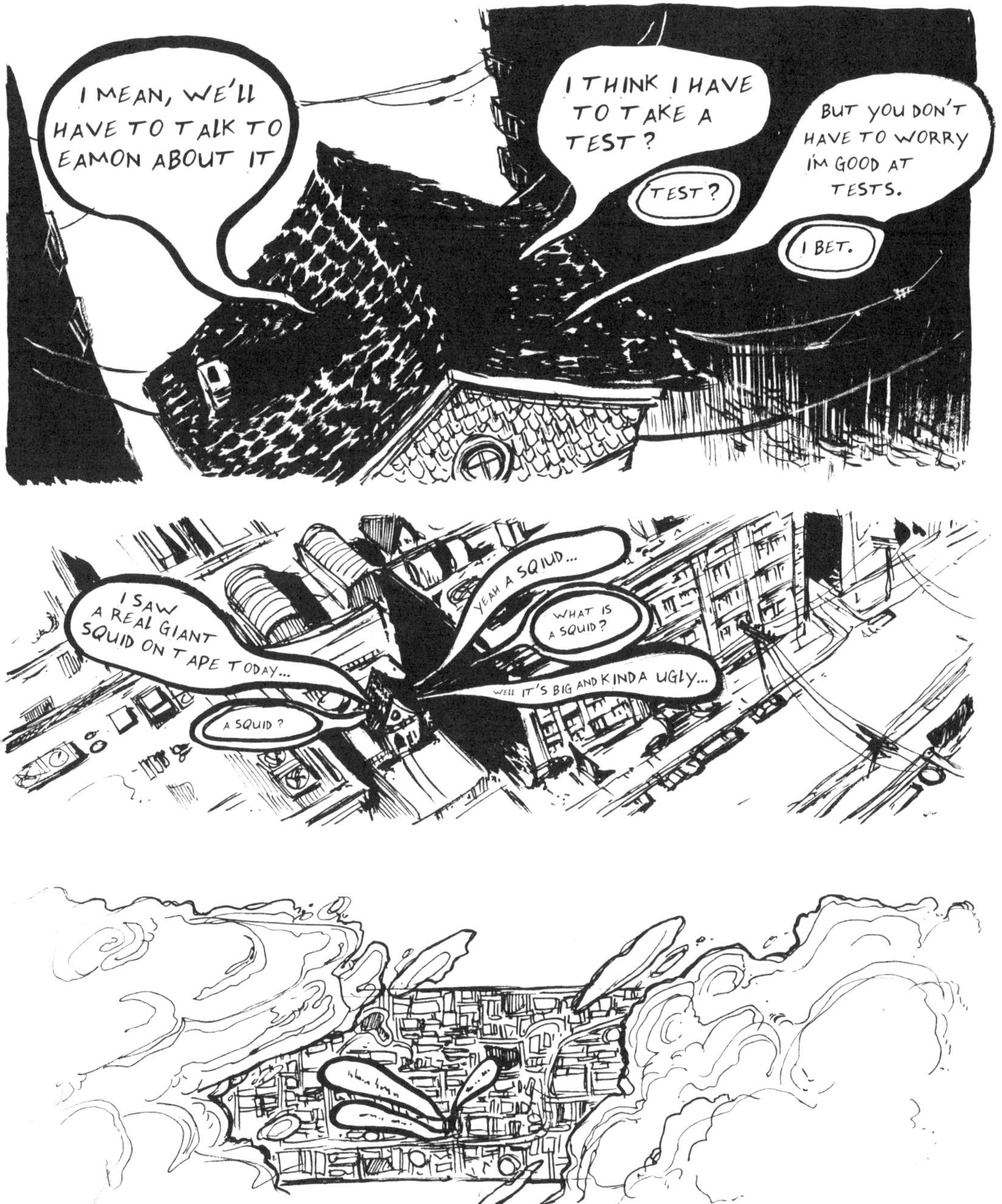
I MEAN, WE'LL HAVE TO TALK TO EAMON ABOUT IT
I THINK I HAVE TO TAKE A TEST?
TEST?
BUT YOU DON'T HAVE TO WORRY I'M GOOD AT TESTS.
I BET.
I SAW A REAL GIANT SQUID ON TAPE TODAY...
A SQUID?
YEAH A SQUID...
WHAT IS A SQUID?
WELL IT'S BIG AND KINDA UGLY...

SPECIAL THANKS:

VICKI & RODNEY ALLEN, MEMA, GRANDMA MAC, MARK KNEECE, JEREMY MULLINS, DAVID A DUNCAN, RAY, ANDREA & AVA GOTO, DOVE McHARGUE, ANTHONY FISHER, BOB PENDARVIS, KATE CASSELS, LAURA ROUTH, BEN FRISCH, JEREMY SORESE, MAC ARTHUR JEWELL, JONATHAN WOLFE, JON DEAN, MARK GEARY, COLEMAN ENGLE, KEVIN PANETTA & BROOK DARNELL, JARED SMITH, FRANK, THERESA, & SARAH SUTTON, YAYA & TIA, LINUS, TESS, BATMAN, TAYLOR, THE EASTER BUNNY, TERRY NANTIER & MARTIN SATRYB + NBM CREW AND LAST BUT NOT LEAST CHRISTOPHER SUTTON

BECAUSE WITH OUT THEIR HELP THIS BOOK WOULDN'T HAVE HAPPENED

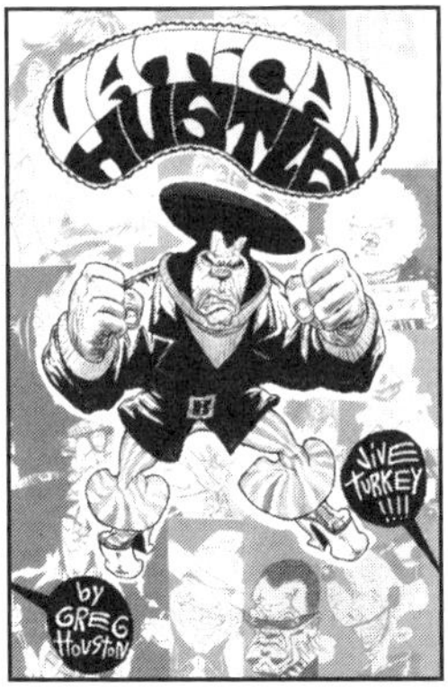
JIVE TURKEY !!!!
by GREG Houston

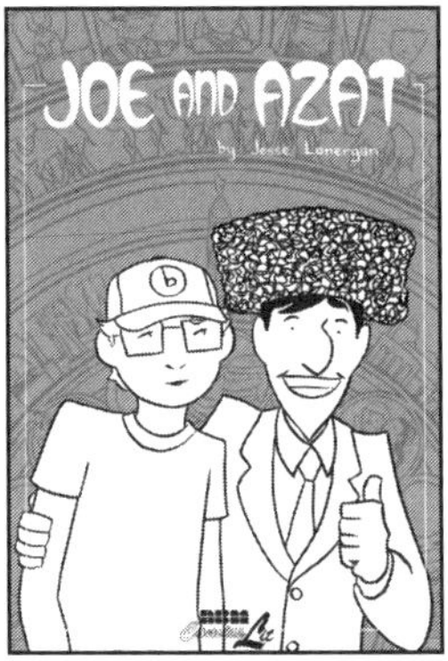
JOE AND AZAT
by Jesse Lonergan

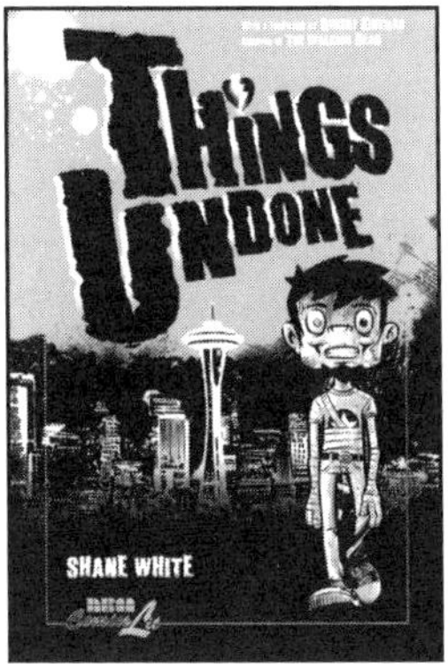
THINGS UNDONE
SHANE WHITE